EPISODES IN MY LIFE

THE AUTOBIOGRAPHY OF JAN CAREW

ACKNOWLEDGEMENTS

The following essays have been previously published:

"Being Black in Belorussia is Like Being From Mars", *New York Times*, Travel Section, September 19, 1971 (New York); "The Weeping Trees", *De Kim*, Litterair pamflet, 1951 (Amsterdam); "The Odd-Job Man", *Pepperpot* vol. 2, no. 1, 1961 (London); "South Kensington Revisited", *Pepperpot*, Vol 2, no. 3, 1963 (London); "Federation: Shadow or Substance?" *Flamingo* (UK), December 1962; "What the Cuban Revolution Meant to Me", *Guyana Mirror*, Oct. 21, 1978 (Georgetown); "Harvesting History in the Hills of Bacolet", *Quaecumque*, winter 1982, Vol. IV, No. 2, Chaplain's Office, Northwestern University (Evanston); "The Coup in Ghana: Season of Violent Change", *New World Fortnightly*, no. 40, May 13, 1966 (Georgetown); "A Long Way To Go", *Globe Magazine*, Feb. 15, 1969 (Toronto); "Culture and Rebellion", *Race & Class*, volume 35, number 1, 1993 (London).

EPISODES IN MY LIFE

THE AUTOBIOGRAPHY OF JAN CAREW

COMPILED, EDITED AND EXPANDED

BY JOY GLEASON CAREW

PEEPAL TREE

First published in Great Britain in 2015
Peepal Tree Press Ltd
17 King's Avenue
Leeds LS6 1QS
England

ISBN13: 9781845232450

Supported using public funding by
ARTS COUNCIL
ENGLAND

CONTENTS

INTRODUCTION

Jan Carew has been referred to as a "Renaissance man" and a "gentle revolutionary". He is a person who has lived many different "lives" over his 92 years, witnessing much of the turmoil of the twentieth and early twenty-first centuries. Depending upon the part of the globe where he was residing, people "knowing" one Jan Carew would be totally unaware of the others and even somewhat perplexed once introduced to them. Carew's many personas included: Jan Carew, the Caribbean writer; Jan Carew, the anti-colonial and anti-imperialist activist; Jan Carew, the early shaper of Black Studies in the United States; Jan Carew, the actor and playwright; Jan Carew, the agricultural evangelist; Jan Carew, the advisor to heads of state in Africa and the Caribbean; and Jan Carew, the investigator of the Columbian origins of racism in the Americas. Like his apparent "rootlessness" and willingness to move so frequently to other parts of the world, his interests and energies could not be contained to one geographical or professional realm. Yet, diverse though these personas might have been, there could still be seen a common thread of a commitment to the struggle of the downtrodden and to giving "voice" to those seldom heard, be it in his creative work, or his activism.

This is the second volume of Jan Carew's "memoirs", though it would be well to note that he was writing his memoirs for much of his life, as autobiographical details embedded in his other works – the histories, essays, and stories. However, this, like the first volume, was specifically written as "memoir". The first volume, *Potaro Dreams: My Youth in Guyana,* was published in 2014. This earlier work, started in earnest when Carew was in his mid-eighties, offers readers a traditional Jan Carew narrative, looking at the first nineteen years of his life in his home country and ending during World War II.

But, as he began crafting Volume II of his memoirs, Jan Carew was already in his late eighties and beginning to face physical challenges. He was also wrestling with the parameters of what he wanted to write. There was a long life with endless experiences that could be shared, but he also had the desire to retain as private some of those experiences. Thus, with a body closing down on him, sapping his energies and, sometimes, his ability to maintain his focus on the task at hand, he settled on the notion of

"Episodes". Here, he would share part of the story, offering selections and titbits that had a particular importance for him. Differently to the first volume, *Episodes in my Life* would not require him to follow a strict chronological narrative, because, as often happened, things did not always occur in a neat, linear fashion. Thus, while sections have been grouped according to certain themes and do have a basic chronological structure, the reader will appreciate that there was much overlap at various tumultuous nexuses of his life.

Differently to the first volume, significant parts of this one were dictated. Some sections had been written by him many years earlier, as he sat before his computer – though he was never really comfortable with reading material on a screen. In the effort to harness the early versions of this electronic medium so that it would match the flow of his thoughts, reams of paper were continuously printed off for a more careful review of work done. In his last few years, though, he was confined to dictating his memoir to various helpers: to me, to his grandson, Alexander Macbeth, to his daughter, Shantoba Carew-Edwin, or to an assortment of graduate assistants from the University. Then, he would read over the transcript or, eventually, listen to the transcript read to him, and make corrections or adjustments as necessary. All along, we continued his other writing – stories, novellas, essays, poetry and tribute messages. As much as his body allowed him to work, he did. But, time ran out for him.

As he came to understand that he would not be able to complete the memoir work in this fashion, he encouraged me to flesh out sections as needed. We had been together for nearly 40 years, and thus he figured that I knew much of what transpired, or could find the appropriate materials from which to cull his story for him. I responded to his request in two ways. I have added to the text of his second memoir a selection of articles, requiems or poetry that were written at the particular time under consideration, or are earlier, reflective pieces that fall within the theme of a particular section. Thus, in many cases, the reader has the opportunity to see not only the reflective commentary that is memoir work, as Jan Carew gazes back over many decades, but also to read some of Jan Carew's "heat-of-the-moment" writing and get a sense of his reactions to people and events close to the time of the event itself. Where appropriate, I have written bridging text to aid in the connections and clarity.

Episodes in my Life is divided into six sections: "Anoke: The Awakening"; "Eastern Bloc Overtures"; "A Third World Writer in Exile"; "In Whose Backyard?"; "From Lotus-Eating into the Jaws of a Coup" and "Offers too Good to Resist". The overall time period of this second memoir stretches from his youth and early manhood in British Guiana in the 1920s and 1930s; to his education in the US and early political awakening in BG in the 1940s; to his continuing education and life as a writer, artist and activist in

Europe through the 1950s and the first half of the 1960s; to the experience of the Cuban Missile Crisis and Nkrumah's Ghana in the early 1960s; and then into his intersections with Black Power in Canada and the establishment of Black Studies at US universities from the latter half of the 1960s through the rest of the twentieth century. For those curious to know more about his voluminous work, a "Bibliography and Special Exhibits" appears at the end of this volume. Besides being a novelist, playwright, poet, storyteller, reviewer, and journalist, Jan Carew was a prolific essayist.

Joy Gleason Carew

I.

ANOKE: THE AWAKENING

Introduction

Section One, "Anoke: The Awakening", includes chapters one through three. It describes the socio-cultural base out of which Jan Carew came and some of the early influences on his life. By beginning this volume of his memoirs with the word "Anoke", Carew pays homage to Guyana's indigenous Amerindian people and to the African and Amerindian cultural blends produced by the importation of Africans in the early colonial period. He also remains true to his Guyanese roots, which are a blend of many ancestral strains. That this melange was important to Carew, can be seen in his biographical statements which often included something like the following: "Jan Carew was born in a liberated village on the Guyana coast called Agricola Rome, where his ancestral blood-seeds were planted. Agricola is a place of polyglot races – Creoles in whose veins run the blood of Africans, Highland Scots, Amerindians, Sephardic Jews, English, Dutch, French, Maltese, and Azorean castaways. Then there are Chinese, East Indians, Hindus, and Shiite and orthodox Moslems. Carew is blessed, he claims, 'with the bloods of the most persecuted peoples on earth'." The reader is thus sensitised to the polyglot and poly-cultural realities of colonial settlements whose overlords moved people into and out at a moment's whim, but in which an inadvertent cross-fertilisation occurred.

Carew's life was at once precarious and yet filled with enormous promise and anticipation. At each stage, he presses on, ever compelled to find that future. The reader sees the beginnings of his widening world view as he stretches out from the village, to the regional centre, to the capital city, and, finally moving abroad.

His studies in the United States brought him into contact with a number of remarkable teachers and mentors. At the same time, though, they also brought him face-to-face with American racism and the stultifying effects of being constantly under threat, as he dared to seek higher education and choose his friends on his own terms. When an opportunity came up for a scholarship to study in Prague, Czechoslovakia, he didn't hesitate, for it solved the problem of insufficient funding and offered the intriguing possibility of sampling a socialist society.

Jan Carew returned home in 1949 while waiting for his scholarship to come through. He had been abroad in the US for several years. Now, impatient and sensitised to the new post-War expectations, he was frustrated by the various barriers he faced abroad, and questing for a role in the anti-colonial struggles of his homeland. His encounters with Cheddi Jagan, Eusi Kwayana, Martin Carter and Miles Fitzpatrick, along with other political actors in British Guiana, excited him over the possibilities of shaping a new home society.

Three poems are included in this section: an introductory poem evoking the cultural mix of his homeland and his mother's role in his early development, and two requiem poems written to honour President Cheddi Jagan and the later President Janet Jagan, upon their deaths.

DRUMS

When you listened to the drums in Agricola
you were listening to the heartbeat of the villagers.
There were Muslim drums
singing praises to Hussain and Hassan,
and Hindu drums
beating out rhythms to Lord Krishna.
My mother did not know the languages,
but somehow the drums spoke to her
and she sang aloud.
Inside the rhythm of the drums
she found solace.
Then there were Amerindian drums
with their primordial messages.
The speakers of these drums
the singers of the coast
sang nonsense-rhymes
and played them on radios
that were so loud
you couldn't hear them.
The singers sang
and their song played into
the wee hours of the morning.
Then musicians created
calypsos on their pans,
and Bob Marley sent messages
back to Africa and home.
When I left the village
I carried memories of home
with me,
and the most enduring things
that I carried in my brain,
and in my memory
were my mother's voice,
and Myah's voice,
Myah's sing-song voice,
and the smell of special dishes
curry, cumin, and dahl.
And when my mother died
her voice continued to echo inside my head.
a soft voice
a scolding voice
a voice ordering us to behave
death can never silence that voice.

CHAPTER ONE

MY ROOTS

Looking back over the ninety-plus years that I have lived, I have spent the majority of this time in households that were dominated by women. One of my earliest memories was of a cluster of women peering at me through a mosquito net during a bout of malaria. There was my mother, her sister Aunt Iris, Myah, my Hindu nurse, Jules, a distant relative from the Corentyne and Cousin Maria, who was a distant cousin of my mother, but whom everyone called "Cousin". Then there was the cook, who was a black Carib, and she had two teenage assistants.

We lived in my maternal grandfather's house. My grandfather, Steven Armenius Robertson, had seven children, four women and three men and when he died, all three men had gone abroad. My uncle Eric became a minister in the colonial government. Another son, Cecil, studied law and became a judge in Tulsa, Oklahoma in America.

My grandfather was unstinting with praise for the young men in his household. In addition to the three males, he adopted three others and a fourth that was an illegitimate child of his. Gilbert James and Peter Smart – two of his adoptees – qualified as teachers, as true for all of my grandfather's children, this being a requirement of his. But Gilbert's passion was the sea, and after studying at a technical school in the capital, he got qualifications as an engineer and went off to work on ships sailing in Caribbean waters. Gilbert and Peter remained bachelors until they were well into their forties. Peter eventually became a Deputy Minister in the government, and Gilbert migrated to America and the family lore has it that he became a millionaire.

Stevie was different from the others. He was a voracious reader and had an annoying habit of cornering you and discussing the most recent literary works that he had discovered in our grandfather's library. One of his regular evening chores was to read aloud to grandfather, and a favourite was a history of the volcanic eruption of Mount Pelée in Martinique. I'll always remember hearing his voice in every room in the house when he recited the drama of a lone survivor announcing, "I just came from hell!" There was a tale that prior to the eruption, all living things on the mountain top began escaping from the death by fire. And that the lone survivor had been a prisoner in an underground cell. This was a living example of the hand of the Lord reaching down to free a sinner.

Stevie also wrote poetry. He and Ethel, his youngest sister and my mother, had a special bond. They were the youngest and grew up when Steven Armenius' strength was spent. They were more their mother's children than they were their father's. And, from breast to death, their mother had dinned into their heads that their main hope for salvation was to go abroad. But, Stevie died from meningitis. He was the youngest son and had even won a scholarship to study in England, which meant he was on the eve of greatness, but he died before he had a chance to take it up. Stevie was my grandmother's favourite and his premature death left her with an aftermath of grief from which she would never recover.

Every household also had some kind of handyman around the property. Ours was Doorne. He was a migrant from Suriname, and, like most Surinamers, he spoke several languages. He planted a kitchen garden in the backyard and he had what the cook called a "green hand" because everything he planted flourished. Doorne had lost a part of his left arm below the elbow, but his right arm was powerfully developed, and he could wield a cutlass with skill and precision. He always kept his cutlass sharp enough to shave with and to "correct" the bullies in the Agricola rum shop. As a result, the villagers in the neighbouring villages treated him with a profound respect, no matter how drunk they were.

I was frequently bedridden from recurring bouts of malaria between the ages of seven and twelve, and I had developed eavesdropping into an art. I would pretend to be asleep and the servants and other household members would talk freely while I lay there perfectly still, with my eyes closed. Cousin Maria was the chief gossipmonger and she knew all the wickedest and most delicious stories about relatives past and present. It was by listening to her that I learned about the scandals in Aunt Iris' life. According to Maria, Aunt Iris had fallen in love with a worker on the family plantation. His name was Pride and he was a tall and powerfully built brown man. They had tried to elope, but had been intercepted by the police as they were about to cross the Berbice River into Suriname. In the altercation that developed, Pride had managed to escape to Suriname, where he remained. Apparently, he later died from malaria while working on the Panama Canal. Cousin Maria was the child of that star-crossed love affair. The self-appointed guardians for the family morals never forgave Cousin Maria for being a child out-of-wedlock, and Maria struck back at them by collecting and exposing family secrets.

Our village, Agricola Rome, was situated at the bend on the east bank of the Demerara River in British Guiana – the only British possession on the mainland of South America. Agricola was the largest and most important village close to Georgetown, the capital. We had an electric tram that connected Agricola to the Stabroek Market in Georgetown. Stabroek was known by locals as the "big market" because it was the largest market in BG. In the daytime and early evening, you could hear the tram car singing its way to and from Georgetown and Agricola.

Agricola boasted three denominational churches with their attached schools – Wesleyan, Anglican, and Jordanite. My grandfather was the schoolmaster in the Wesleyan school, and he was the most important spiritual and intellectual leader for miles around. In addition to being headmaster at the Agricola Wesleyan School, my grandfather became the founder and first President of the National Teachers' Association of British Guiana, a vanguard anti-colonial organisation. His authority in Agricola was unquestioned. His relationship with the village people was not unlike that of the schoolmaster in the British poem (Oliver Goldsmith's "The Deserted Village"), "And still they gazed/ and still the wonder grew that one small head could carry all he knew." When he went for his regular walks through the village, arm-and-arm with his wife Louisa, the men would tip their hats and lower their voices respectfully. All would bid them, "Good afternoon or good evening, Mistress and Schoolmaster."

British Guiana, as true even now, was a country of villages and districts. One famous village was Buxton, which is located in a district to the east of the capital city. This village and the neighbouring village of Friendship were established on land purchased by formerly enslaved people in 1840. Once the British abolished slavery in 1834, the plantation owners began paying the former slaves to continue the work, though some of the former colonialists were so anxious to get out of Guiana that they were more than happy to sell their holdings to these slave communes – even at reduced rates – and hightail it back to England. To most people, the incident when the women of the villages of Buxton and Friendship "stopped train" is the epitome of the special, resilient Guyanese personality, though I've often wondered whether this was a myth created by Buxtonians to enlarge their notoriety. Still, it must have hit the country like a thunderbolt when accounts began circulating about those hundreds of village women, armed only with their courage and kitchen and garden utensils, actually stopping the train on its tracks. (BG was one of the first countries in South America to have a light rail system.) The train simply could not go any further and they got the British Governor's attention in their call for the abolition of an oppressive tax.

I tried checking on this through the Guiana archives at one stage, but did not find anything on record. I have often wondered how is it that this story so impressed itself on the Guyanese imagination, and is passed down generation after generation, yet there appears no formal record of it? I remember that some of the living village elders were asked about it, too. At the time, several were over a hundred and they all regarded the story as fact. One, Aunt Jessie, said she was a school girl at the time of the incident and was able to point out the spot on the tracks where the train stopped. Because this seemed to have happened in 1862, this was probably during the "*rates war*" when the British governor found it fit to send troops to put down the growing discontent against the government's tax measures. The revolt was not against the tax rate as such, but against the high-handed way in which it was imposed. The myth had it that as a result of the disruptions, the governor was forced to back down and withdraw some of these measures. And that is the message that people like to hold on to – people power. I have a painting that the late African American artist Tom Feelings did of this momentous event and it still thrills me to see it.

Hindu village life in BG had its own texture and character, too. Even well after World War II, when I became involved with Cheddi and Janet Jagan, life in those villages was very much like the life of a century before. People still lived in *logies*, those single-room huts-from-hell that were built to accommodate slave families. When slavery was abolished, indentured labourers from India were brought in and cotched themselves in these dark corners. The children, who shared those huts with their parents, learned to wash the mud from their feet and dry them before they entered. They had meals of dhal puri, and homemade lemonade, and this was rounded off with ripe mangos. Their parents were still at work in the fields with the youngest carried on their mothers' backs, and the young girls would be left to look after the home. So these school-aged girls were responsible for preparing dinner, the most important family meal of the day, and maintaining the household, since their elders had awakened at foreday morning, and left home before sunrise. All the females in the family had duties assigned to them, helped somewhat by the men who would do some of the heavier work like fetching firewood from the riverside.

Our house in Agricola nestled in a grove of fruit trees and no matter how hot it was, the shade trees lowered the temperature inside the house. A wide veranda formed a semicircle around the front and sides of the house. There were lots of louvred shutters, sash windows and coolers in which pitchers of water would be stored overnight. There were mango trees, Ethiopian apples, star apples, a cluster of tamarind, breadfruit, guava and, along the edges of the backyard, papayas. Inside the back-garden bed were coca plants, bananas, and plantains. There were also jamoon trees whose fruit was highly prized for making wine. In the old days, one shared the ripe fruit with neighbours and friends.

Nearby Georgetown, the country's main city, was known as the "garden city" because of the fruit trees that flourished in the back and front yard gardens. In the old days, the houses were built of wood, and no one used air conditioners since the two- and three-storey houses had excellent cross ventilation, and you followed the sun as it moved from East to West. An afternoon siesta after dinner was a very necessary part of the daily routine.

Differently to my maternal grandfather, my father, Alan Carew, was an Empire Loyalist and he believed that living under the British crown was the greatest blessing that life had to offer. My mother, on the other hand, was a nationalist. She thought that colonial rule was an abomination and that the colonial civil service used colonies, like BG, as dumping grounds for their mediocre lower middle classes. All of the senior government and commercial posts were held by white British. Then there was a hierarchy of colour, caste and class that structured our local population. My mother's great grandfather was a German-Dutch sea captain who had retired and bought an estate on the Corentyne coast. When Louisa, his daughter and my grandmother, had fallen in love with a black man, he instantly cut her off without giving her a penny. Louisa then married Steve Armenius Robertson, my grandfather, who had become one of the youngest school-masters in the colony.

My father's father sailed schooners between the Caribbean islands and the Guiana coast and liked to call himself a buccaneer. He kept a coffee estate on the side. My father's name was Charles Alan Carew and on my birth certificate he was listed as a planter. He had spent some time in the US and Canada working on the railways, and returned one time flush with money and a car. Cars were quite rare in those days. He had owned a general store on Camp Street, one of the principal commercial streets in George-town, but a cousin cheated him out of the business and fled to Brazil. My mother always said that if she had known enough about business, she would have tried to save it, but, shortly after they were married, he lost it and they could no longer afford the same lifestyle, losing his car and chauffeur.

My father married my mother after he returned to Guiana following World War I, and we three children came along in 2-year increments. My sister, Cicely, was born in 1918; I was born in 1920 and my youngest sister, Sheila, was born in 1922. My father was a widower when he met and married my mother and he had two grown children by his first wife – a boy and a girl. My mother maintained friendly relationships with her two stepchildren, possibly because they belonged to an age group closer to hers.

My maternal grandmother, Louisa, had several children by Steve Armenius, but she died from cancer before I was born. She was kind and gentle and her marriage to Steve Armenius was often referred to as a "Venus and Vulcan" marriage. Her good looks and mild temperament were contrasted with his dark skin and stern demeanour. He was a mixture of Amerindian, Scottish and African.

During wartime, my family got shipments of foodstuffs from relatives in the countryside, and grandfather's house became a waystation for visiting relatives from the Corentyne, like the Smarts, the Hinzens, the Selmans, and the Gonzaleses.

When my father lost his business, my mother became the main bread-winner in the family. Like her siblings, she had qualified as a teacher. My grandfather contended that his children all needed to do a stint of teaching, because they were members of a privileged middle class and it was their duty to contribute to the wellbeing of the underprivileged. It was also taken for granted that the women of the family would make what they called "good marriages", and that the men would eventually take up professions like medicine, law and the ministry.

My mother was the youngest of the women in the family. She was also the best looking and it was taken for granted that she would marry a husband who was well-off and that she would become a housewife. After the collapse of his business, my father leased land on the Corentyne Coast and tried growing rice. However he was ill-suited to work as a farmer. He was a denizen of the city and his rice-growing business collapsed, too. My mother then took up a teaching job at my grandfather's Wesleyan Method-ist School. She did this soon after my grandfather retired, but the new headmaster did not treat her with the respect she demanded. So she took up the job of headmistress of a smaller school in a neighbouring village called Mocha. Meanwhile, my father would take a bus to Georgetown in the mornings, and return in the evenings.

While I was in my grandfather's house in Agricola, suffering from bouts of malaria, there was a special maid who looked after me. Her name was Myah and she was a Hindu. I became very attached to Myah, since I spent more time with her than my mother or the other females in the household. Myah had married when she was twelve years old and her husband, Lalgee, who came from the Essequibo Coast, was twice her age. In their twelve years of marriage, she had presented him with a girl and a boy, though both children died during the twelve years of the marriage. Myah used to sleep on a rug by my bedside. In my malaria delirium, I would see ghosts sitting at the foot of my bed and I would call out to her, "Myah, that woman is there again", and she would say, "Close your eyes and go to sleep. Is your grandmother keepin' watch over you." When the malaria left me, I did not see the ghost again.

Growing up in a colony, you developed a sharp awareness of race and class. One of the ways in which colonial power perpetuated itself was by inflicting petty insults and humiliations on the subject people.

My mother had also become profoundly aware of racial differences after having lived in the United States for a few years when I was still a toddler. She used to tell the story of the bitterness she felt when a bus driver had ordered her to sit at the back of the bus. She said that for the first time in her life, she actually had felt like killing someone. On the other hand, I never once remember my father talking about a racist incident. He belonged to the Georgetown upper crust and was very loyal to the British, often announcing that if the local people wanted the right to govern themselves, he would declare, "Lord, let thy servant depart in peace".

I grew up through adolescence and early manhood sharply aware of racial issues through family anecdotes. My mother's father, Steven Armenius, for example, had clashed with a young English education official. This young man, who could not have been more than twenty-eight years old, was on an inspection visit to my grandfather's school in Agricola. He had, before the entire school, condescendingly called my grandfather by his surname alone – "Robertson." My grandfather had refused to answer any of the questions this young inspector asked until he called him "Mr. Robertson".

My father's brother, Steven Fitzroy Carew, was a prominent citizen of New Amsterdam at the time, owning a general store on the main street, several houses, a sawmill, and an estate on the Corentyne Coast. He had four children: two girls, Vera and Gertrude, and two boys, both called Steve. The sons, Little Steve and Big Steve, excelled in all sports: cricket, football, tennis and athletics, but their academic abilities, in contrast to my side of the family, left much to be desired.

There were three sawmills in New Amsterdam at the time, including the one my uncle owned. There was a gentleman's agreement between all the saw mill owners that when rafts came from the interior of the country, they would take turns to buy the load. A young Englishman reneged on the agreement and took a raft ahead of his turn. When he came to discuss it with Stephen Fitzroy, he was very rude. My uncle, who was tall and powerfully built, kicked him, literally, out of his office. Uncle Steve was taken to court for assault and had to pay a large fine. In earlier times, he would likely have been thrown in prison for daring to hit an Englishman.

For a while, Stephen Fitzroy was a national hero. And, though these were petty episodes, they had a profound influence, helping awaken the national consciousness of our country from its colonial torpor. These incidents were occurring when former ex-servicemen and women, who had served in the British Armed Forces, were returning home after World War I, having seen the freedoms that people enjoyed in metropolitan societies in Europe.

My mother was certain that once we wrested power from the British, we would stumble down the freedom road for a while. But, if we selected the bravest and the best, and, the most patient and compassionate amongst us to serve side-by-side, there was nothing we could not achieve in the long run – no goal to which we could not aspire.

My mother was strict to the point of being tyrannical. She did not allow me to play regularly with other children in the village. I had to do homework. Most of it was set by her, and other teachers. The children who were the offspring of the lowest ranks of workers did not have playtime in their daily activities, but they were very clever in mingling work and play. When they went to gather firewood from the riverside they would play a game of bat and ball. They would improvise wickets by putting three sticks in the ground. The bat was shaped from a piece of driftwood, and the ball was usually made from balata-tree gum. Occasionally, I was allowed to play with them, but they were clear about the social divisions. When they were amongst themselves, they would refer to me as "that red boy" who was the schoolmaster's grandson.

After graduation from Berbice High School, I, like most of my friends, joined up in the local militia forces. World War II was on and they needed us to man coast artillery posts. But my service was not very long, as I was discharged early on medical grounds.

I moved from New Amsterdam to Georgetown and got a job in the British Guiana Customs Service, thanks to my Auntie. But though the Customs Service was considered a good job, my ambitions were broader than to just stay home. My mother, too, knew that I'd have to leave Guiana to make something of myself and had often told me so.

CHAPTER TWO

FROM CUSTOMS OFFICER TO STUDIES IN AMERICA

The war had ended for me after I was discharged on medical grounds in 1943. I had had three operations after signing up for the Coast Artillery and they deemed me too much of a bother to keep on. But, at the end of the war, I still had responsibilities to my mother and my younger sister.

So, I took a job in the colonial civil service in the registrar's office in New Amsterdam. This was one of the most unpleasant experiences of my life. The registrar was a large Dickensian figure who reminded me of someone coming out of Dickens' counting houses. He seemed to have dedicated his life to making things unpleasant for junior employees. But this was a time when veterans were returning home and jobs were scarce. The euphoria of victory had petered out and though knew I had to leave Guiana if I were to make something of myself, I had obligations to fulfil.

My aunt, Harriet Maude Dingwall, then managed to secure a job for me as a customs officer in Georgetown. These jobs were considered the pinnacle of opportunities for the Creole middle class. She was married to Rev. John Dingwall who was the superintendent for Moravian churches in BG and a member of the legislative council. My uncle was considered one of the most highly-educated black men in the country. Prior to being posted to BG, he had been a schoolmaster in Jamaica, his native country. The Moravians had sent him to Germany as part of their missionary work, and he was ordained in their parent church in the latter half of the nineteenth century. After returning to the Caribbean, my uncle spent several years in Guatemala before assuming his post in BG.

My aunt knew the wife of the chief secretary of British Guiana, the highest-ranking officer in the colonial government. It was through this connection that she secured this job for me.

Being a customs officer gave me some new and unwanted distractions. Seeing the ships come and go made me more anxious than ever to leave home. A job in the customs might have been highly prized, but I hoped it would be my ticket for one of those boats that docked in the harbour.

I met Carl Bradshaw on the first day in the customs office and he showed me the ropes. Carl was the scion of an upper-crust Georgetown family and, I discovered soon after we met, also a gifted artist. The local elites treated him like a maverick. He let everyone know that he was planning to go to America as soon as the war ended. He took me to a bar opposite the customs office and I was amazed at the familiarity with which he treated the director of customs. The director was a white Guyanese, a strange figure – short, rotund, and very red in the face. This was a typical redness, a combination of sunburn and rum. The man was obviously an alcoholic and never went home immediately after work. Instead, he would go straight to the bar and remain there until Carl took him home. Deposited outside his house, he would be greeted with a torrent of abuse by his wife. This was a scenario that never changed. Drink plays a very interesting part in Guyanese and West Indian culture. It is a kind of leveller. The cynics say that the rum shop and the mental hospital are the two places where everyone was equal, and all consideration of race, caste, and class are ironed out. So, I went to the pub in the afternoons and Carl, the director and I would drink and then we would take him home. I never had any great passion for drinking and would fake taking the drinks, but the relationship between me and the Director changed totally as result of these bouts.

It was an interesting time in Guiana because the war had opened up things and there were great changes taking place in our country. The customs and the treasury were departments where you traditionally had the Creole middle class – mixed and lighter-skinned folk – but this was breaking down after the war. For the first time, you had people with darker hues coming in. Forbes Burnham, the man who would become the first prime minister and then, later, president of Guyana, was brought in in this period, and I was one of the people to break him into the job. Burnham was dark-skinned and the kind of candidate who, previously, would not have fitted into the customs elite, but he was also one of the winners of the rare national scholarship that entitled him to go to Oxford and he was filling in time while waiting to go off to England. We met again in England and later on in the United States when he was returning home after qualifying as a lawyer. Burnham was a very brilliant scholar and he not only excelled at law at Oxford, he became very involved in the anti-colonial struggle. At one point, he and I shared a lecture circuit.

After my sister graduated from high school, I knew my time had come to look for ways to leave the country. When I received my first civil service long-leave, I went to Trinidad and with the help of a friend of my father, and secured a job there with the special wartime price control board. Things were rationed and the board controlled the prices of commodities for the population. In the British colonial services, you secured a government job and then were entitled to two leaves a year: a short-leave and a long-leave, as part of your benefits. These civil service jobs were really jobs for English expatriates who would be going back home to England for the six-month period of their long-leave. What many British colonials in the civil service did was to save up their money, and go on a holiday somewhere – if they didn't go to England.

For the first time in my life, I was assiduous in saving a large part of my salary. I lived in Curepe, a village just outside Port of Spain, since it was cheaper living there, and commuting to and from Port of Spain was easy and inexpensive. I was acquiring double the pay that I got as a customs officer in BG, which enhanced my objective of saving money to go to America to study.

Trinidad, because of its oil, was more advanced than BG and the Americans had leased land for naval and air bases on the island. Thousands of Trinidadians got jobs working for the Americans, but, for the first time, the people of Trinidad were also exposed to the American brand of racism, and there were many racial incidents when American servicemen came into contact with the local people who were working on their bases. Racism between the British coloniser and the colonised had also not departed. The British also did what they could to encourage a strong racial animus between the Indians (descendants of indentured labourers from India brought in after the abolition of slavery) and the Blacks (descendants of African slaves). Like BG, which had a similar history, this racism would carry on with particular venom for generations to come.

I had applied to both Howard and Columbia universities in America and was accepted by both, but I couldn't afford Columbia in New York City. Another attraction of Howard was that they were doubling up their programmes to accommodate those of us who had been in the armed services. You could get two years of study in one by continuing through the year without a summer break.

I resigned from my jobs and set my attentions on getting to Howard in Washington, DC. After a brief stay at home, I returned to Trinidad. From there, I set out for America on a Dutch liner that was scheduled to dock in Brooklyn, New York. The war was still on and our ship had to dodge German submarines that were sinking Allied ships indiscriminately. The Germans were also sinking schooners which plied between the islands. They were determined to prevent oil and bauxite – both in high demand for the war industry – from reaching their destinations. So, any ships travelling had to move in convoys. The convoy that escorted us to Brooklyn had a number of vessels travelling together protected by the Allied navies.

I had met a Guyanese sailor, Danny Jackson, in Trinidad, who had shown me around. He had also helped me get papers as an "Able-bodied Seaman". Small tankers were sailing to Murmansk in the USSR, and he told me that if you signed on as an oilman with one of them, you could make thousands of dollars in one trip. He had made one these journeys and survived, but there were many others who did not. I was all set to sign on to one, but an old seaman I'd befriended talked me out of it and I later learned that that particular boat was torpedoed. I wrote a story about this dangerous run while I was at Howard and Arthur P. Davis, who ran a small community publication, printed it. That was my first published piece of writing. Davis also taught journalism at Howard and he read my story to our class. Many years later, I met Danny again in London where he had settled after years at sea. He told me hair-raising stories about his life during the war years.

When I landed in Brooklyn, it was my second visit to America. But, I have only vague memories of the first time I landed on these shores. It was 1924 and I was four and my younger sister had been kidnapped right in front of us. Our stay was cut short when my parents sent me and my older sister back home to stay with other family members, while they stayed behind to look for my missing sister. Miraculously, she was found a year later in Florida and my mother and father returned to Guiana with her.

Now, I was back to try my luck in America almost twenty years later. I tried to get a taxi to take me to Harlem, but the first three I hailed refused to take me. The pace of life in New York City was almost overwhelming and I was relieved when the driver of the fourth taxi I stopped listened to my plea, and agreed to take me to H.C. Cameron's house between Lenox and Seventh Avenue. When I knew the situation better, I found out that there were black taxi drivers and white ones. The driver who grudgingly agreed to take me to Harlem was white, but if I have known the custom earlier, I would only have tried to hail black drivers. Still, my accent helped and my apparent "ignorance" of the social rules allowed me to step briefly out of the Jim Crow-like conventions.

It was a long drive to Harlem and the city lights around me looked like fallen starlit galaxies. I noticed that the lights dimmed when we reached Harlem. It was as if we had left the bright lights and entered a darkened cave.

H.C. came out to greet me and to pay the taxi. His broad Guyanese accent was reassuring after my long journey.

"I was expecting you since yesterday. I had to make sure there was somebody at home to greet you. How is your family? I hope you left them all in good health."

"They all send greetings and wonder when you'll be coming home on a visit."

"Every year, when the winter's cold begins to bite me, I promise to make that visit a reality, but something always comes up. Some business crisis forces me to postpone it."

H.C. was a black Chinese who had been living on the same street in Harlem for the past thirty-five years. He and my father had grown up in a village on the Corentyne coast back in BG. He owned a travel agency and a real-estate business and had offices for both on the ground floor of the building in which he lived. He owned several properties in New York, and in the summer he would keep one of his larger houses in Harlem vacant. This was the house he kept for students; it had a cricket pitch in the back garden while inside were billiard tables and sleeping quarters. His African American neighbours would look out their back windows and see this strange ball game being played. But H.C. was careful and had put up nets to catch any wayward balls, because if any windows were broken, that might had caused a riot.

H.C. always selected one of the senior boys as the head-boy, so to speak, and he, in turn, would select who would be chosen as residents during the holidays. H.C. also owned a restaurant at the corner of 133rd Street and Lenox Avenue, which provided meals for the residents of the student house. He also had a club which he called "The Royal Exiles", which only admitted West Indians who were born in the West Indies. A band of us took up the issue with him, pointing out that the club was discriminating against 2nd and 3rd generation West Indians. The club eventually became famous and would cover the expenses of having the leading cricketers of the Caribbean come play cricket on Randall Island nearby.

H.C. would provide sumptuous dinners for his student guests, expensive steaks and lavish plates of fruit and vegetables. He was a kind of "godfather" for Guyanese students in America. Anyone who stayed at one of his places, or found a job in New York through him, was known as one of "H.C.'s boys". Even living in his district of 133rd street between Lenox Avenue and 7th Avenue, meant you were protected by being one of "H.C.'s boys." He used to parole dozens of gangsters from the street and once you were known as one of H.C.'s boys, people would generally leave you alone. One fellow, Jeffery Lord, who was a champion athlete, was surrounded by some fellows intent on robbing him, but he broke away and outran them. I had an incident where I saw two fellows about to fight and I stepped in between them and asked, "Why don't you fellas find some other way to sort this out?" They were so surprised that they stopped fighting and left.

On another occasion, I had gone to visit a girlfriend in Brooklyn on Lafayette Avenue, and three fellows tried to hold me up. It was around three o'clock in the morning. I tried to talk to them.

"Where are you from?" they asked menacingly.

"I'm from a poor-assed country called British Guiana," I replied. "Why don't you fellas go down to 5th Avenue where Rockefeller lives?"

"Aren't there any black people in your country?" they asked.

"Yes, there are plenty of us," I said. They looked a bit confused, as if they didn't know I was black. The situation became increasingly tense. "Look," I bargained, "I've got thirty dollars on me. I can split it with you. I'll give you fifteen and I'll keep fifteen." There was a café that was open nearby and I suggested we go in for a coffee.

"Fine," they said. After our coffee, they escorted me to the nearest subway, saying, "It's dangerous around here," and waited until the train arrived. We shook hands and they watched me leave.

There were complex racial codes in Harlem, but being associated with H.C. could help you bend the rules. I remember later, when I was a student at Western Reserve University in Cleveland, I took a white student to H.C.'s house and he stayed a couple of weeks with me, walking around Harlem without ever getting mugged or hassled. But a lot of this also depended upon the spirit of the white visitor. Years later, in the 1960s, when I was showing Feliks Topolski, the painter, around Harlem, Harlem had changed over those two decades. I took Feliks to meet John Henrik Clarke and Tom Feelings. Clarke was the doyen of militant black scholars in New York and Tom was an artist. Feliks asked Tom if he'd take him around some of the places on 133rd Street. Tom replied, "I could, if we could rent a Sherman tank." Feliks went around all the same. He was determined to hit some of the dives in Harlem, and it was his foreign accent and open manner that saved him. He felt welcomed and the people he encountered didn't feel threatened.

I spent my first summer in New York, staying with H.C., and then travelled to Washington by train to start my course at Howard University. Howard is one of the oldest historically black universities in the United States, and is financed by the US Congress. It had distinguished professors and well-known scholars like the African American scientist, Charles R. Drew who discovered how to preserve blood plasma that would save the lives of millions of people. The story went that Dr. Drew died in 1950 after a car accident in North Carolina, when the white hospitals would not treat him and it took too long to get him to a hospital that would treat Blacks, though this account has been disputed. Ralph Bunche was another. He was working for the United Nations and ended up as the diplomat who represented the UN in mediating between the Palestinians and the Jews to partition the land that would become Israel. A fellow BG student, Wally Francis, and I went to hear him speak and we questioned him.

Howard was like an island in Washington, D.C. As a black person, you were safe if you were on the campus and stayed in the area around the university, but you had to be careful when venturing further into the city. H.C. had made arrangements for someone to meet me when I got to Washington and I was met by Aaron Peters, who was studying medicine. I stayed in the same dormitory as he. Peters had worked as a chemist with a pharmacist in the BG countryside. During that period of his life, he had gotten hold of a medical dictionary and studied hundreds of cases by heart. Later, when he finished his medical studies, he turned out to be a brilliant doctor with an encyclopaedic memory.

The other West Indians at Howard were very helpful in trying to induct me into the black-white morés of the US. You had to know where you were, where you could go, when it was safe to go there, and where you couldn't go. If you tried clothes on in a store, you would have to buy them. They taught me how to get a cab that *would* take me to the Howard University area. Even my clothing was an issue. Because I didn't have a lot of money when I left home, my father had arranged to have some clothes made for me by a local tailor. But, these made me stand out as a foreigner. They insisted that I get American clothes and took me to a second-hand place.

While I was in America as a student, I was stopped by the police several times in different cities. However, I always made sure to walk around with my passport, because it was still dangerous in segregated America, particularly in Washington DC. They could shoot you first and find out you were a foreigner, later. Incidents of racial profiling were thrust upon me and most of the black students residing in Washington at the time.

In my two years at Howard, I learned a lot about racism in America. It was dangerous to be a black man on the streets in Washington, DC. I always felt I was walking across a minefield. Washington, DC. was like the deep South. There was this web of hatred and bigotry, with white Americans acting out racist fantasies.

One time, I was walking with a Norwegian girl I'd met at the International Students' House. The building was in downtown DC and any international student from any of the area universities could go there. They had dances and other entertainments. There were other West Indians there besides me, and I imagine that some African Americans went, but not many. You didn't experience any racism there, although they were predominantly white students from various countries. We students from the West Indies felt that we had to take full advantage of any educational opportunities we could get. When the police stopped us, I was escorting my friend to the bus stop. The three policemen approached us with guns drawn, but after inspecting our passports they let us go.

One day, when there was a rush of students in the hall in between classes, I saw a strikingly beautiful white woman walking down the stairway and our eyes met. I went up to talk to her. She was a professor of Classics, and from that initial meeting, we became very close. I remember going for walks with her around a reservoir behind the university when she would recite poetry by Catullus. It was a lasting affair throughout my time at Howard.

Intellectually, my time at Howard was stimulating. Eric Williams, who went on to become Prime Minister of Trinidad & Tobago, was there, as was the historian Merze Tate and other remarkable professors. The Howard Library seemed to have an endless supply of books and I regularly took armloads of books home to read. One of the best jobs I got was to work in the US Library of Congress. Whilst I was at Howard, I started thinking I would do medicine, but I did not restrict myself to just science. Like many others, I attended a wide range of lectures on the Howard campus or at the International Students' House.

But I was also always broke and looking for jobs to pay my university expenses. My mother was not in a position to send money to help, although she did manage to send some occasionally. There weren't many jobs on campus. Once, I took a job as a dishwasher at the Statler Hotel. When I went for the interview, the head fellow asked me if I was familiar with the mechanical dishwashing unit they used. I had never seen one before, but wanted the job, so I said that I was more familiar with a newer model than theirs, but could manage with this one. I also learned from my co-workers on the dishwashing line that eggs were the hardest to clear off plates and that, as they were allowed a certain amount of breakage, these were the plates they broke most often, rather than fight with the egg.

I made my decision to leave Howard because I was spending so much of my time and energy looking for jobs or working at them. Seventy-five per cent of my time was spent on this job search, while only twenty-five was left for my studies. This is when I decided to get on a bus to go to Cleveland, Ohio. My friends were afraid for me, but I was determined to leave racist DC. I had enough money for bus fare and one of my classmates, who was from Cleveland, had told me about Western Reserve University. He said that people at Western Reserve were more liberal, so I decided I would leave Howard and try to get a meeting at Western Reserve. After two years in DC, I said goodbye to all my West Indian friends, packed my trunk, and set off on a Greyhound bus for Cleveland.

I met an African American girl on the bus who lived in Cleveland. She had a brother who was a seaman in the merchant marines in the Far East and she told me that I could have his room. I took her up on her offer. Her family made its living by numbers running and they had a loft apartment on the top floor of a building. I could hear the calculating machines chattering.

Once in Cleveland, I went to see the Director of Admissions at Western Reserve. He was from the New England section of the country and had a patch over his eye. I told him, "I came to this country for an education and all I'm receiving is insults and affronts to my dignity as a human being." He told me that they were willing to accept me. I signed up, but I only had enough money for one semester.

One of my classes was taught by Danish professor, whose name I think was Denkliffson. This was a course in political geography and, at one point, she was dealing with the Amazon basin. I was questioning her quite a bit and she asked how I knew so much. I told her, "I was born in that region." Then she asked, "Well, why don't you give a lecture on this for the group?" So, I went to the library and boned up a bit in preparation for the designated class. A few days later, when I was giving the talk, I discovered that she had invited the dean and two or three other faculty members. After my talk, they asked me where had I got my command of English. I told them that I came from an English-speaking country, British Guiana. They were impressed with my presentation and offered me a scholarship and this was how I managed to continue my studies at Western Reserve. Here I was, the only black student from South America in this very good college, and they had only let me in because I was from British Guiana. They didn't know where British Guiana was. To them, I was something exotic and that was good enough.

Studying at Western Reserve was very different from Howard. It had a different ambience. They gave you more latitudes for intellectual activities. For example, I went to the concert hall – it was on the campus – and I became friends with a young conductor. It was more eclectic, too. Western Reserve allowed me to operate differently. You discussed books. I knew the vice president, a man from Wales. The average student – black or white – didn't have the kind of contacts I had.

I had the money for my tuition, but I still needed a job to cover my other expenses. I got a job shelving books at the Cleveland Public Library and got to know Dr. Fern Long, who was in charge of International Relations for the library. She was a white American from the Midwest. She invited me to speak to her monthly group – which attracted people from the universities and the Cleveland business community. This was another talk about the Amazon basin. I was often asked to speak to different civic groups.

Another time, when I was speaking to a mixed group of both Blacks and Whites, there was a short fellow there. His name was William Pierson, and afterwards we spoke. He was a brownish fellow and in South America he wouldn't be considered black. I talked politely to him but never really got to know him until later. I actually came across him several times and each time, he invited me to have a meal with him, but I didn't go. About a year later, I met him downtown, and he said "What about a dinner invitation. I'm going to pin you down right now; why don't you come tonight." I learned that Pierson was prosperous member of the local business community. He took me around his holdings. He had shoe stores downtown and a range of other businesses. He took me to one building and there was a white elevator operator who greeted him. When we got to his office upstairs, he told me that he owned this building. When he bought it; the elevator operator didn't know he was now the owner and tried to bar him from entering. Pierson didn't fire him because he was fighting with big racists downtown and didn't see the need to fight some working-class man operating an elevator. It was an eye-opener to hear his tales of Mexico, too. He was happiest spending time in a place where he didn't have to face discrimination. In Mexico, he wasn't white or black, but simply a rich American.

I told Simeon Booker, one of my house members, about meeting up with Pierson. I remember saying to him, "I'm going to dinner tonight with a man named Pierson", and his eyes lit up, and he said "That's the richest black man in the country." He was a multimillionaire and yet, if you saw Pierson, you wouldn't even have noticed him in a crowd. Pierson was also a friend of Henry Wallace and Henry Wallace was the US Vice President under Roosevelt at the time.

So I went to this house. I really thought I was going to the wrong place. It was on South Boulevard, just overlooking the park. He had bought that house from a white millionaire. It had a swimming pool on the roof – that takes some money. He had a bar downstairs big as his whole house. The refrigerator was built into the wall. You could press a button and the refrigerator came out and then he had drinks of every kind.

He was very gracious, but he had also checked me out, since it was most unusual to have black students at Western Reserve. He found out that I was very popular with the other students, because I was telling the truth about situations; I never pretended anything.

Pierson was living in this house alone, so he said, "Why don't you come and live here? I can help you out with extra money." So, I went to live there for a while. Now, he had several cars and he let me use this custom-built Chrysler, but I knew I'd have to give it straight back to him, because I'd have to take a second job just to keep this car running. I was working in the ice cream factory at night, but that wouldn't do it to keep it in gas.

I said, "Look, why should I be working for a car?"

"You work for something," he said. "You can take the gas in my car." In short, William Pierson had money to burn.

I said "No, no, you've done enough. I don't want to. I'll take the streetcar or get a bicycle."

At another point, I was doing some sketches of temples in Cambodia and showed them to Dr. Long. She was very impressed with my work, and shortly afterwards presented me with a large packet of art supplies. She had a soft spot for artists. She had been engaged to an artist, but on the way to the wedding, he was killed in an accident. I did several paintings, one of which was a hillside of yellow flowers I had seen in Trinidad. I sold several paintings to the Library and to the Director of the Library who had become a friend. I didn't keep any of them, although I still have photos of two: a fellow shouting, and a painting of a sugarcane field. I was also writing in this period – stories and poetry. Dr. Long took over mentoring me, and I seem to recall that some of these pieces were published in a magazine, but I don't remember which.

But, I also experienced racism in Cleveland. I went to a restaurant in downtown Cleveland with some friends from the student co-op where I lived at one point. I was the only black person in the group and they served me dishwater – and they made sure you knew it was dishwater. I poured it on the floor and we all walked out. Another time, I had accompanied a white female student home in the Cleveland suburb of Shaker Heights and was on my way back home. The police stopped me and asked what I was doing in that area and I told them that I was visiting friends in Shaker Heights.

To this they asked, "Do these 'friends' know you?"

They took me to this student's house and her parents answered the door. They asked the police why they were wasting public funds arresting guests to this country when there were real criminals all over the city. The police then offered to give me a lift back to campus, which I turned down.

At this point, I was staying in the Hough district with the family of the African American girl I'd met on the bus from DC to Cleveland. They had provided me with an apartment of my own. If anyone came to the door of the building downstairs, before they would open it, they made sure that an armed guard was at the door checking to see who it was. Whilst normally it was very risky, I could walk around with ease; because I was going to the university, the family and the community-at-large were very proud of me.

There weren't many Blacks at Western Reserve University. There was one light-skinned fellow who had been passing for white and he came to me secretly to confess. But, after watching how I moved around the university so easily, he let it be known that he, too, was actually African American. There was also an African American professor at the Medical School, but some people tried to burn his house down when his wife and baby were there. Happily, they were saved.

A particularly nasty event occurred to me and another friend, a white student from California, when we were crossing a white working-class neighbourhood between Shaker Heights and the university. We heard people shouting, "Nigger! Nigger!" She and I had to walk fast to get out of the area. Though she was an American, she had not been inducted into the racial patterns of Cleveland, so we were both caught unawares.

It was very difficult to find accommodation close to the university. I had befriended two African American students, Simeon Booker, who studied journalism and ended up an editor for *Jet* magazine, and Earl Dearing, who studied law and became a judge in Louisville, Kentucky. We decided to join with some of the European students we knew and buy a house and turn it into a student co-operative. This co-operative would own the house in perpetuity, so that when one group of students left, another would take it over. Some twenty years later, my future wife, Joy, also attended Western Reserve (by then known as Case Western Reserve University) and the student co-operative was still running.

I organised this. It was simple, really. If twenty-two of us put forth about $70 each to make the down payment on the house, that would cover it.

Then, paying the mortgage was less than we would have individually spent in regular apartment rental. We had single bedrooms and shared the bathroom, kitchen and main-floor living spaces. The house was near the university. We raised some more money because I went to the president of the university and got some funds from him. This was to be an International House; i.e. for international students; it was also interracial and students from any of the universities in the area could stay there. So, we bought this house and this is where I lived during part of my time in Cleveland. It was very cheap; we also got food in bulk from mid-Western co-operatives at a fraction of the price. Our experiment in inter-racial living was so impressive that *Jet* magazine published an article on us in 1946. The bonds formed so long ago have remained and several of my fellow house-sharers have stayed in touch with me

One day, the neighbours complained to the president that there were white women and men living in the same house as Blacks. The president passed it onto his vice-president, who was a Welshman and somewhat more liberal. He ignored the complaints, saying it was perfectly legitimate. He left it to us to deal with the situation. We had a party every Saturday, so we just invited the neighbours. They had such a good time that they soon forgot their complaints. The problem was solved amicably.

One summer break, Klaus Angel, a German student, and I decided that we should go on a tour of America to get to know it better. We took one of his parents' cars for our tour. Both of his parents taught at the Western Reserve Medical School. They had been contemporaries of Freud, and Klaus remembered Freud bouncing him on his knee. Klaus complained about having two parents who were psychiatrists, since they tended to analyse his every action. Klaus was fed up with being told why he lived the way he did and he was in open rebellion against them by not telling them anything. He would more regularly confide in me than his parents. They used to call me to try and find out what he was thinking and doing – to no avail.

In preparation for our journey, which would take us through some of the southern and western parts of the country, I decided I needed a disguise. So, I fashioned a turban for my head and placed a jewel on the front of it. Together with my accent, which was decidedly not that of an African American, and that of Klaus, the whites and blacks we encountered never thought we were from America.

I was at Western Reserve for about two years. I became friends with the son of the Consul General of Czechoslovakia in Cleveland, Martin Spitzer. Martin told me about the Czech Student Union scholarships to attend a university in Czechoslovakia. Through him and his father, I received a scholarship to study at Charles University in Prague in 1949. The Prague opportunity was both economical and political. As a poor student from a colonial society, I was willing to go anywhere I could get a scholarship. I was also interested in socialism. The Czechs, as the Soviets would do in the next several decades, understood that by offering these scholarships to study in their country, they would be building allies among peoples wrestling to free themselves from colonial rule. I was, in fact, the first person to take up one of these scholarships from my region of the world.

CHAPTER THREE

ENCOUNTERS WITH CHEDDI

My involvement with Cheddi Jagan came in three phases. The first was in the late 1940s, after studying in the USA but before leaving to study in Prague. The second involvement came in 1952 when I returned to British Guiana after my time in Prague and before I left to continue my studies in Europe. I stayed for a time again in 1962, and then in 1966 – this last time recalled in a later chapter.

My excitement over the political developments in Guiana began in 1949 when I first returned home after being away nearly five years. I had applied for a scholarship from Charles University in Prague and decided to go home while I waited for a response. This was a time when anti-colonial turmoil was brewing and serious agitation for universal adult suffrage was taking root. I was curious to see what was happening.

I stayed with my aunt who lived in the family house on Almond Street in the Queenstown section of Georgetown. One night, while I was walking home, there was a political meeting at a street corner. It was there that I heard Cheddi for the first time. His was a lone, mesmeric voice in the legislature, denouncing the arrogance of British colonial power. He was discussing the question of land ownership and how the colonial government reserved the best lands for the elite of the country, leaving only a fraction for the masses. The manner in which Cheddi spoke to the crowd accorded them a respect that I hadn't heard before, and I was very impressed. Cheddi was Indo-Guyanese and he was addressing a predominantly black crowd calling for Indians, Blacks and Creoles to pool their strengths in the fight against the British.

I resolved to go to his house and visit him that very night. He and his wife, Janet, invited me in and I offered to help him in any way I could. There began my relationship with Cheddi and Janet. I began working on a journal they edited, the *Political Action Bulletin*, and attending village meetings with them.

Cheddi was a dentist who had done his studies in the US. The son of indentured workers from India who had been settled on the sugar estates in BG, he was fortunate that his father had been able to scrape together enough funds for him to attend Queen's College in Georgetown. He began his studies at Howard University in the mid-1930s. There he became steeped in African American culture and social life. He also became quite popular with his West Indian classmates by being a very clever poker player. Cheddi was not alone in this; there were several of the brightest students in medicine and dentistry who were attending Howard and who were also brilliant poker players. Some of them were so good, that they made enough money to cover their rent and school fees.

H.C. Cameron, our patron in the US, and at whose apartment houses we stayed during the summers spent in New York City, always appointed one of us as his "head boy". During Cheddi's time, the head boy was Claude Denbow. Denbow, who studied cardiology in the US, and Cheddi were to become lifelong political opponents when they returned home later.

After Howard, Cheddi went on to Northwestern University to do dentistry. He fell ill during his time there and had to spend some time in a convalescent home, where he met Janet Rosenberg, who was one of the nurses. A Jewish American, Janet was one of the first white women to take the side of the ordinary folk in BG. This impressed me, and it impressed the Guyanese working people.

In the early days, Cheddi worked as a dentist during the day, but at nights he and Janet would go out to the countryside and hold meetings with the peasants. These were always mixed groups: Afro-Guyanese, Indo-Guyanese, and Creoles. Going out at night to the villages with Cheddi in 1949, I developed a respect for the ordinary people of Guiana, and I realised no one had ever listened to them before. From those early days, I have had a lifelong connection with that movement and it continues until the present time. They were crossing racial, ethnic and class lines, bringing people together in a common struggle against British rule.

It was also during this early period that I met Eusi Kwayana and the poet Martin Carter, who became our national poet. Eusi was an Afro-Guyanese from the famous town of Buxton on the coast. The emancipated slaves of Buxton had pooled their money and actually bought out the plantation owners. Martin was a Creole from Georgetown who worked as a civil servant. He could read his powerful poetry to thousands of people and they would listen enthralled. One poem said, "*I come from the Nigger yard of yesterday/ leaping from the oppressor's hate/ and the scorn of myself/ ... naked like a stone or a star...*" I had just published my first collection of poetry, *Streets of Eternity*, and was glad to be in his company.

These three together – Cheddi, Eusi and Martin – represented a goal for our nation as we tried to extricate ourselves from the colonial mentality that threatened to pull our country apart. Cheddi was preaching socialism and I wanted to be a part of the movement. I was so keen on this that I would ride my bike from Georgetown to villages some the twelve or more miles away. And, as Cheddi and I got to know each other better as we did these village meetings, I proposed to him that I formally join the movement and could represent it abroad.

Another close friend and activist during this hectic period was Miles Fitzpatrick. Miles was unabashedly Marxist and one of the leaders in our anti-colonial struggles. Miles had studied law in England, and had only recently returned home to establish a practice. In the normal course of events, he would have been expected to settle down to a respectable middle-class existence and marry into a middle-class family. But he had been radicalised during his stay in England and had become a part of the anti-colonial student movement. While he was a law student in London, his flatmate had been Kenyan Joseph Murumbi, who was a leader of a radical group that was fighting to end British rule in Kenya. Miles had also been active in the Movement for Colonial Freedom (MCF), a movement headed by Fenner Brockway, a radical Labour member of Parliament.

Miles had honed his skills as a political speaker by doing a lot of speaking to various radical groups in London. His radicalization had taken place in the aftermath of World War II when large and small eruptive movements had awakened young professional students from their dreaming torpor in London and the British provinces. The winds of change were affecting colonial societies throughout the world. Even a high-coloured student like Miles suddenly encountered racial prejudice in England and the rest of Europe, because the average Brit lumped middle class and working class, pale faces and dark ones, creole speakers and well-spoken colonials all together, and treated them all alike. In other words, people like Miles found out – as the students liked to say in the vernacular – "there ain't no black in the Union Jack!" Miles took the side of the have-nots against the have-gots in the world struggle. He made the choice and stayed with it for the rest of his life.

After a few months in BG, the scholarship from Charles University in Prague came through. But, I still needed a recommendation from a progressive group. British Guiana's contacts with Prague and the Eastern Bloc were then tenuous. Cheddi had not yet formulated a foreign policy that included communist countries. The intellectuals in Guiana at the time were all some version of Marxist, but, in 1949, the left-wing parties weren't as cognisant of the value of communist party linkages – though many were Stalinists. But, the Communist countries in Europe had not yet awakened to the possibility of alliances with British Guiana, either.

In the late 1940s, BG had two basic parties. There was the PPP – the People's Progressive Party – which was a united party of all of the left-wing groups, and there was a small middle-class party, the National Democratic Party – led by Rudy Kendall, and there were still many independents. But, because of Cheddi, Guiana soon began to become known around the world as a Marxist-led country.

Eusi and his village had made some interesting overtures to the Soviets on their own. Eusi had written to the Kremlin leadership asking that they send books to his village school. Somehow, the British Communist Party got a hold of the message and sent him sets of pamphlets and other books. Some years later, in the early 1960s, when I was about to return to Guiana to work in Cheddi's government, my friends the Klautkys, who were prominent in the logging industry in Guyana, sent me £16,000 sterling to buy books for the library of the new university that was being formed in Georgetown. With the help of the British Communist Party, I bought the books and had them shipped down.

Though British Guiana was in this period of anti-colonial ferment – which was exciting – I still had my mind set on Prague. Cheddi wrote a letter of support for me and so did the African American artist and political activist Paul Robeson. One of the students at Charles University, Samuel Bankole Akpata from Nigeria, had written to Robeson for a recommendation before, and this seemed like a wise idea in my case, too. When my visa came through, I ended up doing a two-year stint at Charles University and after a return to BG in 1952, then stayed on in Europe for almost a decade more.

When I returned to BG in 1952, I was less happy with what I found, and for a time there was something of an ideological rift between Janet Jagan and me, and relations with the Jagans were a bit strained. Janet felt that since East Indians were the largest ethnic group in BG, they would, for the foreseeable future, vote along racial lines, and that class and ideology would be secondary considerations. My concern was that the result of this would be ever-mounting animosities between Blacks and Indians. I had proposed that we should have a government of national reconciliation, that Blacks and Indians should share legislative and executive power equally, and the main focus of the newly-elected Marxist government should be the formation of a united and popular government. Blacks and Indians would then represent the constituencies they served without fear or favour. Unfortunately, the old colonial legacy of race, caste, colour, class, and gender were still very much at play. It was, as an English MP once said, "A policy of divide so that no one might rule".

1952 was also when I first met Maurice Bazin, a French physicist and political activist who would play important roles in my life over the next few decades, including not only in Guyanese politics, but also in drawing me into the US at the height of the Black Power movement. He and his wife, Nancy, were friends of Cedric Belfrage, a famous English left-wing journalist, who had recently been deported from the US. Jagan had sent the Belfrages to me and asked me to extend a genuine Guyanese hospitality towards them. I agreed to help out somewhat. As such, I was the contact person for foreign visitors. I would perform a similar function in Nkrumah's government in the 1960s. Guyana was still then British Guiana, but as it was left-leaning, it was of great interest to people on the left. Belfrage and his wife were planning to settle in Mexico.

Sallie and Cedric Belfrage tried to affect an ideological reconciliation between the Jagans and me on this question. They urged us to consider making racial harmony the central focus of our left-wing party, instead of a united front in which it was assumed that all the Guyanese would be represented. Though the Belfrages did manage to open up a friendly dialogue between the Jagans and me, the animosities between the two races have lasted now for two generations, and continue to create a situation of "division so that no one might rule."

Cheddi was freely elected in April 1953, but I had been so uncomfortable with the rising racial divide that I had already decided to go back to England. In October of 1953, the British also landed in Guiana to wrest control from Cheddi and the new PPP government. Jagan's left politics as the Cold War intensified could not be tolerated. The constitution was suspended and an interim government of unelected, unrepresentative middle class politicians was installed. The Jagans and others were imprisoned and then placed under house arrest for three years.

Back in England, I wrote a piece for the *New Statesman and Nation* in 1953, called "The Story of British Guiana", in which I told an anecdote that Janet had shared with me earlier. This told you a lot about the conditions the Jagans were fighting against in BG. On returning home in the later part of the 1940s, Cheddi had applied for the job of company dentist with the bauxite company and he had returned to BG first to prepare for Janet to join him. The company housing was strictly segregated according to race and when they found out that Janet was white, they insisted that she had to live in the "white" section, while Cheddi would have to live in the section for the local people of colour. At the height of the furore about Cheddi's being a "communist", the result of the publication of this anecdote in a prominent English journal was that it forced the company to hastily recruit a local man of colour, thus, ending the colour bar. They had been operating a kind of apartheid system like South Africa and this incident broke it forever. It just so happened that the engineer they had chosen for this "historic" mission was a classmate of mine from Berbice High School named Gordon Kennard.

Over the next four years, the British did everything they could to break up the PPP. Forbes Burnham, who had been the Chairman of the PPP, was encouraged to form an alternate political party – the People's National Congress, PNC – taking a large part of the Afro-Guyanese electorate with him. But, in 1957, Cheddi was re-elected overwhelmingly – although now by a majority Indian vote.

Again in 1961, Cheddi was re-elected and I was invited to be a part of
Cheddi's new government. I had been heavily involved in the anti-colonial
movement in Europe and the recent Cuban revolution had left me
enthused about the possibilities of social change back home. Though
family relations were a bit strained, Sylvia, my second wife, and the children
joined me and we settled into a rental house. This was at the height of the
Cold War and it was amusing when the right wing planted the warning that
"The Cubans Have Landed" in the local paper. My aunt was quite alarmed
and would not believe that the "Cubans" were Sylvia and me. My Jamaican
wife, Sylvia, had been born in Cuba, though she was raised in Jamaica.

While British Guiana was not yet fully independent, the British had
allowed – in face of the global anti-colonial push – the Guyanese people the
prospect of full independence in the next few years. I went back, hopeful
that the non-racial sentiment of the earlier years could be recaptured, now
that the people had spoken again so forcefully. But our country was too
fractured to be able to accept a government of national reconciliation, and
a new middle-class party, the United Force, was further fanning animosities between the Peoples Progressive Party and the Peoples National
Congress.

I saw this directly when Maurice Bazin and his wife were in Guiana and
I took them to a mass meeting at one of the large sugar estates, Skeldon. The
workers at Skeldon were predominantly Indian, and many of them were
hearing me speak for the first time. I stood on a platform and before me was
a multitude of faces. First, Brindley Benn, one of the leaders of Jagan's party
spoke, and then it was my turn. There were a number of people in the
crowd who had come to act as *agents provocateurs*. They were followers of
another right-wing group that some believed was financed from abroad.
Their leader was a lawyer named Balram Singh Rai. As soon as I stood up
to speak, Rai's faction began chorusing, "We will die for Rai! We will die for
Rai!"

Making political speeches in the Third World can be a hazardous
business. Mischievous groups in the crowd can throw a speaker off balance,
and also throw missiles at him or her. So as a speaker, you have to remain
outwardly calm, and find a way to win over enough of the crowd so they,
in turn, will help silence the noisy dissidents. So, I retained my equanimity
and said to the crowd, "I left home and went abroad for nearly ten years, and
nothing seems to have changed here. We still want to die for small
causes…" There was a ripple of laughter that went through the crowd. My
supporters silenced the dissidents and I was allowed to speak. "If it's dying
that you're after, I can give you something big and noble to die for: Die
fighting against imperialism, against racism, against the oppression of the
poor and the needy."

After I spoke that Sunday, certain factions were calling for me to run for premier. The Bazins were also impressed with the meeting, and I remember that Maurice made a point of giving me some notes on his impressions and future strategies. But, despite that kind of adulation, I felt it would be dishonest to act like a messiah. I just wanted people to work together. I wanted more internationalist policies: solidarity with Africa, Latin America, Asia and the Caribbean. The leaders of other parties wanted to isolate Guiana and turn it into a satellite of the United States.

Later, breaking with Jagan's party was a painful affair, because I had been connected to it from its inception. The kind and quality of intellectuals, activists and farmers I remembered from the earlier period seemed to have dispersed themselves into quiescent groups. My niece, Denise Harris, whom I used to take to the villages with me when she was a little girl, likes to tell me that I had a greater and more sincere following than those who later took over reins of power. There is a story that Engels, while travelling by train through Germany, saw the cathedral at Cologne and remarked, "Germany is a beautiful country. It's a pity one can't live in it." Right then I felt like that about Guiana: "Pity the nation divided into fragments, each fragment deeming itself a nation."

Communal riots between Black and Indian, fanned by outside agents, spread across the country. At the talks leading up to independence, Cheddi was persuaded by the British to accept a new constitution that involved proportional representation. The British had calculated correctly that whilst the PPP would be the largest party, a cynical alliance between the PNC and the rightwing United Force party, led by Peter D'Aguiar, would have a narrow majority. Cheddi was thrown in a kind of political limbo for nearly 28 years as Burnham's party, the PNC, took over, and for nearly three decades controlled Guyana.

In 1992, though, several years after Burnham's death, Cheddi again won the elections – even under international supervision – and was named President of Guyana. He remained in that office until his death in 1997. Shortly after his death, Janet became President, but had to resign due to poor health in 1999. She passed away in 2009. I saw them one last time in 1994.

Jan and Joy Carew with Cheddi Jagan in 1994.

Photograph: *Guyana Chronicle*

REQUIEMS

After Janet and Cheddi passed, I sent requiems which were read at the memorial ceremonies held in their honour. Janet Rosenberg Jagan was the first woman President of Co-operative Republic of Guyana, 1997-1999. Cheddi Berret Jagan was President of the Co-operative Republic of Guyana, 1992-1997.

Requiem for Janet (2009)

She was an angel
to women huddled in dark corners
of the logies
She brought unfamiliar light
to those in hell
and took up cudgels
for the lowliest and most despised
blinded by flashes of darkness
those following her
were for the first time
blinded by light.
They unfurled red banners
to Krishna,
Lenin, Stalin, Mao Zedong.
The proconsuls of empire
sensing how dangerous she was
imprisoned her.
But the red banners multiplied.
They were masters
of the art of virtual perception
and they even tried playing anti-Semitic cards
but she learned from the working women
who she led
to be steady as a rock on a riverbed.

Requiem for Cheddi Jagan (1997)

The river, amber-tinted by the rains,
garlands the falling tide with water hyacinths
and sings requiems for him on his way home
to ricefields and savannahs and bitter-sweet sugarcane
where refrains of suffering still echoed in the wind
and streams veining forests and a marecage
flowed in time to the rhythms of rebellious hearts.
They laid him on a funeral pyre
and north-east Trades
gusting down corridors of Atlantic tides
touched his embalmed face
while lashing winds and rain
transformed prayer flags to Shiva
into red banners of his pristine dream
that the torment of the poor and the despised
must be redeemed forever.
His eyes were closed
the orisons of priests
echoed across plumed arrows of the canefields
but showers of sparks rained down upon the mourners
reminding them
that deep inside the swaddling cotton shroud
was a dauntless heart of fire
and fire is never timid when it bonds with the winds of
       time.
Riversong and windsong
rhythms of rain
drumming on his funeral pyre
and a Swami and his acolytes cantoring poem-hymns
sang requiems for him at Port Mourant and home.
But showers of sparks and burning embers
fanned by an insurgent wind
deluged the bereaved, warning them
that hearts of fire never rest in peace
that embers hissing in the rain
can always burst into agile flames again and again
and leap as high as stars.
When a host of mourners melted in the mothering dark
the fire's glow brightened the night
and starlight jewelled dewdrops on petals of wild
       flowers,

a watchman of dayclean swore
that ancestor Acabre had come
in the witching hour
to greet a kindred spirit of fire.
"Look out for them," the watchman said,
"for from this day onwards,
the two, ever vigilant,
with their fearless mothers beside them
will walk hand-in-hand from Waini Point to Akari
Orealla to Roraima
I tell you, they'll make sure
that we unite
to realise their undying dreams."

II

EASTERN BLOC OVERTURES

Section Two, "Eastern Bloc Overtures", which includes chapters four through six, explores the changing geopolitical dynamics of a post-War world in which the socialist nations of the Eastern Bloc and the Soviet Union were making direct overtures to nations engaged in anti-colonial struggle. Along with the escalating imperatives of the anti-colonial ferment had come the search for new political and social networks, both at home and abroad. Jan Carew, as true for many colonial artists and intellectuals, was curious about the new social models being developed by the Soviets and their allies. By opening himself to the two-year scholarship to study in Prague in the late 1940s, Carew became the first student from Latin America to have a scholarship to study in the Eastern Bloc.

It was an opportunity that thousands of Third World students would later take, as the Eastern Bloc offered scholarships to study at its universities, ranging from four to as much as ten years depending upon the area of study. The Socialist world was reaching out to these populations in the recognition that once they gained their independence from their colonial masters, they could be valuable allies in the bi-polar world taking shape after WWII. In the colonies, students and their sponsors were equally pragmatic in accepting this invaluable opportunity to build their country's intellectual capital.

As Jan Carew's writing gained increased recognition in the late 1950s, the Soviets made special overtures to him as a means gaining favour with the Marxist Jagan government in British Guiana. With the translation of his breakout novel, *Black Midas*, into Russian, Carew was invited as a guest of the Soviet Writers' Union. He marvelled at the enormous cache of royalties generated by his work and enjoyed the interaction with the writers he met. Later, back in London, he heard accounts from a cousin about the difficulties faced by Third World students in the USSR, and he took advantage of a second invitation by the Soviet Writers' Union to look into the allegations. With his cousin as his guide and interpreter, he gathered some of their stories and produced a documentary novel critiquing race relations in the USSR. As in the novel, Carew chose to use a pseudonym for his cousin as he recounts some of his cousin's experiences here in the memoir.

Two other pieces are included in this section: "Green Winter Epilogue" published in the 1965 US edition of his 1964 documentary novel, *Moscow is Not My Mecca* (US edition entitled, *Green Winter,* 1965); and the 1971 *New York Times* Sunday Magazine piece, "Being Black in Belorussia is Like Being From Mars".

CHAPTER FOUR

PRAGUE STUDIES

I was on my way to Prague, but I had to go to London, first. The Czechoslovakian visa that I had obtained earlier in the US had expired and I had to apply for a new one. So, I left for London to wait while my new visa was processed and to organise my passage to Prague. But then I decided it was cheaper to wait in Paris and I journeyed there.

I finally got the visa and set out by train for Prague. I was excited at the prospect that I could do a programme in which I would study radio isotopes – the Carbon 14 method of judging the age of organic matter. I was also not too worried about the language since I was told that the courses were being given in German as well as Czech, and I had studied German at university.

I had kept in touch with Martin Spitzer's fiancée and I gave her my itinerary so that she could meet me at the train station in the Czechoslovakian capital. Half a dozen times during the journey I was awakened from a restless sleep by border guards who were checking our papers as we traversed France, West Germany and East Germany. I remember that the East German guards were dressed in immaculately tailored uniforms. They looked as if their outfits had been hung on Nazi manikins and they had not been allowed to display a single crease.

I arrived in Prague on a dismal afternoon. The first thing I thought as I stepped off the train was that it was rather bleak and grim-looking. There were few passengers but many guards. When I stepped off the train with my heavy suitcase, I looked around to see if there were any porters but there were none. So here I was, a lone Guyanese man in a country that my mother believed was somewhere close to the end of the world. My suitcase was a leather one that my aunt had used a generation ago when she had travelled to England to visit a stepson. It still exuded the smell of the shoe polish with which it had been cleaned. Two young women came up to me and asked if I was "Jan Carew". The smaller of the two picked up my heavy suitcase and with the greatest of ease carried it to the end of the long platform. The one who spoke to me in English was Martin Spitzer's fiancée and the two were university students. I was rather stylishly dressed in an outfit that I had bought in New York – a fur hat, a dark blue overcoat with a fur collar, highly polished boots and a knitted light-grey scarf.

It was, in fact, early springtime in Prague in the late 1940s, and food and clothing were still rationed. The young women meeting me just assumed that I was well off because of the way in which I was dressed and, as they explained to me afterwards, they thought that anyone dressed like me had to be some kind of diplomat or foreign dignitary. Actually, I had bought the outfit at a second-hand shop in New York. I was wearing what my classmates at the University had called derisively "dead man's clothes". It was a stroke of luck that I visited the shop soon after a wealthy patron had passed away, and he happened to be my height and build. The proprietor had, in addition, made slight alterations to the garments for me. So I arrived in Prague wearing a double-breasted blazer, cavalry-twill trousers, and a fur hat. The two Czech women were somewhat taken aback. They had expected to see a downtrodden man from the Third World, not a being who, apart from my darker countenance, was dressed like a member of the English upper-middle class. In this city with its castle and its grim Kafkaesque shadows lurking in doorways, I must have seemed like an apparition or a ghost. Later, I discovered that American clothes were very popular in Prague and there were people willing to literally buy them off my back.

Spitzer's fiancée, not wanting to disappoint her seemingly grandiose guest, had taken me to the Alcrona Hotel in Wenceslas Square, one of the finest and most luxurious hotels in the city. I didn't have enough money to stay there for any length of time. Happily, I had another contact in Prague. I had met an Australian woman in London who had spent two years there and she had given me the address of a professor at the university, Ivan Svitak. My Australian friend phoned Ivan and he picked me up and took me to his building on the outskirts of town, where they had a vacant apartment. It is an irony that during the Prague Spring of 1968, Ivan had become one of the anti-communist revolutionary leaders and he moved to the US, taking up a professorship at a university in California. At the time I met him in Prague in the late 1940s, he was twenty-three years old and he already had two doctorates. We became close friends, but I lost touch with him when he came to America.

I met Jorge Amado, the Brazilian author, in Prague. He was in exile and staying as a guest of the Czech Writers' Union. We used to have meals together from time to time. One morning, he invited me to breakfast and he said he had a friend visiting. His friend was Picasso, but I didn't realise this at the time. His guest asked me about British Guiana and we talked for a while. He was cordial and friendly. Though I've heard stories about Picasso being difficult, I didn't find him so at all. I found him to be nothing but pleasant. We even discussed art and I showed him a photograph of one of the paintings I had done and about which he announced, "That black man's shouting for his freedom." Years later, I put this painting on a new edition of my novel, *Black Midas*. Picasso and I would encounter each other a few years later when I moved to Paris and became good friends with the Brazilian artist, Tiberio, who was one of his proteges.

The street where I lived on the outskirts of Prague was renamed just after I settled there. It was originally called "Titova Street", after Tito's triumphant trip into Prague. But, when Tito later broke with Moscow communism, it was renamed "Yugoslavski Partizano" Street. This inaugurated a kind of code among the locals. If you asked for "Yugoslavski Partizano" Street in Prague at the time, the average man on the street wouldn't give you directions, as they still had strong communist sentiments. The only way to get the right directions was to ask for "Titova Street", referring to it by its original name.

It was amazing how many nightclubs and parties Prague had. There were four people of African descent in the city at the time: three African students and me. Nba, a Yoruba, was a denizen of the Prague night life. The local ladies felt that if you were black, you had to know how to dance, though, as it happened, Nba wasn't very good with his feet. He did pretty well all the same. Nba wanted to do engineering, but didn't have the training in mathematics, so he did political science, and later, studied agricultural sciences in the US. The other African students were Olu Smith who studied medicine and Bankole Akpata, who was studying political science, and who had helped me get the recommendation from Robeson.

At one stage, I got a job in a night club. The owner approached me one night and asked me if I knew how to sing, and I told him "No." But when he told me how much he was paying, I changed my mind. For a while, I was singing at this night club with my shirt unbuttoned halfway down. My signature song was "Nature Boy". *"There was a boy/ A very strange enchanted boy/ They say he wandered very far/ Very far, over land and sea."*

There was also a large contingent of Chinese students. This was the time when Mao Zedong was in power and all the menus in the restaurants in Prague were written in German, Russian, English, and Chinese. These students were incredibly studious, spending hours in their classes, taking meticulous notes and studying afterwards. When they left, they took trunks full of these notes, which I am sure helped educate generations of other students in China. I remember one of them telling me that, in the old days on the Bund in Shanghai, there used to be signs, "No Chinese, no dogs." Now, since the people had seized power, they would make sure that this never happened again. I had a sneaking suspicion that the Chinese didn't trust the Czechs all that much, and the mistrust was mutual.

But Ivan Svitak was very fair-minded. He was a brilliant teacher. He, Bankole, and the other black students, steered me through the troubled waters of Czech society. We had another friend in Prague, Prodot Mukherjee from India, whose father was in the Indian army. Prodot had come to Prague before all of us and spoke Czech fluently. But, they were very racist in Prague against certain people and they thought Prodot was a Roma (a Gypsy). Interestingly, the Roma's origins are thought to have come from the northern part of India centuries ago. Once, when we were on a train to Bratislava, this racist man tried to order him off the train. I straightened the fellow out by roughing him up a bit and he backed off. I met Prodot again in England after I left Prague.

I learned to ski while I was in Czechoslovakia. Things were pretty rudimentary and you had to walk up this slope in the Krkonoše mountains and then ski down. So the trip up took some time, while the trip down was over before you knew it. There was a restaurant about halfway down and the plan was to stop there for some refreshment, but if you missed the turn, there was only one way to get back there. One of my friends made a point of inducting me into some survival tips and demonstrated how if you were stranded out on the mountain you should carve out a snow cave where you'd wait until daybreak. He said it was amazingly warm, but I hoped I would not have to use one. At one particularly cold stage, I was feeling a bit sorry for myself and I thought, "What am I, a man from a country near the equator, doing here, freezing my ass off!"

But, in fact, I had a great deal more freedom than the average student. The Czechs had never heard of British Guiana before and they didn't know what to make of me. They couldn't tell where I stood in the East/West divide. I came home one night after a session with the local Czech-made brew. It was about 3 o'clock in the morning. This tall fellow in a grey-coat uniform insisted that I had to tell him my life story, which was part of the secret police investigation of foreigners. I told him, "I've been drinking that terrible alcohol you fellows produce. I really couldn't tell you a coherent sentence, let alone my life story. If you let me get some sleep, I could recollect more truthfully later." Luckily, my landlady came out and offered him some coffee and I went off to sleep. When I woke up he was still there. He said he'd help me write a coherent life story.

"What work did your father do?" he asked.

"He was a dental technician," I said.

He frowned, "Did he have any hobbies?" he persevered.

"He liked to sing," I said.

Again, he frowned, "Anything else?"

"He also used to make the boats he sailed," I added.

"That's a good proletarian operation," he concluded, and with that he wrote something down and left, and I didn't hear further from him, or anyone else, though at one stage, I had a girlfriend who was in the secret police.

I spent just under two years in Prague before returning to London, via Paris. Svitak, who was my mentor, was getting into political difficulties, so I thought it best to leave the country while I could. I had to cross the border to East Germany at Pilsen. At the crossing, there were American guards and German guards across the no-man's land. My exit from Prague had been dramatic. I had to get an exit permit, and I could only get this from the head of the communist party who had an office in a former bank in the middle of Wenceslas Square. One had to appear in person to get this permit. I waited for about an hour and they didn't call me, so I went home. I went a second time and it was the same story. The third time, I dressed in very formal wear and nobody called me, but this time, I got up, opened the gate where this nabob, as the Hindus would call petty officials, was sitting. I asked her why she wasn't calling me after two days, and now it was three days, and nobody called me. The guards were surrounding us and ready to grab me when she told them to leave me alone. I got the exit permit. Little did I know that when I got to the border, the Czech guards inspecting my passport said I was missing a certain document and that I would have to return to Prague to get it before being allowed to leave the country. But that was half a day's journey to go back and then the same to return the border, which meant that I'd lose at least a full day. I told them I wasn't going back and started arguing with them loudly enough for both sets of guards at the border to hear. That way, there would be eyewitnesses to any incident that arose. So, the Czech guards had a brief discussion between them, and decided to let me go. Dealing with the bureaucracy each time was like taking a journey into Kafka's castle.

I was welcomed by the other guards, who, after glancing at my passport, waved me on. As British Guiana was still a colony of Great Britain, I was travelling under a British passport at the time.

I left Prague in 1951, not expecting to return, but I found myself returning in the mid-1980s. I had wanted to write a book on Grenada following the US invasion in 1983 and was invited by the International Organisation of Journalists to complete my work in Prague. Therefore, as a guest of the IOJ, I was provided comfortable lodging for several months. And two years later, the IOJ published my history, *Grenada: The Hour Will Strike Again.*

Prague

Thirty years passed
And the city remained
As I had left it
Chained to the Vlatava
By bridges
The Charles still
Brooded over the mill race
And the castle
Was pasted like a postcard
Against the autumn sky
Pale sunlight
Touched gilded baroque towers
And Jan Hus' Van Dyck's beard
Glittered fiercely after the rain.

CHAPTER FIVE

GUEST OF THE UNION OF SOVIET WRITERS

In the early 1960s, while I was living in London, the Soviet Writers' Union invited me to the USSR for a visit and I decided to take them up on it. Earlier, the Soviets had notified me that they were going to translate my novel, *Black Midas,* into Russian and have it come out in serial form in their journal *International Literature*. Afterwards, following their usual policy, they would issue the complete book in a Russian edition. Things are done the other way around in the West.

In preparation for this, I received a number of letters from my translator, requesting further details on the many botanical terms, and Creole words and phrases that different characters used in their dialogue. It was also clear that she had obviously had some training in both liberal arts and science, and she made great efforts to find comparable terms in Russian. When we met in Moscow on my second trip to the USSR, she and my former wife, Joan, who accompanied my daughter, Lisa, and me, became quite good friends and the two corresponded for some time afterwards.

Meeting my translator in Moscow was quite intriguing. Though I do not remember her name, I remember her clearly. She had all the graces and good manners of the grand bourgeoisie about whom one had read in Russian novels. Noticing how intrigued I was, she told me, with an amused smile, that of late she had been making extra money by holding Emily Post-type classes in etiquette and good manners for the new class of bureaucrats: the former peasants and workers who had become high ranking officials. Paradoxically, with increasing diplomatic duties, they now needed to take a crash course in the manners of the very bourgeoisie they had been taught to despise.

One day, after having been in Moscow for a few days, she took me for an afternoon stroll. We arrived at the Novodevichiye cemetery with its expensive marble tombstones. We wove our way between them until we came to her father's grave. Placing flowers on it reverently, she confessed that both of her deceased parents were aristocrats. Her father had been a general in the Tsarist Army, but after the revolution, he became a general in the Red Army. That father of hers, I thought, must have been very adroit in escaping Stalin's secret police, because during the great purges, the upper ranks of the armed forces had been decimated, and he would have been a prime target. In a strange juxtaposition of the military and the creative, Chekhov's tomb, surrounded by a cherry orchard, was a mere twenty yards away from the general's. This habit of taking friends to visit the tombs of close relatives seemed to be a cultural ritual in the Soviet Union; it happened a few times on my visits there. On another occasion, I was taken to this same cemetery to see Nikita Khrushchev's tomb. As Khrushchev had fallen out of favour by this time, replaced by Leonid Brezhnev, he had been stripped of all privileges, including not having his remains placed near other political luminaries in the Kremlin wall. Still, he was accorded some special recognition by being placed in a cemetery graced by famous writers, musicians, and other luminaries of Russia's past.

On my first journey to the USSR, I was travelling alone. Victor Ramzes, a young Soviet Jewish writer, met me at the Moscow airport. The Union of Writers had assigned him to be my escort and guide for the rest of my time in the USSR. He took me to the Hotel National off Red Square and installed me in a suite.

I knew that the VIP treatment I was receiving was not only because of my novel, but because my Soviet hosts were out to win my political support. These Soviet invitations and visits, plus my relations with Soviet writers and artists, were taking place against a backdrop of their desire to establish political relations with British Guiana, then governed by the Peoples Progressive Party (PPP), which had openly declared its allegiance to the communist cause. Both sides in the Cold War were aware of the fact that British Guiana, situated as it was on the northern coast of South America, had a symbolic geo-political, and strategic importance – in spite of its relatively small size, with a population of under a million. While this situation was regarded as an opportunity for extending influence by the Soviets, it was seen as a "communist threat" by Great Britain, the United States, neo-colonialist governments in the English-speaking Caribbean, and right-wing military dictatorships like that of Brazil.

The Hotel National was one of the old and ornate leftovers from Tsarist times. My three-roomed suite was large enough to accommodate half a dozen guests. Its old fashioned décor included an armoire, a chaise longue and heavy brocade curtains draped on windows that almost reached from the floor to the ceiling. From any of the tall front windows, I could see the Kremlin, the endless queues snaking along towards Lenin's tomb, the gilded Byzantine domes of churches inside the Kremlin walls, the towering Spassky Gate and, at an oblique angle from a corner window, I could see a statue of Pushkin. It was the last week in April, and workmen were putting finishing touches to an underpass that would make it easier for the crowds to spill out of Red Square after the May Day parade. So there I was between the bronze statue of Pushkin, a descendant of an African and revered literary figure and an aristocrat, and anonymous workers preparing for a celebration of labour and the October Revolution – the tsarist past jostling at every turn with the contemporary Soviet experiment! From the windows of my suite, I had a front-row seat where I could see the centre of power from which this drama was being enacted.

I often wondered how Stalin, living inside the Kremlin walls, had tolerated the statue of Pushkin so close to him. But I told myself that Pushkin was safely dead and Stalin, a former seminarian, had discovered long ago that there are only two races on earth: the living and the dead, and in the dark unconscious dreams that had germinated in his soul when he was a young priest in training, he had also discovered that he could always trust the dead more than he could the living.

I am six-feet-four inches tall, and the top of Victor Ramzes' head only reached to my shoulder. He was olive-complexioned, and because his head was too large for his body, it seemed as if a third of his neck was buried between his shoulders. He had gentle eyes that could glitter with intelligence and dance with laughter, or become neutral and guarded in a trice. He was the son of a railway superintendent, and had recently graduated from the elitist Moscow University School of Languages, where diplomats, top journalists and translators were trained. The languages in which he specialised were English, French, Hindi, and he had learned Amharic later on. In the decades I came to know him, he translated several literary works from Hindi and Amharic into Russian. He had become an official escort with the Writers' Union after graduating, and his first assignment had been to escort the American writer, John Steinbeck, when he visited the Soviet Union for the first time.

After unpacking, Victor took me to a bank on Tchaikovsky Street where he withdrew a large wad of rubles and handed it to me. I was casually shoving the money into my pocket when he told me how much it was. I was shocked and handled the funds more carefully. This handsome payment was taken from an account they had established for me and represented the royalties my novel, *Black Midas,* had earned so far. The original English edition of *Black Midas* had come out in 1958, and now in Russia it was very popular and I had collected a large sum of royalties. In fact, the Russian version collected more royalties than the British and American versions put together. It was also published in Georgian.

However, I soon found that this bonanza of rubles could only be spent in the Soviet Union, since it was illegal to take Soviet money out of the country. The Soviets had not signed the international Berne Copyright Agreement. In the light of this, I felt compelled to find ways to spend these funds. For one, I changed my room into a more sumptuous suite at the hotel and, with Victor's help, plotted out some visits to other parts of the USSR. I wanted to spend these funds, and I was curious to see the country for myself after reading about it for so many years.

Afterwards, I contended with the head of the Union of Soviet Writers that by refusing to sign the Berne Copyright Agreement, the Soviet government appeared to be either inadvertently or deliberately exploiting Third World writers who were already being squeezed and underpaid by capitalist publishers. That's why, I insisted, it would be a great boon to us, the victims of a double exploitation, if we were paid in a currency that we could use outside of the USSR. Unfortunately, it was only decades later that the Soviets finally signed international copyright conventions.

I have always been interested in birds, and seeing grey-necked crows winging their way around the Kremlin domes and rooftops, I asked Victor about them. He told me they were features of Moscow life. When they returned to nest around the bases of the onion-shaped domes of churches inside the Kremlin walls, everyone knew that spring would soon follow.

I would take long walks across the city, past its splendid monuments and its charnel rows of wooden shacks. It was early spring and the snow, dirty and wrinkled, still clung to iron rooftops and maintenance men would climb up to the spine of rooftops and send avalanches thundering down on the pavement. It amazed me to see the nimble footwork that old and young pedestrians displayed to avoid being smothered by snow and ice. In addition, cylinders of ice, disgorged by fat down-drains, lay across the pavements like fallen tree trunks, an extra hazard for the drunk or unwary. In the mornings, the rusty iron roofs glowed red, blushing after being released from the icy grip of a long winter. From the depths of my suite, I could sense the whole of Moscow stirring, like a polar bear awakening from a long hibernation. Winter was releasing the city from its icy grip for two seasons before returning. The crowds moved freely, since they were no longer encumbered with massive overcoats and boots. At the same time, they seemed unaccustomed to crowded city pavements, as if they had only recently left the countryside, and collided and jostled along good-naturedly.

My suite in the Hotel National became something of a salon as the weeks went by. An Ethiopian student with whom I had dined early on, returned some days later to call on me. "You probably don't remember my name, but it is Tsegaye Selassie," he said with a twisted smile. "There are thousands of us who bear the Emperor's name, but I am actually a relative – a distant one, mind you. You remember that you invited me to visit you at any time?"

"Yes, of course. I'm delighted that you could come," I lied, because I wanted to get rid of him as soon as possible. I did recall, though, that I had invited him to come and visit me after a fellow Ethiopian student had whispered to me that Tsegaye knew everything about the recent revolt of Emperor Selassie's palace guards.

Tsegaye's perfectly shaped, dark-brown face mirrored all the age-old refinements of a decadent Amharic ruling class – one of the most ancient on the African continent. It betrayed its refined antiquity in a delicate bone structure and the big cruel eyes like those rapacious saints one sees staring out of ancient Coptic tapestries and icons. Generations of inbreeding had created an exquisitely wrought androgynous being.

Tsegaye did tell me about the revolt of the palace guards with all of its bloody details and all of its treachery. This African aristocrat did not say if he had been involved, but he spoke with such authority that there was no doubt in my mind that he was. He told me that the Emperor had gone to Brazil on a State visit and it was common knowledge in palace circles that he owned coffee plantations in Brazil as well as Ethiopia. The palace guards, who were an elite corps and who looked down on the army, took advantage of his absence to stage a coup d'etat. The Americans stepped in and encouraged the army to fight the palace guards, while the Emperor, certain that the army would support him, was flown back to Asmara in an American plane. The conspirators were tortured and then hanged; their bodies were left on display for several days. Tsegaye said that the punishment might have been medieval, but had the other side won, it would have done the same things. This was a strange conversation for a spring morning in Moscow, especially as we were almost in shouting distance of the palace of the Russian Tsars.

Three Russian writers, friends I had met at the Writers' Union, came to my suite and met the Ethiopian. They liked people who were sophisticated, urbane and aristocratic and disliked freedom fighters types with cloth caps and coarse manners. They preferred their revolutionaries to have a certain amount of style, and hence of all the Blacks they met, they preferred Haitians and Ethiopians, both of whom, they felt, had exquisite good manners. The Haitians spoke French with an elegance and ease that was matched by few Frenchmen. Then, there was the legend that Pushkin's grandfather was an Ethiopian prince. Russian communists, it seems, shared the Americans' reverence for royalty and aristocrats. They regarded them as part of the circus of civilisation, which should be retained and imitated.

We drank Armenian brandy and mineral water, an excellent drink which Vladlen, one of the three Russian writers, had introduced us to in the clubhouse of the Writers' Union on Vorovsky Street. Vladlen, speaking in French, told us the story of a Russian millionaire. Starting from humble beginnings, he had made millions, a considerable achievement in Tsarist times, and had been noted for treating the hereditary ruling class with an affectionate disregard. One night, a prince had ordered the finest wine in a restaurant for his friends. The millionaire, not to be outshone, ordered the entire stock of the same wine, told the waiter to pour it into a pail, and when he had done so, washed his hands in the wine, gestured to him to take it away, and got up and walked out. The millionaire later fled to Paris after the Revolution and committed suicide.

Having grown up in a British colony, I was anxious to see what life was like in a Soviet Central Asian Republic. These were regions that had been colonies of Tsarist Russia. So, Victor and I flew on to Tashkent, Samarkand and Bukhara in Soviet Central Asia. I also wanted to go to Khiva but was told that its tourist facilities were just being refurbished and modernised, and they wouldn't be ready for foreign visitors for another year.

Earlier, I had met George Padmore in London. This dapper Trinidadian revolutionary had served as a mentor for my generation. He had been a Communist and a member of the COMINTERN (the Communist International), and while living in Moscow, he had been elected to that city's Soviet, which was the City Council. Stalin had appointed him Commissar for African Affairs. But when he disagreed with Stalin, contending that race would still be a burning issue, even after the issue of class was more or less resolved, he was summarily expelled from the party and had to flee for his life.

Padmore liked to tell amusing anecdotes. He told me how he fell out with Molotov when this high-ranking comrade and ardent Stalinist had ordered him to make a special trip to Berlin in order to buy him razor blades. Padmore had told him quite coolly that he wasn't an errand boy.

"The comrade was obsessed with being clean shaven," Padmore had remarked mockingly.

When Padmore left the Soviet Union with Stalin's hit men hot on his heels, he had escaped to Copenhagen. When he finally landed in London, the British authorities put the word out that he was under their protection. This 007-type of escape by a Black revolutionary from Trinidad who was married to a Jewish wife was truly unique.

As it turned out, Padmore had done important comparative studies of the Soviet and British Empires. During long sessions in his London apartment, he contended that the Soviets were far more generous in modernising backward societies, since the women were emancipated and education and health services were free and available to all. The Soviet rulers also encouraged the preservation of indigenous languages and culture. While the British, through their Christian missionaries, had offered the natives whose countries they colonised, treasures in Heaven, and urged them to eschew material things on earth, the Soviets preached that when socialism redistributed the world's wealth equitably and released the creative energies of the world's peoples, then all of us would enjoy paradise here on earth.

But, Padmore also pointed out that both the British and the Soviets still governed their empires through indirect rule, and despite the vast differences in geography and history, language and culture, a colony by any other name was still a colony. He insisted that as long as the vast majority of the people did not have the absolute right to govern, or even misgovern, their homeland, then a foreign government that arrogated this right to itself was a colonial one, no matter what name it pinned on the rulers and the ruled.

Still, I was anxious to see what life in Soviet Central Asia was like, and Tashkent was as good a place as any from which to begin, since under Soviet rule it had become the largest industrial city in Central Asia.

Under Soviet rule, a tenuous unity had been imposed upon the vast territory from the Baltic to the Yellow Sea. One crossed seven time zones. The Soviets had revitalised the ancient cultures of the peoples in Soviet Asia but at the same time had tried to suppress the new spurt of nationalism that this revival was bound to inspire. But, for the time being, the dominant Russian culture, with its superior technical skills, was still acting as a magnet for the polyglot ethnic groups – Uzbeks, Tadjiks, Buryat-Mongols, Turkmens, Bashkirs, Yakuts, Kazaks, Kalmucks and numerous others. Their Mecca was Moscow, but with China pushing her way towards the forefront, I could see that it might not be too long before Beijing would take over from Moscow. However, no matter how those societies evolved in the future, the contribution that the Soviets had made to a new flowering of indigenous cultures would be a lasting one.

Reading some of the contemporary fiction, non-fiction and poetry coming out of Soviet Asia, one got a more profound understanding of the tremendous changes taking place in this vast region than if one pored over the learned treatises of contemporary scholars. I read a novella entitled *The Camel*, while I was in Tashkent. Victor had given it to me. The author was a young nomad who lived in the border region between the Soviet Union and Iran. His simple tale was vivid, terse, and evocative, with that almost magical quality that a writer achieves when he or she has moved within a lifetime from an oral to a written tradition. The author had, somehow, brought the riches of both into his prose. Reading that story of a young nomad's awakening to a new consciousness of self in a changing world, it occurred to me that his was a voice breaking out of a long silence that had been imposed upon millions, and that after him, a plethora of other eloquent voices would be heard.

When we were flying back from Bukhara to Tashkent, Victor recalled that a year ago he had accompanied John Steinbeck on a flight in the opposite direction and that Steinbeck suffered from claustrophobia. So, after their small passenger plane had landed on a grass runway on the outskirts of Bukhara, and the hostess had taken a long time to open the door to let the passengers out, Steinbeck, in a panic, had pushed the other passengers out of the way and rushed to the front of the plane. After that frantic outburst, Victor said, some of the Uzbek passengers who had witnessed that scene, looking at the greying Steinbeck with awe, thought that he had been possessed by an evil spirit, and they were impressed with how quickly he had exorcised the spirit and returned to normal.

One of the highpoints of my visit to Tashkent was my meeting with Sergei Borodin, the author of the *Donskoi* trilogy. Anticipating my question, he told me with an amused chuckle, "No, I'm not related to the composer." He was, however, a Chekhov devotee, and lived in a house surrounded by cherry orchards.

Victor told me later, "Borodin's a very brave man. Years ago, at the height of the purges, when he was attending a reception at the Kremlin, he refused to shake Stalin's hand. He's one of the few writers to have openly defied Stalin and lived to tell the tale. Luckily, his writer friends convinced him that he'd be safer if he lived as far away from Moscow as possible. So, now he lives here in Tashkent."

When I met him, Borodin was a very tired man. Keeping his integrity during Stalin's reign of terror had probably cost him several years of his life. Deep in his eyes was the same sediment of fear, the same opaque, mindless exhaustion that one found in the eyes of heroes of the anti-Nazi underground movement. Along with writing, his great passion was collecting old coins, and he had a priceless collection. He showed me a Victorian penny that someone had found in Siberia.

Borodin's wife was a Tadjik and daughter of a chieftain. She was a marvellous and gracious woman who managed to do everything with elegance and subtlety. Their youngest son, Sasha, who was eleven, was studying English at school, and while he could only speak a few words to me, his mother explained that her son's English teacher was Chinese. Then, almost inaudibly, she muttered, "I always knew that one couldn't trust the Chinese." The irony of that remark was that, except for her dark, Turkish eyes, she looked like one of the elegant Mandarin women that Chinese artists liked to depict on their rice paper scrolls.

Borodin and his wife invited me for cocktails one evening, but when Victor and I turned up, we found they had prepared a sumptuous surprise party to welcome me. There was a table groaning with food and drink in the centre of a large room. In a corner of the room there was a group of Armenian dancers, singers and musicians. The lead singer, I was told, was one of the most popular entertainers in the Soviet Union. Walking on air after several drinks, I danced with the troupe, sang Guyanese folk songs, and partied into the wee hours of the morning.

The secret of Russia's ties with her Asiatic peoples was not difficult to discover. Almost at once, the Russian settlers in Asia have been intermarrying on a larger scale that any other colonial rulers have ever done. So, the bond holding autonomous republics together is not only one of language, culture and technical skills, but of blood. All Eastern and Western conquerors learnt this lesson ages ago – Alexander, Genghis Khan, Tamerlane (they were conquerors from West and East). Stalin and his successors had the added advantage of a new weapon in their arsenal – an ideology with a widespread appeal for poor and backward peoples. But the ideology by itself would never have won over all the disparate tribes and nations of Asia. When people like Ghulam were conversing, they often said, "Before the arrival of Soviet power," or "after Soviet power was established," and what they mean by this was an army equipped with modern weapons, technicians, teachers, modern transportation, schools, hospitals and a new faith with new gods and devils, saints and sinners... and all of these emanating from Moscow and spreading outwards.

I still had a lot of royalties. So, in Tashkent, I decided to buy some of the famous silk of the area. Silk was part of the dowry for brides along the Silk Road. The women would have a carved trunk filled with silks and jewellery. I brought this silk back to London with the intention to sell it, but the various women in my life, including my daughter, Lisa, descended upon me and took it all.

I spoke to a gathering of Russian writers, journalists and translators about African, Caribbean and Latin American literature, and about the political situation in British Guiana. I could tell the professional journalists from the rest; they had that harassed look of individuals pursued by a surfeit of information. The editor of *International Literature*, one of the foremost literary magazines in the Soviet Union, was there. This was the magazine, with a circulation of over two million, that had published *Black Midas*. The editor had an air of quiet authority about him, and he was treated with that respect that Russians accord to those walking the corridors of power. I also found him extremely hospitable and helpful. I met the translator of my novel and the editor who had worked on it. Both were handsome young women. The first edition of my book came out in 500,000 copies. It was not unusual for books to sell two million copies in the Soviet Union. Yevtushenko's poems would sell out within days of publication, and then there would be a lively resale trade with the same book changing hands three or four times at five times the original price.

I had seen Yevtushenko on several occasions as he was entering or leaving the Writers' Union in Moscow. He was invariably surrounded by a coterie of admirers. My writer friends were anti-Yevtushenko. They said, disparagingly, that his wife was a far better poet than he was. He was, they claimed, a Narcissus gazing at himself in the myriad eyes of his devoted followers. In fact, my friends envied him for his reckless courage, his youth, his popularity on both sides of the Iron Curtain, not to speak of his freedom to travel all over the world, and especially to America. But Yevtushenko, as he himself often declared, was a tough Siberian, capable of enduring any amount of praise or contumely.

My friends pointed out a poet from a remote area of the Caucasus. He was a member of a tribe that numbered fifty thousand, and he had won the Lenin prize for his poetry. He was thickset, blonde, blue-eyed, with a large head, the neck of a wild bull and broad shoulders. Whenever I saw him, and we were to meet again in the Astoria Hotel in Leningrad, he seemed to be drunk and dreaming his life away in the strange and unaccustomed setting of big cities. He reminded me of the bandit chieftain from the Caucasus in Dostoyevsky's *Memoirs from the House of the Dead*, the one whom Ali, the youngest in the clan, looked up to with awe.

Then I met Irakly Andronikov, a Georgian writer, historian and a very popular television personality. He claimed that, quite by accident, he had come across some papers that proved that the Tsar had instigated Pushkin's death at the hands of a professional French duellist. By sheer coincidence, of course, this new discovery happened to coincide with the official party line on the subject. Andronikov was a man who scattered goodwill around him like confetti. We went for a walk one afternoon. Many people on the street recognised him; even the chess players, intent on their game as they sat in a garden enclosed by a circle of old buildings, looked up and waved to him. He was short, swarthy and energetic; his friend, Sergey Smirnov, who had joined us, was the exact opposite; he was tall, blonde and taciturn. Smirnov had won the Lenin prize for his book *Heroes of the Brest Fortress*. He had written about those gallant soldiers who kept on fighting in the deep tunnels under the fortress for months after the German armies had swept deep into Belarus. He hosted a popular TV programme about forgotten heroes of World War II, and one of the most riveting stories he had unearthed recently, he told me, was about a German soldier who had knocked out his senior officer, swum across the Bug River to the Soviet lines and, when he was captured, told the commanding officer that the Germans were going to attack the Soviet Union within seventy-two hours. The Soviet officer got in touch with Moscow, and his message was carried all the way up to Stalin who ordered that the German soldier should be shot as an *agent provocateur*. The Soviet officer did not obey Stalin's orders, but decided instead to wait. He told the soldier that if the Germans did not attack he would be shot. The Germans did attack and the soldier's life was spared. Years later, a stranger rushed up to this German veteran at a railway station in Berlin and thanked him for saving his life. The veteran was mystified until the stranger explained that he had been the young officer this German had knocked out before deserting and swimming across the Bug River. He had hit him so hard on the head that he had spent the war years in a hospital.

One night, in the restaurant of the Intourist hotel in Bukhara, Victor and I sat at the same table as an American Embassy official and his wife. We introduced ourselves and in a short time sparks began to fly, and the Cold War almost burst into flames. Victor told the American that he thought it was bad taste on the part of American diplomats to have shown such open distrust of Steinbeck's Soviet hosts during that author's visit. The American diplomat's reply was that the Soviets were in the habit of attributing statements to visiting writers that bore no relation to what the writers had actually said. The two reminded me of faces on an Egyptian mural, with the profiles facing in opposite directions. It became a verbal contest with each of them adamantly defending his system and his "way of life". I found myself playing the role of a non-aligned referee, and in the end, our parting was almost cordial.

Many decades later, when Northwestern University in Evanston, Illinois hosted the African Studies Association annual meeting, I was able to arrange to have Victor invited so that he could come to the US for a visit. He was ecstatic and happily soaked up every experience, but, most of all, he seemed mesmerised by Chicago's architecture and the palatial homes of the northern suburbs.

In 1979, accompanying my wife, Joy, as she led a group of fifty Black American medical doctors and their wives on a visit to the USSR, I made a point of taking her around to the Soviet Writers' Union. I did not see anyone I had known from my earlier visits, although they were cordial. It had been a tradition to invite visiting writers to leave their autograph or small message on the cafeteria wall, and I was pleased to show Joy my drawing of a man in a hammock that was still there after all these years.

"Being Black in Belorussia is Like Being From Mars"
New York Times, Travel Section, September 19, 1971 (New York)

The Third World students studying in Moscow say that the season they like best is the "green winter" – the summer. This was the season I chose for our journey through European Russia in my silver-grey Daimler 104.

Driving across the Russian countryside in July, I felt besieged by space. The skies were too wide, the forests too vast, the rolling plains too infinite for my imagination to encompass them. The highway was like an asphalt peninsula thrusting into a green ocean, and the towns and villages like clusters of barnacles clinging to it. The villages were far apart and each one had a wide unpaved dirt road cutting through it and petering out in the surrounding fields and forests. It was as though no single village had the collective energy to conquer the space around it.

There was a startled look on sunburnt peasant faces as I sped by. I was a black man in the heart of European Russia, where strangers like me were as rare as orchids in the winter. When I stopped in a town or village, a crowd would surround the car, keeping a respectful distance until someone left the circle of onlookers to ask where I had come from, if the car was mine and where I was going. It was obvious that my presence in a car puzzled the Russian peasants. The image somehow did not fit. They had been told that black men were universally oppressed; that they lived in a kind of destitution that made the lowliest Soviet citizens seem affluent by comparison. I had to explain that my poverty existed on another level; that the difference between the poor peasant in Guyana and myself was that I had escaped into a wider indifference to become a writer. I always left knowing that my explanations were unsatisfactory; that I would need years, instead of hours, to explain the phenomenon of my strange presence in a car somewhere between the river Bug and the Urals. But, the intense curiosity of the Russian peasants was without affectation or malice and, hence, gave no offence.

One rainy night, when the road glistened like an obsidian mirror, I drove across a bridge that spanned a wide river. Two armed sentries, one at either end of the bridge, were so astonished when they saw me that they could not make up their minds whether they should stop me or not. But they must have alerted the guard post ahead, for I was stopped at a roadblock farther on. The guard commander, who came up to me, was alternately jovial and cautious – the joviality seemed natural, whilst the caution was something his epaulettes and rank demanded.

"Where are you from?" he asked – this was a perfectly natural question with which to open our conversation. It was after midnight and we were in the middle of a silver birch forest in Belorussia. Looking at him closely, I thought that he was handling the situation with remarkable equanimity. He must have received a phone call from the sentries on the bridge, saying that they had seen a black man in a foreign car racing through the night. This, I was sure, was not a commonplace occurrence in Belorussia.

"I am from British Guiana," I replied.

If I had told him that I was from Mars, he could not have been more baffled.

"Is that in Africa? he asked, and four soldiers who had been admiring the car joined him to listen and stare.

"No, in South America."

"And where are you going?"

"Moscow."

He signalled the soldiers to remove the roadblock and coming closer he asked:

"Is the car American?"

"No, English."

He looked at it appreciatively.

"Is it yours?" he asked, and I knew that although he was more sophisticated than the peasants, he too was puzzled by what must have seemed to him an image that was slightly out of focus. Many ordinary Russian citizens believe that the very publicised aid their country gives to developing countries, especially to African ones, was used by a handful of spendthrifts to buy luxuries that they themselves were denied. In the cities, the usual reaction to the smart clothes and the expensive cars of black diplomats is one of bewildered resentment. But, I, coming from a country the guard commander had never heard of, was treated to a friendly handshake, and he and his soldiers waved as I drove away.

In the daytime, I would sometimes see half of the highway fenced off for two or three hundred yards and a carpet of grain spread out inside the enclosure to dry in the sun. Old women and young girls bent over their wooden stakes to spread the grain more evenly, leaving twisted furrows and footprints. When other parts of the highway were fenced off for repairs, the road workers were almost invariably women.

In the early morning, flocks of wild birds flew in arrowhead formations above the treetops and the old peasant women with huge bundles of produce would wait at the roadside for lorries to take them to the free markets in the towns. It seemed as if, over this whole countryside, a generation was missing between the very young and the very old. Also, there were far more women than men in this Russian countryside. The war had turned the villages into communities with far more single women than could ever hope to find husbands.

I liked driving through the night, though. It gave me some respite from the vast, shapeless landscape. The darkness, pressing in upon me, restricted my vision to the narrow stretch of highway that was forever being sucked into the beam of my headlights. And when I stopped at the roadside for a while, I was protected by the looming forests of silver birches, firs and pines – gigantic black curtains with a helmet of stars.

When I was somewhere between Smolensk and Moscow, I stopped in a small village at one o'clock in the morning. I went over to a house with cherry trees in the front garden and knocked on the door. It was the only house with a light on. A young woman came to the door. She looked about 23 and was short and sturdy. She was wearing a head scarf and a quilted cotton jacket. Had she just come home or was she about to go out, I wondered. I had expected her to look surprised when she saw me, but there was no more than a note of caution in her voice when she asked:

"Have you come from the gas station?" And since my Russian was indifferent, and I couldn't read my phrase book in the dark, I didn't answer but asked if she spoke any English, French or German.

"A little German," she said, looking straight at me in a way that I found characteristic of many Russian women. It is a direct look without a trace of shyness or coquetry, and yet it is not without freshness or charm.

"I'm on my way to Moscow, and I'm very tired. Could I sleep here until sunrise?"

She turned aside and burst out laughing, and then she began speaking a mixture of German and Russian so that I only caught snatches of what she said: "If I tell them they'll not believe me… A big black man comes to my door long after midnight and asks for a bed for the night… They will say to me 'Gala, you were dreaming!'… Don't you know it's against the law? I would first have to apply for permission. Which country do you come from?"

"British Guiana."

"Where is that?"

"In South America."

"If I were to tell the authorities that a man from British Guiana stayed at my house – they will say that I am mad… so come inside."

She led the way into a small room with two large upholstered chairs and a long, wide divan. I could hear a man snoring in the adjoining room. She fetched clean sheets and a heavy blanket and spread them out on the divan.

"I work at the gas station," she said, "half a kilometre from here. I had just come home from work when you knocked." She offered no further information about herself, and mentioned nothing about the snoring man. But when she brought me a glass of lemon tea, she asked:

"Is this your first visit to the Soviet Union?"

"No, my second. "

She looked tired, and I did not ask any further questions. When we finished drinking the tea, she said goodnight, turned off the light and went out. I woke up before sunrise, and as soon as I started moving about the room, she appeared again with glasses of lemon tea. With only about four hours' sleep, she looked rested and in much better shape than I was. The uneven, mysterious snoring in the next room was still going on.

"You work very hard," I said, for she had on her quilted jacket and headscarf and seemed impatient to go.

"The other worker at the gas station is sick," she said.

I didn't ask for her name and I knew that it would be wise to leave while it was still dark. When we were exchanging gifts – she pinned a badge on my shirt and I gave her a dozen ballpoint pens (a valuable commodity all over the Soviet Union) – I said:

"It was very kind of you… and brave," but she brushed aside my thanks.

"We have an old tradition of hospitality in my village," she said simply.

"Have you got a family?" I asked, determined to find out some more about her, even at the risk of seeming rude.

"A grandfather," she said, pointing to the room from which the snoring came. "My parents were killed in the anti-Fascist war. There're mostly the young and the very old in villages like this."

I offered her a lift to the gas station, but she declined, saying that she preferred to walk across the fields. By sunrise, I had left the nameless village and my nameless hostess far behind.

As I neared Moscow, the wild countryside merged into sprawling villages and these in turn gave way to a forest of new suburbs. Window boxes and trees softened the harsh lines of the new buildings. Along the Leninsky Prospect, taxi drivers coming from the airport – old and young, men and women – drove as if furies were pursuing them like Cossack roughriders.

I left the car in the hotel parking lot and wandered around the city on foot. Mingling with the Moscow crowds, I was conscious of the country-side I had left so recently impinging on the city. The masses of people around me were colliding like tadpoles in a pond. They pushed and jostled and trod on one another's toes with good-natured indifference. They had brought with them the patience and even temper of a people who had learnt their lessons in time and motion in backward villages where cruel winters and a wild countryside had imposed slow, secret rhythms upon their lives.

Walking along the embankment of the Moskva river, I met a young man who somehow symbolised the eternal link between the Russian land and the cities. He had been pacing up and down with measured strides the way I had seen students do in the corridors of the Leningrad university library; but he was reciting poetry. He seemed oblivious to the Sunday afternoon crowds around him, and no one apparently minded his strange behaviour.

"Whose poetry are you reciting?" I asked.

"My own."

"Are you a student?" I asked, because his pale countenance, the blonde forelock drooping over his left eye, his Cossack-style shirt and boots, looked like the affectations of a student, a young man striving to be different.

"No I am a hunter," he said, "I work as a guide for hunting parties in the Caucasus…"

Then he went on to tell me he was born in the Caucasus, and he belonged to a tribe that now only numbered 50,000. Before the advent of Soviet power, he said, his people used to be famous bandits. "Bandits and poets have a lot in common," he said cryptically. He liked solitude, and when he was in Moscow in between his hunting expeditions he knew that the loneliest place was always amidst a large crowd. That was why he had chosen the embankment for his poetry recitation.

"We are the Third World islanded in Europe," he said, "just as the Negro and the red Indian are islanded in the Americas."

We continued swapping views about the Third World, and then he declared, "I think that *Uncle Tom's Cabin* is a fine book."

I laughed, and he looked bewildered until I explained to him that it was not the kind of statement that would endear him to an Afro-American. I had heard of a Soviet cultural attache saying the same thing in Accra and coming to blows with an Afro-American. The fact is the Russian translation of *Uncle Tom's Cabin* is based on the French translation by George Sand. In the process, through the literary magic that translators are capable of, Uncle Tom, in the Russian edition, became a freedom fighter.

I explained this to my friend from the Caucasus, and we parted on reasonably cordial terms.

CHAPTER SIX

RETURN TO THE USSR

The Soviet Writers' Union had invited me for another a visit and as before, I was to make the arrangements to get there, but once there, they would take care of my expenses. Before going this time, though, I called a meeting of all the Caribbean writers in London. We met at Andrew Salkey's apartment. The idea was that we should press that these writings be presented as a body to publishers in Europe, Africa, Asia, and Latin America. With the Soviet Union and Eastern Bloc countries, then, the matter became even more crucial. Though the Soviets had still not signed the Berne Universal Copyright Convention, we could still collect royalties in-country. And, it was likely that such a convention would be signed at some point in the future and then we could receive our royalties elsewhere. In any case, after noting how enthusiastic the Soviets were about my writing, I wanted to encourage others to get into this arena as well. It was after this meeting, that I introduced Vic Reid's, *The Leopard,* and John Hearne's, *Stranger at the Gate,* to Soviet readers. These were the 2nd and 3rd Russian publications of Caribbean works after my *Black Midas.*

Also, for my second visit to the USSR, I decided I would drive and take my daughter, Lisa. When I raised the idea of taking Lisa, and having my former wife and her mother, Joan, join us, both were quite excited. I felt badly that with Joan I had been broke so often and I thought that taking her and Lisa on this journey would be a good thing. Besides the journey across, I thought they could stay about three weeks, before returning to London. After that, I would stay on to do some research on my new novel.

Lisa played an important role in the planning of this intended journey. I did not have a car at the time and she decided that I should buy one. One night, after her weekend visit, she made me stop to look at a Daimler in an auto sales dealership. The next day, I went to my bank to get a loan so that I could buy the car. I told my banker that I was having a bit of a slump and that having the car would allow me the opportunity to travel and rekindle my writing. With the help of a good Italian mechanic who lived close by, the car was serviced and made ready for the long journey. In fact, the journey was over 1,500 miles and took about 10 days. I planned to take the ferry from Harwich to the Hook of Holland. From there, we were to drive across the two Germanies, Poland, Belarus and on to Moscow. I was following in the footsteps of the Russian army fighting back against Hitler. The names of places were familiar because you used to hear them on the news, but the journey was much longer than I expected.

At one stage, after I had entered the USSR, I was driving at high speed and the cops were trying to stop me, but I easily out distanced them. I had my Daimler and they had Russian jeeps. So they radioed ahead and other cops put up a roadblock to stop me. Which they did. They asked me if I knew I was driving above the speed limit and I said no. Driving at night, though, was very dangerous because they didn't have markers on the road to show the centre of the road, and I was driving a right-hand drive car with the headlights slanted for British roads. So, my lights were directed right into the eyes of the incoming drivers and were directed in such a way that I couldn't see both sides of the road clearly.

Because the trip took longer than expected, I was running out of money. Along the way, we camped out at waystations which were well-appointed. Occasionally we stayed in the wooden cottages, the izbas, where there was room for us to stay overnight. We arrived in Moscow and I was despairing because it was a Sunday. Though I had a lot of royalties to collect from the bank, we still needed to economise and we were eating soup and bread until I could get my business affairs in order. We booked ourselves into a hotel and I sent word to the Writers' Union to let them know I had arrived. The next day, Victor came around and we got things sorted out.

Victor also took me to his apartment where I met his wife and son. Since we first met, I had maintained communication with him, but over the subsequent years I had to learn to be very cautious. Originally, I was very enthusiastic in my letters to Victor. Then I noticed that he seemed to back off in the way he was responding to me. There was one time when there had been an earthquake in Tashkent and I had written to him to ask about Borodin, whom I had met on my first trip to the USSR. I wanted to know if he was alright and if there was anything we could send to help. There was no reply and it occurred to me that I was being too insensitive and too informal. So, I changed my tone to a more formal one. Then, his correspondence to me resumed.

As before, the Writers' Union had a big reception for me and I was asked to give a series of talks on Caribbean literature – which I was more than happy to do. My Russian friends also insisted that besides the standard sites of Moscow, that I be sure to take Lisa to see the Black Sea resorts in Sochi before she and her mother returned to London. I thought I would drive, but our hosts insisted that flying would be wiser. Sochi was a delightful stop and dramatically different to the cities we saw in the north. After a few days there, I accompanied Lisa and Joan to Leningrad where they were to catch a ship back to London. I was staying on longer and took the overnight train back to Moscow where I was to meet up with Victor Ramzes again.

I was keen to meet up with Danny, my cousin, who had been studying in the country. Decades have gone by since then, but I can still remember Danny's first coming to my house in Wimbledon one spring morning in 1963. He had rung the doorbell and when I opened the front door, there he was, trying to look self-possessed while involuntarily shifting his weight from one foot to the other. The picture of him standing there under an untidy arch of wisteria whose blossoms had just begun to burst into flowers remains with me to this day. He was wearing a wrinkled sky-blue suit and an open necked shirt, and there was a large battered suitcase beside him. He reminded me of the Syrian peddlers back home who used to go from door to door selling fabric and trinkets to housewives out of dilapidated suitcases like his. I also remember that in order to compensate for his shyness, he was effusive one moment and withdrawn and reticent the next. With his head lowered, he had recited titbits about his twelve-day voyage from George-town, glancing up every so often to be sure I was listening. He told me that my mother, whom he called "Aunt Ethel", had given him my address and instructed him to contact me as soon as he arrived in London.

At the door, I remember him pitching a line at me and, with a rush of words, declaring, "Cousin, I'm Danny James, and I'm too glad to catch you at home, man! I can tell from the likeness I saw in the papers back home, and the pictures Aunt Ethel showed me, that you must be Ian Carew! Well, Ian, here I am on your doorstep!" His ebullience sounded so false that it aroused my suspicion, and left me wondering if this "cousin" business wasn't some kind of ploy. Even if he was using the name most people knew me by back in Guiana – Ian – why hadn't my mother written to tell me about his coming or given him a letter of introduction? So I recall asking him bluntly, "And who did you say you are? Danny James? Because, to tell you the truth, I can't remember any James to whom I'm related."

My rudeness obviously offended him deeply, and with eyes flashing and muttering under his breath, he picked up his suitcase and was about to leave when, in an instant, it dawned on me that he might, indeed, be a relative.

"Wait a minute!" I pleaded, and asked in a conciliatory tone, "You wouldn't by any chance be related to Gilbert James?"

It had struck me that he bore a strong resemblance to Gilbert, who was one of the seven children my maternal grandparents had adopted. In addition to this marked resemblance to Gilbert James, it seemed that Danny had also apparently inherited his quick temper that everyone who had lived in the Agricola family house knew about.

Danny put the suitcase down and confessed gruffly, "Gilbert James is my father, and Dorothy Gulliver is my mother, and I'm the product of one of his hit-and-run adventures, because he left for America before I was born."

"Well, do come in and tell me about this philandering father of yours and step-uncle of mine; haven't been in touch with him for years," I said, leading the way into my study. And for a long time afterwards, I remembered the fleeting expression of anguish on his young face when he described himself as "an accident of one of his father's hit-and-run affairs." It was one that no amount of bravado could disguise.

Once he was comfortably seated in an armchair, we chatted a bit and then I invited him to have brunch with me, and he agreed. So, over a meal of rice and peas, pork chops and fried plantains, and a lively homemade pineapple punch, I enquired, "Wasn't there another James? A Reverend James who was married to Aunt Edith, my father's sister? For a moment I thought you might have been related to him."

As soon as I mentioned Parson James' name, Danny's serious and brooding expression dissolved into an infectious burst of laughter that made lights dance in his eyes. "No, that old reprobate's not related to me. With all kind of scandals swirling around him, he's still managing to threaten sinners with monsoon rains of fire and brimstone, while he himself is a champion lover man and a scamp."

The Danny James who came to my Wimbledon house that morning was a handsome nineteen-year-old Guyanese Creole. He was six-feet tall and sturdily built; and he had a mop of unruly black hair, restless dark brown eyes and bushy, V-shaped eyebrows that gave his face a permanently quizzical expression. I remember being envious of the suntan he had brought with him from the tropics, for, even though it was already fading after his twelve-day voyage from BG, it still tinted his complexion with a rich brown afterglow.

"When did you arrive in London?" I had enquired, and in true Guyanese fashion he treated me to a long and detailed account of his journey from Georgetown to London's West India Docks; of the smells and the bustle at the docks; of waking up with no sun in the grey skies; and of his long cross-town subway ride to Wimbledon.

He turned out to be a good guest from the very beginning, and while he was helping to wash up dirty dishes that were cluttering up the sink, he had asked rather haltingly if I'd mind if he stayed with me until he found a job. I told him that he was welcome to be my guest for a while.

I suggested to Danny that he spend a month or so getting the feel of the city before looking for a job and signing up for night school. But I had quite clearly failed to discern how resourceful he was, for, within a week, he got a job with an American construction company. Once he started work, our busy schedules made lengthy talks possible only at weekends or during the odd after-dinner occasion when we both happened to be at home.

One night, when we were relaxing in my study after our evening meal, Danny closed the book he was reading and confessed that he couldn't understand half of what the author was trying to say. It rankled in his mind, he said, that although he had been near the top of his class when he finished Junior High School, he'd been forced to drop out in order to add to his mother's meagre weekly income.

"Child labour and a good education don't go hand in hand," he declared bitterly, and since he was big and sturdy-looking in his early teens, he had forged his age and found work with a "Yankee" corporation that was mining manganese in the Kaituma area of the British Guiana North-West District. While working in that wild and isolated region of swamps, hills, rivers and virgin rainforests for six years, he had, in that relatively short time, managed to master a variety of invaluable technical skills as a machinist, a mechanic, and a driver of large and small bulldozers.

So, having served a varied and invaluable apprenticeship with this mining company in the BG bush, he had, by sheer coincidence, secured another job with a branch of the same company in London. But first, they had tested him by having him cut up a large steel girder with an acetylene torch. Wearing the prescribed safety gear and taking every possible precaution, he acquitted himself well. It helped that the equipment was much more efficient than the one he had used back home. When the foreman had asked him jokingly why he didn't seem to trust the company's safety equipment, Danny had told him that in the six years he had worked in the manganese mines in BG, he had been an eyewitness to several accidents, one of which had been fatal, and these tragedies had taught him that when working with gas or electricity, your first mistake can be your last. However, he passed the test with flying colours, and won high praise from the Scottish foreman.

After a few months on the job, one evening he came home looking glum. He replied to my repeated enquiries by saying that whereas he hadn't faced any racial discrimination while working for the Yankee company in BG, he had begun noticing ominous signs of racism on his London job. Of course, he admitted, conditions were somewhat different in the Kaituma jungle, and skilled workers willing to put up with the poisonous snakes, the hot and humid climate and the isolation, were hard to find – and even harder to keep when you did find them. Another fact was that those white Yankee co-workers who had sweated it out, side-by-side with him, naked to the waist, were the first whites he had seen doing manual labour. Like most colonials, he had grown up believing that the Almighty had ordained that white British colonial officials should always be decked out in their immaculate proconsul attire while they supervised the *natives* doing manual work on plantations, or in mines and factories.

However, Danny's worst fears came to a head after six months when his fellow workers threatened to go on strike, unless he was fired for breaking union rules. To his surprise, his Scottish foreman and a shop steward summoned the malcontents and listened patiently to their complaints about how the "darkie" was spoiling things for everyone by speeding up and working like a fiend. That canny Scot and shrewd union official told them that since theirs was not the first complaint about Danny they had received, they had both monitored his work pretty closely, and this was what they found: he was smart and diligent and, in any eight hour shift, he did the work of any two of them put together. So, they proposed a tongue-in-cheek solution that would resolve the Danny dispute once and for all. Since Danny was doing the work of two of them, then one or two of the protesters could undertake to do three men's work – and the management would then be willing to sack Danny on the spot! That was the end of that! Danny told me that after being tipped off in advance of two attempts to sabotage machinery he was working with, his policy was to be vigilant on the one hand, and to win new allies in the majority camp on the other.

Danny moved into a second-storey room that overlooked the back garden and a large copper beech that shut out the early morning sunlight and screened him from our neighbour's prying eyes. He then settled down to a routine of work in the daytime and attending extra-mural classes in the evening.

A representative of the PPP was in London at the time, and he had told me that the Eastern Bloc countries were offering more scholarships to study in their countries. I suggested to Danny that he look into getting one of these scholarships, but, at first, he was a bit hesitant. He listed several things that would be a problem: his race, Communist education, the Cold War. But I introduced him to this PPP representative, and after talking with Danny and getting a sense of his background and interests – noting that Danny had been working at a mining company – the representative recommended that Danny apply for a scholarship to study engineering in East Germany. Danny applied and was accepted. This was a rare opportunity, because working a job and attending school in the evenings, it would have taken him several years before he could get a degree.

I saw him off for East Germany, and I didn't see him again until the summer holidays. As it turned out, when he got to East Germany, the quota had been filled, so they offered him the opportunity to study in Moscow at the Patrice Lumumba University instead. All of these programmes required that Third World students enrol in intensive language studies before being able to enter their formal areas of study. Despite the fact that several of Danny's classmates had already studied at universities before, Danny had done better than them in the Russian language courses. But he was disillusioned with the treatment he received as a black foreigner in the USSR and was complaining about the hardships of living there.

Danny's letters had kept me up-to-date on his studies, and that first year at Patrice Lumumba University seemed to pass rather quickly. One afternoon in the early summer, when I answered the doorbell, there he was again, broad smile on his face and suitcase in hand. But, I noticed at once that there were scars on what had been his unblemished mahogany-brown countenance. The scars looked as if he had been cut with a razor. When I asked him about them, he explained that they had been made by frost in the air during the Moscow winter.

"These are scars from that same brute of a winter that defeated Napoleon and Hitler before my time," he said.

The construction company, for which he had worked, agreed to employ him for three months every summer and now that he had become a university student, the other workers treated him with a new respect.

At first, he was fairly reticent about his experiences in the Soviet Union. He knew that I was a socialist and tended to be lenient about flaws in the USSR. The difference was that my concept of it was a dream, while he had the experience of living for a year with the day-to-day irritations of that badly flawed experiment. One night, when I asked him about his relationships with other Guyanese, fellow Third World students, and ordinary Russian folk, his response surprised me. First, he mentioned very casually that he had done so well in his first year studies that he was being transferred to Leningrad University where he was going to be the first Guyanese student to attend that historic institution. He then announced that he decided to major in history and political science, since he would've needed two extra years of mathematics in order to study electrical engineering. After talking about academic issues, he then launched into a litany of complaints about life in the Soviet Union. Most of his anger was directed against the mounting racism that was affecting his life and that of the other Third World students. Initially, they had all gone there with great expectations that, in the socialist world, racial discrimination would have been completely abolished. But alas, this was not to be, and the stories he told about students being attacked by thugs, and the police intervening belatedly and then arresting the victims and not the attackers, had familiar echoes of life in the West. Things had come to a head when an angry Russian father had murdered a Ghanaian student who was dating his daughter, and there was an attempt at an official cover-up of the crime. Danny had played a leading role in organising a seven-hundred-strong Third World student demonstration. The protesters assembled at Red Square. Both the police and ordinary citizens were taken completely by surprise. They had looked on as though mesmerised by the sight of the first non-governmental demonstration in Red Square since the Trotsky riots of the 1920s. This peaceful and well-organised protest, taking place four decades later, exposed the growing problem of racism in the Soviet Union very effectively, and made it impossible for the Soviet leadership to keep on claiming blithely that this problem did not exist. When Premier Khrushchev was told about the demonstration, he declared angrily that the students "Could stand on their heads when they were in their own country, but when they were in the Soviet Union, they would have to obey Soviet laws which prohibited all demonstrations." Nonetheless, the Soviet government was forced to respond and, after denying that there was a problem, it grudgingly took steps to remedy it. Needless to say, Danny and those other students knew full well that the international press would pick up the news of their demonstration and, though it would be distorted, this would help them make their case.

Being the naïve and trusting soul that I was, I was appalled when Danny told me about the devious black market currency transactions in which some Third World students became involved. "They don't declare the foreign currency they bring with them, and using this, along with the generous monthly allowance the Soviet Government gives us, they wheel-and-deal in the black market. That's what Marx would call their 'primitive accumulation'. But starting from that modest beginning, some of them are cunning and unscrupulous enough to have become quite wealthy. They dress in Western styles and carry out these illegal currency exchanges with impunity. Russian girls are drawn to this flamboyant lifestyle and flock around the student apartments near the university, though there are also idealistic ones who are choosing to marry foreign students because they want to work side-by-side with their husbands to help them build their new societies when they go back home. Still, there's a funny side to this sordid business. I often have to remind myself that here am I in a communist country witnessing Third World students learning and practising the crucial basics of capitalism day after day. Many of them who started out as ardent socialists, end up being worshippers of the almighty dollar."

Despite Danny's revelations, I continued to believe that some of the ideals of the October Revolution were still alive, but as a writer and activist, I decided that I had to find out more. It was all the more important that I tell the truth about how this vast corrupt Soviet bureaucracy had been slowly imploding for years and, in the process, was discrediting socialism. I decided that the best way in which to analyse these complex happenings, and bring them to the attention of a wider public, was to write a documentary novel based on Danny's experiences as a black student in Moscow and Leningrad. So, night-after-night, we had long question-and-answer sessions during which I took notes, and it was during these sessions that the first chapters of my novel, *Moscow Is Not My Mecca,* began to take shape.

I could sense, as the end of the summer holidays approached, that Danny was in two minds about whether he should return to the USSR. But one night after dinner, he told me that after weighing and balancing the pros and cons, he intended to continue his studies at Leningrad University. He was doing so, he said, knowing full well that life was no bed of roses, and that the gulf between the propaganda about the creation of a new socialist society and the tawdry reality of a corrupt bureaucracy suffocating the creative talents of a whole nation was wider and deeper than the Pacific Ocean. And, yes, there was increasing racism, the winters were vicious and the day-to-day bureaucracy unbelievably petty and obstructive. On the plus side, though, in spite of the political and social problems, the quality of education was very good, many of the ordinary people he met from time to time were warm-hearted and friendly, and in five or six years, he could earn the equivalent to an M.A degree. If he were to stay in Britain, he acknowledged, working full time and going to night school, it would take him three years to get the required "O" levels, another three to pass the "A" levels for university entrance, and then another six years to earn a BSc degree. That could add up to a total of twelve years. Then, in a lighter vein, he confessed that the Third World students had tipped him off that the young women in Leningrad were more sophisticated than those in Moscow, and men of colour were in great demand. With a devilish gleam in his eye, he assured me that this last bit of information had only played a small role in his decision.

Danny had been at Leningrad University for over a year when the Union of Soviet Writers invited me to pay another official visit to the USSR. My novel, *Black Midas,* was still doing quite well in Russia. This invitation could not have come at a better time, since I had also started work on my documentary novel based on Danny's experiences. I had been particularly intrigued by Danny's parting words as he left to return to his studies in the Soviet Union: "Here in London, I had to look out for gangs of Teddy boys roaming the streets and attacking anyone of colour they ran into, and now I'm on my way to Leningrad to face more of the same – Russian thugs prowling the streets in search of students of colour. It's a hell of a world we're living in!"

Now that I was back in the USSR, I was sure that with Danny being fluent in Russian and showing me around, he could also arrange meetings with a cross-section of Third World students who could provide me with invaluable material for my new book.

Victor Ramzes was to be my escort and interpreter from the Writers' Union again, and he booked us on that luxurious midnight Moscow-Leningrad train of which the Russians were very proud. Since my cousin Danny was the only Guyanese in Leningrad, it wasn't difficult locating him. I found him living in a university dormitory on the right bank of the Neva River. It was one of the relatively new and grim Leningrad buildings. I was delighted to see him. But I noticed that there, closer to the Arctic Circle, the scars on his face made by frost were more pronounced. Bursting with family pride, Danny introduced me to several of his friends.

My first official visit to Leningrad was a short and hectic one. The mornings welcomed me with grey skies and a fine, misty rain. When the palest of sunshine burst through the clouds, it created patches of sunlight, and very quickly, eager sunbathers commandeered those precious patches and stretched out to bask in their warmth. The Neva River still had some chunks of ice jostling their way towards its estuary, and yet those ardent sunbathers didn't seem to mind exposing their half-naked bodies to temperatures that were still only in the upper forty degrees Fahrenheit.

A Russian-speaking Danny and Elke, his East German girlfriend, joined us for dinner at the historic Astoria Hotel. It was while staying at this hotel that Yesenin, the Russian revolutionary poet who had married the American dancer Isadora Duncan, had committed suicide some forty years before. Interestingly, Danny and Elke could only communicate in Russian, because she couldn't speak English and he couldn't speak German. Somehow, when Danny spoke in Russian to the waiters or to Victor and Elke, his whole persona seemed to change, and he became more assured and sophisticated. He had an open personality and had not restricted himself to the university community, but had gone to the houses of workers. He also got to know some of their children who were attending ballet school free of charge. He was pleased to note that they were not being restricted because of their parent's socioeconomic status.

I remember Danny complaining that the most difficult challenge he had to face in Leningrad was adjusting to the new cycles of light and darkness. "The sun sleeps through nights and days in the winter and it stays awake twenty-four hours a day in the summer," he said. Elke, speaking in Russian with Victor translating, added, "He has difficulty falling asleep in the summer because the light creeps under his eyelids, while his body keeps telling him that it's time to sleep."

There were students from over fifty countries at the university, and with Danny's help, I met and mingled with those from Latin America and the Caribbean, Africa, India, and other Third World countries. They were young and idealistic, but they all agreed that the streets of Leningrad were becoming more and more dangerous for people of colour. Thugs had recently set upon the three of them and all three had bruises and broken ribs. But, they admitted, they also had an allowance more than twice the amount the Russian students had.

Though many of the black students I interviewed seemed more concerned about what was happening back home than the immediate situations around them at the university and the community at-large, several of them did complain about the quality of the education. But, how could they judge quality, if they had had no formal education before? I could see how Danny was benefiting from his education in Russia. He didn't have a wide background in high school before he came to Britain. He had to drop out of school to go to work. His communication with me, after almost two years of studies, was much more sophisticated than when he first arrived. You could see his intellect expanding and his English improving. He'd had to learn English grammar better in order to learn Russian.

As I questioned these students about the racism they were facing in Leningrad, I kept looking into their eyes and wondering which of them, on returning home, would end up as a corpse by a roadside, or in a garbage dump after being murdered by right-wing death squads. Because of their education in a Communist country, they would be branded as "dangerous subversives", and nowhere in their homeland would they be safe. But at least, the hatred of those "communist educated" students would be based on ideology and not on skin colour. For the first time, being a "communist" was something worse than being a "nigger" or a "coolie".

However, there were also magical moments during that Leningrad visit. I saw the Kirov Ballet Company's performance of Romeo and Juliet, with music by Tchaikovsky. Echoes from the music still linger in my brain, and images from the final scene will remain with me forever. I also visited the Hermitage Museum, which was the former Winter Palace of the Tsars. It had some three hundred galleries and twenty-seven kilometres of corridors, and must be the world's largest museum. There were spellbinding exhibits of Rembrandt's paintings, while in another gallery there was the largest collection of paintings from Picasso's blue period that I had ever seen. It's interesting that the Tzarina, Catherine the Great, whose agents were given *carte blanche* to buy any piece of art that they deemed to be worthwhile, did so with impeccable good taste from the earliest days, while she herself remained a dilettante who knew little about art apart from its price. And yet, the art she collected remains a priceless legacy for all time. Catherine and the Hermitage! The two have become synonymous. One would hardly have expected the Bolsheviks to follow in Catherine's footsteps, but, in fact, they did, and it was under their rule that the large Picasso collection was purchased.

It would have taken a lifetime to see even a small part of the collections that the Hermitage housed. I felt exhausted after drifting in and out of half a dozen of the larger galleries. But equally striking were the large photographs that showed the damage to the buildings from the bombardment by Nazi artillery during World War II. Looking at these, one could appreciate the dedication, skill, creativity, and expense it had taken to restore the buildings to their original state.

Danny's dormitory room, which he shared with a student from Ecuador, was small and austerely furnished. They each had a single bed, a desk and a small cupboard. The students I met were polite, but guarded at first, but after some humorous exchanges, they relaxed and the stories and anecdotes made it difficult for me to keep up with them. When I mentioned this to Danny, he laughed and said, "You came when spring fever was pushing cabin fever aside, and that's when even folks with lockjaw will talk."

The Leningrad branch of the Union of Writers hosted a reception for me, and I gave a talk on Contemporary Writing in the English-speaking Caribbean. When we were leaving, Victor apologised, saying that several of the writers had availed themselves too freely of the free drinks. That's why, he said, the questions they asked had nothing to do with my talk. Many of the questions were, in fact, about my student life in the United States as a black man and being a writer in exile from my home country. The naiveté of some of the questioners was astonishing, but I told myself ruefully that almost half a century of crude negative propaganda about the West had backfired, and a cynical population was now believing the opposite of what they were being told by their officials. Later, when I saw my hosts collecting leftovers from the reception, I couldn't help but think it reminded me of a scene from Mikhail Bulgakov's novel *Black Snow*, where a drunken partygoer was trying to stuff a piece of salmon into his pocket.

Danny broke the news to me that he and Elke were planning to get married. I wished him the best of Guyanese luck, but pointed out that he would be adding a fifth strike to the four he had listed when he was first awarded a scholarship. Now, he would be a black man from British Guiana with a white wife from an ostracised communist state, in addition to having studied behind the Iron Curtain during the Cold War. Elke was a graduate student in mathematics and was two years away from earning a Ph.D. She was quiet and a foil to Danny's gregariousness. But she also had a wicked sense of humour. Once, when the three of us had gone for a walk along the waterfront, a security guard, after examining our papers, had turned to her and asked, "And who are you?" She took Danny's dark brown hand in her lily-white one and replied, "I'm his sister." The guard, who had been stern and unsmiling up to that moment, cracked up, and waved us on with a wide grin.

I said goodbye to Danny and Elke, wishing them the best of luck once more.

I returned to England and completed my new novel, *Moscow is Not My Mecca*. Secker and Warburg published it in 1964 and Stein and Day in the US brought it out as *Green Winter* in 1965. Stein and Day was a new publisher and my book, they told me, was the first book they published. I knew the book would be controversial and had added an "Epilogue" to the American edition. I was determined not to produce a knee-jerk anti-communist work, but to tell the truth about the rise of racism in the Soviet Union. The regular Communists were against it. But, the Socialist Workers Party in Toronto, Canada was for it and had done a favourable review of the book in its journal. The SWP was Trotskyist and thus anti-Stalin. Their journal was also one of the few white journals to recognise the impact

Malcolm X would have as a black leader and they had, for example, bought the rights to most of his speeches.

John Wolfers, my agent in London, told me that he had received another offer to pay for publication of the book, but he had turned it down. He didn't tell me this until long afterwards. I could only guess who the alleged publisher had been, Wolfers was quite principled. Later, I discovered that a pirated copy had been published and it had been adapted for teaching English to African students. Perhaps, the publisher of this one was the same as the one who had approached Wolfers? I actually saw a copy of this pirated edition when I was browsing through contemporary publications in a shop in Lusaka. I looked over and saw a nun standing close by who had taken it from the shelf and was looking at it. It was called *Winter in Moscow* by Jan Carew. So, I begged her to sell it to me, since it was my book and I had never seen it before in this edition. She graciously agreed to do so. Many years later, a fellow professor at George Mason University presented me with another copy. The book had been published by Avon books in 1967 and even had an introduction ostensibly written by me, though I had not written a word of it. Furthermore, the title was totally different from my intention – though, perhaps more closely associated with Cold War perspectives on Moscow.

At the time of *Moscow is Not My Mecca*'s initial British publication, Danny was in the midst of a school year at Leningrad University. The first time he heard about the novel being in print was when he was summarily expelled from the University. Instead of returning to London immediately, however, he decided to contest the expulsion at the centre of Soviet power. So, taking the train to Moscow, he went to the Kremlin and insisted that he wanted to speak to President Brezhnev or to Premier Kosygin. After being passed from one astonished secretary to the next for over an hour, he finally got through to Premier Kosygin on the telephone and, according to Danny, the conversation went something like this:

Danny: Good morning, Comrade Kosygin, my name is Danny James, and I am a student from British Guiana –

Kosygin: Guinea? In Africa?

Danny: No, British Guiana, in South America, and I was studying History and Political Science at Leningrad University. But I was expelled last week –

Kosygin: Expelled, Comrade?

Danny: Yes, I was given a week to leave the USSR, and all because my cousin wrote a book about the day-to-day problems of racism that we Third World students are facing here.

Kosygin: And why are you approaching me on this matter?

Danny: Because friends I trust have told me you are honest and fair-minded. Comrade Kosygin, I haven't read the book my cousin wrote, but I know that he's not afraid of telling the truth in his writings. What I would like to suggest is that you and I first read the book, and then we can meet and discuss the issues it raises, objectively, before a decision is taken.

Kosygin: Perhaps. But, maybe I should meet some of those fellow students of yours? Apart from toadies seeking favours, and sycophants, there are not that many people who have nice things to say about me.

Much to Danny's surprise, the Premier laughed out loud before pleading that he was too busy with affairs of State to take up his suggestions. But, he added that he admired how this student from British Guiana had been bold enough to walk into the Kremlin compound and insist on pleading his case with him directly. He then said he would recommend to the Minister of Education that the expulsion order be dropped and that Danny be reinstated.

It was interesting to hear about Danny's experiences with Premier Kosygin, because, years later, Kosygin was mentioned in a letter that Michael Manley, the Prime Minister of Jamaica, had written to me. Manley was describing his meetings with Premier Kosygin during his first and only official visit to the USSR. Kosygin had apparently been Manley's principal host during that visit, and Manley had described him as being warm, thoroughly versed in world affairs, considerate and having a subtle sense of humour. By sheer coincidence, Victor Ramzes, who had served as my guide and interpreter since my first visit to the USSR, and who became a lifelong friend, happened to be a friend of Kosygin's daughter. At Victor's behest, when her father died, I sent her a copy of Manley's letter along with my condolences.

Danny did indeed receive a letter from the Minister of Education cancelling the expulsion order and he rejoined the student body. However, much to his annoyance, for the rest of his years as a student, the faculty and administrators treated him with a special deference since he was rumoured to have powerful friends in the Kremlin. Perhaps his success, as a lone Guyanese student who had confronted the Kafkaesque Soviet bureaucracy, was a portent of things beginning to fall apart in the Soviet Union, though at the time no one recognised it as such.

By the time Danny graduated with the equivalent of a Master's degree, I was living in Canada, and he had written to me saying that he had run into difficulties getting a visa for Elke, his East German wife, to join him in Britain. In fact, after he applied for the visa, he said, a stranger had approached him and offered to get the visa immediately, if he would agree to mingle with foreign students and pass on information about the militants among them to designated agents from time to time. I wrote to a friend in the British Parliament, explaining the situation, and he, in turn, took the matter up with the Home Office. As a result, the visa was issued and Danny was able to ignore the proposal that he should become a spy.

I also speculated that my book's publication might affect my relations with the Soviet Writers' Union and I was correct. I also knew that once the book was published, I would also have to be very cautious in my correspondence with Victor Ramzes.

On the other hand, however, the controversy made the Germans suddenly very interested in me. A West German version of *Moscow is not My Mecca* was published in 1965. *Black Midas* had earlier been brought out in a German edition in 1959, and there was also discussion of translating *The Wild Coast* too. First, the Cultural Department of the West German government invited me for a visit. Subsequently, the Cultural Department of the East German government invited me there.

While I was staying at a very posh hotel in West Berlin, a strange woman phoned me to invite me to her room after midnight. I didn't go; a friend from the Cameroons had just been poisoned after an invitation like that. I tried to look around the dining room at breakfast the next morning to see if I could detect who she might have been, but to no avail.

It was a tense period all around, and outspoken black people had to be careful. A few years earlier, the African American writer Richard Wright died suddenly from a heart attack in Paris in 1960. His close friend, the black artist Ollie Harrington left Paris in 1961, deciding he would be safer in East Berlin.

"Epilogue"
Published in the novel *Green Winter*, 1965 (New York)

"The Russians have been the most generous of all peoples to those who were poor, backward, illiterate... My people were dying out before the Revolution. Soviet power established itself here in the early twenties, and now illiteracy has vanished... There are over a million of our students studying at Higher Education institutions... You saw the canal that separates the old and the new city? Not so long ago my people lived on one side of the canal and our czarist overlords on the other... This has all gone forever."

Hamid Goulam, the Uzbek playwright, was sitting in his large office in Tashkent talking to me. He was a man in his early forties with a thickening waistline and the clear eyes of a plainsman accustomed to scanning the vast distances of the steppes. He succeeded in being calm, dignified, controlled without ever being pompous. And that peculiarly hooded expression, which many high Soviet officials seem to wear like a mask, was completely absent from his open intelligent face. He kept his hands together with his fingers interlocked, and occasionally a single finger would wag an accompaniment to some point he wanted to emphasise.

At no time listening to Hamid Goulam did I get the impression that he was just a Party hack trotting out a tired hymn of praise of Soviet Power. But while he spoke I tried to put myself in his place. Suppose I had been like him, a proud Uzbek, forty-three years old, a distinguished playwright, and a high and trusted official in the Soviet hierarchy! I would have been born in 1919 a year before the Revolution had travelled East to Tashkent (for it had travelled as fast as the Red Army could rout the White rebels, unseat the local emirs and generally impose order on a chaotic situation); and growing up from childhood to youth and then to manhood, it would not have taken much propaganda for me to realise that the Revolution had brought fantastic benefits to Uzbekistan; that almost overnight my people had been thrust out of the muddled twilight of waiting years into the twentieth century; I would have known in my bones that for centuries my people had been sunk in a slough of stupor, so that the only excitement offered was the shriek of innocents cast down from the high towers, the public executions, and the macabre rivalries between the local emirs, khans, mullahs, and their czarist overlords to outdo one another in the imaginative cruelties they practised against my people. I would have seen factories, schools, technical institutes, universities, hospitals, housing projects in which multi-storied apartment buildings were replacing the traditional mud houses; and would have heard the grumblings of the older generation when the women first cast aside their veils (the first actress who appeared onstage without her veil was torn to pieces by the audience); but looking into the old peoples' eyes as they squatted in the tea houses, too polite to show their bewilderment at the fantastic realities around them, I would also have known that my people had somehow to pay a high price for the swift changes, the progress, the great leap forward. Perhaps the old people would have realised that once the Uzbeks had crossed such a great distance in time so rapidly, then enormous voids are left in the spirit, and a people would need to fill these voids with the rich things of the imagination. Educated in the autonomous Republic of Uzbekistan, I would have known the songs, the legends, and the folklore that sprang from the conquests of Genghis Khan and Tamerlane and felt an almost atavistic pride in the fact that my ancestors had conquered and then ruled the Russians for four centuries.

It is not difficult for me, a British Guianese, or for an ex-colonial from Asia, Africa or Latin America to understand the underlying tensions that exist between the Uzbeks and their generous Russian benefactors. One can argue that the Soviets are supreme empiricists, that their plan for economic and ideological integration of the great land mass they controlled had nothing to do with any sentimental fondness for Uzbek, Kirghiz or Tadjik nomads; but if the other colonial and ex-colonial powers had shown the same enlightened self-interest when they controlled such large areas of the world, the gap between the haves and have-nots would not have been as wide as it is today. The late Lord Beaverbrook's forlorn crusade for the economic integration of the "Empire" through a programme of expansion, investment and overall development is not unlike the one the Russians actually implemented in Asia.

For two decades, Russian propaganda has claimed that the victory of the working class in the Revolution has swept away, along with the panoply of czarism, the Russian Orthodox Church, the injustices of the rich against the poor, the inequities of racialism and colonialism. Well, has it? The revolution and Stalinism has indeed eliminated many things, including millions of the innocent and guilty alike, but they did not get rid of nationalism. Stalin, the ex-student from a seminary, made a religion of Russian chauvinism. And it was only natural that the more xenophobic the Russians became, the more strongly the different races and nationalities inside the Soviet borders would react, by themselves, becoming more and more nationalistic. And it is a fact that the Russians have never distinguished themselves by their subtlety. Peter the Great, a sword in one hand and the tools of a shipbuilder and artisan in the other, imposed progress upon the backward serfs and boyars he ruled. And Stalin, that archetypal tyrant, was later to force the Russian peasant into becoming an industrial proletarian almost overnight, by using famine, firing squads and terror unlimited.

The attitude of the Uzbeks and other coloured peoples inside Russia is not fundamentally different from that of coloured peoples in the rest of

Asia, in Africa and the Americas. If foreign students of colour encounter discrimination in Russia, it is safe to assume that the roots of this discrimination lie in anti-Semitism and the racial contempt of white Russians for their own coloured citizens. Racialism is never a spontaneous growth. It is rather an aberration born of the arrogance and guilt of the haves towards the have-nots. Communism was used as a plaster to cover up the sore of racialism. But with the thousands of students from Asia, Africa and Latin America arriving in the Soviet Union as students and living side by side; with the collective frustration of the vast majority of African students making itself felt publicly in a demonstration in Red Square; and with the Sino-Soviet rift becoming one of the facts of life in our time, even the most dogmatic hot gospeller of communism is having to admit that slogans are not enough to cure racialism.

After the student demonstration, Mr. Khrushchev blurted out irately that the students "Can stand on their heads in their own countries if they liked", but in the Soviet Union they must abide by Soviet Laws; and then he added once again that the Russians were more interested in class than in race. But a more profound analysis of the situation is required if there is to be a working relationship between the Russian peoples and coloured students from Asia, Africa and the Americas. There is a great deal of speculation about the Sino-Soviet rift, but one very important aspect tends to be overlooked. Thousand of Chinese students studied in the Soviet Union during the past decade, and many of them had to face the same crude racial arrogance with which the present crop of coloured students has to contend. After all the other explanations are offered, there is still the fact that some of those students hold positions of power in China today; they might well be the starch that stiffens the Chinese attitude to their once fraternal neighbours.

The Russian case against the Chinese was put to me by both officials and ordinary Soviet citizens I met by chance, and then there was the lengthy Suslov speech, which was published in full in April 1964. Suslov portrayed the Chinese as xenophobic ingrates. Having denounced gratitude as a bourgeois vice for nearly half a century, and having themselves used gratitude for exclusively political ends – to reward the faithful and to punish the heretic (and sometimes, as in Tito's case, the reward and the punishment almost collided, the one riding so hard on the heels of the other), why should the Chinese, still burning with the zeal of new converts, adopt the bourgeois vice of "gratitude"? Besides, the Russians should know that poor nations have little but their pride to give them solace for their backwardness. What the rich nations call ingratitude, the poor countries regard as a show of pride.

The Russians, and this includes Hamid Goulam when he was discussing the Chinese intransigence at a recent writers' conference, sound like self-righteous Western Europeans talking about the vagaries of coloured peoples. They talk of "WE" and "THEY" and the only coloured peoples the "WE" embraces are the Japanese, who are admitted into the fold as "honorary Aryans". And yet the Russian case against the Chinese is logical when it deals with the curious economics of "the great leap forward" and the question of foreign policy. It is only when, in the full flush of the argument, racialist statements escape, that one begins to understand how profound the Chinese suspicions are. However, countering one brand of racialism with a more dangerous Herrenvolk mythology is a dangerous game in the escalation of hatreds.

It is against this background of Soviet relations with the coloured peoples within her own borders, the Sino-Soviet dispute, the Cold War and future relations with the African, Asian and Latin American peoples that one must see the twelve thousand or so foreign students in the Soviet Union. Joseph Robertson's story in *Green Winter* is highly personal, incomplete but objective. For those from both East and West who are genuinely interested in how the Twentieth Century black man feels about the Cold War and its protagonists, this story offers opinions, not because they are necessarily right, but because they are our own.

III.

THIRD WORLD WRITER IN EXILE

Section Three, "A Third World Writer in Exile", includes chapters seven through ten. The title is reminiscent of Jan Carew's famous essay, "The Caribbean Writer and Exile", in which he describes the contradictions for many writers of his generation. Not only did they not "fit in" at home, they later discovered that they often did not fit in abroad – what Carew termed "a wider indifference". They had grown up in colonial communities where the local mantra had been that they had to "leave home" if they were to make anything of themselves. The restrictions of colonial hierarchies were sapping their energies and so they had to find ways to be free of these limitations to realise their true potential. But, as many were to find out, they were both "exiles" at home and abroad.

This section stretches from the early 1950s into the latter half of the 1960s. Having now committed himself to art and literature following his university studies, Jan Carew decided to make Europe his home. His London connections, especially those at the British Broadcasting Corporation (BBC), made it possible for him to receive a periodic income which he would collect through Western Union in various cities. Through connections with other Guyanese or writers he met in London, he was introduced into the arts scene in Paris and Amsterdam, and this helped him to find housing and literary outlets. Each stage led to another set of connections that would prove invaluable later in life and in other regions of the world. Having met the millionaire and left-wing activist Mike de Swaan in Amsterdam, for example, he then had connections to the de Swaan brothers later in New York, when he went there with Olivier Productions and in Mexico when he was on his way to Cuba to report on the missile crisis.

In London, his widening circle included a whole coterie of artists and students, many of whom would go on to be the intellectual and political leaders of newly-independent nations in Africa, the Caribbean and Asia.

A chance encounter with a Guyanese friend brought him into acting with Laurence Olivier and meeting his first wife, Joan.

His activism in the anti-colonial struggle encompassed the international relevance of the struggles of black Americans. He describes his renewed contacts with W.E.B. Du Bois and Paul Robeson as a result of London-based campaigns to have them released from their internal exile in the US. A new relationship developed with the iconic Claudia Jones, who bridged both the anti-colonial and black American struggles, when this Trinidadian activist was expelled from the US and set up her political organisation in the United Kingdom. A special memory comes from the night he was launching the first Black newspaper in London in 1965. Malcolm X, the African American Muslim Leader, was in town and, having been invited to the reception, became a close friend in a short span of time, as the two met frequently afterwards.

Lauded for his novels, recognised for his broadcasts, editing of newspapers, and commissioned to write plays for radio, TV and the stage, Carew's artistic life was full. But this was also a time of great political turmoil as he and his fellow activists reacted to the Mau Mau rebellion in Kenya, to the Sharpeville massacre in South Africa, and to Patrice Lumumba's assassination in the Congo.

Included in this section are his 1951 poem, "The Weeping Trees", the article "What is a West Indian?" published in 1959, and two short 1961 cameos describing London life in the late 1950s-early 1960s, "The Odd-Job Man" and "South Kensington Revisited".

CHAPTER SEVEN

TRESPASS TO PARIS AND AMSTERDAM

I must go wandering again
Across green pastures of my mind.
I must hurl words
across drawbridges
of wild imaginings

I returned to London after leaving Prague in the early 1950s, and managed to do some broadcasts of my work on the BBC. I didn't plan to stay there, but needed to make some money so that I could return to Europe to continue with my studies – this time at the Sorbonne in Paris. I was excited at the prospect of studying radio isotopes under Juliot-Curie.

This was the beginning of my literary career in London. I received enough money to pay my rent and put food on the table. I was cotching – staying with friends who had somewhere for me to stay. I lived in Amsterdam off and on in this period and I was also travelling back and forth between London and Paris. Though France had been devastated by the war and there were shortages of things, living as an artist was more rewarding in Paris.

I had been in London a couple of weeks when I met another Guyanese who had been a classmate of mine at Berbice High School. Hanuman was Indo-Guyanese and came from a family of 16 boys and girls. They were rice farmers and ranchers. When I told him that I was about to go to France, he gave me the address of a French student, Roger Baudoin, whom he had met while he was studying in France. This contact turned out to be an invaluable one for me.

So when I went to Paris, I thought I should go to Roger's address, and thinking that he was a student, I assumed he would be living in some tiny garret. To my astonishment, he was living on one of the most expensive streets in Paris – Rue du Faubourg Saint-Honoré. Roger was, in fact, the son of a director of a steel cartel in Europe. However, Roger wasn't there at the time, as he had gone off to do his National Service. Still, his family invited me to dinner. The Baudoins had a sumptuous duplex and with Roger away, they invited me to come stay in Roger's apartment while I

Jan Carew in Paris, with Wilson Harris and his landlord, M. Baudoin

Personal photograph

pursued my studies at the Sorbonne. I lived with the Baudoins on and off for nearly three years. When they went on their holidays, they left me in charge of the apartment – and they gave me permission to entertain friends while they were away. Some of my Guyanese visitors included John Carter, the famous jurist, and Wilson Harris, the novelist, who had married my sister. Wilson, like John, would later become famous and be knighted by the Queen of England. Both of them happened to come to Paris at the same time.

Wilson came to Paris while he was on long leave from his job in the colonial civil service. We had met originally in the mid-nineteen forties when I was working for the customs office in Georgetown and Wilson was courting my sister. In the beginning, it was a family relationship, although later, when I returned after several years abroad, Wilson and I became quite close and our literary relationship began to develop when we spent an extended time together in the interior of BG. In Paris, we frequented the book shops in the Latin Quarter, visited places like the Rodin Museum and the Expressionists' museum. I used to visit the latter frequently; it was an easy walk from where I lived on Faubourg Saint-Honore off of Rue Haussmann. I later introduced Wilson to the Baudoins and I have a picture of Wilson, me and M. Baudoin standing on a bridge.

At another point, John Carter came for a visit and he stayed with me too. We went to the Folies Bergère, which he paid for, since I, as a penniless student, could have never afforded to go. John had studied French at Oxford, but he couldn't speak it very well, so when we went to restaurants or other events, I would have to translate things for him.

I would meet John again in London. I had a girlfriend who was from the aristocracy and the two of us went to see him one time. I was amazed at John's behaviour. He was almost obsequious with her and this annoyed me no end. I started being rude to her to counter John's obsequiousness. He was upset, worried that we might be insulting this upper-class woman. I told her to go, since John and I had things to discuss. John complained, "You can't treat these people like that." But, when I went home later, she was waiting on my doorstep and I let her in. I saw her many years later and learned that she had married an upper-class fellow.

I had a girlfriend from home – Eula – who came for a visit while I was in Paris. She came along with another Guyanese girl, Joan. The two of them came from families that were pretty well off and they were prepared to stay in a hotel. But, after discussing the possibility with the Baudoins, I convinced them to stay in my apartment at the Baudoins' house. I moved into a small pension for the time being. We would all take our meals with the Baudoins and Mme Baudoin was very pleased to meet these well-brought up young ladies from British Guiana.

Joan had met a young Frenchman, who was a barber, on the boat they took to come across to France. She had a crush on this fellow, but the

French bourgeoisie were very strict about these matters and the Baudoins decided to invite him around, basically to see if he had the right class. Barbers tend to be very garrulous, but they do not often have the opportunity to learn the social conventions of the upper classes. So, at the dinner table, this fellow was telling his whole life story and while the Baudoins were urbane and proper, we exchanged occasional glances and it was clear to me that this fellow would not be invited back. I am certain that Mme Baudoin also pulled Joan aside to let her know that this young man was not suitable. After having lived in the United States, it was interesting for me to see how class could matter more than race.

So, I registered at the Sorbonne University– which was free – and lived in the lavish mansion of the Baudoins. My friends at the Sorbonne thought I was some kind of American millionaire slumming it with them in their student quarters. What they didn't know was that I had very little money, though I was receiving occasional cheques from my work in London. So, while I was eating and sleeping quite comfortably, my movements across the city were restricted to long hikes because I couldn't even afford the metro fare.

One great friend who was also taking courses at the Sorbonne – although not on a regular schedule – was an artist from Brazil named Tiberio Wilson. Tiberio had been living in Paris since World War II and he taught me how one could live in Paris on a very low margin. One morning, he came to take me to breakfast, but instead of going to a café, he took me to a number of the fine department stores where they had food exhibits. We nibbled our way through the various items on offer. At one point, Tiberio appeared with some serviettes that he had taken from a packet he had opened. Tiberio turned out to be a good friend of Picasso's and Picasso would come to his gallery openings. But, as Tiberio pointed out, having a good sale or sales at one point did not guarantee a regular income, and so his life frequently went from bang to bust. Tiberio was also an ultimate optimist when it came to relations with women. He had what one might call a "difficult beauty", and so may not have seemed attractive at first glance. We would go to local dances and I would watch him go around the hall, asking young ladies to dance. Often, they would turn him down, but when he got to the end of the line, he would clasp his hands together and rub them with a look of anticipation on his face, and then proceed around the hall again. This second time, there was invariably one young lady who said, "Yes," and off they would go. As Tiberio explained it to me later, those that said yes were not only agreeing to a dance or two, but would also agree to other activities later on. Several times I left the dance hall on my own. Tiberio so intrigued me that I drew upon him in my novel, *The Last Barbarian* (1961). He had a painter's passion for women but all the time I got to know him, he never had an enduring relationship with one. His affairs went like this: one of his handsome Brazilian friends would be in love with a woman and when the affair broke up, Tiberio would act as a shoulder to cry on. He was good at consoling brokenhearted women, given that he was very kind-hearted and generous.

During my Paris sojourn, I met a very beautiful woman. I was, in fact, with Tiberio when I first met her. We had gone to Cafe Fleurs on the Left Bank, which was famous for Jean-Paul Sartre's and Simone de Beauvoir's meetings there. The French, who have great respect for literature, charged twice the price of a cup of coffee thereafter, for you might catch a glimpse of these luminaries while sipping on your *café allongée.* Tiberio and I went to the cafe one Saturday evening and as soon as we entered, we saw two beautiful women sitting at the far end of the cafe. Tiberio, who was always what West Indians call "bold as brass", walked right over, introduced himself and me, and asked if we might join them. They invited us to sit with them. One of the two was a Contessa and they were both divorcees. In this company, I did not feel my French was up to scratch, but the friend of the Contessa had spent a while at Cambridge and spoke English fluently. Over the course of the evening, the one who spoke English leaned over and said to me, "We would like you to come with us, but we do not want your friend to come."

I soon realised that I would have to betray Tiberio that night. I pretended that I wanted to go to the toilet and left in the ladies' *Delage* sports car. Tiberio later told me that to cover the bill, he had to cut down his allowance for two weeks. Irene, who was the Contessa, had a chalet in the Alps in Chamonix. She invited me to *sejour* there and I had no qualms in accepting.

I also met Ollie Harrington in Paris. He was a well-known black American cartoonist and artist and a close friend of the novelist Richard Wright. Ollie took me to Wright's apartment one day. The author of *Native Son* had just moved in and things were in a bit of disarray, which possibly explained why Wright wasn't particularly cordial. Wright had also recently returned from the 1955 Writer's Conference at the Conference of Non-Aligned Nations held in Bandung, Indonesia. Years later, Ollie told me that he suspected that Wright's death in 1960 had been the result of an assassination and that he had not died of a simple heart attack. Wright was one of the most eminent and outspoken figures in the Non-Aligned Movement and there were many in the West who were not pleased that he had been one of speakers at this conference.

I met Alioune Diop, the Senegalese writer and founder of the long-running review, *Présence Africaine,* and some of the other key figures in the Négritude movement. There was Gaston Monnerville, who was a lawyer and Minister in the French government. Monnerville was from French Guiana, but had settled in France after World War II, where he represented a constituency in France. He was the most powerful black man in European politics at the time, and had been president of the French Senate since 1947.

He would hold this position until 1968, and though his politics and those of President Charles De Gaulle clashed, he was second in line of command, should something have happened to the French President.

Once, I went to see Monnerville in his office. He had a son who was studying in the United States and he wanted to solicit my advice about some problems his son was having. Despite the eminence of his father in Europe, the boy was encountering problems of racism in America. In Europe and in the colonies, class was more important than race, and one could have access to housing, education, and be treated more humanely if one were seen to be of a proper class – despite being a person of colour.

When I was in Paris a second time, I did some drawings which I left with the Baudoins. They were all about the rivers of Guyana. I left them with the Baudoins because I felt it was a way to pay them back for their hospitality. This was in the late 1950s, at a time when I had recently returned from BG and my travels into the interior with Wilson Harris.

Though Wilson was writer, he worked as a hydrographer and land surveyor. He was charting the currents in several rivers in BG, and he had been living in the rainforest on and off for seventeen years. I had accompanied him on two of these journeys and in the midst of these primordial forests, remember watching him hold forth on esoteric topics like Spengler's *Man and Technics*, with his men listening in rapt incomprehension. Wilson was at home in this solitary world of the rainforest, and the men who worked with him were devoted to him. Travelling with them, you could see this vast and magical world through his eyes as well as through theirs. Wilson didn't carry a weapon, not even a penknife, though his men were well armed.

That journey with Wilson to Tumatumari swept me into feeling that I'd entered into a magical world that called for a different kind of language. Wilson had invented a language that affirmed itself on your conscious and unconscious mind. It found its way into my first booklet of poetry – *Streets of Eternity,* but when I tried to adopt this new language more fully, I simply did not have the courage to stand up to the storm of cruel criticism that greeted us. So I ran away from it and produced an outpouring of prose that was a mixture of the new and the old. What a shame, I tossed much of it away! Those Canje poems remain alive and the most authentic. That Canje river journey left me without fear of Guyana's primordial hinterland and the men and women living and working in it. It made me understand people like Gerald Loy, who worked for Wilson, and his explosive reaction to life in the interior. I have often thought of writing a story about Gerald's magical love of an Amerindian woman, and of his seeking redemption through her powerful feminine role as a mother and lover.

During this period, I was not only painting but also working on novels, short stories, poetry and features for the BBC. Living as an artist was much more rewarding on the continent. People appreciated art and artists more overtly. Basically, I was a nomad, occasionally sending things to Henry Swanzy who produced the *Caribbean Voices* programme at the BBC and living off the periodic cheques which would be sent to me via Western Union.

I had heard that Amsterdam was a good city for artists and writers, too, and I thought I would go there and try to make a living. I arrived in Amsterdam in winter and had barely enough money to last me two weeks. Luckily, I met a young woman on the train who offered to help me get my bearings.

I had a letter of introduction from a prominent artist for Nola Hatterman who was living there. Nola was also a good friend of a Guyanese law student in London, Ralph Morrison. I knew Ralph's family back in BG. The house in which Nola lived had rooms that were supposed to be occupied by a merchant seaman from Suriname who was working on a ship that sailed from the Far East, but he was always away and not occupying the apartment, so Nola let me have it.

Nola was living with an architect and a political activist, Arie Jansma. Arie was a specialist in designing International Trade Fairs. Arie was also a communist who had been one of the leaders of the Dutch underground resistance during the Nazi occupation of Holland. He was Jewish, but he looked like a perfect example of a blue-eyed, blonde Nazi – or the epitome of a German SS Officer. So, Arie, who was trained at a Russian spy school, was able to go underground during the war disguised as a Gestapo officer.

Arie had saved the life of many people. Dick Alpheus, who was a painter, was one of those. Dick was in hospital and Arie came dressed as an SS Officer and told the Nazi commandant in the hospital to release Dick into his custody immediately. Arie was playing the part of the officer so well that the nurses begged him to let Dick stay until he was better. Even Dick didn't realise it was Arie until they were driving away from the hospital.

Arie had also been saved by someone. There was a rendezvous of factions of the Dutch resistance in Amsterdam and, for once, Arie was late. As he was approaching the building where the meeting was scheduled, he realised he was surrounded by the Gestapo. Arie turned and walked away with a Gestapo officer trailing him. Because he was one of the leaders of the Dutch resistance, he always had a bodyguard shadowing him. In this case, it was a plainclothes woman who shot the Gestapo officer in the head, and she and Arie were able to flee.

That strong sense of camaraderie from WWII survived well after the war. There was, too, a sense of sympathy stretched between the left-wing intellectuals and colonial people. I always felt that people in Amsterdam understood our plight in British Guiana. One night at the artist's club, this Dutch fellow made some racist remark about me and the whole club rose up and expelled him. I wasn't accustomed to having white people taking up cudgels for me.

There was a Surinamer, Caya, who lived in the house with Nola, Arie and me. He, too, called himself an artist. He was a fire-eater and an archetypal survivor. During the war, Caya would steal coal from German buildings to survive the coldest months of winter. His real name was Frohm. He was a huge man, but he knew how to dodge the tax-collector and other fastidious officials. When the tax-collector came looking for someone named "Frohm", Caya would meet him at the door and say, "I know Frohm very well. He's a very irresponsible man. The only time you can get him at home is between midnight and five in the morning." The tax collector never could find "Frohm", but this didn't stop him from trying repeatedly – and missing him. Caya also used to go to Rotterdam when the American ships came in. They used to have black American kitchen hands on the transatlantic liners, and Caya would volunteer to work in the kitchens while the black Americans went ashore for their R & R. He had a good time, since he would take huge quantities of food from the full American larders. The story went that Caya, to get past the head of customs at Rotterdam, would say, "Look, we're both small men trying to make a living. If you give me a permit to pass, I will share some of the bounty with you." So he had free passage for his goods.

Through Nola and Arie, I met a lot of writers and poets. I also met Michael de Swaan. Mike was a millionaire and a left-wing activist. Though he came from a very wealthy family, his interests clearly leaned more towards the masses. He was one of four brothers and they had helped to finance the underground movements during the war years. They were short of cash by the end of the war, but were very clever at business and remade millions in a short space of time. Mike made his fortune trading in jute and he was very generous with the artists and writers by subsidising their works. I had an eye infection at one point and Mike arranged for me to be seen by the top opthamologist in Amsterdam. It would have been impossible for me to pay for it otherwise.

There was a kind of fraternal bonding with this group of men and women around Mike de Swaan and I was closely affiliated with them. We met in Mike's spacious apartment every Sunday night and we reminisced and had long drawn-out discussions about arts and politics.

Stories of heroism and sacrifice were common amongst the Dutch artists at this time. For example, Mike and his wife, as Jews, had to send their young son to a Dutch peasant family and the boy never knew his parents until the war had ended. Though he was reunited with his family, he never recovered from the alienation. Misfortune further haunted them, because their next child, born during the war, drowned in a canal. Then, there was the tragedy when one of Mike's brothers died in an airline crash in London on a flight from Manchester. I met one of the other de Swaan brothers in New York a short while later, when I was an actor with the Laurence Olivier company. A third brother helped me in Mexico in the 1960s when I was reporting on the Cuban Missile Crisis.

As a member of this artist group, I also met poets like Jan G. Elburg and the novelists Salvadore Herzog and Bert (Lambertus) Schierbeek. Schierbeek became quite famous (he won the Constantijn Huygens prize in 1991). I met him again in the 1960s in Ibiza. He apparently wrote a novel about me, but as I don't read Dutch, I never saw it. There was also a Jewish painter called Jan Meyer, who became a close friend of mine.

The memories of the Nazi occupation were still vivid in their minds in the aftermath of WWII. There was a black fascist who had a nightclub in Amsterdam. He had joined the German SS, though he was very dark-skinned. The Germans had recruited Indians. They had been prisoners of war from Singapore; the Japanese had conquered Singapore. Some Indian anti-colonial fighters became mercenaries for the Japanese and they were sent to Holland to help the Germans. So, this black fellow had a night club that the Germans patronised during the Occupation. After the War, he was paraded half naked through the streets. But, he had a lot of money and bought his way back into favour. Later generations didn't know about his history and patronised his club.

Moreover, the Dutch were themselves still in Indonesia and Suriname as colonial masters. The Dutch government recruited some of the bour-geoisie from Suriname and gave them powerful jobs in Indonesia. I remember one of the artists telling me that when the Japanese wrested Indonesia from the Dutch, they used to interrogate the prisoners and ask, "What nationality are you?" and the middle-class prisoners would say, "We're Dutch" and be summarily taken off to POW camps or concentra-tion camps. But, the ones who said they were from Suriname would be let free. It took a while for the Dutch to catch on, and eventually, they, too, tried to pretend they were Surinamers. Several Surinamers were also in high positions in banks and government offices in Holland. In 1975, when Suriname gained its independence, a middle-class flood rushed to Holland for fear of being ruled by the polyglot Surinamese people. I later learned that Suriname had a much larger middle-class than we had in British Guiana but, like Suriname, our country also saw a large exodus of the middle class on the eve of our independence. This was a double-edged sword. On the one hand, those who left were disgruntled and likely to sabotage the efforts of the new governments; on the other, they were depriving these nascent countries of key professional and commercial skills.

In the 1980s, when Desi Bouterse seized power in a coup in Suriname, he had a gripe against the old intellectual class. The Grenadian revolution had broken out in 1979 and Bouterse, who was left-leaning, extended the hand of friendship to the new Grenadian Prime Minister, Maurice Bishop. He also authorised sending Surinamers to Cuba to study at Cuban universities. But when Bishop was overthrown and murdered four years later, Bouterse, feeling threatened, recalled many Suriname intellectuals from Cuba. One was my close friend, the poet Dobru (Robin Raveles), who was the national poet of Suriname. Unfortunately, Dobru had a disease that required blood transfusions and when Bouterse recalled him, Suriname didn't have the facilities to carry on the treatment and Dobru died about two weeks after he was recalled. As for Bouterse, he too was overthrown in 1987. Yet, despite his 1999 conviction *in absentia* for drug trafficking, his political group won the largest number of seats in the 2010 elections, and Bouterse was elected by a majority in the Suriname Parliament to serve as Suriname's next leader.

The man who started the literary journal *de Kim*, on which I was guest editor for while in Amsterdam, was a Jewish former textile millionaire from Berlin called Lugo Kunst. When Hitler came to power, Kunst sold everything and fled from Germany. With his international contacts, he raised money to found the journal. He wanted to live the life of an artist and had given away much of his money, having just enough to run *de Kim*. He had friends in Amsterdam who had hidden him from the Nazis. There is a story about a rather robust girlfriend of Lugo's sitting on a mattress, with him underneath it, while the Gestapo searched his home. He was squeezed beneath her until the Gestapo left.

I reconnected with Nola Hatterman again years later, in 1975, in Suriname where she had moved and started a school for artists. By this point, she was in her 70s. This was the same year that Suriname gained its independence from Holland and my wife Joy and I were spending a year there. Nola had a theory that the tropical light played havoc with colours and that painters from the tropics had to be trained to deal with the equatorial sun. Nola had a love for Suriname and had a house built in its interior. This didn't surprise me, because even when I knew her in Amsterdam she had always surrounded herself with Surinamers. Though Nola died in 1984, her legacy lives on with the Nola Hatterman Art Academy in Suriname's capital, Paramaribo.

Another Dutch writer and patron of the arts I met was a baroness named Sandrine van de Rijn. She had recently returned from the US where she had attended Smith College and was out "slumming" when we met. She became quite enamoured of me and wanted to marry me. Her mother, who lived in an apartment near the Queen's palace would have me over for coffee or tea and she, too, was very keen on having me marry her daughter.

I was bedridden with German measles for a month during my stay in Amsterdam, and there were three women to whom I had become very attached, who insisted upon attending to me during my illness. German measles is a child's disease in Northern hemisphere countries, but we have no antibodies for it in the tropics. It, therefore, attacked me in a very severe manner, which is especially worrisome, since contracting this as an adult can affect one's ability to have children later. The women who looked after me included a Parisian model, Milenka; there was also Sandrine, and a Finnish girl who was a relative of Jean Sibelius, one of the great composers in music in the late nineteeth and early twentieth century. But although I was now living in great luxury in Holland, I didn't want to continue living there. As soon as I recovered, though, I went back to London, starting a new chapter in my life.

"The Weeping Trees"

De Kim, Litterair pamflet, 1951 (Amsterdam)

The weeping trees
Are weeping tears of blood again
And the tears gush
From a fountainhead
In Mincing Lane
The Companies of Putumayo
Are not dead,
They live again
To draw fresh tears of blood
At a fountainhead
In Mincing Lane
Blood that besmeared
The hands of potentates of Putumayo
Leaves the same crimson stain
On greedy hands
In Mincing Lane.
The weeping trees
Stand like columns
In leaf-roofed factories of death
Where young Malayans
Serve their apprenticeship.
And lads from England in the name
Of potentates of Mincing Lane
Stoke fires in these factories of death
With hot and searing flames
And bombs and bullets.

In the old days
Arawaks and Accewayos died
And only the wind and the trees
And the dark-bosomed,
Myriad tributaries
Of the Amazon,
Heard the echoing anguish
Of their soul's cry.
In the old days
The potentates of Putumayo
Turned unhearing ears
To inarticulate cries

From the hearts of the Arawaks
And Accewayos
Dying in the cathedralled glooms
Under the weeping trees.
But now
The potentates of Mincing Lane
Breathe many an uneasy sigh
When young Malaysian partisans die.

The weeping trees
Are weeping tears of blood again,
And the wrung tears
Shatter mirrored pools
Of the Zingu and the Trombetas
No more,
But now they pour
In green mansions
At Tangan and Malaka,
At Tapa and Selangor
And the crimson tears
Gush from a fountainhead
In Mincing Lane

CHAPTER EIGHT

LONDON ADVENTURES

My life in England was a combination of work and survival. Between 1949 and 1958, I worked as a freelance writer, contributing regularly to the BBC'S *Caribbean Voices* and other programmes. Henry Swanzy, for one, had been a life saver for me by accepting my poems while I was living in Europe. Ernest Eytle, a Guyanese who worked at the BBC, had taken some of my writings to Swanzy and he had bought them. Many Caribbean writers were saved by this life jacket. Swanzy, who headed the BBC General Overseas Service, paid by the word and so some of us wrote some very long poems, or submitted quite a few. Once I was back in London on a permanent basis, I had to expand my sources of income and began doing regular broadcasts on BBC radio.

I eventually decided to settle in London because I was a British citizen and you could make a living there. My country had not yet gained its independence – that would come in 1966.

For West Indian immigrants making the rent money was a constant problem. In the 1950s, we had "spielers". This combined a means to make one's rent and enjoy a grassroots club activity. A party would be hosted in someone's apartment where drink would be sold. If the police found out, this grassroots club would move elsewhere. We had similar informal gatherings in Harlem in the US. There we called them "rent parties". At the same time, our growing community was having an impact on the local pet shops. West Indians preferred to buy their chickens live, to ensure that they were safe to eat, and these shops started providing live chickens. Eventually, these shopkeepers found that they could make good money supplying immigrants from the West Indies, Africa and South Asia.

When I first went to England, I looked up John Carter, who was a fellow Guyanese and had done law in England. During the war, he had taken up the case to defend a black American soldier who was accused of rape. His case was successful and this brought him some fame. John was later appointed ambassador by the Burnham government, first in London. Later, he was posted to various locations around the world. In 1966, he was knighted by the Queen of England. The Queen Mum was apparently particularly fond of him and used to insist that he stay longer than the usual time she allowed her visitors.

BBC *Caribbean Voices* session.
From the left: Henry Swanzy, George Lamming, Andrew Salkey, Jan
Carew and Sam Selvon.

Photograph: Bruce Paddington, BBC.

I met Vida Menzies in London in those early days. Vida was a Jamaican who used to give the upper-class British physiotherapy treatments; she was also well-known for her soirees, to which various ladies and lords would come. One of her regular escorts was Rudolph Dunbar, a musician from BG. After escorting Vida to one of the ambassadorial parties, Rudolph noted that Vida had a "ruthless flare for the dramatic". While she was at the party, one of the ambassadors took a shine to her and she summarily dumped Rudolph for this fellow.

Vida was also well-known for her broadcasts on health matters, which she had done in Jamaica before moving to the UK. Like many Jamaicans, she commonly dropped the "h" at the beginning of words and pronounced the "th" at the end of words like a "d". Because she was on the radio, she was encouraged to seek a language coach to help her overcome these dialect features. Sylvia, my second wife, used to coach Vida on this. More often than not, though, in her broadcasts, she would regularly say, "Good-day ladies and gentlemen. How nice to see you (pronouncing the "h" loudly)." But, then she would continue, "Today, I am going to teach you how to breed properly." (She had forgotten to watch the final "th" in the word "breathe".)

Immigrants are often painfully concerned about how they will be received in the "mother country" and so take great pains to remove any features in their language that may tie them to home. Fanon wrote about this with people from Martinique who tried to make a new life in France. In Martiniquan creole, there was a tendency to drop the final "r" from words. A fellow, concerned that people in France might mistake him as someone less cultured and educated, was overheard ordering a beer by saying, "I would like a beer-r-r-r." Instead of a simple "r", he drew out the sound, thus calling even more attention to himself. Conversely, the Jamaican upper class often spoke better English than the ordinary English, though there were some who, rather than sounding like the English, chose to keep some of the Jamaican creole features in their language.

Rudolph Dunbar had affected an upper-class British English accent, though he was born in a small village in British Guiana like me. He was also known both for being impeccably dressed in his Saville Row suits and for his famous parties. He particularly liked to serve people with dishes and silverware that had come from Hitler's collection. He had been a correspondent with the Associated Negro Press and had been in the group that first entered Hitler's bunker. He had managed to collect some items with Hitler's initials on them as souvenirs. Rudolph described how, when he was flying back to London, a general sitting next to him offered to give him some souvenirs. But Rudolph told him, "I'll give you some real souvenirs if you place my goods in your kitbag; I'd be most grateful as I could be sure to get them through customs." So, Rudolph had his loot carried through customs by a general.

Rudolph was a highly-trained clarinetist and conductor. He had trained at the conservatory in both the US and in Paris and had even written a highly-regarded book on the clarinet. When he arrived in London in 1931, he started the first school for the study of the clarinet. In 1942, he was the first black man to conduct the London Philharmonic and then, in 1945, he conducted the Berlin Philharmonic. He had persuaded an American 4-star general, who was in charge of the occupation following the war, to allow him to conduct the orchestra. It was quite a symbol to see this black man conducting an orchestra in a country that had just fought a racist war. Rudolph took this symbol even further when he conducted an orchestra at the Hollywood Bowl in the US., the Cuban National Orchestra in Havana, and the world-class orchestras of Leningrad and Moscow.

Rudolph would have been in his 80s when he died in 1988. We last came across each other in a park in London not long before he passed away. He was probably a homosexual, very urbane and had good relations with both the heterosexual and homosexual communities.

Rudolph had lived in London through the preparations for World War II. He was appointed by the *Chicago Defender* newspaper and the Associated Negro Press to be their on-the-spot reporter of events in Europe. He was accepted as a legitimate member of the press corps and dressed in a US officer's uniform. So, he had passes to go wherever he wanted. He could talk to General Eisenhower or whomever and was clearly not intimidated by the establishment hierarchy.

It was Rudolph who introduced me to Lord Cowdray, the publisher of London's *Financial Times,* in 1964, and made the arrangements for the formal launch of our paper, *Magnet,* at the Commonwealth Institute.

Edward Scobie was another of my lifelong friends whom I met in London during those BBC days. Scobie was from Dominica. He was a journalist and a historian. When we met in the early years after World War II, he was an officer in the Royal Airforce. Scobie was tall like me, but his hair had gone prematurely white after the large number of sorties he had flown during the war. He was now an editor and an authority on the history of blacks in Europe. Scobie was another one of my London West Indian friends whom I enticed to come to the America in the 1970s.

In the last few years of his time in London, Scobie had been paying regular visits to Amanda Aldridge, the surviving daughter of the famous 19th century black American thespian, Ira Aldridge. During these visits, he took meticulous notes on the history of the distinguished Aldridge family. I accompanied him on one of his weekly visits to this grande dame of the English music and theatre world because I was doing a feature on her for the BBC and for a popular magazine. Many years later, Scobie and I were in the process of developing two stage plays, one about Ira Aldridge and the other about Amanda, when Scobie passed away.

At the time of this visit to Miss Aldridge, it was early spring when the London weather is capricious. One could leave home in bright sunshine and within an hour, the day could change into one of leaden grey skies and cold temperatures. Amanda lived in a second-floor apartment in Kensington Palace Gardens. "She's been living here for the past sixty years," Scobie told me when he rang the doorbell.

Looking around, it was obvious from the neglected period façade that this six-storey building had obviously known better days. Miss Aldridge's apartment was comfortable and the spacious drawing room (which was the only room in the flat which was heated) was where she spent most of her waking hours. When she was not working as a voice teacher in her West End studio on Hanover Street, attending concerts or visiting friends, she spent the little time she had left at home. Scobie had explained to me that she was in great demand as a voice teacher, teaching upper-class English ladies correct elocution. Amanda's manner of speaking was so perfect that it reminded me of the Hungarian linguist's comment about "Eliza Doolittle", that she spoke English too well to be English.

Above the mantelpiece, was a huge portrait of her illustrious father, Ira Aldridge, who, at the height of his career – between 1833 and 1867 – was known as the "African Roscius" (Roscius was the greatest actor in Roman times). In the portrait, Aldridge was dressed in the costume of Othello. The apartment was filled with gifts her father had received over the years, and other mementos from her and her mother's past, making the room into something of a museum of the Aldridge-Brandt family. Paulina Ericksson Brandt (Baroness Brandt) was Amanda's Swedish mother. She was a gifted soprano who had studied at the Royal Theatre School in Stockholm. She and the famous Jenny Lind were classmates, but she had given up her career as a concert singer after marrying Aldridge. Scobie explained to me later that this had left an aftermath of discontent in the Baroness's heart and a certain sediment of bitterness with which she had never been able to come to terms. She had sworn that she would never allow her gifted daughters Brigit and Amanda to follow in her footsteps by giving up their careers. She had a mother's pride in them and wanted them to do all the things that marriage to a famous man had prevented her from doing. Unfortunately, Brigit died as a young woman. Amanda had a promising career in opera; however, she developed a bad case of laryngitis and lost her singing voice. Jenny Lind was a great help to her and encouraged her, instead, to become a voice teacher. She had taught many hundreds of students by the time I met her, including not only English students and students from the continent, but also Paul Robeson, Marian Anderson, Roland Hayes, and Muriel Smith, when they were in London. I visited Miss Aldridge with Scobie again nine months later and, in fact, I arranged to take one voice lesson with her before I left Britain.

She had raised with Scobie the possibility of getting a larger apartment that he could share with her. "No matter how active I may appear to be," she said, "old age is taking its toll and going to a nursing home is simply out of the question. I couldn't live without all these precious belongings around me."

Scobie continued to call on her regularly, his last visit coming two days before her ninetieth birthday. She passed away in her sleep two days later.

The artist, Feliks Topolski, was a good friend of mine. His death was a great loss to me. Feliks came from Polish-Jewish aristocracy and had come to London from Paris in 1935. I met Feliks in the early 1950s at his studio when Cesar Grant took me there. Feliks' studio was several rooms under a railway arch in Waterloo. Actually, he had two of these studios. One was a working studio and the other was for storage. He also had sleeping quarters in the working studio, but otherwise he lived with his wife and two children in an apartment in Regents Square.

The two of us got on well from the start. He was a gracious host and a gifted raconteur. He believed in the Oscar Wilde adage that you should make every woman you meet believe you're in love with her and every man you meet that he is boring you. He had a passion for women. In a corner of the sleeping quarters section of his studio, he had a huge bed and a gas stove. Feliks was one of those people who – if he liked you – made you feel welcome every time you went to see him. Feliks' guests could cross lines of race, colour, creed and nationality. As for his studio, one day in the week was always "open house".

The day that Cesar had taken me to meet Feliks was the same day that he had delivered one of Feliks' paintings to 10 Downing Street, the Prime Minister's residence. One time, Feliks had been commissioned to do an equestrian portrait of King George VI, and when it was done the King came to inspect it. But, the King didn't like some of the figures in the painting and wanted Feliks to change it. Feliks said 'no' and the two of them fell out. Nonetheless, some time later, the painting was presented to the court unchanged. To this day, Feliks' work hangs in Buckingham and other palaces.

He also had a hand-turned printing press on which he produced a limited edition of his *Topolski Journal* which was his commentary on world affairs or art. For example, he had a special issue on my journey to Cuba during the Cuban missile crisis. He illustrated the book jacket of my book, *The Last Barbarian,* and wanted to do more illustrations, but my publisher turned him down. This proved to be very shortsighted as Topolski artwork fetches a lot these days. He illustrated a children's book by Arna Bontemps, *Lonesome Boy,* before I met him. He also did graphic drawings for the journals I founded and edited – *Magnet*, a newspaper, in London, and *Cotopaxi*, a literary journal, in Toronto.

We met again after I moved to Canada in the 1960s. Feliks had come to NY on a commission to do a study of culture in urban ghettos after the Martin Luther King, Jr. riots. I had a commission from the CBC to interview him, as well as to do a piece on the new voices that were arising in the black community. The commissions were for both radio and television. This was important, because here was a period that saw Black Power risings in the US, Canada, the Caribbean and Latin America. It was something akin to the Arab Spring uprisings of 2011.

So, I flew to New York and met up with Feliks, and we stayed in a flat on 52nd street that belonged to a wealthy friend of his. I had originally come up with the idea of the CBC projects as a means for us to get together and for Feliks to see his daughter who was attending New York University. I took him to meet John Henrik Clarke. Feliks wanted to go to Harlem and sit in the street to draw people, but John had also introduced Feliks to Tom Feelings, an African American artist living in New York at the time, and Tom told Feliks that he could go do the drawings in Harlem – if he rented a Sherman tank. Feliks, a white man, sitting on the streets of Harlem during the Black Power uprisings was asking for trouble. I didn't go with him, but Feliks went and did his drawings. The people treated him with great kindness since he obviously was not a white American. His accent, his whole manner, openness and treating people with respect caused them to relax. That is when he gave me a painting, "La MaMa", which came from a series drawn at La MaMa, a famous black theatre in Harlem. Feliks published some of his work on the black uprisings of the 1960s in his collection, *Shem, Ham and Japheth Inc.: The American Crucible.*

During WWII, Feliks was an aide de camp of General Anders who was the head of the liberated Poles and he accompanied Anders to important meetings with Churchill, Roosevelt and Chiang Kai-shek. The last occasion on which we met in London, Feliks asked my advice on whether he should take up an offer from the Polish government; the communist government was still ruling in Poland. They said that there were many castles around the country and they weren't sure what to do about them. So, Feliks could have one as a gift from the government. But, Feliks didn't take them up on it. Subsequently, with the fall of the Iron Curtain, tremendous changes have taken place; Poland now being part of the European Union.

I do not remember the first time I met Andrew Salkey, but it was probably in the BBC building on Oxford Street more than sixty years ago. It would have been in the early 1950s. That was where West Indian writers and peripatetic journalists, escapees from boring nine-to-five jobs, university dropouts, graduates seduced by life in London and reluctant to return home, ex-servicemen (who had returned home briefly only to find themselves surrounded by a generation of strangers, and who, discovering that you can't go home again, had hotfooted it back to familiar London haunts), and, of course, poets, artists, hangers-on and aspirants to literary fame. We all met at the BBC Oxford Street building where an Irish producer named Henry Swanzy presided over the *Caribbean Voices* programme, which nurtured the entire bevy of Caribbean writers of Andrew's and my generation. That BBC building, which has long disappeared, was conveniently located opposite the Oxford Street tube station, and a cluster of pubs.

What I remember about Andrew is that he moved faster than the rest of us. But his was not the movement of someone in a hurry, because his movements had the natural ease and rhythm of water flowing down a slope. Andrew, without losing an essential Jamaicaness, had adapted to big city life like a hand to a tailored glove. There is a quality of restlessness, of constant alertness that living and surviving in cities (or in primordial rainforests) beats into you. He carried an aura of urban hustle and alertness around with him, even when he was standing still. And yet you sensed that underlying this urban, restive façade, there was a Caribbean ease, an infinite tolerance in dealing with the array of odd characters whom he came across in his daily life as a school teacher, a broadcaster, a journalist, a novelist, a poet and a playwright. He dealt with the whole wide world from a nexus of certainty about who he was as a human being. He was born in Panama, but grew up in Jamaica, and this twin nationality implanted in his psyche a dual consciousness of PLACE that expanded the frontiers of his imagination, and, eventually, enabled him to identify with the sufferings and triumphs of the have-nots everywhere on earth. Andrew came to believe that art and literature had to be like lightning, for lightning was never timid, and it never failed to illuminate the hidden recesses of suffering and anguish in our human world.

The only time I ever saw him in a rage, his eyes enlarged and flashing, his voice harsh and hectoring, was when a senior BBC producer, who was his boss at the time, made a denigrating and stupid remark about James Baldwin's writing. He dressed down the very surprised and contrite Englishman with some choice Jamaican expletives, and at the same time treated us all to a brilliant critique of Baldwin's work. Baldwin was in London at the time and Andrew had just interviewed him. Years later, when Jimmy Baldwin, Andrew and I were having dinner in a restaurant in Amherst, Massachusetts, I reminded Andrew about this episode in between quaffs of double Scotches and lively reminiscences. It was against the law to serve double Scotches in Amherst because of the large student population, but the barmen, with a smile and a wink, told Jimmy that he had "been on the mountain" and was willing to make an exception. My story and the barman's witty remark, was followed by fresh rounds of drinks, and bouts of loud laughter.

During the decade I had known Andrew in England, I cannot once remember his ever mentioning his father. He always talked about his mother, however; she was a school teacher, and very early in life, she had inflamed his imagination with a love of the written word. His education, which she supervised, was exacting, strict and almost Jesuitical; like his mother, he too was a born teacher.

Andrew, the Guyanese writer Roy Heath, the Jamaican writer Neville Dawes and Wilson Harris are, in a profound sense, kindred spirits. Their creative imaginations had to explode out of severe, restrictive classical moulds into which their young minds had been forced by the colonial education system. But once their minds broke out of that stultifying mould, they roamed a cosmos of new creative ideas and plucked from it fantastic imaginings which were honed and shaped into magical offerings in prose and poetry.

Andrew was a *rara avis* amongst West Indian writers. He was a passionate defender of literature's great black proponents, but his passion for literature transcended personal likes and dislikes and his generosity of spirit was boundless. When he took V.S. Naipaul's first manuscript, *The Mystic Masseur*, to Andre Deutch, a London publisher, his bold advocacy opened windows of opportunity, not only for Naipaul, but for others. As a reader for Faber & Faber, he wrote a review of Wilson Harris' *Palace of the Peacock* and recommended strongly that it should be published. Like his friend and mentor, the Guyanese writer Edgar Mittelholzer, (and they both seemed to sense that they would die prematurely), he had to make the most of the time allotted to him. He was infinitely patient and generous with younger writers who sought his help and advice. Andrew never felt that being a successful writer gave him the prerogative to be rude, boorish, a poseur or an exhibitionist. Of all the writers I have known, he was the most responsible when it came to the totality of his life and beliefs, and this included his family commitments, his passion for social justice, and the integrity of his voluminous writings.

In the decades between the publication of his first novel, *A Quality of Violence*, and a final work of his, a novel about a Nicaraguan boy living through the period of the Sandinistas and the Contras (he mentioned this work to me on the phone several times, but as far as I know it is still unpublished), his talent had matured slowly, almost stealthily. He had sent me poems from time to time, but when the *Black Scholar* published a slender volume of his poetry, it was clear to me that he had finally found his own unique, distinctive and eloquent literary voice, for those poems were perfection itself; he was using language as never before, with a pristine assurance and power.

In those poems, and a collection that was awarded Cuba's Casa de las Americas annual prize (*In the Hills Where Her Dreams Live*, 1979), he had achieved a muted resonance that seared spirit, emotion and intellect alike. I am willing to predict that in the aftermath of Andrew Salkey's untimely death, he will eventually be recognised as one of the supreme Caribbean poets of the generation.

Just before I retired from Northwestern University, I spent a year as a visiting professor at Hampshire College in Amherst. Andrew was also teaching there and I saw him frequently. In that year, too, Baldwin was doing a stint as a writer-in-residence at the nearby University of Massachusetts-Amherst in what was called "The Valley", for in this bowl of land, there was a cluster of five major academic institutions in and around the town of Amherst: Hampshire College, Mount Holyoke College, University of Massachusetts-Amherst, Smith College and Amherst College. Both Andrew and Baldwin seemed to be exiled and beleaguered in that Massachusetts rural setting during the final years of their lives. Was this an accident or fate? I do not know. But they both lived through those terminal years amidst New England farms, rolling hills and placid valleys that wore copses of trees, mountain ridges and the occasional lakes that glaciers had gouged out capriciously during a distant Ice Age. I remember Andrew once boasting about the tomatoes he had planted and harvested, and this surprised me. However, by the time I was installed at Hampshire, he had given up this gardening venture. He had, he confessed cryptically, to ration his energies. He lived in a stone house surrounded by untended fields. The closest structure to his was an abandoned barn into which his large cat liked to trespass. Baldwin shared a house with a French professor and her son, in a setting that was equally isolated and rural.

After my stint at Hampshire College, I retired from Northwestern and spent the next two years in Tlaquepaque, a small town of artisans in the Mexican state of Jalisco. All of my contacts with Andrew were by letter and telephone. I could not bear the thought of his life ebbing away, and distance provided me with the illusion that Andrew was still the companion of my salad days in London. I kept him alive in my imagination like Keats' nymphs in his "Ode on a Grecian Urn." When I called and Pat, that extraordinarily beautiful soulmate of Andrew's answered, I could tell from the quality of her voice whether it was one of Andrew's good or bad days. At one stage, he confessed to me that he no longer had the energy to write, and I suggested that he talk into a tape recorder. I do not know if he took my advice. Pat lives on with an enormous lode of priceless memories and I hope she'll spend the rest of her life sharing these with us. Her own story is itself a masterpiece waiting to be written.

I knew two Guyanese artists living in London at this time. Denis Williams was one. The other was Aubrey Williams. They were not related, although both came from Georgetown. Aubrey was the son of a civil servant and self-taught, whereas Denis's talent was recognised early and he won a two-year British Council Scholarship to study in the UK. As a young man, Denis had studied under a local artist, E.R. Burrowes, and then he went abroad to do further study. Later, he returned to Guyana and was appointed Director of Art in the Department of Culture in the Ministry of Education. In that post, Denis was the founding principal of both the E.R. Burrowes School of Art and of the Walter Roth Museum of Anthropology and Archeology.

Denis's and Aubrey's entrees into the British artistic scene were also quite different. Aubrey was gregarious and Denis was studious. Denis submitted a painting to a competition for young painters in Britain, and when he visited the exhibition, Salvador Dali picked out Denis's painting for comment, saying it was really unique because it had no Pre-Raphaelite connections.

Denis and his wife and three daughters were living in a three-room apartment in a house on Oxford Road at the time. One day, when the claustrophobia had become unbearable, and they were on the brink of starvation, Denis decided to ring up Wyndham Lewis, a leading art critic in England at the time. He told Lewis that he had several paintings that he would like him to see. Lewis told him to bring the paintings to his house, but Denis said they were very large and could not afford to take them around. Lewis insisted that he bring them around, but added that Denis should rent a van and that he, Lewis, would pay for the transport of the paintings. Lewis was impressed. While Denis was there, he called one of the leading galleries in London and told the director that he had paintings by a young artist worth seeing. The gallery owner said that while they were booked for the next five years, it was their policy to look at new artistic work and agreed to come around. When he saw the paintings, he agreed with Lewis to organise an exhibition as soon as possible. The gallery owner also wrote a glowing review of Denis' work, and other positive reviews followed. Lewis wrote a review, too, stating that Denis was an artist of genius, and recommended him for a job at the Slade School of Fine Art.

Denis later did a degree in archeology and took his family off to the Sudan and Benin. He also taught at Ife and Lagos universities and had a job in Khartoum. His work, *Icon and Image: A Study of Sacred and Secular Forms of African Classical Art* came out of this period. Later, after returning home to Guyana, he turned his archeological training to research on the Amerindian legacies of Guyana and produced the book *Prehistoric Guyana*.

Denis knew the English artist Francis Bacon quite well, and before he left for Africa, he took me around to Bacon's studio in South Kensington. They were great buddies and, in fact, had lived next to each other at one point. Bacon had just finished his portrait of Winston Churchill.

Much later, after Guyana gained independence in 1966, Denis and I joined other Guyanese in London discussing whether we should go home or not. Forbes Burnham, then the Prime Minister, was offering inducements for us to return. But, I could not work for Burnham with what I knew about how he came to power, with a clear conscience. Denis, however, did finally decide to move back in 1967.

He was in Georgetown when the US Peace Corps sent down some skilled craftsmen from Georgia in the American South to demonstrate the techniques of making bricks out of clay. The Peace Corps had been started by US President Kennedy as a kind of cultural and technical counterbalance to the support offered to developing societies by the USSR. Since Guyana had a left-leaning but at this stage non-Marxist government, it was the "beneficiary" of some of these new US projects. Denis had attended some of these classes and was so impressed by the work that he was determined to use this technique to build his house. The man who headed the group was the oldest member the Peace Corps had they ever sent abroad. There were big write-ups in the press and Denis was happy to take the classes under him, learning how to shape the bricks, to get the right consistency of the materials, etc.

Denis had decided that he would build a house on the Mazaruni River near the Pakaraima foothills in the interior of our country. I also bought some land in the Mazaruni River region when Denis was there, although I never developed it. *Time* magazine had a write-up about Denis and his family's move out there. Denis felt that Guyana had an ethos, a sense of being that was unique, that the forests, the rivers, and the purple mountains imbued it with a magical aura. So, building his house in the Guyanese interior, using techniques brought to Guyana by Blacks from the US South, whose ancestors had brought them from Africa during the slave trade, was Denis's way of physically and spiritually reconnecting the African Diaspora.

However, his house was rather inaccessible. There were no main roads anywhere near it, and in order to get there, you had to go by boat and then take a long trek by foot. In fact, he ended up delivering the last baby of his Welsh wife, himself, because he could not get her to Georgetown in time. She subsequently left him and returned to England. He later married an upper-class Georgetown woman of mixed Portuguese-Creole ancestry.

Aubrey Williams was another Guyanese artist living in London, but his entrée had been quite different to Denis's. When Aubrey moved to the UK in the early 1950s, he was in his late 20s. He died in 1990. Shortly after his death, Joy, and I visited his widow at their house in Hampstead. She was keen on giving me one of the paintings Aubrey had done of me. I hadn't sat for the portrait, but he'd taken the image from the back of one of my books.

When Aubrey left BG, he had been working in the interior as an agronomist for the government. These British civil service jobs not only paid well but, as I've mentioned, they also provided "long" and "short" leaves, when we could go away on paid leave and know that our jobs would be waiting for us when we returned home. However, Aubrey, had no intention of returning to Guyana and his previous life.

Though initially self-taught, Aubrey also studied under E.R. Burrowes, as had almost all local Guyanese artists. When he got to England, he enrolled at the St Martin's School of Art.

Both Aubrey and Denis were involved with the Caribbean Artists Movement in London, which was started by Kamau Brathwaite, John La Rose and Andrew Salkey. Its history was written by Anne Walmsley, an English literary and art critic and another good friend of mine. Denis was involved earlier than Aubrey, but as Anne became a patron of Aubrey, he, too, became involved.

Lord Campbell, reforming Chair of Bookers, the company that owned sugar estates in Guyana, also became a patron of Guyanese art, and he gave Aubrey a scholarship to go back home to Guyana to stage an exhibition of his work. Aubrey was developing a following in London, but he wasn't well-known in the Caribbean. As a result of his tour, Aubrey got a commission to paint a mural at the Timerhi airport in Guyana.

Much later, I did a review of a book about his art by Anne Walmsley called *Guyana Dreaming: The Art of Aubrey Williams*, a book that was widely praised.

I met my first wife, Joan, in London in 1952. Her maiden name was Joan Mary Allen. When I married her, I was her fourth husband and her then surname was Murray, since Andrew Digby Murray was her third husband. When I met Joan, she had three daughters, two by Andrew, and one by her first husband. By the fall of the year we were married, Lisa, her fourth daughter, was born.

This was also the time I got involved with the Olivier Productions. One day, I was walking into South Kensington underground station when, by total chance and several thousand miles away from our previous meeting, I bumped into an old classmate of mine from Berbice, Cy Grant. Cy, who was a very good-looking fellow, was a professional actor and a folk singer, though he had also recently qualified as a lawyer.

During the war, Cy had been an officer in the British Royal Air Force and he'd been shot down over Holland. Miraculously, his life was saved. The bomber in which he was flying was damaged by enemy fire and was falling out of the sky when the escape hatch jammed, but one of the engines exploded and blew him out of the plane. He was given sanctuary by the Dutch, but the Nazis captured him and he was a prisoner of war for about two years before he was liberated. Cy told me that being a POW was tough, but he did have one victory in that the Nazis could not place him in their racial pigeon holes. When they asked him what he was, he began listing his various polyglot ancestors, and they ended up listing him as of "indeterminate race".

Cy told me that Laurence Olivier's theatre company, where he was working, was looking for somebody who was roughly his height and build to act the role of the character opposite him. The original actor had left and there was a vacancy. Here was one of the most prestigious theatre companies, and all of the actors were professionals, so I was apprehensive about taking this audition. The only acting I had done was in high school.

Cy was on his way to visit Andrew Murray, a friend of his, and he suggested I go and have tea with Andrew and his family on Fulham Rd in Chelsea. I was at a loose end so I agreed to go. It was here that I met Joan for the first time.

Later, when I went for the audition, they accepted me, which was miraculous. If they had advertised, there would have been hundreds of professional actors flooding in. Then, being accepted after one audition was virtually unheard of. I would be acting alongside Sir Laurence Oliver, the pre-eminent Shakespearean actor in England. The year was 1952 and The Laurence Olivier Productions Company, of which I was suddenly a part, was due to tour to Liverpool and the US with two plays: Shakespeare's *Anthony and Cleopatra* and Shaw's, *Caesar and Cleopatra*, both under the direction of Michael Benthall. So, out of the blue, I got a well-paid job as an actor, when I hadn't acted beyond school plays before. It was a huge surprise.

We rehearsed in London for a while and then moved to Liverpool. Olivier had warned Cy and me that we might have to endure some racial incidents in the US where we were going to take the plays, but I told him, "I've lived there, I know it pretty well." However, the first racial incident was in Liverpool. I had gone ahead of the company and the woman in the boarding house that the company had booked refused to have me. "We refuse to board blacks!" she said. So I left in a rage and the first person I met was a priest.

"What kind of Christians are you?" I chastised him. "My friend and I are in the Olivier Company and they won't allow us to board in the same hotel as the white actors."

The priest took me to a nearby boarding house that accommodated Cy and me, but I felt the company should have expressed some solidarity and not have stayed at the racist boarding house. But they did all the same.

Cy was a lot more professional than I was. I didn't take the job all that seriously. All the same, we travelled on a Cunard liner from Liverpool to New York. We were due to perform at the Zeigfield theatre in New York. It felt funny to have people rushing to get your autograph when all you had was a few lines. Such was the status of Laurence Olivier. Not many Blacks were actors in any of the leading Shakespeare companies in the world. It gave me a sort of celebrity status.

My old mentor and sponsor, H.C. Cameron, came to see one of our performances at the Zeigfield, with some of his protégés.

I met Langston Hughes, the black American poet, for the first time and he took me around quite a bit. He even threw a party for me and a couple of other people. Arnold Rampersad, Hughes' biographer commemorated the event when he wrote: "The quiet at 20 East 127th Street was broken only by a party in honour of Arna Bontemps, the Columbian writer Jorge Artel, and Jan Carew, a tall, handsome actor from British Guiana and a celebrity as a member of Laurence Olivier's Old Vic [sic] Company then visiting New York."

Langston was a great host and he had a special sense of humour. People considered him the poet-laureate of Harlem. I remember he once told me an anecdote about a black ex-serviceman from the Korean war whom he had met in a bar in Harlem. This war veteran had managed to become a sergeant but he couldn't read or write. His commanding officer only found out when he saw him holding the list of names in his platoon upside down (he'd memorised them all!). This man told Langston he was going to do some studies. Langston asked him what kind of course he was going to do.

"General education," replied the ex-servicemen.

"What's this general education?" Langston enquired.

"Reading and writing," replied the serviceman.

Langston introduced me to some of the key figures in the Black Renaissance in the US, like Ralph Ellison, author of *The Invisible Man*. He also arranged a speaking assignment for me to go to Fisk University and read poetry, where I spent time with Arna Bontemps, another famous writer of the Black Renaissance. I also met Charles Johnson, the internationally famous sociologist, who was then President of Fisk University. Back in NY, I met Harry Belafonte. He was a rising star and was just beginning his career as a folksinger and an actor, singing in a nightclub in the East Village.

There was a benefit held at the Hotel Theresa in Harlem during the time I was there, and I was asked to introduce Josephine Baker, along with Canada Lee and John Garfield. I began and then handed it over to Canada Lee who had a booming voice that presided over the room like a force of nature. The event was a huge success. Baker was world-famous and revered by the French. She was a friend of President Charles De Gaulle who had decorated her for her commitment to the French Resistance during the Nazi occupation. She'd been recently discriminated against by the New York Cotton Club, but when she returned to France there was a large demonstration to welcome her.

The Laurence Olivier company had 48 members. For years after the Liverpool and New York productions, I kept seeing several of them on film and television. Cy, in fact became one of the first regular black faces on British TV.

When I was with them during our rehearsals and tour, the group divided into cliques and my best friend, apart from Cy, was an Irishman called Niall MacGinnis, a medical doctor. Niall acted part of the year and the rest of the time he practised medicine. He loved playing the guitar and singing calypsos. Edmund Purdom was another actor in the Company and he got a big Hollywood role after the production at the Zeigfield.

Vivien Leigh, who played Cleopatra, was a bit of an alcoholic. One night, the Zeigfield hosted a cocktail party in the upstairs of a building on 52nd Street. At one point, Ms. Leigh arrived late and a little inebriated. She was dragging her mink coat, worth more than $50,000 dollars, through puddles of champagne.

Olivier had been right, however, about expecting racism in the US. While we were in New York, one of the millionaire patrons of the theatre invited the company to a function at one of his social clubs in upstate New York. Very pointedly, the whole company was invited, except Cy and me.

Mike De Swaan, whom I had met in Amsterdam earlier, had written to his brother, Mony, who had a huge office on Wall Street. Mony came to see the show and entertained me to dinner one night. To my surprise, Mike had told Mony to book me a ticket anywhere in the world that I wanted to go when the show closed. So, after seven months with Olivier Productions, I went on a holiday to the Caribbean and South America with first class tickets! And, when I returned to New York, I still had my return passage to London on the Cunard line.

I returned to London and Joan came to meet me at Southampton. In the meantime, she and Andrew Murray had separated. When I had met her with Cy, I was immediately drawn to her. She had just returned from a trip to Holland and I had lived in Holland, so we immediately had something in common to talk about. The next day, she had phoned me and invited me to go for a walk with her and her three daughters in Kensington Gardens. I was surprised. Joan was tall and very striking; she had a full head of copper-red hair, and blue-grey eyes. We walked around the lake and the children fed the ducks while we talked about a wide range of topics. After a few hours, I took them back home and returned to my flat. I was attracted to her, but I wasn't very keen on going into a serious relationship. In addition, she had three children and I was only just beginning my life in London. Nevertheless, I did call her after a few weeks and we saw each other several times before I left with Olivier Productions. But since I was scheduled to be away in America with the company for nearly a year, I thought that Joan's and my relationship would end. So, it was a surprise when she met me at the docks.

My life changed after I met Joan. We began living together, first, in the house in Chelsea, and later, in a place in Kent. I used to take the children out for walks. I would push Lallie, a plump baby with bright blue eyes, in the pram and people would look at the baby and then look up at me. Then they would see the other children hugging me, and I could see the quizzical looks on their faces.

In places like Chelsea there was usually a private, fenced-in garden in the square that only children who lived in that neighbourhood were allowed in. You had to pay a small fee and every house owner had a key to the garden. Andrew gave the key to me because he was going out to his office every day and I was at home writing. Joan had a Cockney housekeeper who cooked meals, did the shopping, and so forth, but she didn't take the children out for walks, so I would take the children to the garden. There was a caretaker for this private garden who was responsible for keeping people out who didn't have the right social credentials. He was used to seeing Andrew with the children, but he didn't know my connection to them and he tried to bar us from the garden. Andrew was incensed. He confronted the fellow in a very English scene – how dare this lower-class man bar his children?

Andrew Murray was six-foot-six inches tall; he had been a colonel in an elite corps of the army. He came from old Scottish-Irish nobility and his mother lived in Devonshire where the upper crust had lived for centuries. His father had been a colonel in the army, too. When he met Joan, he was pursuing a professional career in the army. Andrew was a graduate from Winchester, one of the top public schools, and he was a brilliant mathematician. So, he went into the elite corps by virtue of both class and academic excellence. Andrew had rewritten some of the manuals of the British army and was all set to have an outstanding career in the armed forces when he decided to resign. It was a matter of principle, about using nuclear weapons. He would probably have become a field marshall, if he hadn't taken this stand. For a while, he was unemployed, but, with his training in mathematics, the biggest American firm in London hired him. He started out at the lowest level, but within one year he became a director.

Andrew's principles also applied to me. He didn't object to the fact that I was now living in his former house and helping his former wife raise his children. His marriage to Joan was already on the rocks before I appeared on the scene, and they would probably have divorced anyway. He later married a general's daughter.

People often ask me about race relations in this period. People *had* asked Joan, "What will others think?" But Joan had all the arrogance of the English upper-crust. Her attitude was that since the English had suzerainty over one-third of the world for centuries, she should be able to decide whom she should choose to marry and establish relationships with. She wouldn't let any lower-class bureaucrats choose for her. Joan was also naturally kind and generous, and she went out of her way to help people who were less fortunate than she was. Later, after we broke up and she and the children left, she decided to go back to school to take her "O" Levels and then she would go on to university. She was very bright and did a special study on rehabilitating young delinquent women and eventually became the headmistress of a state-run institution.

Married to Joan, I suddenly had four people absolutely dependent on me: my wife and three stepchildren – Gillie, Anna and Lallie. Then, there was our new baby, Lisa. Andrew Salkey had once told me that when you marry a woman, that woman becomes your country. I never knew England the way I did when I was with Joan. I learnt that English women can be very brave in a different way to Caribbean women. Joan's bravery was to have fought for me against her own society. Joan's mother was an English Canadian; her father was a white settler in Kenya. Kenyan whites are some of the most racist of all white settlers on the African continent and he cut Joan off when she began to go out with me.

One of the first things that happens to you when you marry a white woman is that you start thinking about what you look like to others or what you imagine others see. You become "visible" as a person. When people saw me with these white children of Joan's, they had to adjust their lens to comprehend this group as a family. If the woman is upper class and attractive, then being with a man like me doesn't fit into their stereotypes. Then, the "threat" of your blackness is multiplied and they indulge in speculation, saying things like: "This intermarriage is alright, but what about the children? You're placing a handicap on their heads for life."

When my sister Cecily died, I lost the closest person in my family. I was absolutely desolate. She had died of cancer, though I had brought her to London to be seen by the best doctors. I remember the best poem I've ever written in my life was the one I did for her, "*I sent no flowers for her dying/ The withered petals fall into the dust too soon…*" I had already fallen out with Joan by that time, but I had no one else to go to. She, alone, could plumb the depths of anguish that I felt. I stayed with Joan for three days and nights. They tell me that when Joan was dying years later in the early 1980s, all she could talk about was the good times we had together.

I was married to Joan for three years, during which time my first daughter, Lisaveta, was born in the hospital on Earls Court on October of 1953. When Lisa arrived, it was the most beautiful thing that had happened to me in my life. To this day, when I think of her, I still see her face as a newly-born child.

After leaving the house in Chelsea, we lived in Kent for a while, outside Deal. It was there that I developed an appreciation for the rural English landscapes. I also started writing pieces for the *Kensington Post*. The Black American magazine, *Jet,* did a feature on me in 1955, because I was the first and only black person on this London weekly. Kensington was the borough of the royal elite and I had to attend many royal functions as a part of my job.

Sadly, I fell out with Joan while Lisa was still a toddler. I moved out of the house in Kent, and not having any place to stay at the time, I actually moved in with Joan's former husband, Andrew, for a while. Joan and I got legally separated, and she kept the girls with her in Clapham where she moved later. I had visitation rights and Lisa would come spend weekends with me in Wimbledon.

It was around this time that I began teaching on the extra mural programme of London University. One day when I was having lunch at the House of Commons with the famous MP, Fenner Brockway, he said to me, "Don't you have some kind of qualifications? The head of the extra mural programme of London University is looking for someone to teach a course on race relations."

Brockway arranged a dinner with the pro vice-chancellor. The dinner lasted about four hours and I got the job. Conveniently, the classes were being held in Wimbledon, the district where I lived. Upper-crust Wimbledon residents had requested the course and it was they who attended it. It was a time when race relations were souring in England. In the aftermath of WWII, England was now dealing with the increased numbers of immigrants from its colonies flooding in for the jobs to rebuild England. The arrival of the 1948 MV Empire Windrush was emblematic of the impact of these new populations on the UK, and many more were coming in during the 1950s. On my course, I had quite an interesting mix of students, from educators, to solicitors, to bus drivers. Even so, I found it curious that we were offering this course in race relations in Wimbledon, one of least diverse sections of greater London.

I got the Wimbledon house through Roger Cronin, who was a student in my extra mural class. He was a solicitor and offered me a choice of two places. One was a house divided into three apartments. The other was an apartment in Mayfair, where the rich people lived. I chose the Wimbledon house because, by this time, I had four children I was responsible for and needed more space. The former owner of my house was a Trotskyist member of Parliament with a disdain for his middle-class comrades and he practically sold the house to me for a song. I could rent two of the apartments and live in the main part of the building. It was a big house, detached, and double the width of the usual London houses. The main section where I lived, was on two stories and had several rooms. My office was a large room with French windows leading to the garden. It had padded doors to control the noise from the rest of the house and a fireplace. Best of all, was the back garden, which had an apple tree, a copper beach, and luxurious wisteria vines. Off and on, I had a gardener. I also had a handyman who did repairs, who was almost a permanent fixture. One of the two self-contained apartments was located on the third floor, the other in a basement one could enter from the street. The house had two garage spaces and I rented out one.

The house was walking distance from Wimbledon Common and it sat on the top of a steep hill. Visitors arriving on the underground from London, would often arrive at my door slightly winded from the steep hike. Everybody in Wimbledon knew who I was and where I lived. I was the only black man living in the area at the time. People could arrive at the station and not being sure which direction to go to my house, would simply ask a passer-by and be directed the right way.

The Guyanese writer, Ronald Dathorne, was very jealous. He and his German wife came for a visit and he never let me forget how different I was from the average West Indian. Most West Indians living in London at the time were staying in rooming houses, not living among the mansions of Wimbledon.

Ironically, I lived next door to a salesman for Guyana Rum, and his daughter used to play with Lisa. He was very respectful, especially when he saw that I was a good friend of Lord Jock Campbell, the chairman of Booker Brothers, the company that made the rum. He noticed that Lord Campbell would come to dinner at our house.

Across the way from my back fence, was a large property that belonged to Eric Newby, a well-known writer of travel books. Newby was a vigorous man in his mid-forties, a keep-fit fanatic whose explosive energy was a constant affront to my own indolence. A few years back, he had made a journey to the Hindu Kush. Just before leaving Britain, he spent a fortnight in Wales taking his first lessons in mountaineering. After this inadequate apprenticeship, he proceeded to climb near the summit of one of the most formidable of the Himalayan peaks. When I felt energetic enough (which was very seldom), I would join him on runs around Wimbledon. There were times when trailing him up a steep incline, I felt as though I were trying to scale Mount Everest myself. There were a lot of small hills, and you could run by a lake and the riding stables. There were footpaths from our part of the Common and you could follow them all the way to Richmond Park, which belonged to the Royal household and had deer wandering around freely.

Newby's runs were real marathons. Eventually, I began doing them every other day. Not only was I getting fit, but these runs helped me finally shake off my smoking habit and set me on a path of running that would be a constant feature of my life well into my 80s. There was also a local police station near the Common and I used to go running with them sometimes, too. I wore surplus paratrooper boots, which is ironic, because I had made some jumps from airplanes during my training for the Coast Artillery during World War II, and never thought I'd see boots like those again.

I lived in this Wimbledon house for a few years, without a wife or resident family. At one point, I was driving a Daimler and people didn't realise, seeing all of this opulence, that I needed those jobs – in the theatre, broadcasting for the BBC, doing TV plays, and journalism – to be able to put gas in the car.

"What is a West Indian?"
West Indian Gazette, September 1959 (London)

The question "What is a West Indian?" is one that concerns every thinking person in the British Caribbean today. For, we are standing at a cultural crossroads and the direction we take will affect our future, our identity. Here are some of the factors to be examined to discover who we are:

We are made up of cliques and factions who base their claims to being intellectuals on skin colour and shade, social status, wealth and political power; and the claims do not stop at being merely intellectuals, but extend to being arbiters, critics and patrons of all the arts.

According to West Indian values, there are certain incandescent heights – being a doctor, dentist, lawyer, magistrate, politician, judge, businessman – which once attained, entitle the lucky individual to all kinds of magical depths. The artist and writer is even more profoundly involved in the quest for his or her own identity and has the badge of learning which supposedly gives the ability to appreciate (better than anyone else) anything that comes under the heading of "culture".

It has become very popular for West Indian politicians to tell us about a West Indian culture, but I have heard none of them come near to defining for the mass of people what this culture is. Some people evade answering this question by saying that we are a part of Western civilisation, whilst others ask, "Is there a West Indian culture?" It is important for us to know the answer to this question because our society is in danger of passing from barbarism to banality without an intermediary period of civilisation. This, of course, takes into account the last four centuries.

To answer the question, the word "culture" has to be defined in terms adequate for ourselves. Bertolt Brecht's poem always seems to me to go to the heart of what culture is:

Great Rome is full of triumphal arches.
Who erected them?

Over whom did the Caesars triumph?
Had Byzantium, much praised in song, only palaces for its inhabitants?

Even in fabled Atlantis, the night that the ocean engulfed it,
The drowning still cried out for their slaves.

Culture then, is the product of a man's creative labour in a place, in a society where he has lived, and over thousands of generations, where he has put his particular stamp on an environment. To admit there is a West Indian culture is to concede that the foundations of this culture were laid by slaves, and later, that some of the builders of these superstructures were bond labourers. The descendants of the slave owners who still have an honoured place in our society, have taught the great majority of educated West Indians to believe that the millions of slaves were not important, that it was from the masters that all cultural blessings flowed.

But if we accept the master's claims, we find ourselves in a dilemma, for his civilisation is dying whilst ours is now being born. His institutions have become sacred cows surrounded by a host of worshippers, some of whom admit that the sacred cow was not the product of an immaculate conception. Hence Brecht's cry of despair, "Who built them?"

Our immediate problem is to define the culture we have inherited. And this is not easy, for our society during its centuries of historical gestation has been fed by racial and cultural streams from all over the earth. Today, then, it is like an anaconda snake, which having swallowed, mashed, pulverised and digested its first gigantic meal (and ours was a meal of polyglot cultures), must now discover the relationship between the intake and the expenditure of energy.

Because of our unique experience, we find ourselves in the mid-twentieth century not knowing who we are or what we are. When a man or woman says, "I am a West Indian", he or she knows that this envelope of life with a West Indian address is faceless, a cipher. And the West Indian will only cease to be this when, through a creative representation of the smell of his earth and the dreams of his people, he can discover a true image of himself.

Jan Carew in his Wimbledon office. From a *Tatler* magazine piece on Caribbean writers.

Photograph: *Tatler*

CHAPTER NINE

WIMBLEDON LIFE

I met Sylvia Wynter, my second wife, at the BBC in 1957. I was quite busy at the time, doing readings at the BBC, organising courses on race relations in the extra mural department, still writing my column for the *Kensington Post*. I was also very active in the anti-colonial movement. The BBC had a number of services on which one could freelance. There was the Home Service, the International Service, special features, etc. When I was in London, I would do the reading for the broadcasts myself. So, after they agreed to buy something, they would set up a schedule for me to come in. To hear these stories in the actual language of Caribbean people and about things back home, was something new at the time. I had developed quite a following and I later found out that my nephew's generation at Queen's College in Guyana was so impressed with my way of speaking, that they tried to speak like me.

I had gone to the BBC on Oxford Street to read a feature for *Caribbean Voices* when someone met me at the door and said, "There's a Jamaican woman reading your poetry and praising it. You might want to meet her." At the time, Sylvia was married to a Norwegian and had a child, Anne Marie. She was a student at London University, King's College doing graduate work on the Golden Age of Spanish literature, and had recently returned from Spain.

When I met Sylvia, it was like going back home. She was from Jamaica, though she and her brother had been born in Cuba. It seemed to me that Sylvia carried a lot of guilt and was troubled about having married a Norwegian. It was not long afterwards that she got a divorce from him. I married Sylvia in 1958, after divorcing Joan.

Sylvia and I collaborated on several projects, including a documentary on stowaways from British Guiana for ITV's Granada television. But, the most prominent collaboration was probably our play, *University of Hunger*, which would be produced later by the Georgetown Theatre Guild back in Guyana. I had previously done plays at the BBC, but this was the first major stage play. It was later adapted for radio and for television as *The Big Pride* and I had the classical black American actor, William Marshall, as the lead and the Senegalese actor, Johnny Sekka, as the main supporting character.

It aired first on television on May 28th, 1961 as part of the Associated TV's Drama '61 anthology series.

This came when, after years in the literary wilderness, my first novel, *Black Midas*, had been a bestseller, and Martin Secker & Warburg – a prestigious publisher – had brought out two other novels of mine, *The Wild Coast*, 1958, and *The Last Barbarian*, 1961. *The Wild Coast*, had, in fact, been written before *Black Midas*, and several publishers had turned it down, but after the success of *Black Midas*, Secker & Warburg accepted it without reservation and both came out in 1958. An American edition of *Black Midas* was also brought out by the US publisher, Coward McCann, though the publisher insisted upon changing the title to *A Touch of Midas,* claiming that the word "Black" would offend black Americans. At the time, the generally accepted terms in vogue were "Negro," or "Coloured." Little did they know, but within ten years, America's Negro youth would start calling themselves "black" in order to free themselves from the legacies of racism in the US. The first two novels were set in Guiana, while my third novel, *The Last Barbarian*, was set in New York's Harlem.

In addition, among other freelance activities, I was writing regular book reviews for the literary journal *John O'London's Weekly,* was an art critic for the avant-garde *Art News & Review,* and was writing a weekly current affairs column for a local paper, *The Kensington Post*. The most important and rewarding of my many and varied creative activities, however, was the weekly broadcast that I did on the BBC programme, *Caribbean Voices*, where I read my own poetry, short stories and features about life in London. Many of these vignettes were also later published in the BBC's magazine, *The Listener.*

When I married Sylvia, she, her daughter, Anne Marie, and later our son, Christopher, lived in the Wimbledon house with me. We had reverse jobs. We had two small children in the house – a baby, Christopher, and a toddler, Anne-Marie. Syvia would go to bed early and then get up at midnight and work until four in the morning. Then, as I was working from home, I would look after them in the morning and early afternoon. Her mother eventually sent a woman from Jamaica to help out and this really made a difference.

When my novels came out with a splash, there were all kinds of photos and special articles done, showing our happy family, but, this marriage, too, fell apart. I was unaccustomed to this – the boot was now on the other foot. Eventually, Sylvia left with the children for Jamaica, having decided that it would be better to raise them back home in the Caribbean. At one point, when I returned to Guiana to work with the Jagan government, I arranged for them to join me there, but that was not successful and Sylvia went back to Jamaica.

Race relations in England had also begun deteriorating about this time.

Walking with Sylvia on Wimbledon High Street one day, I heard someone shout from a car window, "Nigger, go home!" This would never have happened in earlier years in genteel Wimbledon. Another time, when Sylvia and I were jogging on the common, she stopped to catch her breath and I went on, but something was troubling my mind and I went back to check on her. I found Sylvia struggling against a man who had attacked her. I chased him off and while she was alright, she was clearly shaken up.

I had a number of interesting people renting the flats in my Wimbledon house at various points. After Sylvia left, my life became a collage of love affairs, anti-colonial activity, solitary periods of writing and painting, and wild spells of carousing.

At one point, I had three models living at Wimbledon house with me. One was my girlfriend. She was tall, Jewish, and came from France. I met her when I had opened the French windows in my office one day in late spring and she was passing by. She said "Hello!" And we struck up a conversation. She had actually met another Guyanese, Stanley Moore, who was studying law in London at the time. Stanley's wife had been a close friend of my sister Cicely. This model wanted to marry me and we stayed in touch even after I moved to Canada in the mid-1960s. But, I already had two failed marriages by this time and did not want to marry anyone else at this point. Later, when I started to get lonely in Canada, I tried to reconnect with her, but by this time she had moved to Argentina and was married to an Argentinian millionaire.

The actor, William Marshall, was a temporary renter. It was the mid-1950s and Marshall was in London to take over the Othello role that Paul Robeson was meant to do. Robeson was held up in the US following the McCarthy hearings and the denial of his passport. It was uncertain whether he would be able to come over. Then, when Robeson did win his fight against the US government, he fell ill in the USSR and it appeared that Marshall might still be needed to perform the role. But Robeson's health improved and after delaying rehearsals for the production, he was able to fulfil his commitment for the four-month run.

I first met Marshall at the office of my solicitor in Bloomsbury, an area of London that many writers have written about. Sheridan, my solicitor, was young and making a name for himself by representing artists, writers, actors and clients, some of whom I am sure had future prospects, but were, on the whole, currently risky. My own payments to him were irregular, but he never demanded the arrears that I owed him. I had been contracted to write three plays a year for the ATV company and had brought him the contract to examine before I signed it. I also talked to him about letting my house when I was away, and he told me he had a possible tenant who was about to come to the office.

When Marshall came through the door, the office seemed to grow smaller. He was six-foot-five and had shoulders that could fill an ordinary doorway. His voice, too, had levels of resonance that were mesmerising. His was an interesting case that he shared with me and the solicitor. He was being brought before a magistrate's court on the allegation of a British tycoon who accused him of living off "immoral earnings", when the truth was that this tycoon, from the north of England, was jealous of a mistress who had fallen in love with Marshall. The jealous lover had set Marshall up by inducing a woman to stay overnight in his apartment, and Marshall had fallen into the trap. The solicitor suggested that Marshall should hire a barrister to represent him in court, but Marshall was certain that he could defend himself, and when his case came up, he insisted upon defending himself, much to Sheridan's dismay. But, Marshall was a very impressive fellow – tall and with a booming voice. He appeared in the court wearing one of his Othello capes and won his case.

I offered Marshall a place to stay at my Wimbledon house. He was a pleasant enough companion and would regale me with stories of the young and up-and-coming. I was under contract to ATV to write three plays a year, and *The Big Pride*, which aired in May 1961, was first of the three. The other two that I wrote that year were *The Day of the Fox* and *Exile From the Sun*. The black American actor Sammy Davis Jr., played the part of a black revolutionary fighter in *Day of the Fox*, and opposite him was Zia Mohyeddin, the accomplished Pakistani actor. This aired in December 1961. The English actor, Leo McKern, was booked to play the role of the Brazilian artist, Tiberio, in my play *Exile From the Sun*, but there was a strike in the ATV studios when rehearsals were about to begin, and I left England before the strike ended. Everything was ready to shoot the play, but the play was never performed. I still have a copy of the shooting script.

Working with Sammy Davis, Jr. on *Day of the Fox* was both fascinating and demanding. He was very quick on his feet and could ad lib his parts, but he couldn't read very well, so learning the script was difficult for him. He had been in the theatre since he was a little boy and hadn't had the time for proper schooling. He kept missing his cues in the play and so, once we understood what was going on, we went to his apartment to help him memorise the lines by reading them over and over to him. At one point, I was driving him to the airport and we were running late, so I was pushing it a bit. We careened around a roundabout and slipped on the wet road, but managed to come to a safe stop. I looked at Sammy and he looked ashen from the fright. He had already lost one eye in a car accident, and probably thought that his time was up at this point. Happily, the rest of the journey was much smoother.

Marshall was my tenant in Wimbledon for several months during that hectic period. One weekend, in anticipation of my daughter Lisa's visit, I had baked a chicken and left it in the refrigerator. Marshall came in late

Jan Carew with Sammy Davis, Jr in rehearsal for Carew's TV play, *Day of the Fox*.

Photograph: *Flamingo* magazine (1 December 1961). Photo is credited to Ian Coates and A.T.V.

from the theatre and proceeded to eat the whole bird. The highlight of my week was the weekend when my daughter would come over and that chicken had been very lovingly prepared. When I discovered this the next morning, I was so furious with Marshall that I gave him notice on the spot.

Marshall was tall and handsome, and had a voice like a church organ with deep baritones. He was a perfect man, but lacked that last bit that would have made him a great actor. He was somewhat difficult to work with, as he thought he had more talent than he did.

Johnny Sekka, who played opposite him in my TV play, was also strikingly good-looking. He was smaller in stature, had smooth skin, and was very elegant. He was married to a Swedish woman and didn't womanise as so many West Indians did. Sekka was a born actor and could dominate a play even with the smallest of parts. He went to the Royal Academy of Dramatic Arts and graduated at the top of his class. He also studied in France. I went with James Mason's agent to see him in a play at the Hammersmith Theatre. It was an English play and he had the lead. At one point, he was a runner-up for the lead part in a film by Gordon Douglas, but Sidney Poitiers got the part, playing a Moor who kills General Gordon. Sekka disappeared into Hollywood in the 1970s where he played various roles, but he didn't gain the fame of Poitiers, although he was a better actor. Poitiers did, however, bring Sekka into some of his films. When Black actors in America, like Poitiers, get some success as actors, they start to believe that they can be directors and write scripts, but they are often incompetent when they move outside of acting – though some projects seem to make a lot of money. You don't see so many writers and directors with talent thinking that they can do it all.

In the 1960s, the American actor, James Mason, was very interested in making a film of my novel *Black Midas* and he went to the USSR to see if he could get backing. The book had been translated into Russian and I had acquired a sizable amount of royalties from it. There was another deal in the works at this time, too. Florence Hays Turner, a writer and agent for MGM studios in the US, was also interested in making a film of the book. Florence was from the American east coast millionaire families of the Whitneys and the Hays, and was a devotee of my work. She also wanted to marry me at one point. I've had approaches from black filmmakers over the years, but they, too, have fallen through. Film people can be very fickle. They get your hopes up, take you to lunch at the Dorchester where they pick your brain while flattering you about your talent. Then, off they go to raise the funds, and you never hear from them again.

During this period when I was separated from Sylvia, I met a woman named Florence. She was a student at London University and was a close friend of the Jamaican writer, Orlando Patterson. Her father was a Cockney picture-frame maker who devoted his life to studying early drawings by

Leonardo da Vinci and others of that era. He was so recognised for this skill that he was often pulled in as a consultant for the British Museum. He could have become a millionaire, but preferred to live modestly.

One weekend, when Lisa was at the house, Florence was also staying over. She was jealous of Lisa, and thought I paid far too much attention to her. She wanted Lisa to stay in a separate bed, but I insisted that the two of them share the double bed, while I slept on the single one. Lisa said that my lady friend kept mumbling all night, and trying to push her to the edge of the bed.

Another girlfriend was from Northumberland and married to a Jewish banker. Her husband had been wounded in the 1948 Arab-Israeli war. She came from a region of England that had been settled by Danes, so people from there tended to be very blond and Scandinavian looking. She wanted to leave her husband for me and her mother came to me to plead that I would not see her anymore. I told her mother that it was not up to me to decide this, that her daughter would be the one to decide. Her family, feeling that they needed to get her out of the clutches of this black man who must have put some black magic on her, sent her to New Jersey in the US to stay with her brother who was high up in the medical profession. They could not understand her fixation on this black man from the West Indies. She and I planned to get together in Venice. We were to meet on St. Marks Square. But as I came out of the airplane on my way to see her, I knew that our affair was over and I never saw her again after that.

Other people I knew in Wimbledon included Rosemary and Adrian Seligman. They lived just down the street from me at Wimbledon Common and welcomed me to the neighbourhood. They gave me some of their paintings and once threw a party for me. I met the local Conservative MP there and I remember that later, when the anti-immigrant fever was at its height in Britain, I wrote telling him that he'd obviously forgotten how much he'd enjoyed my company. The Seligmans had also hosted President Haile Selassie of Ethiopia during his years of exile. I remember seeing a statue of Selassie that Hilde Seligman, Adrian's mother, had done and placed in her garden. In 1955, after her death, the family donated the bust to the Wimbledon Borough Council and it was moved to the grounds of Cannizaro Park. Many years later, President Selassie and I would meet when I was at Princeton.

We had a left-wing activist living in Wimbledon who was involved in local politics. He told me that the Trinidadian writer and activist C.L.R. James was the most brilliant speaker he had ever heard – and he had heard Bakunin, Radek and all the Bolsheviks. CLR and I had fallen out, which was too bad. I had attacked him for being a Trotskyist, and he was furious. Later, in the late 1960s, I saw CLR at the airport in Toronto. He was stranded, as nobody had turned up to meet him. I was there to meet someone else and seeing that his local organisers were very disorganised, I took CLR home with me and looked after him until we could hook up with the group that was hosting him. He was very generous towards me afterwards. I last saw him in Jamaica when we were both there for Carifesta in 1976. One of his many writings was the book, *Party Politics in the West Indies*. It's a phenomenal work, and people should be reading it. In it CLR did an analytical study of the black bourgeoisie in the Caribbean and the US. Differently to the white bourgeoisie, the blacks do not own any companies or property, but build their social status based upon the size of their pay-cheques.

It was green and quiet in Wimbledon when the summer arrived. At the bottom of the Common was a pond where ducks, having fled the winter, returned to dally away the spring and summertime. Beyond the pond were fields of grass that bordered a golf course, gently rolling hills, and clusters of forest with dense growths of ferns carpeting the forest floor. This was the largest of the London parks. Walking along the wet and narrow trails in the early morning, it was easy to forget that you were surrounded by one of the world's great cities.

One morning, while running with my neighbour, Newby, we found an old man gasping his life away not far from the highway that borders the Common. While my companion went to phone for an ambulance, I tried to make the old man comfortable. His face was ashen and contorted and his eyes stared blankly at the grey sky. I had to fish loose dentures out of his mouth to prevent him swallowing them. The old man had been walking across the Common during the night, and had had a fit. He had spent hours on the cold wet earth. The police arrived, and after them the ambulance. I never discovered who the old man was or how he fared after that. A big city is an impersonal place. The death of one old man is a ripple in an ocean of wide indifference. At nights, the Common was a place of darkness, of bunched shadows under the trees and furtive figures. The lights that surrounded it barely illuminated it. No wonder it was the setting for so many crime fiction stories.

Beside the park, on the main highway to the city, were many famous houses. There was the Seligman mansion with its six acres of gardens, where the Emperor of Ethiopia lived in exile during World War II. Selassie had made his prophetic speech before the League of Nations warning that they must live up to their promises to help Ethiopia, or they, too, would not be able to stop the Nazis from colonising the world. Black people everywhere had risen up to defend Abyssinia, even in British Guiana. Alongside support for Marcus Garvey, Ethiopia was the most important pre-war cause for black people in the world. I remember the story of the black American aviator, Hubert Julian, who "headed" the Abyssinian air force during the war with the Italians. He was originally from Trinidad and had gone to the US where he built his own airplane. He was a strong supporter of Garvey and used to fly for him during parades. Once part of his plane crashed in the Harlem river.

This fellow not only went to fight for the Abyssinians, but also later went to Finland to offer to fight for them in WWII.

Then there was the house of Wilberforce, the great partisan of emancipation. His house, like many of the twenty- and thirty-room mansions of a bygone age, has now made way for blocks of modern flats. An attempt by citizens of the Wimbledon Borough to save it as a national monument proved futile. I visited the house just before its demolition and walked through the large and empty rooms with their faded murals and ornate ceilings. There was no suggestion of its ever having been occupied. It was a place emptied of reminiscences... no ghosts, no memories were there. Only the greenhouse, long neglected, its plants pushing against the low roof, was an affirmation of life. For a while afterwards, the house was a heap of rubble. When I passed by years later on the bus, even the rubble had been erased and clean, box-shaped, red brick buildings comfortably overlooked the wide green spaces of the common. Perhaps, someday, the common itself will give way to a forest of new houses.

The northwestern end of the common led into Richmond Park with its deer and grazing sheep, and picnickers dotting open fields and sheltering under clumps of trees. This extensive and miraculously preserved green belt kept the frenzies of the day at bay – all except the insistent roar of traffic. Standing in the middle of the common, I often listened to this roar and it reminded me of the distant sound of a waterfall. It is strange that when you are in the midst of this din, you never hear it very much. It's as constant as surf.

I met a West Indian park keeper one day. He had come up from Antigua a few months before. He lived in a small hut close to the golf course and the riding school. He told me he liked the feel of the green wooded expanses around him, even in the winter.

"But you haven't lived through a winter yet," I said to him.

"Don't matter to me," he said, "there's still going to be some green around."

There was a lake on the common. You came upon it suddenly out of a grove of trees. The water was green and untouched by the wind. I never tried swimming there. The water was icy cold, even in midsummer. I preferred to sit on its shores and gaze at the still water, like the trees which leaned over to look at their images. A long and gently sloping hillside led away from the lake. From the top of the hill, one could look at children from the riding school being put through their paces in a bowl of sand and clay, where the ferns and trees have been cleared away. The instructor barked orders and warily the children urged their mounts to canter, to trot, or to jump over low hurdles.

The common was a sanctuary, my sanctuary. Today, I wonder if it has resisted the remorseless spreading-out of the city of London.

When I first moved into the house in Wimbledon, and the Seligmans hosted a party for me, an article appeared in the local paper and I became a bit of a celebrity. My friends saw me on television and, much later, Donald Chesworth, who became a local representative of the Greater London Council, wanted to put up a plaque on my house to say that I had lived there. I lived at 58 Ridgeway Place in Wimbledon up until the time I left England permanently in 1965.

In the 1990s, when I had returned to London for a conference, I took Joy out to see the Wimbledon house. I understand that more recently, it has come up on the market and is priced at 3.7 million pounds.

"The Odd-Job Man"

Pepperpot vol.2, no.1, 1961 (London)

The odd-job man had become a rarity in London by the end of World War Two. This itinerant handyman, a leftover from John Bunyan's age of the tinker, was threatened with extinction before West Indian and other minorities of colour began migrating to Britain in the 1950s. Groups of these newcomers had settled in Brixton and turned this borough into one in which Blacks had become a majority. This creation of a Black ghetto in London had taken place surreptitiously and it inspired an incipient racism that spread to other cities in Britain where black immigrants had settled. The white hosts were not prepared for suddenly having black neighbours and fellow citizens in their midst.

This was an unplanned immigration that had taken place when the British colonial empire was sundering and colonial subjects of colour could still enter the mother country freely. So there were now enclaves where the sounds of black music were everywhere, and the tantalising smells of highly seasoned ethnic foods assailed the nostrils at every turn.

The odd-job men, who were trained as artisans before they migrated, found that they could augment their income by doing jobs that English workers no longer wanted to do. So when I wanted some minor repairs done to my house in Wimbledon, a West Indian friend recommended that I contact Mr. Travis, a Jamaican construction worker in Brixton, who with two companions moonlighted as odd-job men.

We met at the Doctorbird Café in Brixton. This Caribbean eatery was owned by Travis's uncle, and apart from the free meals he cadged from time to time, he used it as an office for making deals with prospective clients. Travis was a loud and hearty individual, while his companions were rather quiet and only spoke in muted monotones when he asked them questions. They agreed to replace slates on my roof, to plaster a wall in my study and to insulate the French windows in my living room. Travis explained that since all three of them had day jobs, they could only work for me at night or on weekends.

They turned up the following Saturday morning in a flamingo-pink Cadillac. Parking it in my driveway caused consternation on this staid upper-middle-class street. This glittering black man's dream chariot, which would have won acclamation in Brixton, seemed to threaten a riot on this street in Wimbledon. In addition, Travis actually greeted and talked to passers-by while he was working on my French windows – and a few of these tight-lipped Wimbledon denizens actually chatted with him and asked him to do small repair jobs for them.

When I got to know Travis better during a break for tea laced with

Jamaican rum, I asked him, "Travis, tell me how you can rationalise that expensive automobile while living in a dingy bedsitter in Brixton."

Travis chuckled and said, "That's the question most people would like to ask me. Well, lemme tell you. I bought it from a Yankee boxer who brought it to Britain and didn't want to take it back to America. When I drive it I feel equal to anybody else on the road. I'm working at three jobs to pay for it, but it's worth it. The eyes staring at me make me feel a sense of power that I never felt before."

When Travis arrived with his dream chariot, I regarded him with some suspicion. But my suspicion was quickly allayed. He talked a great deal but he was also a good worker, the ideal odd-job man. He treated me to a discourse on odd-jobbing. He had worked for years as a carpenter before coming to London, he said, and in Jamaica a carpenter had to be able to turn his hand to a variety of jobs. There was too much specialisation in London, he said. Each man tended to shut himself away in his special skill, doing his particular job as though it was the only thing in the world that mattered. The very fact that specialisation had become so much a part of the whole industrial process made the need for odd-jobbing more urgent. People didn't want to pay a half-dozen specialists to do minor repairs that a single jack-of-all-trades could tackle. There were many odd-job men in Brixton and other boroughs of London where West Indians had settled in numbers, my friend told me. And apart from many of them working in the building industry, there was often the need when a West Indian bought a house to make a slum dwelling habitable.

I discovered after a few meetings that my Jamaican handyman was something of a philosopher. I noticed that in spite of his big shiny car, his symbol of conspicuous consumption, he always dressed like a working-man. When I asked him why, he said that a man who changed his habit of dressing should not be trusted. He took me on a tour of Brixton one evening when the summer sunshine was keeping the darkness at bay. The dark faces framed in open windows, people sunning themselves on front steps, and children, reprieved from going to bed early, playing in the streets, lent an air of warmth and gaiety to the district. My companion was well known and had to stop several times to trade gossip, to give advice on house repairs, on car maintenance, on electrical fittings.

"He's a general," one of his friends told me. "Man, what this guy don't know ain't worth knowing."

We ended up in his bedsitter and in a short while, three visitors, all odd-job men, turned up. They became engaged in a protracted discussion about installing windows in new buildings, about the wholesale prices of nails, putty and window panes. The car was parked outside and a group of children were standing around it looking at their distorted images on its radiator and doors. The Jamaican looked outside occasionally and I thought

I detected a gleam of satisfaction in his eyes every time they lighted on his dream chariot.

And he told me that, "No car is worth having unless children can see images of themselves when they come close to it. It creates a sense of magic and mystery for them. And when they see me driving by, they believe that I am a King of the Road."

CHAPTER TEN

WAGING THE WORLD STRUGGLE

London was a crossroads of the anti-colonial struggle and solidarity campaigns for black Americans. I had been involved with the Movement for Colonial Freedom with Fenner Brockway and others. Fenner was a left-wing Labour MP who was born of English parents in India who were missionaries. Educated back in England, he became a lifelong anti-colonialist. He started the MCF with the basic goal of exposing human rights abuses and racism around the world, as well as to give support to liberation movements.

I remember once demonstrating (and there was plenty to demonstrate against at the time) in front of the American Embassy and I got there early and a senior policeman had a chat with me. I had on a Harris Tweed jacket, cavalry twill trousers, suede shoes and a cravat.

The policeman asked me: "Will you take part in this demonstration?" I perhaps didn't look as I would – because I believed in always looking smart at such occasions.

"Yes, because in America we wouldn't be allowed on the footsteps of Congress. We'll have a very respectable demonstration, Officer," I'd said. "You need not worry."

In fact we were demonstrating against the arrest of communists in America during McCarthy's rage against real and imagined communists and, given the lack of respect that McCarthy had showed in his purges, a respectful demonstration wasn't our main concern. Many of those demonstrating were radical left-wing activists, so the feeling of empathy was very strong amongst those in attendance, who had their own rage to announce to the American Embassy.

Claudia Jones was one of those we were fighting for. Claudia was one of the most outstanding women I had met in the twentieth century. She was patient, dedicated and courageous, and she was not afraid of treading dangerous political pathways. She was not afraid of espousing causes that exposed her to penury, harassment, and a plethora of both open and hidden dangers. She was also tolerant of those with opposing political views.

This Trinidadian-born political activist and former member of the Central Committee of the US Communist Party had settled in London, after being deported from the United States. Always politically engaged, she and her partner, Manchanda, a Maoist revolutionary from India, had become very active in the civil rights struggles of West Indian immigrants in Britain. She started the *West Indian Gazette,* a monthly paper that was widely read by West Indians in London, Birmingham, Bristol and other cities with immigrant populations.

Claudia was soft-spoken in her social conversations, but her voice could ring out and fill a crowded auditorium when she was making a public speech. The last time I heard her speak in public was when she introduced Paul Robeson at a rally in the St. Pancras Town Hall. I have a picture of us at this event. This meeting was a fund-raiser for Claudia's community newspaper in 1959. I do not remember any instance when Claudia raised her voice in the course of a conversation. There was a Trinidadian politeness in the way in which she listened to the person, or persons, to whom she was speaking. She was a mixture of the Trinidadian, the Afro-American, and the woman of the world, but despite the softness in her demeanour, she could be very persuasive.

I remember one of her countrymen telling me, "Claudia can persuade you to do something, and you will go away believing it was your decision and yours alone."

Claudia kept the *West Indian Gazette* alive against almost impossible odds. When her illustrious friends like Robeson and W.E.B. Du Bois visited London, she got them to appear at rallies for the paper. Another good friend was Pablo Picasso, who on occasions would send her drawings that she could sell to help raise much-needed funds. Years later, when she died suddenly of a heart attack alone – Manchanda was in China at the time – rumour has it that her apartment was ransacked. Things were stolen including Picasso's drawings – which she never actually sold, the manuscript of her autobiography, and other private papers. Those who knew her, also knew about her heart condition, and that she was living on borrowed time. She wore the mantle of greatness with ease and dauntless courage. She never faltered in the exemplary choices that she made.

In the late 1950s, Wole Soyinka, the Nigerian writer, and I did a Sunday night performance at the Royal Court Theatre called "Eleven Men Died at Hola Camp". During the Mau Mau Rebellion in Kenya, the men were beaten to death and the British issued a white paper following the enquiry into the case. We turned this into a play, and it was explosive. The man who subsidised the Royal Court Theatre threatened to withdraw his funds. Wole and I sat on either side of the stage and read from the report. At the end, there was total silence, then the audience erupted into applause. It was one of my best performances. Wole later turned the white paper findings into a documentary drama.

I was still married, though separated, to Joan at the time, and the Mau Mau struggle was intruding into our personal life. However, there was also an English comrade named Donald Chesworth, and he stayed with me most of the day because he had a deep understanding of the way I felt. The Hola Camp Massacre was a horrific event and shocked the country. Donald was a very upper-class white Englishman and very principled. He really devoted his whole life to the struggle.

Around this time, there was another Guyanese, who had studied in the US and had an Masters of Art degree, and who had applied for a job as a fireman in London. The fireman's union was the most left-wing of all of the unions in London, but they refused to take this fellow. So, we sent him to take the fireman's exam, which he passed with flying colours. Donald located the head of the union – who was knighted and was one of the main forces against having a black fireman – and invited him to lunch and twisted his arm by warning him that it would look really bad if the word got out in the press. So, the fireman's union took this black fellow and he became the first black fireman in London.

Our activist community demonstrated almost every day during the late 1950s and into the 1960s on issues as diverse as immigration to apartheid in South Africa. In one speech, quoted by the *Telegraph*, I said something like "What is happening is that the slums of the Empire are coming too close to the doorsteps of the English." In another demonstration, following Patrice Lumumba's assassination in 1961, we placed marbles on the streets to trip up the police's cavalry. It was an organised affair.

These atrocities were coming one right after the other: the Mau Mau rebellion in Kenya of the mid-1950s, the Sharpville Massacre in South Africa in 1960, and now, Lumumba's death.

When Lumumba was killed, I was deeply upset and felt that we should take some violent action. I was walking around the streets, wanting to insult white people, and looking for a fight. Unfortunately, the first person I saw was Joan, and I couldn't really pick a fight with her. The next person I saw was Donald and he was one of the most radical members of the Labour party, so I couldn't fight him either. I really felt Lumumba's death more than any other political tragedy that had occurred.

I remember Anthony Sampson writing in a piece that Lumumba was the most brilliant negotiator to have arisen in the Third World. I was with Sylvia when I first heard of him. She showed me a newspaper, saying, "We must rescue this man or he'll die." Lumumba's rhetoric to silence the Belgian opposition was outstanding. At the Ghanaian embassy, with a group of interested parties, we had drawn up a policy statement in support of Lumumba calling for, among other things, the demobilisation of the *Force Publique*, which had brutally tortured the Congolese people. Lumumba was the first democratically-elected Prime Minister of the Democratic Republic of the Congo, and his untimely and horrific death cut short so many African and Third World hopes.

Three months after Lumumba's death, the Bay of Pigs invasion took place in Cuba (an event whose consequences I would witness the next year, as a correspondent for the London *Observer*). I attended a pro-Cuba demonstration with Sylvia. Michael Foot, the Labour politician and activist, was one of the guest speakers. "Hands off Cuba!" was the motto at the time and when Sylvia, who was born in Cuba and passionate about the Castro revolution, addressed the crowd, she had them on her feet saying "It's not hands off Cuba! It's *Viva* Cuba!"

At one stage, some of us in the MCF got access to the Labour party – which was the leading party at that time – and I was asked to address the House of Commons about British Guiana. I went to great lengths to provide accurate details about our physical location, history and current colonial status, making every effort to disabuse them of the common misconception that BG was an island, like Jamaica or Barbados. After spending so much energy educating the members, the next day in Parliament, a Labour MP got up and still described Guiana as an "island". It showed how ignorant colonial rulers could be. They were supposed to be these superior people and they didn't know the difference between an island and mainland territory. British Guiana had 82,000 square miles.

After *Black Midas* was published, Cheddi and Janet Jagan asked me to be the Guiana representative to the West Indian Committee. This body was set up in London by companies with West Indian interests, dating from the days of slavery. Now it was made up of some bigwigs from the big companies. I was the first black person from the Caribbean; the others were Brits.

I was also very active in local solidarity campaigns for the black American activists Robeson and Du Bois. They had been very outspoken about the liberation of African peoples and the right of people to choose their own allies. Both had been subjected to McCarthyite scrutiny, had their passports withheld, and were shut off from their legions of fans and supporters in the US and abroad. For Robeson, this prevented him from appearing in theatres and concert halls across the United States and throughout the world. So thousands of fans had been denied the pleasure of listening to his deep, melodious and uniquely expressive voice. Du Bois was shunned, too, and people were afraid to invite him to give lectures at their universities.

But, in July 1958, Robeson and his wife Eslanda Cardozo Goode, *Essie*, finally arrived in England after their eight-year long fight against the US government. I met them at several receptions and public events at which they were the guests of honour. I had last seen Robeson almost a decade before, and now, though he was at least thirty pounds heavier, he was still a magnificent specimen. The natural friendliness and warmth he exuded made everyone he met feel that he or she was a cherished friend.

Robeson's arrival in Britain was at the behest of Glen Byam Shaw, the

General Manager of the Shakespeare Memorial Theatre, who wanted Robeson to play the role of Othello to mark the opening of the 100th anniversary season, though it was Peter Hall, the new artistic director who directed the play. When Robeson had agreed to play the role a year earlier, the membership of Equity, the British actors union, had voted unanimously to allow him a special pass – because he was not a member of the organisation – so that he could act in Great Britain. He couldn't come then, because his passport had not yet been returned to him. Needless to say, his welcome when he finally did arrive in the summer of 1958 was warm and tumultuous.

True to form, shortly after his return to London, Robeson was the main speaker at a mass rally for peace in Trafalgar Square, and his great voice, filling that historic square and echoing beyond it, seemed to touch everyone in the huge crowd personally. Macdonald Stanley, the blind Trinidadian trade union leader, also spoke at that rally. Stanley, tall, lean, ascetic and looking like a black Jesus, his voice trained to speak to large audiences without a microphone, had also thundered across the square with a surprising clarity and resonance.

I took Robeson shopping in London on a couple of occasions, and I was always surprised about his reluctance to hail a taxi. When I asked him why he seemed to be boycotting London taxis, he laughed and said, "I'll show you why." Then he hailed the first cab that came our way. But when he reached our destination, I only then realised that the meter had been turned off since the moment we sat down in the cab. The driver opened the door for Paul, shook his hand and, refusing to take any money from us, said, "It's a great honour, Paul Robeson. Here is my card. Anytime you want a lift just call me."

"That's why I don't hail cabs here – unless I really have to," Robeson explained genially. "You know, when I try hailing a cab in New York, the white drivers won't take my money either, but they also refuse to take me as a passenger because I'm black."

He was affable and restless, and every day he and Essie had to contend with a new array of invitations to social and political events. Claudia visited them daily. Robeson, in the midst of his busy schedule, gave two benefit concerts to raise money for Claudia's paper. The St. Pancreas Town Hall event was memorable. Robeson was in good voice and with the Town Hall full to overflowing, he sang spirituals, folk songs – and sustained applause greeted his rendition of "John Henry". Having listened to the melodic resonances, the lyricism and the passion in the songs he sang, one left the Town Hall with a sense of poignancy and sadness. It was as though Robeson had bared his soul to the audience and revealed that this was one of his final performances before the curtain would come down forever.

In retrospect, I can now see that during those final London visits,

Robeson was living on borrowed time and trying to complete as many tasks as possible while he was in charge of all of his faculties. At the time, however, I had no inkling that his affliction was one that could have been secretly induced. Now, no one will ever know. What is certain is that during those final thirteen years of his life, he had been pushed inexorably into a limbo world of forgetfulness and fantasy. I only caught a glimpse of how ill he was when I saw his performance at Stratford later on.

The Robesons only stayed in London for about a month in 1958, and then they went to the Soviet Union for what was supposed to be a short visit; however, he fell ill while he was there, and he was not able to return to England until the spring of 1959 when his doctors pronounced him well enough to return to his arduous routine. So, he began rehearsals at Stratford, and the play opened in April and ran for four months.

When the season was well under way, Robeson invited Patricia Burke and me to see the play as his guests. Patricia, a popular actress and musical comedienne, was a close friend of mine, and she had known Robeson since she was a child. Her mother, Marie Burke, had acted with Robeson in the musical *Show Boat* in the nineteen thirties. The fearless and politically committed Patricia had more time to spare than usual during that Robeson visit, because, after attending a World Peace Council meeting and speaking out against nuclear war, she too was being blackballed by theatres in Britain where a trans-Atlantic, copycat McCarthyism was in vogue. I remember her telling me that only a few principled BBC producers had defied the ban and offered her work from time to time.

Sitting in the front row, we could see by the end of the early acts that Robeson was a sick man who was, by sheer grit and willpower, acting this most demanding of Shakespearian roles. Perspiration was dripping into his eyes, soaking his costume and making parts of the stage wet and slippery. There was something at once heroic and profoundly moving in that Robeson performance, for it was his swan song – the last time he would ever act in a theatre. I could not help thinking that there were also shades of *King Lear* in that emotionally wrenching portrayal of Othello, something of the anguish that suffuses the soul in the wake of a great betrayal. For fleeting moments, Robeson must have been aware that not only was his great physical prowess betraying him, but also that the certainty of his beliefs, which had sustained him for a lifetime, was being assailed by doubts.

After the show, Patricia and I visited Robeson in his apartment on the outskirts of Stratford. I had expected him to be exhausted, but instead he looked refreshed and was in an ebullient mood as he entertained us with stories from his past. He told us about football matches he had played at Rutgers University, but also sobering accounts of confrontation with racism in the US and abroad. One, was about his encounter with Nazi Brownshirts at a Berlin railway station in 1934 when he was on his way to the Soviet Union. It was the year after Hitler had come to power and he was travelling to Moscow with Marie Seton and his wife, Essie. A group of Brown Shirt thugs surrounded them menacingly. He was sure that it was his cool demeanour, and the fact that the women with him were not German, that made the thugs hesitate, and they were able to board the train.

"That was my first encounter with that brutish lynch-mob phase of fascism," he declared, "and it made me all the more determined to fight against it."

I could see that he had a steely resolve behind that façade of affability, and at that moment, I decided to bring up another matter about which I had long been curious.

"Paul, my West Indian countryman, Peter Blackman, told me that he was in Moscow in 1949 when you gave a concert and tried to save the lives of Feffer and Mikhoels, two of your friends (one was a writer and the other was an actor and director). Peter said that despite your knowing that you would incur Stalin's wrath, you had made a point of mentioning Feffer and Mikhoels before singing the Warsaw Ghetto resistance song as the finale to the concert. Peter also said that it was the first time that song was ever sung in the Bolshoi Theatre, or any major Soviet theatre. That was a very courageous thing to do."

"Oh, yes, I remember," he said, but the tone in his voice made it clear that he didn't want to pursue the topic any further. But I wasn't willing to drop it entirely.

"That episode reminds me of another that took place in the Royal St. Petersburg theatre a century before. Ira Aldridge, your black predecessor on the European stage, was playing the role of Shylock in *The Merchant of Venice* – this would have been in the 1850s. He had decided to rewrite some lines in the play, and portray Shylock as a resolute, fearless and articulate speaker for the rights of Jews, and not the snivelling caricature that Shakespeare had created. The Jews there were so pleased that they presented Aldridge with a golden plaque saying that it was the first time that a Jewish character had been portrayed in that theatre with the dignity and the indomitable spirit of his people."

On the one hand, there were the endless anti-communist litanies and a cacophony of voices telling Robeson that a corrupt oligarchy of bureaucrats had arrogated to itself the absolute right to rule in the name of socialism, and that this could not last. On the other hand, he had made clear choices and was convinced that his support for the Soviet experiment would ultimately be very effective in internationalising the fight for the freedom of black Americans.

He offered us refreshments, and changed the subject to lighter reminiscences.

"When I first played Othello on Broadway, Jose Ferrer acted as Iago opposite me. Ferrer kept criticising my acting techniques, until I finally pointed out to him that if my name were removed from the billboards, the show would close in a matter of days." Listening to this anecdote, I couldn't help feeling that despite the worldwide fame he had achieved, he was still vulnerable.

He was in a subdued and thoughtful mood by the time he mentioned that one of his great regrets in life was not being able to act the part of Toussaint L'Ouverture in a film based on the novel *Black Majesty*. His Russian friend, Sergei Eisenstein, the towering genius in the art of filmmaking, had agreed to direct the film. But when Eisenstein had the time and resources to start shooting *Black Majesty* in the Soviet Union, Robeson was already under contract to make *Saunders of the River* with Sir Alexander Korda in England, and he could not get out of the contract. *Saunders of the River*, he said, was an "unmitigated disaster", because anything progressive in it had ended up on the cutting room floor.

After his successful season at Stratford ended in November of 1959, an exhausted Robeson returned to the Soviet Union for treatment. It was an ailing Robeson who came back to England some two years later, and he was only able to make occasional public appearances and to greet the occasional guest. He left England for the last time in 1963 and returned to the US where he basically lived in seclusion for the next thirteen years.

Back in 1958, though, when Robeson's sixtieth birthday was approaching and he was still restricted by the investigations of the US House UnAmerican Activities Committee, Indira Gandhi organised a national committee to sponsor an All-India Paul Robeson Celebration. The US State Department documents, when they were examined many decades later, showed that Ellsworth Bunker, then US Ambassador to India, had assured John Foster Dulles that the embassy would do everything possible to stop the proposed celebration. The American Consul General of Bombay had told Chief Justice Chagla, president of the celebration committee, that many would regard the celebration as evidence that India was going communist. India's Ambassador to the US had also been summoned to the State Department and told that Robeson was an unfortunate selection for an American to be so honoured, and that it would appear that the event was inspired by communist groups. To complicate the matter, Mrs. Gandhi told me that, at the time, India was in the midst of negotiating loans from the United States. Despite of all this, Prime Minister Jawaharlal Nehru endorsed the celebration honouring Robeson. The courageous and principled actions of Ms. Gandhi and her father in honour of Robeson played a significant part in having his passport returned and the ban on his travel lifted.

Indira Gandhi later became Prime Minister of India, until her assassination in 1984. With her death, black peoples everywhere, and the millions in the Non-Aligned Movement lost a great and noble champion. Mrs.

Gandhi was a champion of African liberation and of the liberation of African peoples in the diaspora. She told me that when she was a student in England, Robeson, who was also living there at the time, had been her mentor and a kind of father figure for many students from the Third World. He had, she said, always been particularly kind, patient and generous with her. At the time, Mrs. Gandhi was just another student in England, while Robeson was at the height of his fame as a concert singer, actor and political activist. She never forgot his warmth, great artistry and his compassion. Besides, he could sing Hindu folksongs brilliantly – they recalled to her the smell of the earth, the dreams of the people, and filled her with a pride and nostalgia that was almost unbearable. All her life, she saw Robeson as the embodiment of what was finest and best in the emerging Third World peoples.

I met Indira Gandhi in London in the middle 1960s. She was President of the Indian Senate at the time, and had come on a short, unofficial visit. Her two sons were attending an English public school, as had their great grandfather, grandfather and mother had before them. Nehru, their maternal grandfather had attended Harrow, the same school that Churchill had attended. One of the teachers she remembered most vividly, Mrs. Gandhi told me, was one who taught her to value a certain fierce, female integrity. She was small-boned, her features irregular and every movement controlled and graceful, but her eyes were compelling.

Our first meeting took place shortly after I had seen *The Queen of Jhansi*, a memorable Indian film. The heroine was a Hindu warrior queen who had resisted the English conquest of India long after the male leaders were overcome. Before the Moghul conquest of India, Hindus had, for a thousand years, been leaders – diplomats, outstanding rulers, military commanders, movers and shakers in the corridors of power. There was a quiet assurance about Mrs. Gandhi that said she came from this tradition and she knew she was destined to rule.

But she also had a graciousness and ease about her. She gave the impression of being genuinely pleased to have escaped her official functions and to be spending the evening at my Wimbledon home with a polyglot group of irreverent artists, writers and folk singers. Mrs. Gandhi even helped me carry dishes into the kitchen and volunteered to lend a hand with the washing up.

After dinner, the mood of the gathering became even more relaxed. Feliks Topolski was Mrs. Gandhi's escort for the evening. In fact, I met her through Feliks. He was a longstanding friend of the Gandhi and Nehru families. His easy, urbane presence helped everyone lose their awe of the great woman, except Jitendra Arya, an Indo-Kenyan photographer whom I had invited to join us. Jitendra, who had been educated in India, treated Mrs. Gandhi with a speechless reverence the entire evening. Prior to this,

I had discounted the strength of the Indian caste system outside of India, but this display showed how very powerful these traditions could be.

I had also invited the Frats Quintet, a Jamaican folk group that had been visiting London for a few days, to give my Indian guest a rare and genuine flavour of West Indian folk culture. They were on their way back home after performing at the Eisteddfod in Wales, where they won an award. When we gathered in a half circle on the carpet, the Frats began their repertoire for the evening with an old English hunting song. Through what linguists would describe as discreet non-verbal communication, Mrs. Gandhi, Topolski, Sylvia and I shared glances and a private joke about the vagaries of colonialism. The English upper class had inflicted these hunting songs on a rainbow array of people and cultures in that dwindling British Empire where the sun was setting on colonial rule. But, I was able to prevail upon the Quintet to play some songs closer to their Jamaican culture.

Feliks' relationship with Indira and her family was interesting. He had recently made a series of unforgettable family portraits while accompanying Prime Minister Nehru on a tour of Kashmir. Topolski's paintings and drawings of Third World peoples, leaders and events have been unrivalled in their scope and range by the works of any other artist. Topolski had been commissioned by Prime Minister Nehru to do the mural in the Indian Parliament that depicted the death of Mahatma Gandhi at the hands of an assassin. It is one of the great paintings by a 20th century artist, and a work of genius that will survive the ages. It was, also, for India, a prophetic work that captured the profound inner contradictions of the Hindu soul – the demonic and, at the same time, creative spirit of Kali, the Destroyer, on the one hand, and the spirit of eternal serenity, embodied in Lord Krishna, on the other. One could also discern in that painting essences of materialism and sensuality constantly colliding with the ascetic, the austere and the spiritual. It is extraordinary that Topolski, an outsider, could capture all of these elements with such authenticity and power.

As with the campaign to free Robeson from virtual house arrest, I had been part of a committee agitating for Du Bois' release from the McCarthyite-imposed strictures. Du Bois and his wife, Shirley Graham, had been denied their passports, too. They were all freed with the Supreme Court resolutions in the Briehl and Kent cases that stated that the US government could not deny US citizens their passports because of their political beliefs. As Judge Edgerton said, "Iron curtains have no place in the free world." And, like Robeson, Du Bois made a point of making the Soviet Union among his first stops with his new passport.

Du Bois and Robeson, those two iconic figures in the black liberation struggle, had returned to Britain at a time when there was growing racism. The British had always prided themselves on being more "civilised" than the Americans when dealing with people of colour in the "Mother country." But with a *dark million*, mostly from the West Indies, India and Pakistan, settling in their midst after World War II, the racial attitudes of white Brits had begun, more and more, to resemble those of southern white Americans a generation ago. However, the visit of those two black luminaries had a profound and positive effect on both the leaders and the rank-and-file members of the civil rights movements in the UK. It made them understand that in order to succeed, they had to have both a local and an international focus.

When I met Dr. Du Bois in London in the early 1960s, he and his wife were on their way to Ghana where they planned to live permanently and, among other projects, to work on the publication of an African Encyclopaedia. During that stopover, the Du Boises lived in a modest basement apartment off Baker Street. It was there that I visited him on several occasions.

I reminded him that I had last seen him about fifteen years ago, when I attended a public lecture he gave at the New School in New York. Dr. Alphaeus Hunton, a distinguished black American scholar who had chaired the event, had introduced us. Hunton had also joined Du Bois and Robeson in forming the Council on African Affairs to stress the connections between the liberation struggles of black Americans and people in Africa and elsewhere in the world.

I was a university undergraduate at the time, and was spending the summer vacation in Harlem with H.C. Cameron. I had taken a long subway ride to uptown New York in order to hear Dr. Du Bois lecture on Marx's theory on the withering away of the State. He spoke in measured tones, and used irony and wit to explain Marx's penchant for "mixing prophecy and cold, hard facts in an intellectual crucible and producing ideas that would change the world."

Before meeting the renowned Dr. Du Bois, I had imagined him to be a powerfully built combination of John Brown and Frederick Douglass, but he turned out to be short, with delicate limbs attached to a compact frame. His Louis Napoleon goatee and neatly trimmed sideburns framed a pale brown countenance, and his bald pate made his forehead seem higher and more magisterial. His dark brown eyes had the calm, reflective quality of one who'd seen too much, and knew too much about the human condition in one lifetime.

Dr. Du Bois was in his nineties when we met again in London, but age had spared his countenance most of the usual disfigurements – wrinkles and spots – and one could easily have mistaken him for a well-preserved individual in his early seventies. His face remains imprinted on my memory when so many others have been erased by time. When I looked at that visage of his in repose, I wondered what was his secret of survival? What were the hidden strengths, the intellectual and spiritual reserves that he had dipped into in order to survive decade after decade? We know so little of his mother, Silvina Burghardt Du Bois, the single parent who brought him up and shared with him the pristine dreams and the first ineluctable expectations of a better life. But even the scattered bits of information about her point to the fact that she had to be an extraordinary woman. However, there are still empty spaces on library shelves waiting to be filled with biographies of this remarkable woman, of the father who left before he was two, of his teachers and his mentors. But after reading all the texts that could fill those empty shelves, there will still be secrets that will elude the most prescient of researchers.

Dr. Du Bois told me that a member of the House of Lords had arranged the British visa for him, and that this Lord – who had started out as a worker – was one of the few that the English class system had allowed to make that rags-to-riches leap in a lifetime. I told him that the English aristocrats like Winston Churchill were much better than their European peers at letting a few lower–middle-class or even working-class individuals into their ranks – a few at a time, but no more! A good example of this was when Churchill was First Lord of the Admiralty and a memo had landed on his desk asking whether it would be all right to admit qualified Indians as officers in the Royal Navy. Churchill declared readily that he had no objections whatsoever. But on the bottom of the memo, he had put "P.T.O." and on the back had scribbled, "As long as there are not too many of them."

"We have similar situations in the United States all the time, but we call it tokenism," Dr. Du Bois had commented with a smile. "But, we haven't been at it long enough to be as urbane and as cynical as the British."

I wanted to know about his visits to the Soviet Union and the Peoples Republic of China. Both were triumphal visits. He received the Lenin Prize in Moscow and Chairman Mao Tse Tung had decreed that February 23, 1959, his 91st birthday, should be a national holiday. This tribute to a patriarch and a man of learning was very much in the ancient Chinese tradition in which age and scholarship were respected. Editions of his *The Souls of Black Folk* and his other voluminous writings had been published in translation and were on display everywhere he went. He said he had been accorded more recognition and acclaim on his visits to those two countries than he had ever received at home.

I remember him saying, "I found the Soviet experiment interesting, and I've watched it evolve over my visits since the 1920s. Now, I'm grateful to the Communist bloc nations for the aid they're giving to Third World countries, and to Africa in particular. But China is flesh of our flesh and blood of our blood. With hundreds of millions at home and millions scattered in dozens of countries overseas, the Chinese know better than any other peoples – except Africans – the insults, the racist epithets, the raw manifestations of racial prejudice. But they have managed to put these things in perspective, and to move forward against daunting odds. They didn't need European and American missionaries to teach them about religion and to frighten them with the threat of hellfire for sinners. After five thousand years of suffering, the poor have been in hell too long not to believe in a heaven of their own making here on earth. That is why their experiment with socialism is the one that interests me most. It seems as if they're bent on proving Napoleon right when he said that, "China's a sleeping giant, and when she awakens she'll shake the world." The only thing I would add to this is that if China is to achieve a genuine greatness, she can only do so by sticking to her socialist principles.

Fifty years have gone by since I visited the Du Boises in their London apartment, and looking at my notes of our conversations my spirit never ceases to be uplifted by the old man's optimism and his certainty that socialism was bound to win out in the end.

I also managed to attend one of Dr. Du Bois' public lectures in London, and there was still enough fire in his belly to hold the audience spellbound. He spoke about his visit to the Caribbean and how Norman Manley, the Jamaican premier, had welcomed him, whilst a few other heads of state in the Eastern Caribbean had gone to great lengths to avoid meeting him. They were afraid of arousing the US Government's ire by appearing to be too friendly with a world-famous black American scholar who also happened to be a Communist.

I continued to visit Dr. Du Bois and his wife in their London apartment during the rest of their stay, but after they left for Ghana, I never saw him again. I didn't know at that time, though, that some years later, I would be living next door to his widow, Shirley Graham, in the Cantonment area of Accra, the capital of Ghana.

In addition to doing my writing, I had an organisation that I ran from my basement in Wimbledon. I had connections with the Chinese news agency, Xinhua, Reuters, AP, and I would send them dispatches on events in the Third World and Black America and these would be published all over the world.

One time, in 1957, the Anti-Apartheid organisation in London asked me to meet Ezekiel Mphahlele, the South African writer, at Heathrow Airport. It was a rather awkward meeting and I had to keep reminding myself that millions of migrants like him were contending with a situation like ours in the Caribbean. I tried to see the situation through his eyes. He had just left a society in which the racial divide was absolute, and the daily situation of whites trapping Blacks in an intricate network of humiliations was a commonplace happening. I could see that the way in which I talked freely to Whites sounded alarm bells inside his brain.

The sponsors of his journey into exile should have created an easier transition from one society into another. He thought that he had escaped a racial situation in which he was "shrivelling in the acid of his bitterness", and seeking wider skies in which he "could soar". He had made his escape through this journey with certain expectations, but he was beginning to suspect that it was far more complicated than he had dreamt.

I had realised that from the first moment we met that he was subjecting me to an intense scrutiny. I could sense the tensions and suspicions mounting inside him every time I spoke to a white person the way I did. When he spoke to whites, I could also see him bracing himself for a confrontation. When that did not happen, an almost overpowering state of bewilderment overtook him. But he had evidently assured himself that this state of affairs would not last, so he, therefore, could not afford to let his guard down. In the midst of his chagrin, he admitted that he was sure that I would soon have the police bearing down on me.

On the flight from South Africa, he and the other black passengers had been assigned to segregated seats on the plane. When they arrived at Heathrow, they were the last ones allowed to leave it. While on the plane, he had waited until he saw a person of colour use the lavatory before he ventured to follow suit. But what more positively he carried with him from his flight was a sense how immense the African continent was, and how, hour after hour, the plane had crossed its immense distances – Southern, Central, and Northern expanses. It was as though it was a world unto itself.

Ezekiel's sojourn abroad, which began with that meeting at Heathrow Airport, was to take him on journeys in Britain, to Europe and to the United States. But, in 1977, at the height of the Apartheid regime, he chose to return home to South Africa. He had won a certain amount of acclaim for his memoir, *Down Second Avenue*, which had received good reviews in papers such as the *New York Times*. However, despite the encomiums he received abroad for this and other literary and critical works, he found living abroad intolerable and he managed to make peace with the Apartheid government. He was allowed to return home and to teach. Ezekiel was excoriated by other exiled individuals and groups, but in writing his own epithet, you could understand that pull from home, "I have not come [back home] to die, but to reconnect with my ancestors while I am still alive."

I remember meeting Hastings Banda, who became President of Malawi. He was a family doctor for the West Indian community in London. Banda was a decent fellow and friend of Nkrumah. But when he went home to Malawi in 1963 and became president, he turned into the worst tyrant in Africa in the post-colonial period. They say "power corrupts" and he is a classic example. He was the only African leader who maintained contacts with the Apartheid regime in South Africa. He established a school which was a copy of Eton College and the students had to wear uniforms as at

Eton. Banda and Eric Williams of Trinidad both followed the same pattern of being very progressive before they were in power, and then, very tyrannical when they came to power.

I also knew Jomo Kenyatta in London. Later, after his arrest in Kenya in 1952, I remember going with Joseph Murumbi, who was a Kenyan politician, to the house of Lady Duff-Scott to get her help to make sure that Kenyatta was being treated decently. It was the same thing with Lord Jock Campbell and me when I was arrested in Ghana during the coup. Andrew Salkey went to Jock to get him to intercede on my behalf. Lady Duff-Scott did help out with Kenyatta, though he was imprisoned for six years. But he was freed in 1959 when the popular uprising in Kenya brought about freedom from colonial rule and they had free elections for the first time in 1963, and Kenyatta won the election. I remember when Kenyatta was making his first visit to London after his election, Cheddi Jagan, who had won the 1961 Guyanese elections, sent him congratulatory messages through me.

Malcolm X arrived in London just as I was launching the paper *Magnet* in early 1965. Rudolph Dunbar had organised a reception at the Commonwealth Institute and it was a very British affair. We had a majordomo announcing the guests. I met Alberto Moravia, the Italian writer, at the reception. He joked that he'd been at a reception for his own work and Warburg, who was his publisher, had talked to him about nothing but his own – Warburg's – work. I knew Warburg because his firm had published my books. Warburg was a descendant of one of the key banking families that had financed the Napoleonic Wars. He told me that, once, when the German novelist Thomas Mann came to his house for dinner one night, he had spent the whole evening playing footsie with Warburg's wife.

Magnet began when three wealthy Jamaican businessmen approached me, saying they wanted to start a paper and they wanted me to edit it. I told them I'd do it if they gave me a free hand to establish it. One of the things that was crucial in Black enterprises, and always should be done, was to project the best of everything in the community; in this case the best typesetters, writers, lay-out artists etc. Rudolph suggested that we should have dinner with Lord Cowdray, and ask if we could use some of the *Financial Times'* resources. Dinner was arranged, and Lord Cowdray agreed to let me use the *Times'* printing press to publish my newspaper *Magnet,* the first nationwide Black paper. When we made the case, I had told him that this was probably the smallest project he had ever supported and he laughed, but he did allow us to use the presses at night when the regular *Financial Times* was not in production. As a result, *Magnet* didn't look like some fly-by-night rag that was published on a shoestring. It was certainly not a fly-by-night, although we did have a very small budget. So Lord Cowdray's contribution was very important in making a splash with the paper.

Magnet's first issue was dated February 13, 1965. It was very striking in appearance and was printed on good quality paper. You couldn't miss it on the newsstands as the paper's title was written in bold red ink that filled up most of the top half of the paper. As this part was above the fold, it was really noticeable on the stands. I had Wilson Harris, the novelist, writing book reviews. Feliks Topolski did drawings. In fact, the first edition had a drawing by Feliks of Martin Luther King on the inside cover. This edition also had a black Mr. Universe on the back cover. It was a time when white racists were assaulting Blacks on the streets and I felt that this black muscleman would act as a deterrent. The articles covered matters of importance not only in England, but also in Europe, Africa, the Caribbean and the US.

Unfortunately, the *Magnet* project fell apart after the first few issues. The men who had joined me in developing the paper had tried to sell it to Lord Cowdray behind my back. To make their case, they accused me of being a communist, but much to their surprise, Lord Cowdray told them, "What self-respecting black man wouldn't be a communist?" These people weren't interested in the paper, they only wanted to get money. They never believed they were capable of having or maintaining a high-quality news-paper like *Magnet*. In the contest that goes on, you have to see your efforts as being part of a larger world struggle and you have to keep focus. Unfortunately, some people are incapable of this and remain wrapped up in parochialisms. They cannot envision themselves as being on the win-ning side.

As I mentioned above, the launching of *Magnet* coincided with Malcolm X being in London. It was Dermot Hussey, my assistant editor, who brought me this news. Dermot was well-connected and could track people like radar. I told him to fetch Malcolm and bring him over. Malcolm X had come to London to give a speech at the London School of Economics, and I was pleased to be able to invite him to our reception. His participation at the Oxford Union Debates in December had had a tumultuous effect; people were still talking about it, and, no doubt, the Africa Society of the LSE was looking forward to similarly spirited experience.

When Malcolm entered the hall and we first met, I was struck by how different he appeared from the standard media representation of him. Instead of the dark, menacing figure, here was a man with grey-green eyes and the kind of light complexion that reminded me of my grandfather. He could have been one of my relatives. When I introduced him to my eleven-year old daughter, Lisa, who was also attending the reception, he chatted with her, and after initial halting exchanges with him, she relaxed, and they chatted like good friends. He told her that he had several daughters and one of them looked a lot like her.

Over the next several days, Malcolm and I spent quite some time

Jan Carew with Malcolm X, at the reception for *Magnet*.

Photograph: Dermot Hussey

together, as I kept him company while he was fighting a case of flu, and Dermot and I joined him when he went over to the LSE to give his talk. As we were about to leave the hotel near Marble Arch, he told us not to go out at the same time. There was a contract out on him and he didn't want us to be in danger. We went out with him anyway and insisted upon driving him to LSE.

There, the African students had taken the lead in inviting him, but it was clear that he had quite a following among other progressive students and faculty. Looking at that sea of young faces from behind the curtain on the stage – white, black, yellow and a range of shades of brown – I could see them appraising him as he launched into his talk. It was a little over a year since he had broken away from Elijah Muhammad and the Nation of Islam, and he had founded his Organisation of African Unity. He had made his second pilgrimage to Mecca and visited Nkrumah's Ghana, along with several other African nations. This talk was one of the most important ones he made.

I was able to get a copy of Malcolm's debate speech at the Oxford Union. My friend, Ed Scobie's first wife, Mollie, was a cousin of Anthony Amstrong-Jones, 1st Earl of Snowdon, and she was able to get a hold of the transcript. The BBC, which was obviously there, claimed it didn't have a copy, but she was able to procure it. I also got a copy of the London School of Economics speech.

Malcolm was in high demand and he was invited to tour the town of Smethwick in the Midlands of England where there had been racial strife. It was a few days before he was due to return to the US, but he wanted to lend his solidarity. Malcolm knew that the photos of him touring the area would be sure to give the black people heart, while worrying the racists. One of the first articles I wrote for the *African Review*, when I moved to Ghana, was about Smethwick.

A week after our London conversations, Malcolm returned to the US and he was assassinated on February 21st, while he was speaking at the Audubon Ballroom in New York. My memoir, *Ghosts in Our Blood: With Malcolm X in Africa, Europe, and the Caribbean*, was an attempt to recapture that special time and to provide fresh perspectives on Malcolm who was far more complex than most biographies have presented him.

"South Kensington Revisited"

Pepperpot, Vol 2, no 3, 1963 (London)

I returned to my old haunts in South Kensington and many changes had taken place since I first lived there more than ten years before in the early fifties. On a day of bright sunshine, the atmosphere was febrile, slightly alien. I strolled around Hereford Square where I had once lived at number fourteen. The garden which the square enclosed was unchanged. Its copper-beach trees with sprays of russet leaves sheltered immaculate lawns and flower beds. Children were playing in the sun and their voices were shrill as sea birds. I remembered how, looking out of my window across the gardens, I used to be able to see the big rambling artists' studios. But these were torn down and new, expensive maisonettes had taken their place.

I saw a few coloured residents coming out of one of the houses. It wasn't so long ago that I was the only coloured person living on the square and that one of my neighbours tried to draw up a petition to have me evicted. I wondered if that old eccentric still peered out of his window, worried by fantasies of a coloured invasion.

Past the square and further up Gloucester Road, was my old bookshop where the bookseller never sold novels before he read and approved of them. Further on, was Queensgate Terrace, a wide and splendid street. I had lived at number forty in the days when it was owned by a Baroness from Eastern Europe. The house used to boast the most disreputable façade on the street. But its new owner had painted it and the columns on the front porch were no longer scarred and leprous. This was the most interesting house I ever lived in. My flat was on the sixth floor and the lift never worked. The caretaker inhabited a dark cavernous basement where ancient dusty odours were as indestructible as his good humour. He was an Irishman with a larger-than-life imagination, an ex-boxer, jockey, para-trooper. He thrived and grew fat in his sub-world while his wife became gaunt and withered, her eyes growing large in her thin face, burning with the fierce resentment of a trapped animal. The Baroness, herself an unusual, witchlike creature, exulted in having the strangest types around her. On the first floor, was a West African prince and medical doctor, a furtive man whose patients always looked like conspirators. The other residents were shadowy, faceless, asserting their presence only when I heard their footsteps on the stairs or doors closing behind them. I never met the prince formally during the two years I lived in the house, but the caretaker told me a great deal about him, how he owned diamond mines and was planning to liberate the whole of the African continent. The Irishman was a Sancho Panza to this self-effacing African Don Quixote.

One day, he came up to my flat to tell me that the prince had left. His Amazonian sisters had taken him back home forcibly to prevent him from being sent to a mental hospital.

The prince's departure was the beginning of a profound change in the house. Soon after, the caretaker emigrated to Australia. The atmosphere of mystery, which at times bordered on terror, vanished with these two. And before I left, the Baroness sold the house. As I walked up Queensgate Terrace towards the Commonwealth Institute, I wondered if the Irishman would ever again find a Don Quixote to whom he could attach himself, whether he would find a wild and feverish imagination to compliment his, because this was for him the breath of life.

Near the top of the street was a mews. Most Londoners had long forgotten that mews were originally outhouses where the falcons were caged. The echoes of falcons mewing must have died away in lost centuries. It was fashionable not to care about the derivation of a word that described fashionable dwellings. Across the mews were the offices of the United States Marines. There was a sign which said: "U.S. Marines, London, England" and enormous flashy cars littered the street in front of the offices.

The discreet, urbane face of South Kensington had changed in the last decade. The cards in the tobacconists' windows advertising rooms and flats were pointers to one of the significant changes; many of them stated: "No coloureds, no Indians, No West Indians or no foreigners." These forlorn postscripts were vain attempts to hold back the inevitable. The flood of coloured students continued to pour in. Topping the bell tower of the Commonwealth Institute was the new College of Science, a skyscraper rising out of the debris of old, vaulted, Victorian buildings. Students from their high towers of glass and concrete now undoubtedly look down on the museums, the Albert Hall, Kensington Gardens and the Albert Memorial which an architect once said was the most ghastly monument ever erected.

I walked up towards the Old Brompton Road. There were coffee shops everywhere. A stone's throw from South Kensington underground station was a Dickensian shop with dusty harps in the window. The last harp-maker in Britain worked on the floor above. His shop was a monument to the past.

IV.

IN WHOSE BACKYARD?

Section Four, "In Whose Backyard," includes chapters eleven through thirteen. The title, "In Whose Backyard?" recalls the struggles of Caribbean nations to assert their own identity despite pressures from the US. It explores Jan Carew's attempts to come back to British Guiana and the Caribbean region. Though living abroad had become the norm, Carew retained a fond hope that he would be able to return to his home region, not just for visits, but on a more permanent basis. The year 1962 presented one of those windows of opportunity. Cheddi Jagan has been elected again in BG, despite the efforts of the US and Britain to prevent this. Jagan wanted Carew to be his director of culture, but, as Carew subsequently learnt, his good fortune was coming as a result of political retaliation against someone he admired. Furthermore, the British Guiana that he had hoped could be still structured around national unity was too splintered for this to happen. With his second wife, Sylvia, and his young family, his attempts to resettle back in BG were aborted as the political and physical tensions of living in a "battle zone" become untenable.

His family returned to Jamaica and Carew soon followed, once again trying to settle down. But, Fate, in the form of the Cuban missile crisis and a commission from the London *Observer*, stepped in, placing him – the only Western reporter – in Cuba at this very heated moment in world history.

It was the "agricultural specialist" Jan Carew who returned to the Caribbean over a decade later, during the period of 1975-1983. Under the aegis of the Caribbean Society for Culture and Science, Carew mounted a number of projects to improve the nutritional base and to encourage a more sustainable and energy-efficient farming. Beginning with an initial effort in Suriname, CSCS engaged in projects in Guyana and Jamaica before the more expansive project work in Grenada. Impressed with the energy for social and political change being exhibited by the young New Jewel leadership in Grenada, Carew was pleased to be invited to mount a project there in 1979. However, four years later, in 1983, the coup overthrowing the Grenadian Prime Minister, Maurice Bishop, his execution along with some members of his cabinet, and the subsequent invasion of US forces, brought the Grenada project to an abrupt end.

Close to Jan Carew's heart was the introduction of the winged bean from

Indonesia, and the reintroduction of the pre-Columbian crop, grain amaranth, two highly nutritious and protein-rich plants. He was keen on
finding ways to reintroduce more traditional fertilisers and techniques to
local farmers, as well as develop ecologically-sound and sustainable communities. Special partners in this latter work were Professor Steve Slaby, a
former colleague from Princeton, and Dr. Ernest Wakefield of Linear
Alpha, Inc. Together, they founded the Third World Energy Institute and
developed the "Synergein project". The projects also benefited from
Carew's contacts with a former Princeton graduate student of his who had
risen into the leadership of the National Council of Churches. As the NCC
was actively engaged in agricultural projects around the globe, there was
interest not only in providing funding and other supports to Carew's efforts
in the Caribbean, but also, to find ways to replicate his Caribbean projects
elsewhere in the developing world.

A latter-day "Johnny Appleseed" of grain amaranth, Jan Carew grew
amaranth wherever he lived for the last forty years of his life – in tropical
and temperate climates – and was known to press packets of the tiny seeds
onto anyone who expressed interest.

Included in this section are Jan Carew's London *Observer* articles on the
Cuban missile crisis written in 1962; the 1962 article, "Federation: Shadow
or Substance?"; "What the Cuban Revolution Means to Me" published in
1979 on the 20th anniversary of the Cuban revolution; and "Harvesting
History in the Hills of Bacolet" published in 1983, which encapsulates his
philosophy and service to Grenadian communities.

CHAPTER ELEVEN

RETURN TO BG

Cheddi Jagan was re-elected Premier of British Guiana in 1957 and in the early 1960s, he contacted me to come to serve as the Director of Culture. But when I arrived in Guiana, I found there were some unsavoury underlying requirements that came with the job. First of all, they had to oust A.J. Seymour, who was the current Director of Culture. Seymour's poems were the first Guyanese ones I remember reading. They had a quality of gentleness and ease which I found almost mesmeric. I told Cheddi that Seymour was the most highly respected cultural figure in Guiana and that using an underhanded method to oust him would reflect badly on me. As far as I knew, the only crime Seymour had committed was in penning a cunningly disguised poem which criticised the new government. I told Cheddi that unless there was absolute transparency in the government's dealings with Seymour, I would not accept the position. I also reminded Premier Jagan of a letter I had written him earlier, saying that culture could not be spread by decrees from above, for its roots lie deep in the collective psyche of the people where the rhythms of creativity originate.

I had returned to BG at various earlier times, in the late 1940s and again in the early 1950s. Each time, I had felt a strong urge to rediscover my homeland. Wilson Harris, who was working as a Government surveyor helped a great deal in this respect. I went up the Potaro River with him, and later, up the Canje. These were two of the most important journeys of my life. The rainforest and the swamps of Guyana have always provided me with a creative matrix from which I could write and paint. Besides Wilson, there were other surveyors, like Sidney Singh and Keith Carter (Martin Carter's brother), who had a lot to do with my impressions of the coast/ hinterland relationships. The surveyors were different from coastal people. They were able to break out of the stultifying colonial strictures of Georgetown, New Amsterdam, and the coast, and to penetrate into Guyana's heartland. Then, in this self-imposed isolation in these primordial landscapes, they read, wrote, and could live a life of self-discovery.

Now, on my return in early 1960s, I moved into a house in Kitty on the outskirts of Georgetown. The Jagan government was very unpopular in

Georgetown when I first moved back, and members of the governing party warned me not to walk around the streets. But I defied their advice.

I told them, "I just came from England where I had to put up with discrimination."

So the first day I moved into the house, I decided to walk down the main street and into the centre of town. I could feel the tension as I walked. But, the chemist, who had a drugstore on the main street in Kitty and who came from the Berbice region of my country – which was where my family had roots – came out of his shop and greeted me. He was a leading member of the Burnham opposition party – the PNC. But Berbicians are very loyal to their roots and there is a strong solidarity between them. I asked him to arrange a meeting with his group so that I could then tell them what I believed the country needed.

I remember him asking me, "Jan, are you a communist?"

I told him that all the brouhaha about communism in BG was exaggerated; that there were about a dozen communists in total. It's a travesty, I said, that so much time and effort was being spent fighting an illusory enemy.

Soon after this, he arranged a meeting with his group at his house. The group was Afro-Guyanese. It was by no means a secret meeting – such a thing is hard to keep quiet in such a small place as Georgetown – and the meeting didn't last long. I told all present that I was for the unity of the different factions in our country.

"We are 500,000 people in Guiana," I said, "and we are divided. New York City, where I was recently, has that many people in one borough or district and they come from over 40 countries. If they can live together, why can't we?"

One of those present pointed out that there had been race riots in New York not long before.

"That's true," I agreed. "The riots in New York left a trail of senseless violence and destruction that Guiana would do well to avoid."

I remember hearing my mother tell stories about living under Jim Crow in America and I didn't want that experience to be repeated in Guyana.

That hope wasn't to be. There was serious inter-ethnic violence in the early 1960s and Forbes Burnham, the leader of the PNC, went on to become an evil, murderous dictator. Luckily, I never worked for him. My infrequent returns to the country in the 1970s and 1980s were often associated with some potential difficulty because of the actions of the Burnham regime, and he never seemed really at ease when I was in the country. I would occasionally see Forbes at some event and he would say to me, "Ian, how nice to see you. When are you leaving?"

I had originally met him when we were both young men working in the customs in Georgetown in the early 1940s. In those early days, we had much in common. The first political discussion I had had with him was about an incident when a local magistrate had ruled against a British judge. This was quite revolutionary in BG. Joe Brand, one of our seniors at the customs, had been queuing up for the cinema when he was pushed out of the way by this British judge. Joe accused him of assault and, remarkably, the magistrate declared the judge guilty and imposed a fine. Burnham and I were both delighted about this and considered Joe a hero. Burnham and I left BG around the same time. I went to the US and he went to England. Our next meeting was in New York in the early 1950s. He had qualified as a barrister and was on his way home. He had become highly politicised and was an accomplished orator, and together, we went on a speaking tour. Some US high schools had teachers who were part of the worldwide movement for colonial freedom and they wanted to expose their students to progressive ideas. At one of the schools we visited in New York State, a teacher was escorting us down the hallway when we heard a student remark, "There are two niggers." Burnham, who had a kind of sharp Oscar Wildean wit, said as an aside to me, "The Black man's burden." Burnham had joined Jagan in the efforts to form a government in BG in the early 1950s, but his politics – largely encouraged by the British in their divide-and-rule tactics – had taken a dramatically different turn by the mid-1950s. Finally elected by some behind-the-scenes wrangling in 1964, including the unlikely coalition of the left-leaning PNC and the right-wing United Force of Peter D'Aguiar, Burnham held the office of President for over twenty years until his death in 1985.

At one stage, whilst Jagan was still in power, I went to meet with leaders in the Amerindian community in the interior and to tell them that Janet Jagan was a socialist and that the government would be redistributing the land – to have land reform – but, that her policy was to leave the Amerindians and their land alone. I also tried to explain what democracy meant. You put an official in power to serve and if that person doesn't serve you, you vote him/her out. D'Aguiar used to put loudspeakers up into the trees and make pronouncements and some of the Amerindians thought that these were magical and that the people who operated them were very powerful. They were afraid of these city officials – both the British colonisers and then the local Guyanese officials, once they came to power. One local official had sexually assaulted an Amerindian girl, and I tracked him down and insisted that he marry the girl. My mother, when she was a teacher, frequently had twelve-year-old girls in her schools in the interior who had babies. My mother was committed to making their lives better and brought several of these Amerindian children to Georgetown where she oversaw their education and helped them get into training in nursing, teaching or some other area of employment. In the other direction, I took a delegation of Amerindian leaders to make their case for support from the

Jagan administration. They were being harassed by Venezuelans who were doing gold and diamond mining in their area.

When foreign visitors arrived in Guiana, Cheddi would send them to me. This was somewhat like my experience in Ghana with Nkrumah. People, especially people of African descent, were excited about the developments in Ghana and British Guiana and they wanted to be a part of it. Some were so anxious to come that they would get on a plane without any real plans or contacts and just arrive. This was problematic for us and was, I think, the reason why Jagan in BG and Nkrumah in Ghana asked me to meet with these people early on. I was to ascertain how serious they were (some could be there as *agents provocateurs*) and what skills they had brought with them that could be of help. Then, there was dealing with the more mundane things, like where would they live, whether they could find jobs, how long they could afford to stay, etc.

Cheddi Jagan was freely elected several times, in 1953, 1957, 1961, and then in 1995. During Cheddi's third period of rule in the early 1960s, there was an attempt to overthrow his government when my wife, Sylvia, was there in the country with our children Anne-Marie and Christopher. I was not there at that time. Cheddi was living in what they called "The 'Red' House" – the Premier's residence – and mobs of the Burnhamite-D'Aguiar faction, which was very violent, were in the streets. Cheddi's supporters had sharp-shooters at the windows of the Red House. It would have been a massacre. Sylvia said that this was where Cheddi showed his mettle as a leader. He was in the Red House and the armed defenders were at strategic points of the building; he remained very calm and collected and concerned about the women and children.

Before the mobs surged out to attack Cheddi at the Red House, they had also threatened the lives of my wife and children. Fortunately, the guards who had volunteered to protect Cheddi were mostly from villages where they had been hunters from their earliest youth. One such guard, Ruben Walton, came from Kiltern, which was the village of my Aunt Henrietta. He had been my aunt's estate manager and he had come down to Georgetown to protect my wife and children. He sent a message to the Burnham-D'Aguiar faction to say that if one hair on the head of Jan Carew's children was touched, they would pay dearly for it.

When the crowd was threatening to get out of hand and moving towards the Red House, there was a British warship in the harbour with the highly-trained soldiers of the Scottish Black Watch, the regiment which the British usually used to put down colonial uprisings. As the mob was about to storm the Red House, the Black Watch troops spilled out into the streets. You could hear their boots thumping on the pavement as they rushed to disperse the mob. It was not so much to save Cheddi, since the British were totally against him, but more that it was their duty to "keep law and order". At any rate, they prevented the massacre and Cheddi and his family and others at the premier's residence were spared.

Cheddi Jagan was a communist and since the split of the party in 1955, he had felt that Burnham's party, the PNC, was a reactionary one and that it would be better for the PPP to go it alone. To do that, he had to mobilise the Indian population. The Indo-Guyanese were the largest group, outnumbering the Afro-Guyanese, and if they voted as a bloc, they could win the elections and power. That's why in the late 1960s Eusi Kwayana was for a time part of Burnham's PNC government, out of his belief that there was a need to defend Afro-Guyanese rights. Later he broke with Burnham and became one of the founding members of the Working People's Alliance, committed to combating what he saw as the racism of both main parties.

When I first joined them in 1949, Eusi and Cheddi were committed to forming a government of national unity in which Indo-Guyanese and Afro-Guyanese would share power on an equal basis. By 1960, you could feel the depth of the animosity that Blacks had towards the Indo-Guyanese government, and vice versa.

Trinidad is somewhat similar, with this basic Indo/Black divide, although in Trinidad, the Black leadership tends to be Creole, the lighter-skinned descendants of the Africans. The same thing happened in Fiji in the South Pacific. Fiji and Guyana are alike in that indentured Indian workers were brought in the 19th century to grow sugar, and alike in the tensions between ethnic groups. When a party supported by the Indians won a majority in the 1987 elections, because they were the biggest population group and commercially wealthier, there was a military coup led by the army (which was dominated by ethnic Fijians) to override the election results and take power. This has happened a number of times in Fiji.

In Guiana, I arranged to have Sylvia and the children move to Jamaica where Sylvia's family still lived, and I planned to follow. With the political situation as it was, I simply could not take up the post of Cheddi's director of culture.

"Federation: Shadow or Substance?"

Flamingo (UK), December 1962

Jamaicans noted NO to a Caribbean West Indian Federation in a bitterly contested referendum. The anti-federalists won by 35,000 votes though 40% of the electorate stayed at home. Mr. Norman Manley, the Chief Minister, staking his political future on the twin issues of federation and independence, barnstormed up and down the island, talking himself hoarse, pleading, cajoling, threatening, trying to explain, somewhat belatedly, the question of federation and its relevance to Jamaica's future. But Jamaica's antipathy to federation was a reflex based on negative impulses of fear and confusion. Successive conferences during which a federal constitution was hammered out merely provided opportunities for parochial discontent to emerge and coalesce. Jamaica and Trinidad, the two largest units, were already awakening to the realities of the twentieth century while striking postures which would have been in keeping with events at the turn of the century. The Windward and Leeward Islands are political and social anachronisms with top-heavy administrations, the problem of a population explosion and stagnant economies. They provide a classic study in the geography of hunger when Nature is kind and man cruel.

At the beginning, the idea of federation was based on sound concepts. Dr. Eric Williams, Prime Minister of Trinidad, envisaged first a union of the West Indian islands and the two mainland territories of British Guiana and British Honduras and then a confederation with Cuba, Haiti, the Dominican Republic, Puerto Rico, and the French and Dutch Islands and mainland territories under the premise that the larger and more populous the unit, the more economically viable it should be, and, the more powerful as a political unit. But federation, as it developed, became a shrunken travesty of this big dream. The first federal constitution sowed the seeds of its own disintegration. Individual West Indian leaders, while trumpeting their advocacy of the idea of a centralised government, made sure that enough power remained in their hands to make this impossible. Standing in the wings was the Colonial Office which, one West Indian chief minister admitted to me privately, was anxious to be rid of these "slums of the Empire".

"It's not that they don't understand," he said, "it's that they don't care."

The years since the inauguration of the first federal constitution provided the unusual spectacle of West Indian leaders clinging to their colonial rulers, reluctant to brave the winds of change. In the meantime, British Guiana and British Honduras circled further and further away in their own orbits.

Federation, such as it proved to be, was more shadow than substance. The Trinidadians, perhaps, came closest to knowing that it existed at all. The Governor General, the Federal Prime Minister and their entourage of civil servants lived in Port-of-Spain, in a temporary limbo world, waiting to move to Chaguaramas, one of the sites the British leased to the United States government during World War Two in exchange for fifty obsolete destroyers. The Americans, at first adamant about keeping this base, subsequently agreed to let the federal government share half of it. Thus the West Indian Federation was a superstructure with flimsy foundations. It had an able civil service but no viable state in which this civil service could function. To the vast majority of West Indians, federation was a political fairground where the educated middle class could find pleasant and lucrative jobs. They could not relate this fairground to their feelings of claustrophobia and frustration in small, stagnant, overcrowded islands in the sun.

Jamaicans, the most politically conscious of the West Indians, a thousand miles to the west of this nebulous federation, had from the beginning been extremely reluctant to join. Both Sir Alexander Bustamante and Mr. Manley, who succeeded him as chief minister, spoke with two voices on the issue of federation. One voice was directed at Jamaicans, the other at their distant brothers and sisters to the east. Bustamante stated openly that since the British Government was so anxious to foist the burden of the smaller islands onto Jamaica and Trinidad, then they should underwrite the transfer with sizable grants in aid. Federation caught Mr. Manley, a more urbane negotiator, in the posture of a brown Hamlet who could not make up his mind. He could have become the first federal prime minister, rationalised the contradictions in the federal constitution and made what was little more than a concept on paper take root. But general elections were due in Jamaica and he had serious rivals in the right wing of his party. His rivals were anti-federalists who, while he was cutting through constitutional Gordian knots in Port-of-Spain, could have made him a leader without a following by winning the election at home and withdrawing from the Federation. Then there was the Mephistophelian Bustamante, always a formidable rival, a leader who had emerged out of the intestines of Jamaica, a man with a common touch, a sense of drama, with an intuitive understanding of the poor. True, Bustamante was in decline, a leader who had become the victim of his own confusions, but he was still a rival to be reckoned with. Manley tried to get the best of both worlds. He remained in Jamaica and won the elections while Sir Grantley Adams, a Barbadian, became federal prime minister. Manley won the Jamaican elections with an increased majority, even though the Federal Party which he headed lost to Bustamante in the federal elections.

Since the 1959 general elections in Jamaica, new political and social forces had been erupting in this crowded island society. And although the alignment of forces is somewhat different, the situation has political undertones reminiscent of the 1938 social unrest which projected first Bustamante and then Manley into the forefront. The discontented black majority are murmuring not only against white imperialists but against their black and brown successors. The social changes since 1938, the new secondary industries, the tourist trade has sharpened the differences between rich and poor. Immigration to Britain since 1952 has blunted the edge of this discontent, but has proved a short-time palliative. The Rastafari movement with its "Back to Africa" slogan was one symptom of this discontent. And just as Mr. Manley was trying to come to terms with the Rastas, a more articulate champion of black men in Jamaica arose, Millard Johnson, a Negro barrister and a disciple of Marcus Garvey. Johnson is now the third man in the Jamaican political arena. He is a Pan-Africanist, a neutralist, a man who wants to see the realities of black power in his homeland, who sees Jamaica as an extension of an emergent Africa.

It was in the midst of these local tensions that Manley held the referendum. And now that a majority has voted NO, the Manleyites are doing some painful rethinking.

There is a feeling that if another attempt at federation is made, it must be built on firmer foundations. The West Indies can no longer afford to carry on by plastering sores; cures must now be effected in the bloodstream of the society. We live in an age of emergent coloured peoples, of revolutionary social change. On a clear day you can stand on a promontory on the Jamaican north coast and see the shadow of Cuba rising out of the blue-green Caribbean sea. These islands, once sugar and slavery were forgotten, had ceased to have any but an historical importance. They were forgotten until World War Two when their strategic importance was hastily acknowledged. The American bases are leftovers from this period of passing interest. They are not just islands with sunshine for sale, but the homelands of uprooted peoples being pushed into the twentieth century.

The island archipelago stands astride two continents, one of the haves and other of the have-nots. In a very fundamental sense the problems of any one island are the problems of all, with slight variations. The logic of a federation with a strong central government, planning for the whole area, giving to an uprooted peoples who were drawn from all over the earth a sense of nationhood, of identity, still remains unassailable.

CHAPTER TWELVE

THE CUBAN MISSILE CRISIS

Everything seemed to be going wrong. It was during a hiatus in my life after the anticlimactic end to my experience in Guyanese politics. My marriage to Sylvia was in disarray again and I feared that a reconciliation was not possible. Still, I did fly over to Jamaica to see if we could pick it back up and, for a while, we did have a house together.

I was writing, and had a regular column in the leading Jamaican paper, *The Gleaner*, under the pseudonym of "John Patmos". I was also doing broadcasts on the JBC, the Jamaica Broadcasting Corporation.

I was caught, though, in a political bind. My wife's family was deeply embroiled with the right-wing party in Jamaica, whilst Sylvia herself was a keen supporter of the revolution. Even though she had been offered a regular programme by the BBC, to be produced by Lord Mountbatten, she was determined to stay in Jamaica.

I considered leaving Jamaica and going back to London, but the thought of being separated from my son, Christopher, and my stepdaughter, Anne Marie, made me feel like I was a total failure in life. It was strange how I was now wading in pools of despair so soon after literary triumphs had made me a figure who could be recognised on the London streets by people who had seen me on TV. My novels *Black Midas* and *The Wild Coast* had come out to great acclaim just a few years back, but this was all ephemeral and made the present crisis all the more wrenching.

It was a time of life when I didn't care about living, and driving around Kingston I often thought of suicide. But, my mother's voice, gentle but firm, scolded me, "You have a whole lifetime ahead of you, boy, but you must always bear in mind, that you're not just serving time, rather you should be making time serve you."

I had a German car, an Opel, and one afternoon, I drove it at eighty miles an hour down Spanish Town road. When I arrived home, I found that one of the front tires had a bulge, and it was a miracle that I did not have a blowout. If I'd had that blowout, it would have meant certain death because I did not have seat belts in the car.

"How is my life to end?" I asked myself. "What worth does your life have at this stage?" I found the answer particularly galling as it became clear that there was no repairing the marriage to Sylvia since she was involved with someone else.

I asked myself whether this was the life I was supposed to live after receiving so many accolades. Besides my life as a writer, I had attended universities where I had won some acclaim, and had associated with some of the most brilliant scholars of the twentieth century, like J.D. Bernal, who was the father of Martin Bernal, the leading scholar of Black antiquities.

I had been in Jamaica for just a few months, but it became clear to me that I did not want to live there for the rest of my life. Then, world events came to my rescue. I got a call from the editor of the London *Observer* newspaper who commissioned me to go to Cuba.

"Something big is about to happen there," he said. He wanted me to go to Cuba to cover the missile crisis from inside the country. Money was no object, he said, and, in fact, he recommended that I hire a plane to get in there. However, as I knew that the Cubans had Czech-made anti-aircraft missiles, I was reluctant to play James Bond.

So I left my job at the JBC and set out for Cuba. First, I went to Puerto Rico where I learned that one of the anti-Cuban groups, ALFA 66, was planning a terrorist attack against a British ship that was ostensibly carrying a strategic cargo to Cuba. I met with the head of ALFA 66 and I wrote a piece for the *Observer* about that impending crisis.

★

"Raiders: We will Sink British ship"
London Observer, SAN JUAN, Puerto Rico, October 20, 1962

SEÑOR Antonio Blanch, head of Alpha 66, the Cuban exiles' commando group, told me today, before leaving for the United States: "Alpha 66 plans to sink a British merchant ship in the next week." He said: "We have no quarrel with the British people, but their merchants must learn that we are at war with Castro. We will sink the ship of any nation once it is in Cuban territorial waters." The main target of the group's future operations, he said, would be British shipping carrying supplies to Cuba.

Señor Blanch is going to the US to launch an appeal for a Latin-American boycott of all British goods and to raise funds for his organisation. He said that after his return, "We will organise large-scale landings in Cuba in November."

Alpha 66 has already promised two raids on Cuba this month, but the raid planned for this week was called off when it was reported that one of its boats had been intercepted and disarmed.

Any raid on British shipping is likely to be carried out from the British-owned cays north of Cuba. These tiny islands are part of the Bahamas group.

There are an estimated 15,000 Cuban exiles in Puerto Rico, many of them well-off men from business, the professions and the civil service.

Their main meeting place is the Church of San Juan Basco, in the old section of the city run by Cuban priests. Next door is the Villa Palmers, which acts as Alpha 66's operational headquarters. Señor Blanch, 34, is a mild-looking Cuban with the thin and mournful face of a Don Quixote.

★

From Puerto Rico, I flew to Miami and then on to Mexico City. At the time, one could get a visa in Mexico to travel to Cuba, as the two nations had diplomatic relations. In Mexico City, I was hosted by Mony de Swaan, the brother of Michael de Swaan whom I had known in Amsterdam when I was living there in the 1950s. Mony offered me a place to stay and an automobile while I waited for my visa. I had applied for my visa, first off, hoping that this would expedite the process.

There I met the sociologist, Gerrit Huizer, who was doing a study of peasant communities in Middle America for the United Nations. I chose one of de Swaan's Alfa Romeos and on the night I arrived, I drove Gerrit and his wife to a commemoration for the Day of the Dead. The event was being filmed by the Russian director Sergei Eisenstein. It was fascinating to see him work. He was shooting some scenes through a white skull, and the final cut had significant power.

Driving in Mexico City was a hazardous business. I remember having some trouble with the car; I couldn't get the car into reverse and I had to get some men to push it while I turned it around amidst the chaos of the celebrations. Eventually, we drove to the famous burial ground to see the ceremony that Eisenstein has immortalised.

Mony told me he had pretty cordial relationships with Che Guevara and he offered to put in a good word for me to help me get a visa. Another friend I cultivated in Mexico City was a Yugoslav journalist who was pretty close to the Cubans. He was telling me what was happening in private meetings that were taking place between representatives of different governments that were mostly sympathetic to the Cuban revolution. I got the visa soon after I arrived, but I stayed on in Mexico City for three weeks before I left.

I boarded a plane to Havana and then travelled around Cuba by car for a while to get a feel of what was going on. What I ended up writing didn't please either the Right or Left. It was a world crisis and nuclear weapons were involved on both the American and Russian sides. A Russian ship carrying nuclear missiles was heading towards Cuba and nuclear war was narrowly avoided. The captain was said to have avoided the orders of his superiors and nuclear war, by not firing the weapons on board his submarine.

★

"Havana angry at Russian 'circus'"

London *Observer*, HAVANA. November 17, 1962

MR. MIKOYAN, the Soviet Vice-Premier, is expected in New York, having apparently reached nothing but deadlock in his talks with Dr. Fidel Castro which ended in Havana on Thursday.

Sources close to the Cuban Government say that Dr. Castro remained inflexible. His letter yesterday to the Acting United Nations Secretary General, U Thant, reiterated his defiant position for the benefit of both of the U.N. and the Soviet Government.

The absence of agreement is reflected in Havana. The city is an armed camp sprouting guns everywhere and striking a defiant posture more in keeping with the pre-crisis period.

There is a general feeling among the partisans of the Cuban revolution that they have been let down by the Russians. Posters advertising the Russian circus (which has been performing here) show a huge bear standing with arms akimbo while its head is turned aside. A man who lives in one of the narrow streets of the old city where politics are discussed fervently and always with a touch of sardonic humour, told me, "The circus is over and the star performers were the two Ks (Khrushchev and Kennedy). Fidel was the man apart. But I was glad to see the missiles go. We Cubans are a very undisciplined people – there was always the danger that one of us would get really mad at America and just shoot a missile off."

A neutralist diplomat summed up the underlying realities when he said that the Cubans, obsessed with their quarrel with the US, had put themselves in a position where they had no room to manoeuvre. They wanted an absolute commitment from the Russians on their terms, and the wily Khrushchev would not concede this.

It is a question of old revolutionaries, who are supreme empiricists, teaching young extremists the art of coexistence in a Latin-American context. It will be a painful business, but Dr. Castro will have to adjust to the Soviet point of view. After all he has no choice, and apart from Russia, the whole Communist movement in Latin America will act as a hidden persuader. Cuba is not only fighting against America, she is also contending with an amorphous bureaucracy which threatens to submerge the revolution under mountains of paper.

Every kind of human activity requires a form. The food shortages are very apparent in restaurants offering austere menus. People queue-up for rations and live on a frugal but adequate diet.

This, however, causes more inconvenience and irritation than any real hardship. The older generation grumbles a great deal, but the young people blame it all on the Americans and in the cause of "country or death" are willing to go on tightening their belts indefinitely.

An official told me, "America had put us in an economic straitjacket. Once we broke out we tried to change things overnight and so made serious mistakes after the revolution. Some of the campesinos thought it would be one long holiday and they killed too much livestock. Then there were the landowners who tried to sabotage the agrarian reform by exporting their cattle. On top of all this, we had to face the worst drought in half a century. But things are improving now we have better educated campesinos and an administration that works."

Havana must be the only city in the world where unarmed males whistle at girls armed with automatic weapons and managing to look both serious and sexy in their uniforms.

There is something impermanent about Havana with its glittering skyscrapers along the sea front facing America… All over the city dated American cars are common, coughing and roaring in turns; low grade petrol and the salt air which corrodes silencers are responsible for this.

Meanwhile the city waits for an invasion or for Dr. Castro to announce that the invasion threat is over.

★

I was a British subject travelling on a British passport, and following routine procedure, I registered with the British embassy. The British ambassador came out to greet me. But I obviously didn't fit his profile of a correspondent for the *Observer*. Before asking me to enter, the ambassador repeated twice, "You *are* Mr. Carew, from the *Observer*?" and to allay some of his discomfort, I said, "I'm afraid so." But he was a typical foreign office type and quickly regained his composure.

I was the only correspondent from the Western press who had been allowed into Cuba. When I took my first taxi ride in Havana, the driver, who was black, scrutinised me in the mirror. After some minutes had passed, he asked, "You're a West Indian, no?"

I said, "Yes."

"Well, if you really want to know what is happening," he said, "I can pick you up tonight and take you to meet some of the brothers. I'll come and get you at 8 o'clock sharp," he said.

True to his word, he turned up and took me to a dive in old Havana. They had Clarin, a white rum. These brothers were cane cutters and tallymen. They had come from different islands in the Caribbean and belonged to different categories of the sugar workers, and many of them spoke English with their Caribbean accents. Their faces, framed against the dim lighting, were veined and notched and marked by working in the hot sun. Between toasts to the revolution, they made it clear that they had come down from the Sierra Maestra to share the fruits of the revolution where they were the most abundant: Havana. They said they trusted Fidel, in contrast to the other revolutionary leaders for whom they had a wait-and-see attitude. In the past, they had been tricked, bribed and brutalised by venal dictators; forever promised benefits that were never fulfilled.

I could see that they sincerely wanted to believe that a new day was coming, but I told them that it would probably take four generations before they had enough technical and administrative skills to run a modern society, and that sometimes all that would carry them along and produce momentum for change would be their enthusiasm for revolutionary changes.

The last story the *Observer* published was dated November 24th.

★

"Like the Yankees…"

London *Observer*, HAVANA. November 24, 1962

I waited for my friends on the Calle San Francisco, and we drove to the old city of Havana. There were shades of Graham Greene in the narrow streets, the signboards suspended across the streets like bunting and people lounging at street corners. The old city is a fragment of Spain surrounded by a fence of skyscrapers.

The streets are clean and the displays in shop windows tawdry. There were short queues outside the fish shops, the grocers and the butchers. The queues moved slowly. My friends, like many others, were Socialists by day and socialites by night. As darkness fell we started our round of friends and clubs. Havana's military posture seemed to relapse into a febrile gaiety. True, Fidel Castro's bearded face gazed at us from a multitude of posters, a tommy gun brandished above his head.

But in the night clubs the dancers and singers performed like hipsters and drinks of "Cuba libre" rum eased the unbearable tensions of the day.

Night life in Havana is still hectic. Night clubs run on a co-operative basis are well attended. The clients, however, are no longer Americanos but young men and women in the militia, office workers and awkward campesinos who come to the capital to share the fruits of the revolution.

We talked in a corner of the club. By its dim lights I could see on the wallpaper a life-sized print of a naked slave girl. "My uncle was chauffeur to one of Batista's mistresses," a voice said. "He thought Batista would be too busy with the bearded ones… Batista sent him to prison."

"Things are getting better," another said. "Three weeks ago the black market rate for the dollar was ten to one. Now it's dropped to seven to one."

"Yes, we support Fidel," my question was answered. "Not all the way, but he's the best of the lot." I asked a man next to me about the Russians.

"They're like the Yankees. You feel all the time they've come to tell you what is best for you. It's funny how they and the Czechs hate each other."

A man with a smooth, ageless, mahogany face said his daughter was at Havana University. He had read and studied to keep up with her. "We are strangers in the same house. She tells me all the time I was corrupted by British and American imperialism. But I say to her: 'It will pass away. No system in which every man's hand is against the other can live long.'"

★

Shortly after this, I returned to Jamaica. But, by now, I was clear about the direction my life should take. I closed up that chapter and returned to London.

"What the Cuban Revolution Meant to Me"

Guyana Mirror, Oct. 21, 1978 (Georgetown)

I had been a British colonial subject living in London when I first read about bearded Cuban guerillas fighting in the Sierra Maestra. My country, British Guiana, was at that time ruled by usurpers who treated us with the utmost contempt. In that decade of the nineteen-fifties, while a war of national redemption was being fought in the Sierra Maestra, the first progressive government that Guiana had ever known was overthrown by British troops. And Cheddi Jagan, like some ancient bell-ringer sounding alarms in cities and villages that had been in the thralldom of a dreaming torpor, was imprisoned. But the message that Jagan had brought to the people had the clarity of a lightning-flash. He laid bare the anatomy of capitalist exploitation in the cities and countryside in a way that the people could never forget.

News about the fighting in the Sierra Maestra was more often than not biased and superficial, but it made our hearts jump, because we could read between the lines. Fidel, Camillo, Che, Abel and other guerillas were fighting for the same objectives as we were – the liberty of the dispossessed in our hemisphere of plunder, usurpation and wide indifference of have-gots for the have-nots. Then I read and reread Fidel Castro's *History Will Absolve Me,* and I knew that the fight in Sierra Maestra against the Batista dictatorship was one that would vindicate us all.

Jagan's government was overthrown in 1953, but he left a heritage of socialist ideas to germinate like seeds of anger in the peoples' hearts. After Cheddi Jagan and most of the leaders of the PPP were thrown into prison, a handpicked puppet administration replaced them for a brief and troubled interlude, before the people returned Jagan to office in 1957.

Fidel, too, had been imprisoned earlier on, after a daring attack on the Moncada Barracks, and at his trial he had spoken with an unsurpassed eloquence for us all in our America. He had become inheritor of José Marti's invincible heart, his enchanted tongue. The history that he spoke about was our history. Not merely the history, as John Masefield wrote, of "Princes and prelates and periwigged charioteers/ Riding triumphantly laurelled to lap the fat of the years…", but the history of "the scorned – the rejected – the men hemmed in with the spears/The men of the tattered battalion which fights till it dies."

As I read more and more about the fighters in the Sierra Maestra, it was as though all the palenques, the maroons, and the quilombos that had sprung up during the Columbian era were gathering in those historic mountains of Cuba, resurrecting themselves, holding hope that they had secreted away in the heart of the Americas aloft like a banner of liberation.

It was as though Bolivar had landed once again at Boyaca; as though Toussaint, Christophe, and Dessalines had returned to sit in conclave with Fidel, and to warn him not to repeat their mistakes; as though the Black and Seminole guerillas, who had fought so valiantly in the watery wastes of Florida right up to the mid-nineteenth century, had gathered their scattered forces again from Oklahoma, and Coahuila on the Mexican border, from the depths of the swamps and bayous and from Andros in the Bahamas, and were picking up their fallen standards and urging Fidel on; as though Zumbi was rising again out of the ashes of the Palmares Republic; as though Boni was shouting encouragement from his forests in Suriname; and along with all these were the distant voices of Caonabo, Anacoana, Farmaconi, Caracas and millions of nameless Amerindians trumpeting their solidarity across centuries.

For many of us, we did not need to know all the details of the Cuban revolutionary struggle that the capitalist press by stealth, half-truths and outright omissions was denying us, because we felt the undying truth of that history with the sharpness and the immediacy of a pain that a man feels in the arm that he has lost. When the guerillas reached Havana in 1959, the thunder of jubilant crowds welcoming them, echoed around the world. But there were those of us who felt a twinge of apprehension in the midst of the jubilation. Would Fidel go the way of those reformists whose eloquence had mesmerised us in the past, hypnotised us with incandescent promises of a bright future, and then reneged on these promises? Would he prune the tree of exploitation, or would he pull it up by the roots?

I remember when the Cuban delegates came to the United Nations Headquarters in New York in 1960, and Fidel and his bearded companeros were asked to leave a downtown hotel. They went to the Hotel Theresa in Harlem, instead. The black people of Harlem had given them a warm and tumultuous welcome, to the consternation of their rulers in Washington, and to compound the problem of these rulers, Nikita Khrushchev had come to Harlem to call on the Cuban delegation. I remember a BBC team trying in vain to find someone in the huge crowd outside the hotel who would make an anti-Cuban statement.

One nameless brother in the crowd had been asked in front of the cameras, "Did you know that Fidel Castro nationalised one hundred million dollars worth of American property?"

"That don't bother me none," the nameless man replied. "I don't own no property. Even the coat on my back I en't done paying The Man for. If them Cuban Cats took a hundred million from The Man, that don't bother me none. The Man done ripped-off ten thousand times more than that from my folks."

It was as though this anonymous brother, a random choice in a crowd of thousands, had become the spokesman for voiceless millions in the

USA. He was, very clearly, defining his relationship to the owners of property who are always surprised that the victims of their system of exploitation are not grateful for the theft of the vast surpluses that their labour creates.

After that historic United Nations visit, it was as though there was a quickening of the pace of developments in Cuba. From our outposts of exile abroad, we saw the promises of the Revolution being miraculously fulfilled; and the Soviet Union stepped in to offer the kind of fraternal and selfless aid that only a socialist country is capable of offering. The new revolutionary regime in Cuba began its task of national reconstruction against odds that were awesome. Generations of Cubans had to be trained to master 20th century technical and administrative skills so that they could run the first free society in the Americas. Looking at Cuba from outside, it was clear that its greatest asset was its people. The working people had become the inheritors of their country for the first time, its land, factories, minerals, all of its resources were now their own. Barriers of race and class were being dismantled forever. These working people set out to construct a new tropical civilisation and at the same time to defend the gains of the Revolution with their hearts, their minds and the incalculable energies it had released inside them.

In the late 1950s and early 1960s, Jagan, as Premier of British Guiana, was beleaguered, and surrounded by enemies. Revolutionary Cuba, herself threatened, surrounded, beset by shortages, penalised at every turn by hostile imperialist forces, with a generosity that was unparalleled since the beginning of the Columbian era, gave Guiana help and succour. The imperialists made pontifical statements, declaring that as long as there were free elections in Guiana, they would abide by the decision of the Guyanese people, but then they promptly changed the rules in order to ensure that a "safe" anti-communist candidate would win the elections. Jagan was driven into the political wilderness by a coalition of British and American imperialists and their local surrogates. And, again Guiana lived through a twilight period of internecine struggle before it re-emerged decades later. But Cuba remained a beacon in the Caribbean archipelago. From the strategic centre of our hemisphere, this beacon shed its light from the Canadian Barrens to Patagonia.

At the height of the anti-communist repression in Guiana, I remember a young policeman in New Amsterdam taking me to his modest home to listen to a speech by Fidel Castro. It was evening and outside there were fireflies and choruses of bubbler frogs. We sat in a small front room, and a dark child with enormous, luminous eyes came very naturally and leaned her head against my knee. We were not far from the Berbice River, and we could hear the evening lispings of the falling tide. The cadences of Fidel's voice rose and fell and that voice somehow seemed to be imbued with the same rhythms of that great and mysterious river. We felt the same irresist-ible force, for that voice which was sometimes hoarse with passion, sometimes ringing like a bell, was articulating the hopes, the aspirations, the dreams of millions of sufferers, so that people who had only slept to dream before the Revolution, could now wake up to change the world. We sat in a circle of silence at the end of the speech. The lispings of the river were louder and more insistent. The falling tide was about to end and the tide was chaffing against the muddy riverbank as if it was impatient to push its way up river. I left the house and walked away into a familiar darkness of stars and fireflies. I kept remembering one line in the speech when Fidel had asked,

"What is man?"

And I began to answer the question for myself, "Man is part of a great collective tide of hope and immortal aspirations, and socialism feeds that tide with invincible motive energies... and since Cuba's socialism is as close to us as the living breath to our bodies, we can feel the movement of that tide in our bones. Their setbacks are ours, their triumphs are ours!"

What was interesting about that meeting in the young policeman's house was that the anti-communist incantations which had risen to a crescendo in Guiana were now falling on deaf ears, and there were no complementary responses. Jagan's teachings, his steadfast advocacy of socialism, had germinated, and a forest of healthy growths was springing up in the minds of the Guyanese people. After the millions the CIA had squandered on turning them away from socialism, the Guyanese people had made their own choice.

I remember when Fidel Castro visited Guyana in the early seventies. I was standing with the crowds lining the road that passes through the Albouystown slum. Albouystown is a kind of living pulse in Georgetown, an accurate barometer for gauging social and political change in Guyana. It is the part of the city that the marginals inhabit. It is an enclave of the poor that can be duplicated everywhere in this hemisphere where capitalism reigns. In this borough of the marginals are charnel rows of hovels with rusty tin cans and rats in the gutters, and here thousands live balanced in an uneasy equipoise between seasonal employment and unemployment, between the simplest common denominator of survival and destitution. As the cavalcade of official cars was passing through, Fidel stopped the car and mingled with the crowd. This crowd, which is often considered menacing, violent and beyond the pale by Government bureaucrats and the new-rich middle class, literally took Fidel its bosom. They had an unerring instinct for recognising one of their own, a soul-brother, a comrade-in-arms in the battle against the bruising indignities of poverty. This meeting of the slum-dwellers with Fidel was spontaneous, warm and tremendously moving, and they have long memories. They'll never forget. When the cavalcade resumed its journey and disappeared around a corner, the crowd did not disperse immediately. It was as though a thoughtful mood had settled upon us all.

An old man who was standing a few feet away from me said indignantly, "But look how they lie to us, eh! They tell us say that Fidel Castro was a white man. That man en't white, because he don't act white."

And a market woman chimed in, "These people wicked for true! Look how they lie to us. They tell us that this man was worse than the devil in hell. But things can change in this life, eh. The very people who was cussing this man blind, now falling over themselves to greet him. What a world we live in!"

The Bay of Pigs invasion in 1961 was a traumatic experience for me. It was as if I could feel the wounds of those defenders of the Cuban Revolution in my own flesh. For forty-eight hours, I lived in whirlpools of anxiety – the same anxiety I felt when Lumumba was murdered in the Congo; when Guyanese youth were being slaughtered by bombs provided by the CIA; when the Vietnamese people were – on a much vaster scale – being made the victims of what seemed like an endless succession of atrocities. The cyclical atrocities continued in the Shaba Province, on the borders of Mozambique and Angola; in Nicaragua – the cruelties, in the name of profits, seemingly endless. But the Bay of Pigs invasion was a milestone in the Cuban Revolution. The victory, costly as it was, made it clear that a united and resolute people can defeat the forces of imperialism. This victory brought us back on a journey down the Road of Hope.

But the real victories of the Cuban Revolution were won in factories and fields and workshops, in schools and universities, in the creation of the enduring foundations of a new tropical civilisation which is being built, not on the backs of slaves and sufferers, but with the creative labour of a free people inspired by theory and practice of Socialism.

The Cuban revolution finally means the realisation of a dream that there should be a country in our hemisphere of slavery and economic plunder where racism has been banished forever. And the finest affirmation of this end to racism has manifested itself in the heroism of those Cubans of all races and colours who fought, and died, side by side with their African brothers and sisters in Angola and Ethiopia after these countries, threatened with dismemberment by imperialism and its surrogates, had asked for help.

CHAPTER THIRTEEN

THE CARIBBEAN SOCIETY FOR CULTURE AND SCIENCE

In 1975, my wife Joy and I embarked in a year's leave, which was to be based in Suriname, formerly Dutch Guiana, South America, a small country to the east of Guyana. Suriname, like Guyana, and French Guiana furthest to the east, had been traditionally known as one of the three Guianas. All shared the same topography stretching from the low-lying coastal Guiana Shield, then going south into heavily forested highlands, and being located between the massive Orinoco river to the northwest and the Amazon River to the southeast. Though originally "discovered" by the Spanish, their colonial status by the 18th century had settled with the British, the Dutch and the French. Their different languages and European-influenced cultures aside, they shared the challenges of having a reasonably well-developed coastal zone where 80% of the population lives stretching approximately 50 miles into the interior, and a sparsely populated and massively underdeveloped interior. This latter had been left to the indigenous people – the Amerindian tribes of the region, the African Maroons, and to itinerant gold and diamond prospectors.

Of the three Guianas, only French Guiana remains a colony and is known as a "Department" of France. It is a country of great contrasts, one where its geographical location near the Equator has made it a favourite of the space industry, and is thus very advanced near those technical outposts. It also served as the infamous French penal colony from which we would occasionally receive escapees in Guyana; otherwise it was a country whose basic development seems to have been left willy-nilly.

When we were in Suriname, I planned to do work for the Caribbean Society for Culture and Science (CSCS) that could have similar benefits for people in Guyana in the future. However, at that point in the mid-1970s, our country was being ruled by Forbes Burnham, and there was no way that I could have established anything on a large scale at this time – although, we did have some smaller grassroots projects in Guyana. Many years later in the early 1990s, when Cheddi Jagan was re-elected, I did raise the question of implementing some of the sustainable models of agriculture developed by the CSCS, such as the possibility of growing anthurium lilies for the export market. I also proposed that the CSCS could offer a number of services in agriculture and alternative energy production by replicating some of the successes we had had in Grenada and Jamaica.

Guyana in 1966 and Suriname in 1975 gained their independence from colonial rule. In fact, Suriname became an independent country in the fall of the year we were there, though as we discovered in the early 1980s, changes of names by independent countries did not always get reflected in the directories referred to at border crossings. Joy and I were travelling to northern Africa and an agent at the passport control found my Guyana passport curious, because his directory did not list such a country. After some minutes of my insistence that Guyana did exist and that the passport was bonafide, Joy offered up the suggestion that he look up "British Guiana". There, he found my country still linked to its former colonial sisters, and agreed to pass me through.

I had been looking forward to spending an extended time in Suriname to begin a project about which I had been thinking for some time. I wanted to find ways to bring more nutritional foodstuffs to people in the Caribbean. I had been reading literature in the organic community about crops that I thought could be very beneficial because they were high in protein, but also because they were already being grown in climates elsewhere in the world that were very much like ours.

My friend, the poet Dobru, had offered to arrange a place for us to stay in the capital, Paramaribo, until we got our bearings, and then, later, to organise a journey into the interior to visit some of the Maroon communities. He had also agreed to introduce me to people who might be interested in helping me with my research into Maroon communities and working on projects to help improve their nutritional base. Besides these projects, I was also eager to induct Joy, an African American who had grown up in the United States, into the real life of Caribbean people.

We ended up living in an assortment of places over the year – in Paramaribo and in the rain forest. The apartments behind the Natural History museum were cool and lovely and were located in a large flowering garden. The garden also had a resident hen, who despite repeated attempts to shoo her away, persisted in laying eggs under a corner table. The doors were always kept open to encourage the circulation of air and there were no screens, and in she would come. So, there I would be tapping away on my portable Olivetti and, in the corner of my eye, I would catch a glimpse of this determined hen coming into the room on her daily task. It became quite normal and familiar, and we didn't mind the fresh eggs.

One of our neighbours was a young Dutch couple who were research scientists on their way into the interior. Their speciality was a certain type of spider monkey, one of which they had as a pet. They also had an infant. In our conversations about their preparations for the long periods in the interior to observe the monkeys in their habitat, they explained that while they had been required to take many inoculation shots, they were not willing impose this on their baby. So, apparently, they were trusting that some saintly presence would look after the newest-born member of their family and to ward off anything that might harm it. We didn't see them again before we left the country, but we often thought of them and their devotion to science. Like Dian Fossey and Jane Goodall, one could not help but admire the fearlessness with which they were determined to plunge themselves into their work.

The small apartment we rented in Nola Hatterman's school was on the top floor of the building. The water pressure was uncertain and we spent much of the time hauling buckets of water up for our cooking and bathing. For Joy, the outsized and unique fruits and vegetables in Suriname must have seemed like something out of *Alice in Wonderland*. The enormous grapefruits, which were the size of basketballs, were what the Surinamers called pamplemousse. Apparently, these were brought over with the importation of indentured labour from Indonesia. No doubt, like the breadfruit that is so common in the Caribbean, this was another of the foodstuffs brought in by the colonialists to feed the new waves of labourers. Another intriguing vegetable from Asia was the yard-long green beans, which they called bora.

We also stayed in a cabin in a clearing on the edge of the rain forest, some distance from Paramaribo. This area, however, was connected to the city by a small road. The two-storey wooden house had most of the city conveniences, including running water and electricity, and it was quite pleasant out there. When we first arrived, Joy thought she saw snakes in the grass clearing around the house. To allay her fears, I told her that most of the animals – snakes included – didn't want to see her any more than she wanted to see them. Once humans established a camp or, as in this case, were coming in and out of the house on a regular basis, the animals usually rerouted themselves to avoid running into them. This little speech seemed to help, as she became less suspicious, and, in fact began to go out blithely to hang the washing without making that extra inspection.

One day, however, as she was heading upstairs, she began to back down the stairs slowly. "I know you said that the animals would avoid us, but there's a snake heading up the stairs!"

I went see what it was, and yes, there was a small snake halfway up the stairs. I captured it and then disposed of it far from the house. On my way back in, I was debating whether I should tell Joy what kind of snake it was, or downplay the event. At first, I thought to downplay it.

"Yes, there was a snake, a small snake. We can keep a look out, but I wouldn't worry about too many more of them. Once they get our scent, they usually avoid us."

I didn't tell her then, although I did tell her after we returned to Paramaribo, that this was a labaria snake, which, while small, did have a potentially fatal venom. From that point on, though, we inspected the steps and tumbled up the bedding before turning in at night. We also added a strip of wood to make sure that there was no gap at the bottom of the front door.

This became a kind of pattern where Joy's initial vigilance would be replaced by a kind of acceptance and willingness to focus on something else. At one point, when we were staying in a cabin in the Brownsberg Nature Reserve, Joy got so involved with her photographs of orchids, that she didn't notice the snakes that I saw in the trees when I was coming up the same path shortly after her. We laughed about this later, although she might not have found this a delightful thought while she was taking the photos. Obviously, we took basic precautions wherever we went, but Americans steeped in Hollywood "jungle" films have a propensity for seeing dangers everywhere, and it would have been a pity if she had been continuously worried.

Dobru had arranged to collect us one morning for a week-long journey into the interior. We were going to stay in one of the villages of the Saramaccan Maroons, people who had scattered along the Lower Suriname River. I had told Joy to expect that we would be taking a small airplane into the interior and from there, most likely a small motorboat or canoe to the village itself. These Maroon villages were purposefully settled in some of the most difficult regions to reach, and although the Maroons and the coastal colonialists were no longer fighting over the former's enslavement, the Maroons had remained in many of these locations well into the last quarter of the 20th century. This, no doubt, was a major factor in the maintenance of their distinctive culture and lifestyle, but it also limited the range of their foodstuffs, which affected the general health of these communities. As we were to discover, the main sources of nutrition were fish and cassava, the latter baked into an unleavened bread, along with wild berries and nuts.

Although we had packed clothing and bug repellent, we hadn't prepared any provisions for our stay, not realising that Dobru expected we would do this. There would have been no problem about doing it, but the breakdown in communication wasn't apparent until we unloaded the plane in the interior. We had just assumed that one or two of the other large bundles in the hold were for us. Regrettably, they weren't and Dobru was not with us when we landed. Our host had sent a young guide to meet us at the bush clearing that was the landing strip, and to help us with our gear. After some halting communication in Sranan Tongo, a local Creole, and some English, he came to understand that we didn't have any food with us. He assured us that the paramount chief of his village would be able to help and that there was a shop near their village where we could pick up things.

The journey now took on a more challenging character. While the airplane had been quite small – just us and the pilot – now the trek was over uneven, heavily forested terrain, and by dugout canoe. Watching the uncertain look on Joy's face when she understood that she would have to get down in one of these narrow canoes was quite amusing, although I didn't show it. All along our journey to Suriname, and to the different places where we stayed, she gamely made adjustments as needed. But, these were adjustments to a local hotel, or to the police chief's house or a cabin in a nature park. Now, she would be travelling in these low dugouts with just enough room for one of us, a local boatman and a bundle or two, plying the mysterious and dark waters of the rainforest river. She was used to sitting much higher and in something much wider. The first of these journeys was the most difficult, but she began to relax somewhat over time.

When we reached the landing place for the village where we would be staying for the week, I could see Joy was totally perplexed about how to balance the canoe and step out onto the muddy slope. The boatman jumped out and with the help of another person, she was safely coaxed up and out of her seat, with only some minor tipping of the canoe, to set foot on the land without slipping back down into the river. Like the rivers of Guyana, the water is dark brown due to the tannin from the falling leaves, and it is difficult to see fish or boulders just under the surface.

We were settled into a room in a guest house that the Suriname government had built for the paramount chief. Evidently, the building lay empty most of the time, as the chief and his villagers were perfectly comfortable in their family compounds and their cluster of small A-frame huts. But we were foreigners. The chief had also arranged for us to have a cook who would regularly bring us fried fish, which turned out to be piranha, and cassava bread. As to our other provisions, we were taken to a shop, actually just a small hut some distance away from the settlement, which had small caches of tinned foods. And there, in the midst of the Suriname rainforest, we discovered tins of Vienna-style cocktail hotdogs and preserved fish, which we grudgingly bought for lack of other options. The guest house had a small camp stove on which we boiled water and heated up the tinned provisions. During our walks, our guides would point out which rivers and streams were safe for swimming. It turned out that piranha fish were quite common in the area and we would see children or some adults with a piece of a finger or toe missing – which they seemed to accept with some equanimity. The lesson to be learned – unless one was fishing for them – was to avoid calm waters. Invariably, we would see children playing in small rapids, and with some trepidation did briefly try that out as well.

Through our organisation, the Caribbean Society for Culture and Science, I had hoped to find communities with which I could work on my goal to introduce a more nutritional and sustainable lifestyle. I had been working for years with colleagues in Princeton and Evanston, who specialised in the development of sustainable communities, to develop assorted models that I wanted to implement in the Caribbean. I had also been reading about the high protein winged bean which could offer so much to small communities. What I needed was a welcoming community and then funding from local or non-governmental agencies.

Included in the plans was a detailed drawing, showing the various fields and other plantings, and where bio-digester systems could be set up to get rid of wastes while providing a source of energy. I was welcomed quite hospitably by the paramount chiefs gathered at our meeting in the village of Santigron – another Maroon village. They, and their bashas (secretaries) and assistants, patiently listened to my explanations, which had to be translated from English into their specific Maroon language and then the bashas would relay the information to the paramount chiefs. No one, other than the bashas, could speak directly to the chiefs at such a gathering. This six-way communication took quite some time. They looked at my garden designs and discussed them amongst themselves.

Then one day, one of the chiefs, speaking to me through his basha and then my translator, told me, "We appreciate your suggestions, Professor, but what will we eat while we are waiting for these new crops and trees to grow?"

To my chagrin, in my zeal to help them improve the nutrition of their community, as well as to have more sustainable crops, I had left out their traditional provision fields. These crops might not have been so nutritious, but they were readily accessible foodstuffs with which they were very familiar and, most importantly, on which they could live while trying out the other agricultural plans. Some of the items I was encouraging them to grow, like the fruit trees to be interplanted with grazing areas for cattle, would take more than a year to mature. I took the design back and revised it to include the much-needed provision field.

I had hoped that the paramount chief of Santigron, which was a Maroon village closer to the coast and Paramaribo, might implement our suggestions. But, whilst it appears that he did not adopt my suggestions, several extremely talented musicians were recruited from this area and their fame brought quite a bit of new income into the community. Also, because of its proximity to Paramaribo and the ability to go there by car, Santigron was on its way of developing a tourist industry.

Visitors were fascinated at being able to step back centuries when entering these villages that looked very much like traditional West African settlements. Not only did the inhabitants look West African, but the houses, clothing, foodstuffs and ceremonies had retained significant features passed down over many generations. For the short-term visitor to Suriname who wanted to sample some of this, Santigron was in a prime location. However, this also meant that the people of Santigron would be more exposed to Western culture than Maroon communities deep in interior, and this could result in an ever greater dilution of their culture. Already, people from Santigron, working in Paramaribo or elsewhere along the coast, were bringing consumer items and new cultural habits back to the village.

We did a lot of reading about these Maroon communities before going into the interior where we gathered oral histories to flesh out the stories of their survival. To our eyes, they appeared to be living in a kind of stasis, as they maintained their centuries-old settlements. The year before, a Dutch researcher, curious to test how connected the Surinamese Maroons still were to their ancestors, had organised a delegation of four of the paramount chiefs and their assistants, from each of the major Maroon groups, to visit Ghana, West Africa. The researcher wanted to see how these paramount chiefs, whose ancestors had been shipped to the Americas on slave ships in the 17th century, might react when they saw Ghana and its people. No doubt, the flight on a huge jetliner and the transfers through busy airports would have been mind-boggling in themselves, but it is evident that when the alighted from the plane in Africa, they experienced a kind of epiphany. Feeling the humid air and seeing people very much like those they had left back home, provoked the Chiefs to chant some praise songs in a language they called "Kromanty". This language was not part of their common parlance in Suriname, but had been passed down by their ancestors and only used for special religious ceremonies. To their amazement, some of their older West African hosts understood them and told them that this was an older form of a local language, also called "Kromanti", which is part of the Akan languages family.

Prior to our journey to Suriname, I had renewed contacts with one of my former graduate students from Princeton, Bill Howard, who was then studying in the seminary. Reverend Howard, by this time, was working in the senior administration of the National Council of Churches based in New York, and in 1979 he became the director of the NCC. Bill and his colleagues were excited about my agricultural project work and arranged for me to meet people in some of the subdivisions of the NCC who might be in a position to provide some funds, advice or other useful contacts. Over the next few years, we corresponded regularly and I would meet him and his colleagues from time to time. From the days of the project work in Suriname and Guyana, and on to Grenada and Jamaica, we worked closely with the NCC's Commission on Justice, Liberation and Human Fulfilment, or "the Fifth Commission", and the NCC's Agricultural Missions.

Through them, we were connected to other organisations committed to similar goals for the redevelopment of Third World societies. Though we were based in Suriname for a year, we did take side trips to Guyana periodically. At one stage, the CSCS was involved in trying to solve the problem of flooding, to which the coastal regions of Guyana were prone. There was also interest in experimenting with the winged bean, but this crop did not do well if it was waterlogged. This led to an investigation of developing raised beds for planting. I had seen this in organic gardening literature and thought we could give it a try. Rather than use wooden railroad sleepers, which were being used in the more temperate climates, we needed a more permanent solution, hence the decision to make these 6 x 3-foot beds out of cement, and with sides tall enough to prevent flood waters entering them. After these large beds dried, we filled them with a mixture of topsoil and organic matter. The winged bean plants were interplanted with a few other vegetables and all survived the next rainy season.

The CSCS work focused on two areas: more nutritious crops and sustainable farming with alternative energy sources, two goals which could be complementary, but could take on a different character depending upon the location and resources. The Suriname and Grenada efforts developed more actively along the nutrition line, initially with the winged bean and then with grain amaranth. Our work in Guyana was a mix of working with nutritious crops and more sustainable farming methods. The Jamaican work, done during Prime Minister Michael Manley's first term of office, focused more on sustainability and alternative sources of energy production. Here, the CSCS, together with The Third World Energy Institute, had laid out a more elaborate plan – the Synergein project – which, with the government's interest and approval, was awaiting the designation of a specific property. Manley was very enthusiastic and put us in touch with various people. Regrettably, this was in the latter part of the 1970s, and with the increased economic pressures from outside, plus the distractions of the political infighting and violence around the elections, our project got moved to the back burner. With the 1980 election victory going to Manley's opponent, there was no question of reviving it.

I initially went to Grenada in 1979. I was very interested in the developments of the New Jewel Movement under Prime Minister Maurice Bishop and thought that this might be a singular opportunity to develop some alternatives to the traditional approach of focusing solely on crops for export. I had last seen Bishop in London when he was a student. Now, he was the head of a new, young government that was determined to avoid the pitfalls of previous Caribbean administrations. Indeed, what struck me over the period I spent there, was that this was a country being ruled by young people with such enthusiasm about the "new day". Even walking the village roads and the streets at night, one didn't have that niggling "worry" about one's fellow man that was so common elsewhere. People greeted you and then went on about their business.

Though I was still growing the winged bean, I was excited at the prospect of mounting a project to grow grain amaranth. Like the winged bean, grain amaranth is extremely high in protein and can provide a much-needed nutritional boost for the poor. It has the potential to be the most important food that ever existed in the Americas. It was widely grown in the region at the time of the Spanish incursions, but was virtually wiped out by the Europeans as part of their genocidal campaigns against the indigenous people. Fortunately, the amaranth plants were still growing in the more inhospitable regions of Central America. Research by the US National Academy of Sciences which was published in 1975 identified grain amaranth as a being an invaluable global resource. If this project worked as I hoped it would, we would be growing amaranth in the Eastern Caribbean for the first time since Columbus came.

Initially, I rented a place in a mountainous region some miles outside the capital city of St. George's in the St. Paul's/ Mardi Gras area, but this was not a prime spot for growing amaranth. The land was uneven and, in the rainy season, was known for sending the top soil of one farm down on another, if the properties had not been properly terraced. Through trial and error, we managed to stabilise our growing area.

I spent much of my time getting know the small farmers and learning how they lived and finding out what stories they remembered from the lives of their elders. I had also put out a request for a more suitable property on which to start the experimental farm. Some months later, the property in Bacolet came up as an option.

Bacolet was located along a coastal road and offered a much larger acreage for the amaranth crop. It had a large house with several bedrooms built around a courtyard and a wide verandah out front. With the help of local farmers, I grew several varieties of grain amaranth to see which was the best suited to Grenada's climate. Surprisingly, some of the varieties grew taller than me and I was 6-feet-4. Some of the farmers had commented that, in the old days, before chemical fertilisers, people had collected seaweed for mulching their crops. I decided to try this for the amaranth, and developed a process where we would collect the seaweed, spread it out in the courtyard and let the rainwater wash out the salt. The courtyard also proved useful for drying the amaranth seed heads, although, in this case, we had to be sure to keep them from getting wet.

Over the next few years, several articles were written about the project which were published in the Caribbean, the US and elsewhere. These generated a flood of letters requesting seeds, or instructions on how to begin projects, and invitations to come to address various organisations. We also reported our results to the experimental farm office at Rodale farms, from which we had purchased the seed. Several different varieties of grain amaranth seed had been purchased from them and, over time, we were able to inform them which were more suited to climates and conditions like ours in Grenada.

Working with our colleague Steve Slaby at Princeton, we organised summer projects for some of his students, who would come down to spend a couple of months to work with CSCS. Slaby was an interesting person. He came from a working-class family, but became a world-renowned engineer. He taught at Princeton for forty years and was on the faculty advisory committee for the Program in Afro-American Studies. Steve was very committed to the world struggle and anti-racism. He wanted to make sure that his engineering students understood something of the consequences of their innovations. So, he had them do projects to address Third World societal needs. For instance, he had his students develop a solar hot water system using an old petrol drum. He developed an electric motor that could run backwards, so that those making electricity at their homes (wind or bio-gas energy, for instance), would not be penalised by extra charges from the electric companies. A right-wing US general once tried to shut down one of his projects and he got the Dean to go tell Steve to stop the project, but Steve just threw the fellow out of his office.

The crops from our early efforts proved to be quite fruitful and instructive to the community of farmers around us. However, our project did run into a snag that required long and complex discussions to effect a compromise. The land we were renting was being reclaimed by the owner at a very crucial point. Happily, we were able to harvest a very fine crop of amaranth (the dwarf grain variety type) and to have enough seed to distribute to a number of local co-operatives. This was precious seed, because it represented the sixth crop, grown under controlled conditions, and monitored from the seed box to maturity. Though we lost this plot, we benefited from the help of a group of dedicated young people who knew about the amaranth experiment at Bacolet, and pledged themselves to help the project move forward. They approached me with the idea of forming a new co-operative and of finding further governmental and other support. We named our new co-operative the "Fedon Co-op" after Julien Fedon, Grenada's freedom fighter of the 18th century. I wrote about Fedon's history in my book *Grenada: The Hour Will Strike Again*. Sometime later, after receiving the approval from the National Agricultural Co-operative Development Association of Grenada, NACDA directed us to another forty-one acre estate and after the legal matters and loans had been taken care of, the property was to be made available to the Fedon Co-op.

We would have continued with the project had not Bishop and several members of his Cabinet been executed as part of a coup led by an anti-

Thursday, May 14, 1981

Prof re-introduces old plant

By Ann Bradley
Daily Staff Reporter

Modern science uses the most sophisticated technology available to try to solve hunger problems in the Third World, but that is not always the right approach, according to a Northwestern professor.

Jan Carew of the Department of African-American Studies says in order to deal with contemporary agricultural problems, we should study agricultural systems of the Caribbean and Central America, which were used before Columbus discovered America.

"Their methods of food production were more effective than the ones we have today," Crew said. "Our agricultural systems have not made all that much progress in 500 years."

CAREW HAS DONE extensive research with the bushy amaranth plant, a grain crop that was supremely important to the Aztec Indians. Amaranth is particularly nutritious because it is rich in lysine (an amino acid) and sulphur-containing amino acids, unlike corn, wheat, rice and other modern grains.

"It is like some plant someone dreamed up," Crew said. "It has something that resists rodents, which cause the loss of hundreds of thousands of tons of grain per year in the Caribbean."

Amaranth was lost when Spanish conquistadors destroyed Indian civilizations in their search for riches.

Carew re-introduced the amaranth plant to the Caribbean islands at St. Paul's in Grenada in 1979. He and a small group of volunteers built stone terraces like the Indians had done and planted amaranth seedlings, which thrived even in drenching rains and yielded the nutritious grain.

THE VARIOUS activities around planting and harvesting amaranth "lend themselves naturally to traditional patterns of communal living and a spirit of self-help," Carew said.

"Agriculture in backward societies has to be woven into the cultural system or it is meaningless," Carew said. He said amaranth fits this description because it can be grown as a "backyard crop" and the leaves can be eaten like spinach.

Carew, who has been at Northwestern for eight years, is a native of Guyana. He studied at Howard University, Case-Western Reserve University, Charles University in Czechoslovakia and the Sorbonne in France. He also taught at Princeton University.

Carew founded the Caribbean Society for Culture and Science (CSCS) which con-

see PLANT on page 14

African-American Studies Prof. Jan Carew examines the Amaranth plant, which he hopes to develop further as a source of food for the world's hungry.

Photograph personal to Jan Carew. The article appeared in the *Daily Northwestern*, 14 May 1981.

Bishop faction in 1983. The instability of the island was further exacerbated by a subsequent invasion by US forces. Grenada's early friendly relations with Cuba had been worrisome to the US. Political infighting had led to the coup and the island was put under martial law. Taking the pretext of "saving" the American students studying at an offshore medical school in St. George's, the US invaded. As with Cuba in 1962, the decision had evidently been taken that it was time to push these countries back in line.

Both Joy and I were in Chicago at the time and, unfortunately, we were no longer able to return to the island and our projects there. I was happy to learn, though, that many of the young farmers with whom I had worked were still growing amaranth and using the sustainable methods in their other plots.

"Harvesting History in the Hills of Bacolet"

Quaecumque, winter 1982, Vol. IV, No. 2,
A publication of the Chaplain's Office, Northwestern University

> Your science can only take root
> when you can speak to the land
> hear it whisper back its reply
> and when you make the acquaintance
> of every sorrow.

St. Paul's and Mardi Gras are joined together like Siamese twin towns on the map of Grenada. The two cling to a winding main road that crosses the parish of St. David's, hugging the green hillsides like a hoop around barrels until it plunges steeply towards St. George's, the capital, and circles the wide arc of the harbour. But despite the large twin dots on the way, neither St. Paul's nor Mardi Gras are really urban centres. They are, in fact, hybrids. Small farms and large ones, and patches of untidy wasteland are interspersed carelessly between clusters of houses, and these are all part of the small towns. Besides the roads that lead away from the main highway, diagonally or at right angles, are either two tracks with grass growing between them or rutted lanes that are likely to stop abruptly in the middle of nowhere.

Beyond these lanes, are, invariably, secret trails made by bare feet and leading to the dwellings of the poor, the landless, the dispossessed, the marginal folk of the countryside. Their houses are hidden behind clumps of hedges and trees, but, occasionally, one stands by itself, ugly and naked and bursting at the seams with children. There was one in particular that I had to pass by every morning, and often I saw different levels of cotton eyes gleaming inside the doorway like snow-white anemones in dark seas. On my way back, these children would be strung out along the roadside balancing kerosene drums full of water on their heads, and in the harsh light, one could see their swollen bellies, hear their laughter and the lilting cadences of their speech mingling with birdsong, the cooing of doves and the occasional harsh cry of a chicken hawk.

Of course, there was a fortunate minority of these marginal peasants who had landed regular jobs as domestics, caretakers, gardeners, artisans and farm workers. Their houses were neat and painted on the outside, and in front of their cottages were anthuriums, fruit trees, fragrant mimosas and vines that bore brilliant bell-like yellow flowers.

What is striking about St. Paul's, Mardi Gras, and indeed all of Grenada, is that it is a society of youths. The average age is under twenty-one. Following trails in the hills of Mardi Gras and beyond, I saw few older people and what appeared to be a host of younger ones. It was the restless discontent, the impatience, the burgeoning expectations of these youths that had sparked off the Revolution of March 13, 1979 and given it its qualities of boldness, of idealism and of reckless courage. The awesome poverty, secreted away in the Grenadian countryside, must be seen against a background of pristine energy and the ineluctable forward thrust of this youthful society standing up to stretch limbs that were stiff from too much kneeling.

A poet-calypsonian told me, while he plucked the strings of his guitar almost absent-mindedly, "It wasn't any longer a question of pruning an old and sick tree, my brother. We had to pull it up by the roots. Every time you touch the earth anywhere on this spice island, you're invading the graves of dead ancestors who suffered too much – the Caribs, the Africans in chains, and the wage slaves who followed them. And now, since the New Day was born, we've turned over the soil with love and care and planted new and healthy growths. It's never going to be the same again."

Following trails in the hills of Mardi Gras when cocks of dawn were crowing and the grass was wet with dew, I tried to reach the peaks of far away hills to greet the sunrise. I was recovering from the painful experience of a slipped disc and, forced to give up jogging for a while, had turned to long walks instead.

It was early October, but the poui immortelles were already flaunting their yellow and russet red blossoms. Against the dark sombre greens of the hillsides, they looked like flames illuminating night skies. The Grenadians call them "Christmas Flowers", and by December, they would stripe the green hillscapes with their bright colours and would carpet the ground with blossoms.

Crossing the green valleys and verdant hills of Mardi Gras, and the villages and estates strewn around it, I became more sharply aware than ever that the history of our Caribbean is still largely an unwritten one. The epic struggle of our ancestors to humanise landscapes, through their creative labour, remains buried in an oral history whose values we are only now beginning to appreciate.

Once the Mardi Gras peasants became accustomed to my presence day after day, they shared with me freely what had been passed on to them by the Old Ones, and what they had gleamed and internalised from their own experiences. Through endlessly flowing conversations, they provided me with a spectrum through which I could peer into a buried past and resurrect truths that were miraculous and at the time illuminating in their simplicity. Few had bothered to listen to them before, and I was providing them with an opportunity they'd been waiting for. The newly formed Grenadian Union of Writers is concentrating on using this vast reservoir of untapped oral material as the basis for a wide range of both creative and academic endeavours. They're taking heed of Santayana's warning that "Those who cannot remember the past are condemned to repeat it."

In every large rural community in the Caribbean, one inevitably comes across an unusually eloquent and gifted storyteller, and Mardi Gras was no exception. I met Marko early one morning when he was on his way to milk his cows. He was tall, lean, grizzled and out of his dark and ageless face, looked enormous sad eyes, like those of a swarthy Don Quixote who had never ventured forth to fulfil impossible dreams. He talked with hoarse eloquence, and sometimes he punctuated a statement with bitter laughter. Walking ahead of me on a narrow trail with his cutlass swinging in its scabbard at his side, he said,

"Ah can't tell you how long we wrestled with these hills and valleys from breast to death. This land makes you old before your time, greyhairs your life while you're still young. And if its not one thing, it's the other –hurricanes, landlords, drought, flood. Farmers are going to have to make a better living or this country will die. This is a country of youths, and yet the age of the average farmer is over fifty-five. Part of it is that before you can buy enough land to make a living you're too old to work it well – but all that is changing. The morning after Gairy fell, I heard Brother Bishop say, 'This is a revolution for land, for jobs, for liberty', and I felt my old heart jump. The land part of it is still to be settled, but this time, me, and all the farmers around – those with land and those without – are a part of the settlement.

"We will take over the land from those who owned it since long time past days, and who used it so badly. Anyway, only He who created the land got a right to own it. Land is for all of we… But, it's not man alone that can be cruel to man – it's the strong wind. When Hurricane Janet came and left, it made a carpet out of my banana trees. All I could do was bawl and beat my chest. Then, I left everything to rot so that the earth could nourish its hungry appetite.

"My neighbour, Belfon, was worse off than me, though. Two acres of his land walk down the hill and settle on top of mine. Before the Good Lord brought us together in this mysterious fashion, I couldn't stand the sight of Belfon, but the heart of the trouble was that I was farming well and he was doing it badly. He was cutting down trees on our steep hillside to burn charcoal, and not making terraces when he planted. So all of us realised that we either had to work together, or the hillside would take a terrible revenge on the good, the bad, and the indifferent. See how that whole hillside is terraced and the trees are springing up plentiful like grass in pasture?"

He pointed to his hillside across the valley, and sections of it were neatly terraced. In the bright light one could see beds of yams, cassava, corn, patches of pigeon peas, sweet potatoes, runner beans, and varieties of fruit trees, coconut palms and papayas were everywhere. The farmers, still remembering the last hurricane, had planted few bananas and some of them had substituted sugar cane.

Many of the coconut palms on the hillside, however, were turning yellow. They were victims of the "yellowing disease" which had originated in Florida, and was now appearing across the entire Caribbean archipelago and into Central and South America.

"You should have planted the Malaysian dwarf variety," I suggested.

"We found out about it when it was already too late," he said. "You see the revolution just brought us back into the human race. Before the revolution, small farmers like me were outside of it, and I, for one, mean to stay here on the inside. I'd rather die then go back on the outside. Anyway, the reason we survived was that we can bend like a reed in a hurricane. Big trees fall down and die in the strong wind, but reeds survive."

After a month of walking in the hills gathering material about the history of agriculture in the region, the Caribbean Society for Culture and Science (CSCS) launched its first project in St. Paul's. The CSCS is a non-profit organisation. Its directors first came together while working on a rural development project in Suriname in 1975, and subsequently, after a stint in Guyana, the CSCS was formed. Its aim was to treat science, technology, and culture as fruit from the same tree; and to hinge all new projects on the idea that agriculture is a culture, a way of life and being, a kaleidoscope of ideas and activities ranging from the metaphysical to the concrete and the objective. There is the added factor, or course, that at the heart of the struggle for the emancipation of the peasant in the tropical world there is usually an oppressive political system.

I had grown up in a village on the edge of the vast forest of the Amazon basin, and working in Suriname crystallised ideas that had been taking shape in my mind for a lifetime.

Marko, the ageless one, was perhaps the most eloquent and articulate of the farmers I spoke to before embarking on the St. Paul's/Bacolet project, but there were others who came and spoke freely and at length from time to time. They talked about old fashioned methods of irrigation, biological control of pests, simple but effective storage techniques and, of central importance, the use of traditional organic fertilisers – animal, chicken, Guinea fowl and duck manure, lime from burnt conch shells, interplanting and methods of mulching during long dry spells, using bagasse from the sugar factories, with grasses and other organic cuttings.

Marko agreed to work for the CSCS, partly out of conviction that what we planned to do was worthwhile, and partly because he was always in need of ready cash. Too much of the energies of small farmers, like Marko, are consumed in a circle of catch-as-catch-can activities – fishing unproductively, hiring themselves out as day labourers when the workforce has always been much larger than jobs available, and engaging in a variety of small artisan enterprises without proper tools, skills or workshops.

Marko, working side-by-side with me building terraces on the ravaged and unpromising hillside we had chosen at St. Paul's, said, "There are two kinds of projects…"

"Two kinds?" I inquired.

"There's that United Nations one at Mardi Gras. A big boss drives up in a jeep every now and then, and tells us poor folk what to do, then he drives back to his air-conditioned office and his drinks and social life. When my cousin, Belfon, told him that what he was doing was wrong, he turned around and said that the U.N. sent him here to tell us what to do, not to listen to what we had to say… Then there's the other kind where you work shoulder-to-shoulder."

Thirty-nine percent of all children between the ages of one and five suffer from malnutrition or hyponutrition in Grenada. Central to the CSCS projects, therefore, was the aim of producing high protein food crops, using for the most part, indigenous resources – readily available and cheap fertilisers, and traditional methods of production, storage, marketing and transportation. The CSCS also concentrated on using, whenever possible, alternatives to expensive fossil fuels. Evanston resident, Dr. Ernest Wakefield has worked closely with CSCS in designing projects to develop bio-gas, wind, solar and mini-hydroelectric power using only local resources. Having done thorough and in-depth research into the history of agriculture in the Mardi Gras/St. Paul's area, the CSCS set out to implement a programme with members of the community ranging from semi-literate peasant farmers to teachers at the local grammar school.

Most of the farmers we talked to knew something about the traditional methods of using organic fertilisers, but all of them had abandoned these methods. They relied instead on chemical fertilisers, herbicides and pesticides. Escalating costs, however, have already placed chemicals beyond the means of small farmers.

"My land became a drug addict, calling for more and more fertiliser," Marko told me, "And when I couldn't afford to buy the chemical fertiliser, darkness set in. But after the hurricane, when the landslide dump my neighbour's two acres onto my land, I saw how the decaying vegetation helped to make things grow again, so I went back to the old ways."

The main high protein crops that the CSCS introduced were the winged bean (a legume which had originated in Papua-New Guinea, and one that is as nutritious as soybean) and grain amaranth (a pre-Columbian grain that is rich in protein). In 1975, my wife, Dr. Joy Carew, and I, carried out experiments with winged beans in Suriname and Guyana, and subsequently helped to introduce this valuable legume to many parts of the Caribbean where it had been unknown.

Both the winged bean and amaranth are hardy tropical plants. Amaranth, in particular, a botanical relative of both the tumbleweed and the pigweed, is drought resistant. Ann Williams writes:

> Varieties can, today, be found throughout the western and southern United States, Central and South America, in Africa and the Far East. Yet, its importance as a grain crop has, until the present, been overshadowed by the large grains – wheat, corn, barley, and rice – in the diets of people in most developing countries. India alone has proceeded to develop amaranth as a serious alternative to wheat and other large grains. (Williams 1981:10).

In the pre-Columbian era immediately preceding the Conquest, amaranth was one of the chief sources of protein for millions of Americans. Williams writes:

> By the time Montezuma came to power in Mexico at the beginning of the 16th century, amaranth was in its heyday there. Tens of thousands of acres of Aztec farmland were planted in tall, leafy, red-flowered, pale seeded stalks. The grain, called *huautli*, was one of the ancient Mexican's four pillars of sustenance, along with maize (*centli*), beans (*etl*), and sage (*chian*). Each year, Aztec farmers brought two hundred thousand bushels of amaranth grain to Montezuma's palace in Tenochtitlan in tribute, along with other produce, game, feathers, fine clothing, and gold. (Williams 1981:10).

Looking at this grain crop after the Conquest, it is important to reflect on the way in which culture and agriculture had been fused together for millenniums in the hemisphere. Williams again:

> For reasons historians have not quite deciphered, amaranth had acquired mystical properties in the Aztec culture, and it was this characteristic that doomed it under the onslaught of the invading Spaniards. Before a number of festivals on the Aztec religious calendar, temple women carefully separated the amaranth grain from the chaff. They ground some of the seed, popped some, then added red colouring from the amaranth flower as well as a sticky sweetener like honey or molasses. Figurines shaped from this dough – seemingly endless varieties of dogs, cats, snakes, birds, mountains, and godlike images – were eaten by participants in the ceremonies who then tithed part of their amaranth crop to the temple.
> When the Spaniards arrived in Mexico in 1519 and began their systematic destruction of the Aztec empire under the leadership of Hernan Cortez, the amaranth was a prime target. As part of the culture's nutritional and religious foundation, the grain had to be eliminated as one step toward bringing about the collapse of the Aztec nation. But although thousands of fields were trampled and burnt and people were put to death for possessing amaranth dough, the plant survived. With what we know today of amaranth's agricultural and nutritional potential, the implications of Cortez's decisions are staggering" (Williams 1981:10).

There are many valuable ancillary usages for amaranth. The Native

Americans in several parts of the Americas believed amaranth to have medicinal qualities, while others "revered it for the mystical properties they believed it to have" (Williams 1981:10). With the great demand for wholesome vegetable dyes in the world today, the CSCS is currently looking into the possibility of producing amaranth's beautiful red dye on a commercial scale. The Indians, for centuries, have tapped amaranth flowers for dyes. The Greek word *amaranthos*, meaning "unfading" may be the root of the modern "amaranth," since the brilliant amaranth blossoms, when dried, never lose their colour. The CSCS is exploring the potential of this and other amaranth by-products.

The initial experiment at St. Paul's was only partially successful. We built stone terraces very much like the ones the ancient Mayans constructed in Middle America, and despite unseasonably heavy rains, the winged bean and amaranth crops reached maturity in a reasonably healthy state.

The first time I took a sack of amaranth grain to the flour mill in St. George's, I had to reassure the owners that the new and unknown grain would not clog up their machines,

"It's the oldest grain in this hemisphere," I declared confidently, "how could it possibly clog up your machines?"

The mill had been grinding cinnamon, cornmeal, saffron, and cloves just before I had turned up with my amaranth. The result was that the first grain from our St. Paul's hillside had a spicy aroma. We made cookies and sweet bread with some of this first flour, and both were delicious.

In August of 1980, the CSCS project moved to a far better site in Bacolet. Because of the distance and the expensive and capricious transport system, Marko left us. But Alban Ettienne, a young Bacolet farmer, took over as farm manager.

Ettienne was short, and built like a gladiator. He invariably spoke softly, and his shy eyes seldom made four with mine. Sometimes, when he stood still, he would lean slightly to one side. He had injured his back when he was twenty-two.

"My mother cured my bad back," he told me one day. "She used hot papaya poultices and gave me a special herbal brew to drink." The "barefoot doctors" in Bacolet are famous for their skills as bonesetters and their ability to cure bad backs.

Ettienne loved the land; I once saw him holding up a handful of earth and offering it to the sun. The sun and the earth were the things he revered above all others. He did not know that I was looking at him as he carried out his primordial ritual. He opened his hand slowly, and the earth filtered through his strong fingers.

The land at Bacolet that we had chosen for our CSCS experiment had been cultivated by an Englishman long ago, the villagers told me. He had grown flowers commercially. Ettienne said, "My father told me that the old

Englishman used to use nutmeg shells as fertiliser. He would take carloads of them after the picking and shelling season, pound them up and scatter them over the land. But since he left, the bush take over."

The topography of the Bacolet area is typical of that of volcanic islands in the Caribbean where because of steep inclines, and sparse natural vegetation (due to the activities of local charcoal burners), erosion poses a serious problem.

In preparation for planting winged beans and amaranth on our Bacolet farm, stone terraces were constructed on the steeper slopes. This was backbreaking work that lasted from "day-clean to can't-see-time" day after day. We were able, from time to time, to borrow a wheelbarrow from a neighbouring farmer. Apart from this, no machines or mechanical aids were used. The heavy clay soil at Bacolet required the addition of approximately two and a half tons of organic matter added to it annually in order to keep it fertile and productive. But the plot of land that the CSCS was using had remained fallow for a long time. We therefore used about one quarter of this amount initially.

The preparation of the soil for the amaranth and other crops was done by four CSCS members and three young farmers who worked part time. In the course of working together we learnt a great deal from one another. This preparatory work was done four weeks before the rainy season started. We had to cut down the thick bush, remove stumps and rocks, build stone terraces and turn over the soil. In addition, we made two large compost heaps and into these we piled large quantities of seaweed, leaves, dried grass, manure, charcoal and ashes, fruit and vegetable skins. We added small quantities of sulphate of ammonia to hasten the breakdown of these organic wastes, then covered the heaps with coconut branches and turned them over every two weeks. We gathered seaweed whenever the sea disgorged it on nearby beaches, spread it out along the seashore and waited for the rains to wash out the salt.

At first, there were sporadic showers that ceased almost as soon as they started. Then the rains came. In the subdued daylight, the heavy rains looked like sheets of glass striking the earth and breaking into scattered shards. Because the sea was capricious about delivering seaweed onto the beaches, we began to investigate possibilities of growing it on bamboo poles as the Japanese do.

The amaranth crops at Bacolet were started in seedboxes, and after twenty days, transplanted in prepared plots. The seedbox was carefully prepared and layered with a foundation of pebbles and small stones at the bottom to ventilate the roots. After a number of trials, we followed the ancient Indian custom of dividing up the surface of the seed box into small squares. This was done by pouring liquid manure over the surface and allowing it to dry in the sun. Seeds were then placed in the middle of each square. Twenty days later, the plants were taken out, with their squares, and transplanted. After another twenty days had passed, the amaranth was mounded, fertilised, and mulched to retain moisture in the soil.

The idea of mulching was relatively new to Bacolet farmers. They believed in leaving the soil bare and exposed on their cultivated plots, although some of the older farmers confessed that they "used to do something liked that", but had discontinued the practice. Some of them later said that they had stopped mulching because agricultural field officers had advised them to do so.

The young Bacolet farmers attached to the CSCS project learned, through new techniques of terracing on different kinds of slopes, to avoid problems of water run-off and erosion. They learned techniques of preparing and using readily available organic fertilisers, and of mulching to nourish the soil and retain moisture in the dry season.

Farming practices varied greatly in Bacolet and surrounding areas, as did local habits of using fertiliser. There was almost a mystical belief in chemical fertilisers (perhaps because, apart from the blandishment of salesmen, they were seldom affordable). Poor farmers were reluctant to use organic fertilisers that were closer at hand and readily available.

Ettienne once said to me, in his soft voice, "I always hate it when I hear somebody say, 'jus throw the fertiliser down and anything will grow like magic. You have to care soil, year in, year out, coax it, nurse it, talk to it, press your ear against it and listen to it talk back."

A field of ripening amaranth grain is not unlike the exuberant and haunting profusion of wild desert flowers after the annual rains have come and gone. In the early morning or late afternoon light, the brilliant red, pink and golden amaranth seeds heads look like iridescent magic wands waving in the wind. There is nothing on earth more beautiful than a field of amaranth in full bloom. One understands why the Native Americans believed that this plant had magical qualities. In addition to being one of the most nutritious, amaranth is certainly the most beautiful of all grain plants when it is ripening.

When the first crop of amaranth grain was harvested, winnowed, and stored in cotton sacks placed inside plastic bags, the CSCS staff noticed that rodents, which commonly attacked cornmeal, rice and flour, did not touch this new grain. And, reports from contemporary Mexican Indian farmers claim that amaranth can, in fact, be stored for a period of up to ten years, once it is adequately dried.

Throughout the 108 days when the amaranth crop was maturing, the leaves of the plant were picked and eaten. Boiled, well seasoned and then fried – this is how the Mexican Indians cook it – amaranth leaves make a tasty and nutritious "spinach".

After milling the grain, the CSCS personnel gave a party to which some

Bacolet farmers and their wives were invited. For this occasion we baked amaranth bread, cake, cookies and sweets made from popped amaranth, honey and coconut. Drummers, acrobats and song-poets entertained us, reciting and chanting special praises of this new grain:

> Listen well, friends one and all
> and hear this story I have to tell
> Amaranth is a power-house of a grain
> if you eat the bread for a year and a day
> let me tell you the things you can do
> without strain:
> with a house on your back
> you can run up a hill
> you can uproot a mahogany with your bare hands
> and hold back the sea with your chest

A few days after this ceremony, I noticed young seedlings disappearing from our beds, and Ettienne explained, "The word's got out that amaranth makes you strong and potent." There was a wicked smile on his face when he added, "We better plant some special beds so that the neighbours can come and take new plants behind our backs."

We prepared the new beds, and after the rains, amaranth plants were springing up miraculously in numerous backyards. One of Ettienne's friends told me, and this was the highest accolade the new plant could have accorded to it: "Amaranth is better than the weed. Whenever I have a hard day or night ahead of me. I put that amaranth tiger in my tank, and I feel like a new man – ready, primed like a sling shot stretched all the way out. Man, that amaranth turns me into a missile!"

For Further Reading

Adams, Robert, "Early Civilizations, Subsistence and Environment", in *City Invincible*, Carl H. Kraeling and Robert M. Adams, eds. (Chicago: University of Chicago Press, 1960), pp. 265-295.

Carew, Jan, "Fulcrums of Change", *Race and Class*, 26, pp. 1-13.

Cole, John N, *Amaranth: From the Past for the Future* (Emmaus, Pa.: Rodale Press Inc., 1979).

Edwards, Anne Duncan, "Grain Amaranth: Characteristics and Culture", research paper for New Crops Department, Organic Gardening and Farming Research Center (Emmaus, Pa.: Rodale Press Inc.) April, 1980.

Jones, Volney H. "Review of "The Grain Amaranths: A Survey of Their History and Classification by Johnathan Sauer", in *American Antiquity*. XIX. 1, pp. 90-92.

Senft, Joseph P., Ph.D., "Protein Quality of Amaranth Grain", research paper for Nutrition Department, Organic Gardening and Farming Research Center, April, 1980.

Williams, Ann R., "Amaranth", in *Americas*, June-July, 1981, pp. 8-13.

V.

FROM LOTUS-EATING INTO THE JAWS OF A COUP

Section Five, "From Lotus-Eating into the Jaws of a Coup", includes chapters fourteen through sixteen. It takes Jan Carew from the European battle lines to Ghana. In 1965, weary of the constant vigilance required to maintain his "balance" between being an artist in an indifferent society and combating direct or incipient racism, Carew found the suggestion of moving to quiet and remote Ibiza quite attractive. He was also still reeling from the shock of Malcolm X's assassination. But the "lotus-eating" in this Balearic island idyll did not last. The offer to work with Kwame Nkrumah in Ghana was too good to resist.

Having led Ghana to victory as the first African nation to obtain its independence from colonial rule, Nkrumah had set an example of Pan-African partnership and collaboration that attracted Blacks from many parts of the world. Jan, as true for so many Pan-Africanists, had watched these developments with interest.

Taking over from the Black American writer and journalist Julian Mayfield, Jan Carew settled into a new life as the editor of the *African Review* and advisor to Kwame Nkrumah. However, much to his dismay, the discontents among the military elite brought his stay in Ghana to an abrupt end when Nkrumah was overthrown in a coup in February 1966.

This section also includes Jan Carew's 1966 essay, "The Coup in Ghana: Season of Violent Change", published shortly after the coup.

CHAPTER FOURTEEN

LOTUS-EATING IN IBIZA

It was 1965 and I was winding up my stay in England. I was fed up with the mounting racism in England and I wanted to find another place to live and write when I first met Carla. I had broken up with Sylvia and had a legal separation from her. My writing was not going well. So, the thought of Ibiza, an artists' hang-out, was very interesting.

I had met Carla Sheckell in London. She was a guitarist and singer who was performing in nightclubs. Her mother had a place in Ibiza, one of the Balearic islands off the Mediterranean coast of Spain, and Carla invited me to come visit her there. So, I sold my Wimbledon house, I sold the car and various items I didn't think I needed, and packed the remainder of my things to ship to Ibiza.

When I first got there, I rented an apartment and spent time moving back and forth from there to Carla's place. Eventually, I moved in with Carla. This was about a year before I went to Ghana to work for Nkrumah.

Carla's mother lived with an artist, a white South African. He was a very unusual white South African in that he had grown up in the slums of Johannesburg and was illiterate. A woman, who became his mistress, had taken him in and educated him. He became a famous artist. He eventually fell in love with Carla and married her, but this was after I had left Ibiza.

Ibiza was once a sacred island where the Greeks came to worship the Goddess Thanis. You can still find shrines on Ibiza where a rock face is marked with a crucifix on one side and the ancient totems to Thanis on the other. Ibiza was the southernmost of the Balearic islands with a coast of rocky indents washed by Homer's wine-dark sea. It is twelve hours from Barcelona by boat and to the south is Morocco.

At first, I lived in an apartment inside the old citadel which was surrounded by massive walls, and from the heights I could see the bay, the parched hills wearing their austere cloak of stunted pines, gashes of red earth, dotted with almond, fig and olive trees and the occasional date palm. There were also the low, Moorish type houses looking like clean white sheets spread out on the dusty earth.

The Ibicencos, the natives of the island, lived a life unto themselves. They are a people without a sense of greed. They have the Spanish sense of pride and honour and the graciousness of the Moors, and there must be few people on earth with their ingrained passion for honesty. When the Spanish Civil War broke out in 1936, my English neighbour left her keys with her friends next door and went to England for ten years. When she returned to Ibiza, she found everything exactly as she had left it, including money and jewellery in an unlocked chest of drawers.

There was a large colony of artists and writers in Ibiza. They, too, lived unto themselves. No one pried into the comings and goings or the day-to-day affairs of one another, and there was no telling who was rich or poor, famous or unknown. You met the same people half a dozen times a day. There was Steve (no one bothered about surnames), an American writer, waiting to hear from the publishers about his last book and drinking himself to death (a very inexpensive pastime in Ibiza since good wine was cheaper than Coca-Cola) in the meantime. There was a retired English solicitor, six-feet-seven inches tall, who ran an art gallery. Another was a blonde Swede who chartered his boat for tourists; an aging socialite who gave up after her sixth marriage and dealt somewhat dilatorily with real estate; and an ex-Chicago gunman who painted primitive pictures. The people who worked hardest, the serious artists and writers, were seen least often. The others, the poseurs and dilettantes, provided tourists with a predictable ration of local colour, walking about barefoot and generally making themselves look ostentatiously dishevelled, long-haired and unwashed. Since tourism came to Ibiza, the waterfront and the bays and coves were being ringed with new apartment buildings and opulent villas.

Although I was born in a country five degrees north of the equator, I found the summer's heat in Ibiza, particularly on windless days, intolerable. It was the dry burning heat of the Sahara, and living in an apartment in the citadel, there was nowhere to escape it. So, I was not unhappy moving into Carla's house. It was a finca, an old farmhouse, off a winding road a few miles from the city. I acquired a motorised bicycle to get back and forth. The finca was an ancient one with a main building that had a roof of earth on which grass grew and was regularly cropped by goats. It began with a cave-like excavation deep into a hillside and then it jutted out with a spread of spacious rooms from which there was a clear view of parched scrubland punctuated with cactus, thorny acacias, and stunted olives. The hillside sloped gently towards a precipitous drop that displayed the rocky faces of pink coves and stretches of seafront. The building did not have an indoor bathroom and toilet, so the large corrales building attached to the main building was transformed into a tiled Roman bath. A professional water diviner, throwing his magical sticks, found a spot close to the farmhouse where we dug a well, and I obtained a two and a half horsepower motor to pump fresh water to a cistern on the roof. I had the pipes painted black so that the sun would help us get hot water into the house. A septic tank was also created.

But after enduring the sizzling Sahara heat of my first summer in Ibiza,

I also rented a farmhouse in the Pyrenees close to the French border, a wild, beautiful setting where in the autumn a demented wind blows from the Sahara and you have to lean against it like a wrestler fighting against an immeasurably strong, invisible and cunning foe. These bouts of wind passed quickly and then for a long time afterwards, the skies were clear and the snow-peaks glittered like Toledo steel. At one stage, I shared this rental with the American actress, Ava Gardner, and another actress whose name I have now forgotten.

And yet I often asked myself, "What am I doing here, lotus-eating so far from my tropical hearth and home, the familiar voices, the land of Guiana that I love?" I often remembered the mountains at Garraway Stream, the distant Kanukus, and the sound of Potaro at Tumatumari. I would like to be buried at Garraway Stream, just beyond the suspension bridge. It is from this point that one can glimpse the unique panorama of the purple Kanuku mountains and the Guyanese heartland.

I have spent more than half of my life in foreign countries – in exile. I left home believing, as so many others had done before me, that the pastures were greener elsewhere, only to discover again and again that the harbours of home were where my spirit had struck immortal roots.

I have returned home five times since 1944 when I left for university. In 1949, just before I moved to Europe to study in Prague, I stayed for nine months, most of them in the interior. The visits, in fact, "*make hungry where most they satisfy,*" for a visit is not a return. It is like a bird alighting on a tree in which its nest is built, looking at the nest and then flying away once more.

I am not alone in my exile. The majority of West Indian writers whose works have been published since 1943 lived abroad. Edgar Mittelholzer, the pioneer and trailblazer of the modern West Indian novel, died tragically in Farnham in England, and he is buried in a quiet country churchyard. He was a zealot with a fierce, passionate integrity and a sense of dedication with which few men have been endowed. He had started out writing and painting in New Amsterdam in Guiana against odds so formidable that a host of others would have given up the struggle, surrendered to despair and disillusionment and immersed themselves in stagnant emotional pools of anonymity. He, however, fought back by disciplining his life to the point where you could have told the time of day by his comings and goings and his daily routine of work and relaxation. No one remembers anymore the long unenviable years of struggle, the multitude of rejection slips, the anguish he endured during those years in the wilderness before his first novel was accepted.

Andrew Salkey, George Lamming, Orlando Patterson, Sam Selvon, Wilson Harris, and CLR James lived in London; only Harris remains. Edward Braithwaite lived in Paris, Ronald Dathorne and Denis Williams in Nigeria, Neville Dawes in Ghana, and Austin Clarke in Canada. And as this list of expatriates grew longer year by year, the new generation of artists and writers came in their wake in the post-colonial era. Many have lived in England while others moved to Canada and the United States. There is no lonelier exile than that of the artist and writer who never left home, but these are divided into two categories: the ones who return after a lifetime of living abroad, and the ones who never left.

I used to frequent the cafes in the evening where we would drink wine into the wee hours. Carla's mother's partner, Douglas Portway, was a very good cook besides being a well-known artist, and he and I used to have cooking competitions. We were thinking of opening a restaurant. In the Spanish way of doing things, you always have dinner at 10 o'clock at night and would not get to bed until two or three in the morning. You would have preferred to awake later the next day, but we had to get up early to catch the fishermen when they first came in, though they would keep fish for you, if you were a good customer. I heard later that Douglas married Carla and she had two sons by him. When I left for Ghana, Carla was supposed to be coming down to join me, but it never came to pass.

Just as I was getting settled in my Spanish idyll, I had this offer from Nkrumah. I had flown back to London to take care of some business when I met Julian Mayfield at the Imperial Hotel on Russell Square in Bloomsbury. Julian was a black American who had been working in Ghana. He was an army veteran, a novelist, an actor and an ardent Pan-Africanist. He was in London as a member of President Nkrumah's delegation to the Common-wealth Prime Ministers' Conference. He had tracked me down, which was not difficult because I was very active politically. Julian invited me to breakfast at the Imperial, and when I entered the hotel dining room, he was already seated at a table, nattily dressed in a silk suit that disguised his bulging waistline. His natural friendliness, his affability and the way laughter came easily to him, made me feel that we had known each other for a long time. However, in the midst of his conviviality, I could detect an air of alertness. Although he was in London and far from the fray in Ghana, I could see that he still felt that he was under surveillance.

I knew that he hadn't invited me to breakfast to exchange pleasantries, and I was anxious to find out what he had in mind, but I also knew that I should wait until he was ready to tell me. In the meantime, while tucking into a breakfast of scrambled eggs, bacon and sausages, I talked about the differences and similarities between the Afro-British and the Afro-American experiences.

"So, Julian, why did you choose the Imperial hotel? I thought the *Times* had the main presidential party staying at the Dorchester."

He replied that staying at the Dorchester was an example of Cadillac pretensions manifesting themselves in a bicycle economy. The presidential entourage should have sought out more modest accommodation since it would have saved Ghana a whole lot of dough. Besides, this was his first visit to London, and over the years, he had read about Bloomsbury and the Bloomsbury set. So, for the couple of weeks he had to spend here, he figured that it would be fun to hang out in the legendary borough where so many literary luminaries used to congregate.

"Your timing couldn't have been better," I told him. "This hotel used to have a whites only policy until Learie Constantine, a black Trinidadian, took the owners to court for refusing to rent him a room because of his colour. Learie was one of the greatest all-round cricketers of all time, very popular with blacks and whites alike. He eventually became the first black Lord here. As a result of the court ruling in his favour, no hotel anywhere in the British Isles can bar a client because of his race, colour or creed."

Julian downed a gin and tonic and I could see he was ready to tell me why he'd invited me.

"Brother, I need a respite from the fray right now. Unless I go to some quiet place and recharge the batteries, I'll just burn out. When the President agreed to let me go, he made it conditional on my being able to persuade you to take my place in the publicity secretariat."

"I'm flattered," I said, mockingly, "but I, too, need a respite from the political fray. That's why I just leased a finca in Ibiza. I thought that a spell of lotus-eating would make my creative juices flow again."

Julian looked me in the eye and said affably, "Don't try to bull-shit me, my Guyanese comrade. Compared to me, you've got energy and motivation to spare. We know you were directly involved with the Mau Mau campaign and the protest over Lumumba's assassination. You've hardly been hiding under a rock."

He knew it was an offer I couldn't refuse, and handing me a contract he added, "You'll have to report for duty in a month's time."

It is hard to recapture the time and the independence movements in Africa – in Ghana, Nigeria, Kenya, Rhodesia. It was all interlocked. Long before I saw Julian, I had done a bit of ghost writing – I had no credit for it – on a film about independent Ghana. We had a political organisation in London. It had Caribbean and African activists, including some of the old-timers who had been in the Pan-African movement in London. There were students and artists, like Ronald Moody from Jamaica, who was a famous sculptor, and whose father had founded the League of Coloured Peoples in London in the early 1930s, which functioned like the NAACP in the US. The LCP came into prominence in the mid-1940s when it hired lawyers to defend a black American serviceman in a US military court in the UK. He had been charged with allegedly raping an English woman. John Carter, a lawyer from Guiana, defended the American and the case was dismissed.

When Julian found me, I was in a different kind of mood. I was living in Ibiza, but I was thinking of returning to some country in the Third World, my own Guiana included, and I was thinking of Jamaica. In any case, I was planning to move from London permanently.

I took Julian around London while we talked about the situation in Ghana. What it had in common with the position of other newly-independent African nations, like Kenya, was that the imperialists were holding the international levers of economic power over them and these countries didn't have the technical and administrative skills to control these levers. Nkrumah had to tread softly because the British had crushed the Mau Mau rebellion with great cruelty in Kenya. Nkrumah had been warned. Cheddi Jagan was known to have relations with Nkrumah, and Cheddi's Marxist party was the target of hostile action from Washington and London, and they were worried that Nkrumah's Ghana and Kenyatta's Kenya would follow in the same direction. The truth was that Guiana hadn't started having any kind of meaningful relationship with the USSR until after Ghana won its independence in 1957. British Guiana was not yet independent, but it was being held up as an example by the imperialists on what an independent country could do and what it could not do. Guiana, at that point, had the most left-wing government of the British colonies.

I never returned to the finca in Ibiza, and my lotus-eating dream became a dream deferred. Instead, I flew to Accra via Rome and arrived on a hot, steamy night. It was as though I had re-entered the womb of Africa from which slave traders had stolen my ancestors three centuries ago and dispersed them across the Amazonian world. The Ghana Airways DC10 had left London on a cold and blustery afternoon and over Italy I remember catching glimpses of snowcapped alpine mountain peaks. No matter how many times I flew, once the aircraft was aloft, I could not help thinking about what it would be like to crash in the coffin space of an aircraft. Death would come suddenly, and violently, and the death wouldn't be personalised because there would be strangers all around you. "What would my last thoughts be," I wondered. But the flight to Rome was uneventful. After a short stopover in Rome, we left for Accra.

Flying over the Saharan wastes was like to crossing an ocean of sand. Before I left London, a friend, a harbinger of bad news and depressing tales, told me that he had read about a pilot who had fallen asleep when crossing the Sahara and had flown a thousand miles off course. Fortunately, he came to his senses and corrected his error without further mishap. On this occasion, though, the plane crossed the sea of sand, soared over green belts of forests, rivers and plains and, at the end of the flight, parted heavy rain clouds and skimmed treetops before a flash of lightning and a downdraft brought it down in a hard landing. When the aircraft began taxiing smoothly towards the main terminal, the relieved passengers cheered.

As soon as an air hostess opened the exit door, the hot and oily African air rushed in and wrapped itself around me like a warm blanket. I took off my jacket and tie. So here I was on African soil for the first time. What struck me immediately was that the pilots and aircrew were African and so were the police, immigration, custom officers and all the other officials at the airport. An official from the Ministry of Information met me. Despite the heat and humidity, he was impeccably attired in a Harris Tweed jacket, cavalry twill trousers, an Oxford University tie and handmade suede shoes. As he ushered me through Customs and Immigration, I noticed that he was very quiet, and had impeccable manners. He was so dark, that when we walked into any of the areas of darkness around the airport, he became almost invisible.

"The minister sends his apologies," he said. "He would have been here to meet you in person, but an unexpected emergency arose and he had to travel out of town in order to tend to it."

While we were waiting for my bags, a group of women, all dressed in white, were singing hymns to welcome a white missionary. The cadences of their singing sounded exactly like those I had heard in country churches in Guiana.

Julian Mayfield had returned to Accra for a while as well and stayed on for a couple of months before leaving again. He went to work on a film with Jules Dassin called *Uptight*. It was to explore the growing activist movement in the African American community and Julian was to take the lead part.

I was tremendously busy in Ghana; it was a hectic period taking over from Julian as an advisor to the President's publicity secretariat and editing the *African Review*, a major Pan-African magazine. I also wrote some pieces for it, including a long piece I did on the town of Smethwick, an industrial town in central England. Here a racist Conservative politician had won a safe Labour seat with the slogan, "If you want a nigger for a neighbour, vote Labour", and a fascist party, the British National Party – which later merged with the National Front – had gained support and was provoking serious racial tension. Malcolm X had been profoundly concerned about these developments and had made a point of visiting Smethwick on the day after he had given his talk at the London School of Economics.

The magazine was extremely popular. I had David Du Bois, the stepson of W.E.B. Du Bois, who lived in Cairo, as one of our foreign correspondents. We had a brand new printing press that was donated by the East Germans and the quality of the publication was extremely high. It went first to Nkrumah's office as soon as a new issue came out, and then it was widely distributed throughout Africa. It was popular with peoples in the independent countries, and in those countries still under colonial rule where it was often prohibited.

There was a vast amount of intrigue in Ghana and there were all kinds of factions. There were difficulties with the Minister of Defence, Kofi Baako. He had studied in the USSR and was a hard-line communist. He had already tried to interfere with my relationship with Nkrumah. We had altercations about the CIA buying editions of *Iskra* (the Spark), a publication which was patterned after Lenin's paper in the USSR and published by the pro-Soviet faction in the government, and when my book *Moscow is Not My Mecca* came out, I believe that Janet Jagan tipped off their political friends in the international arena that I was probably a CIA agent, and there was a cabal in Nkrumah's bureaucracy directly opposed to me, because of the book, and wanted to get me out. Nkrumah, though, did not take the bait, stating that his government was non-aligned and that he was not taking sides. Still, the connection between Moscow, Ghana and British Guiana was interesting. Minister Baako then tried directly to shut down my office at the Publicity Secretariat. In this instance, Julian and I set a trap for Baako. We got an executive order from President Nkrumah signed on Friday evening. Minister Baako came with thugs on Monday morning to prevent me from opening the office. We appeared at the office and pretended to be surprised. I had, though, called General Barwa and told him that here was a man contravening an executive order. General Barwa was going to send men to arrest Baako, but we told him not to actually arrest him, but to frighten him a bit. So, we opened the office and Minister Baako did not try this again.

I originally stayed at the Star Hotel, but once Julian left, I made arrangements to move into his house in the Cantonments section in the suburbs of Accra. Julian was married to Ann Olivia Cordero, a brilliant Latina medical doctor who was in the process of reorganising Ghana's National Health Service. The two, although legally separated, were the doyens of the Afro-American community in Ghana, and everyone, somehow, still regarded them as a couple.

I was encouraged to take over the property, but I felt guilty about living in this sumptuous multi-room bungalow, which had been prefabricated with teakwood from Burma and was far larger than the bungalows I knew back in England. The Cantonments area, which was a fifteen minute drive from the airport, adjoined the outer walls of the presidential palace. Before independence, it housed senior British colonial civil servants like the first secretary, the attorney general, and the commissioner of police. After independence, a new African bourgeoisie had taken over and they were such exact copies of their former colonial masters that the local wits called them Afro-Saxons.

The stewards' quarters, which were located in a small cottage on the property, suited me better. Here, I had two large rooms and a kitchen and both the bungalow and the cottage had large accompanying gardens. I used the bungalow for official functions, but was content to stay in the smaller space.

CHAPTER FIFTEEN

NKRUMAH AND ME

Julian was quite a brilliant fellow, but he was not shy of the bottle. I was never drunk anywhere all my life, but I did smoke. I had seen my father drunk one night when I was about ten years and I took an oath that I would not drink. It was a most unusual thing in the Caribbean and Africa; many people drank in Ghana, with gin being the favourite. Nkrumah drank, but he was discrete about it; he was determined to set a good example for the people by drinking privately.

Nkrumah was very open to everybody and wanted to embrace the whole diaspora, and he realised that Ghana needed a variety of skills to help in its reconstruction. He did not just sit down and wait for people to come, but, instead, went out to get the best people. It is important to realise that Nkrumah couldn't get all the skilled people he needed in Ghana. Not being able to identify this challenge and find a remedy for it was one of greatest mistakes that many African leaders made at the time. They did not look beyond the continent for people of African descent with the right skills to help in the reconstruction of their respective countries. Idi Amin was another president who recruited African expatriates, but Amin was an unpleasant character, a tyrannical bully who spent the rest of his life in Saudi Arabia when he was eventually ousted.

On the other hand, there was a mutual respect between Nkrumah and the expatriate community. Nkrumah liked Julian and Julian helped him with some of his writings, particularly with Nkrumah's writing on "Conscientism". For those of us from the diaspora, it was a real development to have an African leader with a Pan-African vision who was part of the international Black struggle. Nkrumah had welcomed Malcolm X (Julian had been Malcolm's host during his visit there in 1964) who had come to Ghana because he acknowledged that the country was one of the most progressive Third World countries. As a world leader of Blacks, Malcolm was compelled to visit and study the trends in Ghana. Alice Windom, a black American from St. Louis, had also been in the country earlier (I used one of her pictures of Malcolm's 1964 visit on the cover of my book about Malcolm, *Ghosts in Our Blood: With Malcolm X in African, England, and the Caribbean*). There were many of us who believed Nkrumah had the resources to realise the African dream.

I had been in Ghana for almost a year when I experienced my first season of the harmattan. It was a hot and dusty season when sunlight was filtered through a yellow haze and parched winds from the Sahara reduced the humidity and made the nights cool. The sorcerers say that the harmattan winds can turn the sanest mind into a house of troubled dreams and infect an erstwhile calm and peaceful people with an impulse to rage against themselves.

It was immediately after the harmattan and at the height of the Vietnam War that President Nkrumah decided to set out on a peace mission to Moscow, Peking and Hanoi. I told the President that the idea of a peace mission was a good one, but the timing could not have been worse. At what turned out to be our last meeting, I suggested that he think seriously about postponing it.

Our meeting had taken place between six and seven in the evening – the worst possible time of day for a presidential advisor to be the bearer of bad news. The president's working day usually began at four a.m., and by early evening, when waves of exhaustion were threatening to overwhelm him, he preferred to hear the soothing words of sycophants rather than having to listen to hard truths. He sat facing me from behind his large desk, slightly hunched over like a bull about to charge.

"Tell me something, were you elected?" he asked belligerently.

"No, President. But—." He cut me short.

"Well, I was elected. I campaigned in every city, town, village and hamlet in this motherland of mine, and a majority of my people voted me into office. So what gives you the right to criticise me and my government?"

I didn't attempt to answer this patently unfair question.

After a long and awkward pause, I repeated what I had told him at our last meeting, only this time I stated with greater urgency that as a result of the worsening economic situation, there was widespread popular discontent, the full extent of which he seemed reluctant to acknowledge. With a new austerity budget about to be announced in Parliament, this discontent could easily erupt into a rebellion that his many local and overseas enemies could then exploit; that until a peoples' militia was created with branches in every part of the country, the possibility of a *coup d'etat* by the regular army would continue to be a very real one. The regular army, after all, had not been created to fight against external foes, but to quell anti-colonial uprisings and to suppress popular discontents that erupted into violence. I reminded him that the officer corps was, apart from a few cosmetic changes since Independence, a leftover from the colonial era – its CO was an English General with dual loyalties, one of which far outweighed the other. In conclusion, I pointed out – since the President liked historical references – that his regular army was no more reliable than ancient Rome's praetorian guard had been.

In cold and measured tones, his rejoinder was that if the officers rebelled against him, the ordinary soldiers would come to his defence. "Didn't you see the overwhelming support I enjoyed during the rally at Black Star Square a fortnight ago? Over half-a-million people turned out to celebrate the fifteenth anniversary of my release from prison."

"Soldiers are likely to continue to obey their officers right up to the point when a society is being torn to shreds, and only at that juncture are they likely to turn their guns on their officers and join a popular uprising," I said. "So, given the current situation in which the colonial institutions we inherited are still intact, and given the kind of training and indoctrination that the ordinary soldiers have had, they will shoot whomever their officers order them to shoot."

His parting shot before dismissing me was that Judas had given the same kind of advice to Jesus.

President Nkrumah left Accra on Monday the twenty-first of February 1966, mid morning. I was not invited to see him off.

It was true that a fortnight before his departure on his peace mission, the greatest demonstration ever held in Accra had taken place in Black Star Square. He was buoyed and intoxicated by the elation of eyes scattered like stars across black velvet faces. It was the anniversary of the date he was released from prison and was elected as the prime minister of Ghana. The day had been a public holiday and all classes of the people had come together to support him. That was why foreigners became interested in Nkrumah's movement. It seemed genuinely popular, a great mass party built from the grassroots to the top.

Nkrumah had a gift with ordinary people. Early on in his administration, he would go down to the market once a week to listen to the people, but after some assassination attempts, his East German security advisors prohibited him from doing this. There was an interesting story that one of the market sellers was angry with him over something and tried to pelt him with a *kenkey*. He dodged it and his security men rushed to arrest the thrower. But, Nkrumah stopped them, bent over and picked up the bit of cornmeal pastry wrapped in a corn husk, blew it off, unwrapped it and ate it.

Nkrumah also had the advantage of living abroad for some years before he went back to Ghana to lead in the independence struggle. He had lived in United States from about 1935 to 1945 and then went to England from 1945 to 1947, when he was summoned back home to head the UGCC, the United Gold Coast Convention party. The years in the US were rare; African students from the British colonies were not encouraged to travel to America to further their education. Nkrumah had gone to an America that had a nascent civil rights movement growing in its black communities. He had studied at an historically black college – Lincoln University in Pennsylvania – and had then gone on to the University of Pennsylvania, so he had been exposed to the culture of Blacks and Whites in America.

One of the movements that had a profound influence on Nkrumah was that led by Marcus Garvey, one of the first civil rights movements of black people on a worldwide scale. The Garveyite movement advocated that black people should become economically independent, own their own businesses, get education, and participate in international trade. That is why when Nkrumah came to power, he formed the Black Star Line in honour of Garvey's small shipping line of that name. The Black Star Line was the first international shipping company owned by a black country, part of Nkrumah's bid to establish economic independence.

Ghana was a relatively small country compared to other countries from the old empire. Nevertheless, its fight for independence was a significant one. Ghana was one of the richer colonies, with diverse natural resources, including cocoa and gold, though the country never benefited from them. Under colonial rule, the English kept the Ghanaians under strict control and treated them like serfs. Ghana was not allowed to use its resources for the benefit of the Ghanaian people. The excuse the British gave was that Ghana and many other colonies were not fit to govern themselves.

World War II gave impetus to the liberation movements against colonial rule. The handful of the native Ghanaians who worked for the British thought that all people should have the right to govern themselves, and Ghana should not be an exception to this. They demanded that the country should control its resources for the benefit of Ghanaians and the Gold Coast was the place of one of the foremost struggles against British rule.

Nkrumah and the rest of his colleagues were arrested and imprisoned for demanding independence. Even though he was imprisoned, he still had a large following among the ordinary people, making it virtually impossible for the British to govern. Nkrumah also exercised enormous influence on Ghanaians from different walks of life. The intellectuals, teachers, farmers and the labouring classes in Ghana all joined in the nationalist uprising against the colonial rule. People were calling for better working conditions, the right to form trade unions. They formed nationalist political parties. Nkrumah's Convention People's Party (the CPP) and the UGCC party were the first nationwide political parties to be established by the Ghanaians.

J. B. Danquah and others, like R.A. Awanoor-Williams and Edward Akufo-Addo, formed a middle-class party, the United Gold Coast Convention party (UGCC), but they were not interested in freeing the country from subservience to British rule. They wanted an alliance with the whites against their own people. They were fighting for colonial rule, while Nkrumah's CCP party fought against colonial rule. There were Ghanaians who were trying to sabotage Nkrumah's struggle for independence.

Nkrumah's fight against the UGCC connected to similar struggles in England, America and the Caribbean. Elements of the black movements in these countries were inspired by Garvey's ideas of Black self-reliance, shedding colonial rule and, in the case of the Rastafarians, with the goal of moving back to Africa. Initially, W.E.B. Du Bois had come out against the Garveyite movement, stating that its leadership was not well enough educated to lead the anti-colonial movement. But, as time went on, and he observed its growing popular appeal, Du Bois changed his political position and praised the Garveyite movement. So in the midst of the class struggle, there were also race struggles. Du Bois had not been alone; other elements of the middle class also thought that Garvey was uneducated and that the movement needed educated leaders.

The leadership of the UGCC didn't want radical changes in the governance of Ghana and were basically afraid of the power of the imperialists. So, Danquah and his party leadership thought they could have a cordial relationship with the British, with them on top and the mass of the people below them. They wanted everything to be nice and cosy between the different classes in Ghana. Nkrumah, on the other hand, wanted Ghana to enter the modern world as an independent and industrialised country. He gave the trade unions the right to organise for the benefit of the people.

All of this was taking place in the midst of the Cold War. If you made any radical statements, you were immediately denounced by the imperialists as a communist sympathiser. Even though Ghana did obtain its independence in 1957, it still relied on the imperialists for support, on the metropolitan businesses who controlled the key sectors of the economy. Nkrumah knew he still needed to train the society to have a skilled workforce and skilled administrators. But while Ghana still needed some British administrative support, the problem was that the imperialists still wanted to be in charge of the economic wealth of the country.

One of the ways Nkrumah tried to maintain the relationship with Britain whilst making change was keeping a special kind of relationship with the English monarchy. Queen Elizabeth was due to pay a state visit when she learned that she was pregnant and Nkrumah was the first international leader to be informed of this. As part of this special relationship, Nkrumah added extra rooms and kept the air conditioning running at Osu castle, the place where she would be staying. This was several months before she actually came for that visit.

But in the final analysis, guns can always talk more eloquently than a handful of Oxford-trained intellectuals and legislators. The guns were important to the imperialists, though they were also very skilful at controlling the hearts and minds of the colonised through their educational systems and through the churches. They ruled by guns over centuries and shot whatever resistance that came forward. They always had a warship ready. They also used locally-trained troops whose self-interest was connected to their relationship to the imperialists. The British built up the Ghana armed forces, trained the soldiers and gave them some access to arms. The rest of the people did not, of course, have access to arms.

So just a handful of soldiers could seize power and, one morning, the army walked in to the radio station and did just that. But if they possessed military power, they lacked skills in civil administration and put ignorant people in charge. It became like a game of musical chairs when a handful could seize power, and then another group would come along and take power from the first.

So, whilst the crowd had shouted its support for President Nkrumah two weeks before his journey, little did anyone know, except the army plotters, that within a month, the once-revered President, while staying as an honoured guest in a palace of former Chinese Emperors, would go to sleep in power and wake up in exile.

CHAPTER SIXTEEN

THE COUP

On the day of the coup, I was spending the night at The Star Hotel and my secretary, Krumah, had awakened me after midnight and told me that he thought the army was on manoeuvres at Burma Camp. That was a magnificent piece of understatement because, when I looked out of the window, I could see mortar shells exploding in the distance and lighting up the sky like an aborted dawn. So I dressed quickly and resolved to go to Anna Olivia's cottage.

Dr. Anna Olivia Cordero-Mayfield was employed in the Ghanaian public health service. She had graduated from Columbia University in the US and had been a student of the leading specialist in that field. Nkrumah had given her the task of reforming Ghana's public health service. Along with Pauline Clarke, she was one of the most organised women in the Nkrumah administration. Pauline Clarke was a civil servant whom Nkrumah trusted implicitly. Whenever there was an important delegation sent abroad, Pauline would accompany them, seeing to it that the delegates were chosen well and that once they arrived, they performed their tasks assiduously.

When I opened the door of my room, there was a lot of activity going on in the hotel. Before leaving, I telephoned Anna Olivia and she told me that the military was making a bid to overthrow the government of Nkrumah. With her gift for organisation, she said that she was planning to call for a general strike which might bar the army from entering the city and that we should set up a committee to assist those whose lives might be in danger.

I walked over to Anna Olivia's house. There were already a number of people there. It hadn't occurred to the conspirators to cut the telephone lines, so we were able to talk freely to friends and supporters. This allowed us a chance to solicit aid for Geoffrey Bing and his wife, Teddie. Geoffrey was the Attorney General who had prosecuted the men who had threatened Nkrumah's life in a previous failed assassination attempt.

Geoffrey's house was also in the Cantonments area and I volunteered to walk across to this mansion of his. When I got there, there was an Askari guard dressed in full uniform at the gate and he went and knocked on the door for me. Teddy, Geoffrey's wife, invited me in and told me that Geoffrey had been drinking heavily the night before and that it would take some doing to wake him up. I went upstairs to his room, helped him to get up and held him under the shower. He kept saying "Close the window! I don't want to catch a cold." Another magnificent piece of understatement, given that I was there because I feared for his life.

Teddy fixed some coffee and then we all walked from Geoffrey's house to Anna Olivia's. In the meantime, they had called the Cuban ambassador and asked for political asylum for Geoffrey. The ambassador said he could only grant it with permission from his superiors in Cuba. Geoffrey then told them to call the Pakistan high commissioner, who was a classmate of his from Oxford and politically conservative. The high commissioner said, "Of course I can offer Geoffrey asylum, if you bring him over." The old school ties of those who attended Oxford and Cambridge were stronger than some diplomatic and nationalist ties. One of the security guards volunteered to guide us through the back streets of Accra, if one of us drove.

I had just gotten a Humber Super Snipe off a dealer, although I had requested a jeep since I anticipated visiting different provinces of the country. The kind of a car that you drove as a government official was a status symbol and I had thought that a jeep was less ostentatious than the limousines that the higher-ups sported around the country. Julian had warned me that I should be careful to choose the right issues, to make sure that I did not waste time and energy on fighting small battles. So, when I talked to the minister about the kind of car I wanted to drive, he had said, "Why do you want to change our way of life?" So, I ended up with a Humber Super Snipe, and having it probably saved my life.

I had volunteered to drive Geoffrey and Teddy to the Pakistan High Commission. We set out at about five in the morning. By the time we had reached the outskirts of Accra, sunrise was lightening the skies and people were gathered in groups.

The *coup d'etat* was staged in the midst of an all-pervasive season of discontent and even the conspirators themselves were amazed at the popular support for their actions. Yet, it was not so much support for them, as frustration with a leader whom they expected would lead them to the promised land. Their rage was also directed at the sycophants and the fat, sleek men and women who flaunted their wealth before the public with unbelievable bad taste, and a disdain for the poor.

When I turned into a wide street, soldiers were putting up a road block. I decided the best thing to do and did it. There was a gap between two barriers they were erecting, and I drove right through it and then immediately turned right. The soldiers were on foot and for some reason, they did not open fire on us. We reached the Pakistan High Commission, we had breakfast, said goodbye to Geoffrey and raced back to Anna Olivia's house.

Geoffrey told me later that the Pakistan high commissioner took him to the Australian High Commission because Pakistan did not have diplomatic relations with Britain at the time, having broken relations over Britain's position on the illegal white Rhodesian declaration of independence, and he didn't want to embarrass his hosts. So later that day, the Pakistan High Commissioner, Geoffrey and his wife set out for the Australian High Commission. By this time, there were huge crowds gathered all over the city. Geoffrey told me that when they were moving along a one-way street towards the Australian High Commission, the crowds were making it difficult to navigate their way. When they were about a hundred yards from their destination, one of the demonstrators recognised Geoffrey and called out,

"Uncle Geoffrey, I got the job you recommended me for!"

With this call of solidarity, the crowd made space, and the car, with its diplomatic license plate and Geoffrey, made it safely to the Australian High Commission. Geoffrey intended to lie low there for a while and then make his way back to England. But that was not to be.

While Geoffrey was a guest at the Australian High Commission, a journalist spotted him on his way from the toilet and not wanting to embarrass his hosts, Geoffrey decided to give himself up. He was later imprisoned by the leaders of the coup.

After I'd taken Geoffrey Bing to the Pakistan High Commission, I took the car to a garage and locked it up. In Ghana, and I think in Africa at large, it is always easy for people to recognise your car if it is a big one (especially with diplomatic number plates!) so there would be a danger of being identified, and thus a risk to my safety. Later, I began to move around with Preston King, a black American who was a professor of Political Science at the University of Legon, in his more discreet Volkswagen. We went to Nkrumah's palace on the outskirts of town. The city centre was flooded with soldiers and Nkrumah's wife and children were at his palace, where the military had given orders to maintain their safety. Preston, who was studying the African military, was curious to see how the coup makers were going to deal with the absent president's abode. Despite the danger of his curiosity, I decided to accompany him. Driving out of Accra, Preston and I witnessed fighting and horrific scenes at different junctions. I then returned to Anna Olivia's house to see who still needed help. Though the military had seized the radio station, the phone lines were still working, which was a sign of how badly organised the coup was, and Anna Olivia was busy seeking asylum for other friends and colleagues.

After working with Anna Olivia in the Cantonments area where all the high officials were stationed, I returned to the Star Hotel that evening where I met Anthony Abrahams, a Jamaican, who was a BBC correspondent working for *Panorama*. Abrahams had been in Ghana just under a month before the coup, covering the opening of the Akosombo Hydro Electric Project, known as the Akosombo Dam. Abrahams was returning to England the next day and I gave him a coded message and signed it "Black Midas". I wanted him to take it to Andrew Salkey – I knew Salkey would know what I meant. At the hotel, I met William Gardner Smith, whom Nkrumah had hired to start Ghana's first school of journalism. Bill was a black American who had given up his job on the editorial board of Agence France-Presse to take up this challenging appointment. He told me he had been arrested and was under deportation orders. We discussed the day's events before retiring to a much welcome, if brief, sleep.

Three days after the Army coup and the establishment of a National Liberation Council (NLC), I was arrested. My arrest, however, was not lacking in a certain bizarre humour, and decades later I still remember it as though it had taken place yesterday. In retrospect, it all seems as unreal as when it was actually happening. The arrest was sprung on me while I was having a farewell luncheon at the Star Hotel with Bill Smith and Janet Ocran. Bill, who was always an affable and witty companion and a peerless raconteur, was savouring a Cuban cigar and behind a veil of blue smoke was describing how the day after the coup, soldiers had burst into his Pan-African School of Journalism and arrested him and all of the other expatriate members of his staff. After being interrogated by members of the NLC, he was ordered to leave the country within three days.

"I bet Afrifa and Harley delighted in acting like prosecutors at a treason trial when they were interrogating you," I said, and Bill confirmed that they certainly had.

"You're damned right! They were preening themselves in their brand new Brigadier General's uniforms – the two bastards promoted themselves – and they enjoyed pelting inane questions at me. But decked out in his fancy uniform, Afrifa still managed to look like a fop admiring himself in a mirror, and Harlley still looked every inch the policeman that he was."

"Blasted traitors!" I muttered.

"I must say, though, that that son-of-a-bitch Afrifa wears his uniform the way a black mamba wears its skin; the fit is perfect," Bill acknowledged.

"They say he shot General Barwa at point blank range when he refused to join the junta plotting the President's overthrow," I said.

"Afrifa played Iago to Barwa's Othello. The man's a blasted snake," was Bill's cynical response. "But mark my words, with his gift for intrigue and with ambition burning like a bonfire in his belly, in no time he'll outfox the others and take over as president. God help Ghana!" Then he added, "Nkrumah's big dream of a united and powerful Africa has, almost overnight, become a dream deferred while neo-colonists like Afrifa and Harlley scramble and scuffle for crumbs from the imperialist table."

"But Nkrumah's dream will resurrect itself," I declared passionately, "and new generations will take up the fallen standards."

"Not in our time," Bill said gloomily, "Not in our time."

Bill had a broad and pleasant brown face that was dented like a walnut, and his close-cut curly black hair was prematurely sprinkled with white spots that looked like soapsuds. Behind a smiling face and debonair manner was a shrewd and brilliant mind and a serious commitment to the cause of black liberation. He had fought with an all-black unit during World War II, and was stationed in Germany after the war. Like other black servicemen, Bill had great expectations that the end of the war against Hitler would usher in a new era of civil rights for black Americans, and an end to Jim Crow in the southern states. But the racism that he and other black soldiers faced daily from white American Officers and enlisted men in occupied Germany made it clear that the US brand of racial segregation was still alive and well.

What incited violence against Blacks more than anything else was the way in which some German women showed a marked preference for black soldiers. Bill's experiences with hostile white GIs when he appeared in public with a German woman, and the day-to-day nagging discrimination inflicted on him by white officers, had inspired him to write *The Last of the Conquerors*, a novel that was a searing indictment of the way in which apartheid was imposed upon Blacks at all levels in the military. This novel, which was translated into German and French, won him more critical acclaim in France and Germany than it did in the US, and after many visits to Paris, where he met and befriended several black expatriate artists and writers, he decided to settle there. Working as a journalist for Agence France-Presse, he became part of a distinguished black American community that included Richard Wright, Chester Himes, Ollie Harrington and James Baldwin.

Janet Ocran was an executive secretary in the Publicity Secretariat and a close friend. She was in her late twenties, and the African sun had been kinder to her than it had been to many whites, because it had turned her complexion a golden brown and there were barely discernible freckles on her cheeks and forehead. She had the rare beauty of a bluebell that had awakened to greet the morning, a shining intelligence and a lively sense of humour. Although her family had emigrated to Canada when she was a child, a Welsh accent still flavoured her speech. She was legally separated from a husband who was a high-ranking officer in the Ghanaian army. They had met in Canada when they were university students. During the six years of their marriage, she had two daughters by him. Three of those six years had been spent in Ghana, but she had found it intolerable being relegated to the lowly role of a junior wife in a household in which male rule was absolute. She also had a reckless courage that both Bill and I admired, but from time to time, felt constrained to urge her to be cautious. She had come to lunch with us to discuss ways of slipping out of the country with her two daughters.

"My beloved ex-husband has seized our passports and closed my account at the bank, but little did he know that he was making it easier for me and my daughters to escape. The Canadians, bless them, have issued me with special travel documents," she declared airily.

"But have they given you airline tickets?" Bill asked.

"You're playing with dangerous foes, Janet. Ocran wields a lot of power."

Janet lowered her voice and, leaning forward, confided, "Teddy Bing is taking me to the Pan-Am office later on today. We have an appointment with the Manager. Teddy, with her grand manner, and her upper-class English accent, plans to plead with him to issue a ticket to Canada for my girls and me."

"Sounds pretty risky to me," Bill said, "but we could all chip in with some funds, and a safer escape route would be one in which you travelled in a mammy wagon with a hefty bribe for the border guards between Togo and Nigeria. Look here's the address of a reliable bus driver and a contact in Nigeria. The bus driver is the father of one of my students and he owes me. Once you arrive in Nigeria, my contact there will arrange a passage to London for you and the girls."

Janet protested derisively, "Really, Bill! A white woman travelling to the border with two brown children? I might as well go to that border ringing alarm bells. Anyhow, Teddy and I have rehearsed my escape scenario pretty thoroughly. She says that when we're in the Pan-Am manager's office and she gives me a signal, I must burst into a flood of tears. Teddy swears that the sight of a white woman weeping bitter tears will make the Pan-Am manager feel magnanimous."

"Hold on to it, just in case that Teddy project doesn't work. And I'll send word to my Nigeria contacts."

Bill sat back to enjoy his Cuban cigar and a liqueur, and with sardonic good humour described how he was in the midst of a rousing address to the assembled student body at the School of Journalism, when the soldiers burst into the auditorium and arrested him.

"I'm due to fly to Rome tomorrow, and once I arrive there, I'll travel by train to Paris. Watching the landscapes rush past me will give me time to appreciate that my African saga has come to a sudden and violent end and I'm back in Europe again."

He spoke with an amused lilt in his voice. But I could also detect an underlying sadness. Nkrumah had opened the door wide and invited us to come home to Africa, and this coup was booting us out and slamming the door shut behind us.

"Do you think that you'll ever return to America, not just to visit but to live?" I asked him.

He replied, "That ceased to be an option years ago. It's a strange question coming from you of all people, because you and I both know in our bones that we can't go home again." There was a finality in this statement that didn't brook any further questions or comment. After a pause, Bill said, "I doubt whether they're going to arrest you, Jan. One of my contacts, and a reliable one, told me that the soldiers searched your quarters pretty thoroughly and didn't find a damned thing that could incriminate you –"

The words had barely left his mouth when a major and four soldiers armed with Czech submachine guns came to our table, surrounded me, and asked if I was Jan Carew.

"Yes, I'm Jan Carew," I acknowledged.

"I'm arresting you in the name of the National Liberation Council. Would you please come with me?" Before standing up, I tried to pass three tightly folded hundred-dollar bills to Janet. But the polite, soft-spoken, immaculately turned out major saw me and ordered her to hand the money to him.

I thought that I had detected a sympathetic gleam in the major's eye when he announced that he was arresting me in the name of the NLC, so moving closer to him, I said quietly, "Major, I really need that money, but since my bargaining position is rather weak I'd like to suggest that we split it in half, you take a hundred and forty-five and give me the balance." To my surprise, the Major agreed.

I said goodbye to Bill and Janet, and when we embraced Bill whispered, "I'll spread the news of your arrest as soon as I land in Rome."

With the hotel's customers and staff gawking at my dramatic arrest, I was escorted to a waiting car, and with an armed guard beside me, I was whisked away to the Police Headquarters, a spanking new building in the centre of Accra, and taken to one of the upper floors where dozens of high-ranking supporters of the deposed president were lying face down on the floor, stripped to the waist and barefooted. They were as close together as logs in a woodshed. A sergeant, with swollen lips, large white teeth and smelling like a distillery, grabbed hold of me and pushed me so violently, I almost fell, as he ordered with a cruel grin, "You go tek off yuh shirt and shoes, Sah, and lie face down like the others – and mek it smart!"

In the meantime, drunken soldiers were amusing themselves by walking across the naked backs of the prisoners with pigskin boots that had iron cleats, and some of the backs were bleeding where they had been pricked with bayonets after they were arrested.

The major came out of the office just then and I called out, "Major, may I have a word with you?"

He hesitated for a moment, but when the sergeant and two private soldiers moved to seize me, he barked an order to them and they released me and backed away.

Pointing to the bodies on the floor I said, "My ancestors left Africa like that, but this time, I intend to leave standing up. If you want me to lie in that slave position you'll have to shoot me."

In his clipped military accent and with a malicious smile, he taunted me, "That might be a bit messy." Then he berated me, "I forgot that you people are descended from slaves, and yet you put on all kinds of airs. Who do you think you are? A week ago you were lording it over us, and now we're in charge."

I let his anger rise and subside, and said nothing. Then, striking his leg with his swagger stick absent-mindedly, he said brusquely, "Very well, I'll escort you to the general's office directly."

A white man was sitting on one of the two chairs in the room adjoining the general's office, and he looked as if he had stepped out of the pages of Conrad's *Heart of Darkness*. He was wearing a white gabardine suit and there was a pith helmet in his lap. His hair was white as tiger orchids and there was a hunted look in the blue eyes that swam behind the thick lenses of his spectacles. I recognised him at once. He was a Nazi war criminal who was being extradited to the Federal Republic of Germany. I had read about him in the papers. His name was Schumann, and he was a medical doctor who had carried out experiments with prisoners of war and gypsies in Nazi Germany.

Meanwhile, Anthony Abrahams had delivered my message to Andrew Salkey in London, and the *Evening Standard* ran a piece saying I had been arrested. I learned later that there had been demonstrations in Guiana demanding my release. In my message to Salkey, I'd asked him to lobby some contacts on my behalf, if he didn't hear soon of my well being. Salkey contacted Lord Campbell, who was the head of Booker Brothers, McConnell & Company, the transatlantic firm that had extensive holdings in Guiana, and Campbell, in turn, had gotten in touch with the Minister of Foreign Affairs in London. The news of my arrest had also reached my mother in Barbados as she was stepping off a plane.

Confronted by reporters, she tersely told them, "He's been in trouble before, and he'll get out of this, too." Later, I was given a telegram that my mother had sent me in care of Anna Olivia in which she had said, "Love and prayers from us all."

While this was happening, I was taken, under escort, to my office in the Publicity Secretariat to locate some research being done by St. Clare Drake, the sociologist. He had asked me to organise a research project on the migration of people from inland to the coast, to the new deep-water port that Nkrumah had commissioned in Tema. I found the research, but I wasn't allowed to take it with me. The soldiers then wanted to arrest my secretary, Krumah, but I managed to convince them that Krumah did not deserve to be arrested.

The son of the Chief Secretary of the National Liberation Council had done some work for me, and he asked his father to intervene on my behalf with Afrifa. The new Chief Secretary told Afrifa that the World Press had gotten news of my arrest and it was being noised about in various countries and that this would reflect negatively on Ghana. So, I was deported within four days. My contract with the Ghanaian Publicity Secretariat stipulated that the Secretariat would cover my ticket for "home leave", so they bought me a one-way ticket to London via Rome.

In my final hours in Ghana, I realised I had to help Janet Ocran, whose husband and his father were in on the coup. So Teddy Bing and I took Janet and her two daughters to the Pan-American Airways office and Teddy took blankets and made coats out of them so that the girls would have something warm for the Canadian winter. As planned, Teddy told Janet to cry upon her signal, a trick that worked, and the Ocrans got their tickets without paying for them! Several hours later, we were all in the sky, leaving Accra and Ghana in the throes of a violent, British and American-backed coup that stole several hundred lives and devastated Nkrumah's government.

I returned to England and then went back to Guiana for a while. As a British subject, London is where they deported me. Ras Makonnen, one of Nkrumah's advisors who was also Guyanese, was not so lucky. He was held in prison for a year. I met him in Kenya some years later.

There was so much more to be done. The East Germans had just contributed a brand new printing press to the *African Review* and the Ministry of Finance had set aside enough money to make two feature films to be written by Kofi Awoonor, but the coup cut my Ghanaian mandate short. Nkrumah returned to Africa, but could not return to Ghana. President Sekou Toure of neighbouring Guinea offered him asylum and welcomed him to serve as "Co-president". Nkrumah died in 1972, never returning to Ghana.

"The Coup in Ghana: Season of Violent Change"

New World Fortnightly, no. 40, May 13, 1966 (Georgetown)

President Nkrumah left Accra in the mid-morning of Monday the twenty-first of February [1966] on his peace mission to Peking and Hanoi. It was nearing the end of the season of the harmattan on the dry and dusty Accra plains when hot, parched winds from the Sahara bring a haze of dust and lowering clouds; filtering the sunlight and tinting it with yellow; reducing the humidity, making the nights cool; and bringing with it, the sorcerers say, a secret madness, a plague of devils in the brain inspiring an erstwhile calm and peaceful people with an impulse to rage against themselves. The whole land, from the Guinea Coast to the borders of Nigeria, was waiting for the rains. Rainmakers mumbled their ancient orisons, and the meteorological officers forecast further dry days with a monotony that the impatient farmers thought bordered on malice.

A fortnight before the President's departure, the greatest demonstration ever held had taken place in Black Star Square to commemorate the day of his release from prison in 1951. African crowds are a sea of dark faces, bright limbs, eyes like flecks of sea foam and colours like the vivid wild flowers that sprout in varied profusion after the rains; but most of all, African crowds are instinct with a pulsating life force as though every heart was beating to the secret rhythms of drums. And, when the crowd shouted in Black Star Square that day, the chorus of voices drowned the nearby sound of surf and the roll of drums, and it was as though the noise was coming out of the very womb of Africa. And yet within a month, Kwame Nkrumah, staying as a guest amidst the shining rooftops of the Palace of the Rising Sun, was to go to sleep in power and wake up in exile.

The North Vietnamese Mission in Accra had circulated a statement giving their version of the intended presidential visit. The gist of this statement was that Dr. Nkrumah, in going to Hanoi, was taking up an invitation that had been issued a year earlier by President Ho Chi Minh; that whilst looking forward to a visit by a distinguished African leader to their beleaguered capital, there should be no misunderstandings about the purpose of the visit or the issues that President Ho would be willing to discuss; that if Dr. Nkrumah wanted to discuss peace terms, it would have been more appropriate for him to have visited Washington since no Vietnamese troops were occupying any part of the territory of the United States of America. But, Dr. Nkrumah did see himself in the role of a peacemaker, and in this he was encouraged by the Russians. As a neutralist president of an African State, Dr. Nkrumah could act as a disinterested, and hence very effective intermediary between the Russians and the Chinese and the members of the Communist Bloc who were directly involved, and Washington. The Russian Ambassador to Accra had told Dr. Nkrumah, on the eve of his departure, that a big reception was being prepared for him in Moscow on his way back from Hanoi.

In the decade since independence, Nkrumah had transformed Accra from a sleepy, provincial, colonial capital into an important international centre. Within the confines of this sprawling, amorphous city, with wide unkempt green spaces separating one section from another, the whole world met; and because of this, even the political gossip had a special flavour. It was well known in the market places that the former American Ambassador, who was the dean of the diplomatic Corps in Accra, could not leave because next in line to him was the Chinese Ambassador, and Sino-American relations being what they are, it had become crucial that a successor who was more sympathetic to the United States and her Western Allies should take over as dean of the diplomatic corps.

Diplomats in Accra, and they came from the four corners of the earth, tended to be judged either by their popularity with the ladies (and in this respect the situation was analogous to that of Europe in the 17th and 18th centuries) or by the abundance and quality of food they offered at their receptions. On the first score, the Chinese, with their revolutionary zeal and their strict moral codes, were regarded at first with suspicion and sheer disbelief, but later, they were accorded a reluctant respect. On the second count, they fared much better since they had the finest chefs in Accra. In addition there was their natural graciousness, their refined good manners, and their surpassing skill at self-effacement, which won them many friends and supporters. The Russians were neither popular or unpopular. They kept very much to themselves.

One Russian cultural attache, meeting a militant group of Afro-Americans for the first time, had declared that he thought *Uncle Tom's Cabin* a great work of literature. The misunderstanding generated by this innocuous statement instantly destroyed all chances of friendly Soviet-Afro-American cultural relations developing. Later it came to light that the Russian translation of Beecher's *Uncle Tom's Cabin* had most probably derived from the French translation by George Sand who had purged the novel of its sentimentality and so altered the message that it emerged as a model of socialist realism.

The French and Cuban ambassadors were both extremely popular. The former, an urbane greying bachelor, was constantly mentioned in dispatches in the marketplace, whilst the latter, a dashing young revolutionary, was very highly thought of in feminine circles. He got engaged to an African beauty and it became known all over town that a high ranking West German diplomat had expressed his disapproval publicly, saying that he thought the Cuban was taking things too far.

Nkrumạh had been much criticised in the Western press for the sixty-four diplomatic missions he had established all over the world. But this was all part of his strategy to push Ghana into the 20th century. He wanted to expose his people to social, political and cultural crosscurrents from Europe, Asia, Latin America, the rest of Africa, the Caribbean and North America, and he has succeeded in doing this to an astonishing degree. For, whatever happens, Ghana is now wide awake. Nkrumah has opened a Pandora's box of rising expectations to plague his successors and perhaps, to herald his return.

Four days before the Ghana Airways VC10 climbed swiftly into the haze above the Accra plains with President Nkrumah and his party aboard, units of the Ghanaian Army in just under battalion strength began a series of forced marches from Tamale, four hundred miles to the north. Before setting out, the soldiers had been told that they were going on manoeuvres; that they should advance south, towards Accra, with the greatest secrecy, bivouacking far away from the major towns and villages in the daytime and only using the main roads in the early hours of the morning.

The plot to overthrow the Kwame Nkrumah regime had originated in the stewards' enclosure of the Accra Turf Club. The Turf Club was a relic from the colonial era. It was one of those institutions which one would hardly have expected to survive after independence, It was peculiarly British and, in its heyday, it was run by British proconsuls with all the exclusiveness of a tribal secret society. But a decade after independence the Turf Club still survived, and it had become an important social centre, a forum, a bazaar, a focal point for intrigue, political gossip, and illegal trade and currency transactions. Members of Parliament, businessmen and high-ranking officials in the party, the trade unions, and the various public service commissions made their presence conspicuous at the races, and their sizeable bets were a matter of public knowledge. They were in most cases, either themselves or in their wives' names, in possession of large sums of money which they could not have accounted for in a court of law, and of late, senior officials had been charged with corruption with alarming frequency. Their presence at the Turf Club enabled them to claim that they had won their fortunes gambling at the races. The fight against corruption was being spearheaded by left-wing puritans within the Convention People's Party and by a few of the President's closest advisers. Arrayed against these puritans were the old guard, laissez-faire politicians, men who had come to regard certain perks and cutbacks as their due, after the hardships and uncertainties they had endured, fighting for independence. Nkrumah had always played one faction against the other, while he sat in an uneasy equipoise like an African King Lear presiding over the squabbles of his daughters.

After the Adamafio Trial (Adamafio was the one-time heir apparent who had been imprisoned after a questionable trial because he had been implicated in an attempt on the President's life), the left had almost been extinguished as a political force. But they had learnt their lesson and were making a comeback, working with renewed zeal and devotion and making themselves indispensable. The President, however, was constantly restrained from crushing his right wing, by whispers in the corridors of power, cautioning him that the reactionaries, while suffering from a disease that only bribes could cure, were never as power-hungry as the progressives; and he heeded these whispers and took them seriously.

The racecourse society had become more eclectic since the colonial era. Except for the elite in the stewards' enclosure, people of all races, colours and creeds mingled freely and money had become the sole criterion of status. An illiterate Northern trader, with thousands of cedis in his ornate leather purse, could rub shoulders with cabinet ministers, spies (local and foreign), and businessmen and diplomats from all over the world. With the traditional politeness of the Ghanaian deriving from an ancient tribal culture, the trader would reel off socialist slogans to a politician and, a moment later, with equal aplomb, defend free enterprise to a businessman, and deplore the socialistic restraints which were being imposed upon the nation's economy.

The original conspirators who plotted the overthrow of the Kwame Nkrumah regime were (and this was by their own public admission after the coup) J. K. W. Harlley, Commissioner of Police, Major A. K. Afrifa, Colonel E. K. Kotoka and Colonel A. K. Ocran. They are now all members of the National Liberation Council, the ruling junta which replaced the Nkrumah Government. Mr. Harlley is Deputy Chairman of the NLC.

Their foreign backers (and this was hot gossip in the markets and the prisons, two very reliable sources of inside political information), were the West Germans, who took on the job because agents of the CIA and the British MI6 were too well known in Ghana. Besides, the stink of the Nazi regime had never really reached modern Africa. A Nazi doctor of medicine, wanted for war crimes in Germany, had been practising for years in Ghana, and one of Hitler's former pilots, Hannah Reich, was placed in charge of Ghana's only glider school. The toppling of the Nkrumah regime, therefore, represented the first major triumph of the German Secret Service outside Europe since the end of World War II.

The CIA did not distinguish itself for its subtlety in Ghana. It was a popular joke in Accra that this august Secret Service organisation was the leading customer for the Marxist publications put out by the President's publicity secretariat, and particularly *The Spark*, a weekly paper published in both English and French. Sometimes, as *The Spark* was being distributed to the newsstands, a CIA car would cruise behind the delivery truck, buying up the entire issue before anyone could read it. But as the wits in Accra pointed out, the public would have been more effectively protected by the dullness of the journal, and that if the CIA stopped buying it, it would have been an acute problem to find storage space for unsold copies.

Mr. Harlley and Major Afrifa were the two most important organisers of the coup. The two men were quite different in background, experience and outlook. The former belonged to Ghana's *grande bourgeoisie* whilst the latter came from the lower middle class. Harlley was middle-aged, while Afrifa was only twenty-eight.

Harley had started out as a policeman in the Colonial Service, whilst Afrifa was a member of the new ruling elite created by Nkrumah. Harlley had spent most of his working life in Ghana, first under British colonial rulers, and then with the Nkrumah regime, which had endowed him with a high survival potential, an indispensable asset in the uneasy political arena of independent Ghana. Two years ago he had been implicated in a smuggler's diary, but the Government had taken no steps to indict him, so that the charges were neither substantiated nor disproved. It is rumoured that he was once heard to say that since Ghana was in a state of revolution, then survival was the first law of the revolution.

Afrifa, an anonymous senior officer before the coup, proved from the beginning that he had a sure instinct for intrigue and conspiracy, qualities for which the Ashantis are noted (Afrifa is an Ashanti and in this respect a typical one) from time, immemorial. He did most of the inside work within the Army, persuading, cajoling, bribing, threatening reluctant officers and reassuring timid ones that the coup had powerful backers.

Generals Kotoko and Ocran were professional soldiers with a disdain for politics and politicians. They hesitated at first to commit themselves, but afterwards joined the plotters when they were assured that General Ankrah would head the new government once the coup had succeeded.

General Ankrah was a marked man and great care had to be taken in liaising with him. After General Alexander, the English Chief-of-Staff, had been sacked, Nkrumah had installed two heads of the army, Generals Ankrah and Otu, two men with a marked aversion for each other; and when, subsequently, there were rumours that the two generals were about to bury the hatchet, they were summoned by the president and summarily ordered to hand in their resignations and retired. General Ankrah was an old soldier with a brilliant war record. He had fought with the Royal West African Frontier Force in Burma and had won the Military Cross for gallantry. General Ankrah, however, was also more popular with the officer corps than he was with the ordinary soldiers, and the plotters knew, therefore, that if they were to succeed, they would have to win over another general who was still on active duty – General Barwa – a tough, incorruptible soldier, a Christian and a man whose reputation for fair play amongst the rank-and-file soldiers was legendary. He was not approached until the coup was already afoot, and Burma Camp, the main army camp outside Accra, had been surrounded by soldiers from the North. An order from General Barwa calling on the troops to remain loyal to the Government would have ended the rebellion. The troops from the South, in particular, would have remained loyal to him and the security forces and presidential guards would have had time to recapture the airport and seal off Accra.

Barwa was given an ultimatum while his quarters were surrounded by rebel troops who had infiltrated the camp. When a rebel captain and a squad of soldiers returned for his answer, he ordered them out and was assassinated. His personal guards fought to the last man. The news of his death could not be suppressed, and fearing his popularity with the ordinary soldiers, the rebels had him buried with full military honours immediately after the coup.

The Nigerian army takeover, coming immediately after the Prime Ministers' Conference in Lagos, had left an aftermath of uneasiness. The Nigerian and Ghanaian officer corps were linked together by a kind of "old boys' network". Many of the junior and senior officers had met in Britain, at Sandhurst, the top British military academy, or while they were doing special courses at staff colleges. Left-wing activists like Basner, the former South African senator who was one of the President's advisers, began sounding warnings that the Ghanaian army had all the makings of a praetorian guard, and that popular discontent over food shortages and corruption in high places were fertile ground in which plots against the government could germinate. But Nkrumah kept insisting that the army would remain loyal, "and would stay out of politics" and, if the officers revolted, the lower ranks would not support them. Preoccupied with the Rhodesian crisis, the demand for the use of force against the Smith Regime, the breaking off of diplomatic relations with Britain, and the war in Vietnam, the President was trying all too slowly to cure the ills immediately on his doorstep. For the majority of the Ghanaian people, the Unilateral Declaration of Independence in Rhodesia had come like a trauma, but Rhodesia was far away, and their more immediate discontents with the Nkrumah regime were more urgent.

The Ghanaian officers had been greatly encouraged in their decision to act by the swift success of their colleagues in Nigeria, but the vital factor in Nkrumah's fall was his own alienation from his mass support. The army would have had little chance of success without this. Of late, Nkrumah had become a presidential-monarch, locked away in feudal fortresses – Flagstaff House, the Castle at Osu, and the new palace at Aburi. He had also become the prisoner of the bourgeoisie that he himself had created in order to implement the gigantic programmes that were pushing Ghana into the 20th century – the Akosombo Dam, the new town of Tema (a fishing village that had grown almost overnight into a huge industrial complex), the new harbour at Takoradi, the nationwide social welfare programmes, and, the vast and expensive educational programme aimed at giving the youth of Ghana a new sense of purpose. In the meantime, there was inefficiency, chaos, corruption, nepotism, narrow parochial, sectarian and tribal conflict – the bitter harvest that all developing countries have to reap for long seasons before they finally emerge as modern states. In order to accelerate the process Nkrumah was forced more and more to take on dictatorial powers. It was not so much the man himself, as the conditions around him that dictated events in Ghana; the coup was, in fact, a symptom of a developing country attempting its "great leap forward" and then falling backwards for a moment in history. And from neither East nor West was enough disinterested aid forthcoming to make Ghana the independent, neutralist state that Nkrumah dreamed of creating.

Once the decision to overthrow the Nkrumah government was taken, swift and decisive action became a matter of great urgency. The more hot-headed of the conspirators wanted to strike at once, but the sober ones thought it best to use caution and cunning. A fortnight after the plotters had met, the special branch had intercepted a letter to the president which spelt out in great detail all the facts about the plot and named the officers involved. It is impossible to keep secrets for long in Ghana – family groups are too large and interlocked. This letter writer disappeared and President Nkrumah left for Hanoi as planned.

Nkrumah had created an elaborate system of checks and balances to ensure that army should not become a praetorian guard. The security forces and the presidential guards were equipped with the most modern Russian weapons, including rockets and heavy artillery which the army did not have. These units, together with the Workers Brigade, could muster two battalions, and from their strategically located camps they could prevent the various army units from joining up. But two days before the army units were ordered to move South, the plotters found out that both the security forces and the presidential guards would be down to half strength during the President's absence. They also discovered that only small units had so far been trained to use the new weapons, the latest shipments of which had been secreted away in the Shai hills, thirty miles outside Accra.

While Finance Minister Kwesi Amoako-Atta was reading out his budget speech in Parliament on the twenty-second of February, troops on the march south were linking up with other units a hundred miles from Accra. At the same time, President Nkrumah was being welcomed at New Delhi Airport by India's Prime Minister, Mrs. Indira Gandhi. The President had flown to India from Cairo and Karachi, where he had, in turn, been greeted by President Nasser and President Ayub Khan.

The new budget offered the man in the street no respite from the considerable hardships already imposed on him. It called upon the whole nation to pay higher taxes, to continue doing without essential consumer goods, and to further tighten its belt.

There was remarkably little grumbling after the budget speech – people were beyond grumbling; there was, rather, an uneasy calm which could change swiftly into febrile gaiety. They did not really understand why they were being called upon to make further sacrifices. The CPP, the President's main instrument of contact with the people, had become little more than an overgrown bureaucracy – a vast head with tiny impotent limbs. In the remotest villages, people had come to regard party agents as symbols of oppression, or at best as pompous, venal representatives of a government that had lost its inner ear for their needs, longings, rising expectations. The *coup d'etat* could not have come at a better time, for even the conspirators, themselves were amazed at the popular support for their actions; and yet it was not so much support for them as a blind inchoate rage against a leader whom they expected would lead them to the promised land, a leader whom in their atavistic imaginings they had endowed with magical qualities, so that he had become the greatest of their tribal chiefs, a priest-sorcerer, a black David, hurling bolts at gigantic white Goliaths. It was the people who had raised him out of anonymity to light up the African skies, and he had promised to take them all with him; but the weight of their nagging frustrations, their ordinariness, their fear of change that made them clutch at ancient, stultifying banalities, had become intolerable and he had soared into incandescent heights where, after unsuccessful attempts on his life, they were convinced that not even bombs and bullets could reach him. So, their rage was directed not so much against him, as against the sycophants and the greedy, uncaring men around him; men with itchy hands who were constantly rifling the public purse – fat, sleek men who flaunted their wealth before the public with an incomparable bad taste, and a contempt for the poor. In spite of all this, ordinary folks kept hoping that the Father of the Nation would return and put his house in order, and when he did not, they turned against him.

The President and his party flew from Rangoon to Delhi on February 23rd, and then they left for Peking on a Russian jet. They arrived in Peking in sub-zero weather, and a landscape of snows and cheering crowds.

At home, fighting broke out when the troops from the North, having surrounded and taken Burma Camp, fanned out to capture the airport and to move towards Flagstaff House, Osu Castle, the radio and television stations. The battle in and around Flagstaff House lasted from 3:00 a.m. to noon.

It was not a bloodless coup. There were many casualties – military and civilian – before the army finally gained control. Both in Flagstaff House and in the Shai hills, the security forces and the presidential guards, caught completely by surprise, rallied their depleted forces and fought back determinedly. The army had a great fear of the security forces which were Russian-trained. Individual members are still being ruthlessly hunted down. Those who were captured were so strenuously beaten up that others, still at large, prefer to remain in hiding. The chief of the security forces was captured and was coaxed to tell all.

The army expressed its uneasiness by wasting a great deal of ammunition, and by spasms of anger against innocent people. A member of parliament, his wife and twelve-year-old son were shot on the main road outside Flagstaff House. He did not know that a coup was on and when a soldier ordered him to remove the "M.P." label from his car, he refused. The day after the coup, his car still stood in the centre of the road, its windscreen shot away and a bloodstained shoe left forlornly just outside the open car door. Not far from the M.P.'s car was a Ghana Airways van, a lorry that had keeled over, and a damaged armoured car. On the day of the coup, bodies were left for hours where they had fallen. In the Ghana Airways van, an air hostess and two male employees were slumped forward in the awkward postures of death; the lorry driver died gripping his steering wheel, and the soldiers in the armoured car (its whole side had been blown away) had disintegrated into fragments of flesh and splintered bone. There were rumours all over Accra that eleven Russians had fought and died defending Flagstaff House, but no one ever saw them either dead or alive. On the other hand, a British army officer was seen by several eye-witnesses manning a mortar together with a Ghanaian officer outside Flagstaff House, and this was in the mid-morning when no mistakes could have been made.

Mr. Sam Morris, a press officer who accompanied Nkrumah to Peking, describing his chief's reaction to the news said, "A Chinese official took a message to the President in the mid-morning. We could not tell, looking at this urbane official's face, whether it was good or bad news... then the President came out and told us for the first time that the Ghanaian Army had revolted and was making a bid to seize power. He said that he didn't believe it. Later in the morning I picked up the Voice of America on my transistor radio and it was only then that the President was convinced. He then summoned the whole delegation and told us the news."

Will Nkrumah manage to make a comeback? Only a soothsayer could hope to find an answer to this question. But if one were to be asked, one has to take a close look at the personality of the man himself and at the situation that is likely to develop in Ghana.

Nkrumah's successors at the National Liberation Council, all good men and true, are political innocents who start out with the disadvantage of having to learn their political alphabet when in power. They have eliminated what they describe as "a One Party dictatorship" and replaced it with NO PARTY DICTATORSHIP. When they seized power, there were eight hundred people in detention, most of whom have been released. But they are now holding over two thousand people in "protective custody". Ghanaian families are large and complex and every individual held in prison or a detention camp is liable to have, at a conservative estimate, between thirty and seventy relatives who will not feel kindly towards the government; and if the detained relative is rich and powerful, the animosity will be all the greater, for the economic wellbeing of the family group will have been seriously reduced.

Nkrumah had learnt his politics at the source – in the villages, the market places, the slums – and the momentum for change generated by his party had swept from the bottom upwards.

The NLC having abolished and disbanded the CCP, have created a vacuum in a country where, after two decades of Nkrumahism, politics, like food and family, are inescapable facts of life.

The NLC has further abolished most of the other institutions that kept Nkrumah in power – parliament, the Young Pioneers, and the ideological institute at Winneba (an institution that was created to produce young politically conscious cadres to replace the old, venal administrators).

Nkrumah was bound by history, by his own dreams and limitations, to a middle course, between East and West, right and left, public and private ownership, evolution and revolution; he was a neutralist, although for him, and for Ghana, neutralism meant being alternately squeezed and tugged by two great power blocs. The Russians, Eastern Europeans and Chinese extended a rather cautious and tentative helping hand to Nkrumah during his years in power. They regarded him as a "Bonapartist" and viewed with suspicion his attempts to maintain a neutralist stance. Throughout the time he ruled Ghana, he was a man walking in the middle of the political road, threatened by traffic from both left and right.

The coup has now swept aside his illusion of neutralism and the political pendulum in Ghana must inevitably swing either to the extreme right or to the extreme left. The NLC is unlikely to be able to maintain itself in power for more than a year. The contradictions inside Ghana could not be resolved by well-meaning amateurs. If the extreme right win, they may be able to hold power for from five to ten years, but the extreme left will in the end take over from them. Nkrumah has been deposed, but Nkrumahism will continue to decide events in Ghana for a long time to come. The NLC will be able to contain corruption – they are busily doing this already and doing it with all sincerity – in order to present to the public the image of being honest brokers. But they are unlikely to be able to keep it up for more than six months or so. Then the lawyers, the traders, the businessmen, the greedy officials on whom the Nkrumah regime had imposed some re-straints, will swarm back (particularly the lawyers) and will make the great swindlers in history seem like models of integrity. The "socialism" of

Nkrumah, in spite of being preached more than practised, had created an ethos which helped to keep the more naked forms of graft in check.

But amongst the new bourgeoisie created by Nkrumah is a small but influential and dedicated group already entrenched in high positions under the new regime. They had no stomach for the sycophants around Nkrumah, nor the politicians and officials plundering the national coffers, but they shared Nkrumah's dream of a united Africa. They had grown up on a fare of his "magnificent speeches and dramatic actions which had compelled the world to see Africa and Africans as contenders for liberty, equality and, if not fraternity, respect." They were loyal not to the man himself, but to his ideas, and they will continue to uphold these ideas. But the greatest enemies of the new regime are the discontented masses, inflamed by the expectations that Nkrumah released.

There is a tradition in Ghana that when a great chief has been deposed, his memory must be exorcised by a long ritual of denunciation and by displays of public contumely. Equally his successor must be exalted. Both the denunciation of Nkrumah and the praise of the NLC have followed traditional patterns. But it would be foolish to take this elaborate and subtle ritual at face value. In the fulsome and spontaneous praise are implied warnings to the NLC to avoid the aberration that developed under the deposed regime.

Away from the confines of feudal fortresses and the impossible strictures that high office imposes on leaders of developing countries, Nkrumah, the most brilliant political agitator that modern Africa has so far produced, is once more in the wilderness. But it must be remembered that his triumphant struggle to mobilise the whole population of Ghana to terminate British colonial rule dates from no longer ago than 1951. He has been pushed into the wings of history for the moment, but whether he returns to power in Ghana or not, his image had been deep-etched upon black men's minds and will remain a force to be reckoned with for the rest of this century, and perhaps beyond. Ghana – indeed the whole of Africa – will develop in his shadow.

VI.

OFFERS TOO GOOD TO RESIST

Section Six, "Offers Too Good to Resist", includes chapters seventeen through nineteen and looks at the period from the mid-1960s onwards when, following a brief return to England after the coup in Ghana, Jan Carew went back to his home country in 1966. This was also the year that British Guiana was becoming Guyana as it gained its independence from Britain. It was a hopeful time and Carew was happy to contribute to the celebrations by mounting his play, *University of Hunger*, in Georgetown. He also toyed with the idea of resettling back in the Caribbean, but the niggling political tension in Guyana and his ever-present restlessness resurfaced. An invitation from the Barbadian writer, Austin Clarke, enticed him north again, this time to Canada. In a poem appropriately entitled, "Exile (Toronto)", Carew muses, "Why must I leave the sun/ for timeless miseries of winter fog/ And Clarky wrote again/ 'You can't eat the sun or drink the lazy tides...'"

Settling into life in Toronto, Carew wrote plays for the theatre and TV, articles for Canadian papers, and worked on features for the Canadian Broadcasting Corp. One of these CBC commissions, a curiosity to see the impact of the Black Power movement on art and culture in the inner cities, proved auspicious.

Carew then settled in the United States for the remaining forty years of his life, and turned to academe. Initially teaching at Princeton and Rutgers Universities in the late 1960s, he then accepted the chair of the newly-formed Department of African American Studies at Northwestern University in 1973. Fourteen years later, in 1987, he retired as emeritus professor. Over this twenty-year period, Carew played a major role in shaping Black Studies in the US, and on designing programmes for the induction of first-generation Black and other minority students into American higher education.

Jan Carew retired to concentrate on his writing again, but, he did not stay away from academe for long. After two years in Mexico, he agreed to a number of visiting professor stints: at George Mason, Illinois Wesleyan, Lincoln University of Pennsylvania, and finally at the University of Louisville. Also, in this last period of his peripatetic life, he married Joy in 1975 and they had the last of his three children, Shantoba.

Included in this section, in order of appearance, is Carew's poem

"Exile", his 1969 article "A Long Way to Go", the article "Culture and Rebellion" published in 1993, and the 1973 the position paper he wrote for the Department of African American Studies at Northwestern University when establishing the new department.

Exile (Toronto)

November was a dreaming month
when the monotonies of wide blue skies
brought to each day an insane ease.
The sunwheel danced around
eyeless sunflowers, yellow daisies,
flambeaux with stamens like parched tongues
purple anemones, and bumble bees
leeching pollen from chaliced flowers.
November was the month
when sea-drums echoed in my blood again.
And Clarky wrote,
'Dear Jan, Canada's cold, my friend,
and lonely sometimes like canaries
serenading jumbies in hell;
but there's bread...
and Philistines from home can't reach you here.'
It was the season when
curlews thronged southern skies
winging their clamorous way to ripening corn
and harvest-time on the golden pampas.
So I replied: 'Dear Clarky, as I write
the sunwheel's dallying over saffron swamps
on my Berbician coast;
marching crabs jewel the mud;
and herons hurl themselves
like flaming arrowheads
at the approaching night.
Why must I leave the sun
for timeless miseries of winter fog!'
And Clarky wrote again:
'You can't eat sun or drink the lazy tides
rimming your moon-burnished mud;
besides the pygmies and the philistines
multiply, become a host
when hardtime's knocking at your door,
their malice is much harder to endure
than silent furies of Ontario snows.
The people, yes, the people are all right,
but trapped in dreaming torpors of slow time.
Awaken them or leave, my friend!'
I replied, 'Awaken the people?

our awakening will come
when a maelstrom of pain
drives us outside the crumbling bastions
of our crippled selves;
when the New Day arrives
with morning flashing like sheet lightning
from our eyes;
together, side by side,
we'll burst asunder
pale ramparts of heaven
with bare hands and bare feet
and pluck wild orchids
of ultimate release.'

CHAPTER SEVENTEEN

CANADA BECKONS

I'd gone into the Guyanese interior as a kind of respite. My trip home in 1966, came on the heels of being arrested and deported from Ghana and I needed some time to reflect on my future options without distractions. I was also coming off a stressful, but rewarding run of my play, *University of Hunger*.

We were anticipating our country's independence from Britain, which was scheduled for May. These were exciting times for Guyana as the British had finally agreed to our full self-rule. I had also looked forward to being able to direct my play for the February 23rd Republic Day Celebrations at the Georgetown Theatre Guild. As a result, I had stayed in Guyana longer than I was ever to do for the rest of my life (subsequent visits were all much shorter).

I named my play, *University of Hunger*, after Maxim Gorky's *My University* and Sylvia and I were the co-authors. "University of Hunger" was also the title of a poem by Martin Carter. It was about a prison breakout and was based upon a story that Janet Jagan had told me. It was about a man who used his time in prison to educate himself. When he subsequently broke out of the jail, instead of running and hiding like a common criminal, he acted the part of an upper-class gentleman, and with this elaborate disguise, he was able to elude the police. Unfortunately, his young protégé, who had escaped with him, was found out by his mother and their escape was thwarted.

University of Hunger was a great success, although we'd had some rough patches before opening night. I had cast my niece in the play. She would later go on to be "Miss Guyana" in the "Miss World" contest and we had had to deal with some less than professional attitudes on the set. But when I threatened to cast someone else for the part, she relented and the show went on.

The Georgetown Theatre Guild had one of the largest attendances it had ever had. I had insisted that folks from the villages outside Georgetown should be bused into the city to attend the theatre, many for the first time in their lives. There was a part in the play where the leading lady confronted a lover who had abandoned her for another woman, and the women from the villages reacted to this particular moment fiercely. They could hear their own voices in the characters. They were so vociferous that they traumatised the male actors, who feared that these ignited women in the audience would leap onto the stage and attack them. Sometimes, depending on how unsophisticated the spectators were, the audience offered more entertainment than the play on stage.

During this visit home, I had to decide whether I would stay on in Guyana or return to London. I was also mulling over Austin Clarke's advice that it was easier to live as a writer and freelance artist in Canada than it was in England. I had lived as a writer for years before, and during my stay in Ghana, so as soon as I returned to London after the coup, I immediately got in touch with my writing contacts. I had struggled to make a profitable living by writing, and though my first novel, *Black Midas,* had been a great success, it, alone, did not provide me with a living wage. You had to have an agent if you were going to live successfully by writing. The agent arranges all the publicity and marketing for you and creates the platform for you to give lectures or speeches.

I had met Austin in London a few months earlier. He'd been commissioned by the Canadian Broadcasting Corporation to interview Canadian writers in England. Austin also included some other Caribbean writers who were living in the London at the time. The first time we met was when he came to interview me in Wimbledon. Austin was a genial Barbadian and spoke with a distinct Bajan accent that had not changed since he left home. This was a time when your accent told where you stood in the anti-colonial struggle. A perfect British English accent, for example, was an indication of the fact that the speaker had spent more time cultivating the accent, than the content of what he or she had to say.

Austin spent several hours with me on that first occasion and that visit marked the beginning of a friendship that would last for a lifetime. Decades later, Austin remained the only Caribbean writer with whom I corresponded regularly and every letter he wrote, whether in dialect or straight English, was an entertaining treat. The only other Caribbean writer whose letters were as entertaining was the late Samuel Selvon, the Trinidadian writer I had known in Britain and, later, in Canada. Then there was also Jamaican writer, Andrew Salkey, who was the most responsible correspondent of all. Both of them are now gone.

Andrew used to reply as you soon you wrote to him, unlike Austin, who might take a while to reply. But, differently to Andrew, Austin often wrote in handwritten calligraphic pen-and-ink script. One of my friends, the French physicist Maurice Bazin, told me that he and his wife framed some of Austin's letters.

There was a mounting racism in Britain and Austin, in doing this series of interviews, was comparing the racism in Britain and Europe with that of

Canada and the United States through the eyes of the writers who had experienced it. What was striking about Austin's interviews was that he was a gifted broadcaster with warm inflections in his voice that made you feel you were sitting opposite him as he narrated his programmes.

I arrived in Toronto in the autumn of 1966. It was a windy day and walking away from the aircraft, a gust of wind hustled me into the huge glass and concrete cage of the terminal building. A Canadian who had befriended me with some diligence on the journey, gave me his visiting card and an LBJ handshake and vanished. He was returning from a vacation in the Caribbean and all the way up from Antigua to Toronto he had regaled me, in between drinks, in a monologue as persistent as the drone of the jet engines. Snatches of his discourse, and it was very repetitive in theme and content, went like this:

"You people sure know how to enjoy life! Boy, I'm going back to my office treadmill with a sinking heart. By the way, do you know Joe?"

"Joe?"

"Yeah, Joe. You must know him, he's one of your people. Big guy, built like an ox but gentle as a baby... worked at my hotel in Antigua as a beach-boy... a great guy, Joe, one of the best. Can't remember his last name... he was darker than you... big guy... I suppose he does have another name. Boy, he sure showed me a good time, took me everywhere... What do you do?"

"Do?'

"Yeah, what's your racket?"

"I'm a writer."

"A writer?" he asked, looking totally confused, "Anyway, Joe was a good one, real nice guy. And let me tell you something, those coloured chicks can teach ours a thing or two when it comes to good looks. Yeah, Joe even took me home to where he was living and gave me some of the real native food. Yeah, Joe was OK... like he was poor, but he was O.K., and when I was getting ready to cut out I said, 'Joe,' I sez, 'you're black,' and he sure was black, 'but it don't matter what nobody sez, in my books you're still an all right guy.'"

I was subsequently to meet several other Canadians who claimed that their best friends were blacks, and who brought back from holidays in the Caribbean cherished memories of a servant class that acted like a salve to their egos.

My dealings with the Canadian immigration authorities began at the airport. Black people coming into Canada have a profound respect for the Canadian immigration services. They regard it as a kind of white man's "St. Peter's Gate", to which "many are called but few are chosen." And it did not matter what the point of entry was, the gate was always there. Ten years before, I heard a Canadian official state quite openly in Britain that Canada had no intention of letting large numbers of coloured immigrants into their country. Canada needed immigrants he said, but white ones. I have so far not met any Canadians who, face-to-face, were willing to justify their government's immigration policy to me. But in many respects, "The Canadians," as Oscar Wilde once said of the Irish, "are a very honest people, they never speak well of one another."

The day I arrived, I was shunted aside with another black man while the other passengers went through Customs and Immigration. After half an hour of waiting, I asked an official why we were being delayed. No one seemed to know why. The other black man – a Barbadian cricketer – and I both had United Kingdom passports. We were subsequently given permission to stay in Canada for three weeks.

But blaming organisations like the immigration service and the police for practising racial discrimination is like blaming the monkey for performing tricks at the behest of the organ grinder. On my next visit to the immigration office – I went to apply for an extension of my stay – the waiting room was crowded, cold, impersonal, the atmosphere oppressive. The weight of uneasy expectations sat upon all of us like an incubus. Some of the black people seemed anxious that their eyes should not make four with mine. It was as though once our eyes met, we would be inexorably committed to a secret conspiracy against the racialists who might confront us from across any government desk.

The official I was assigned to was cordial, paunchy, with a touch of grey in his complexion, as though dust from the files he dealt with daily had entered his pores and secreted a pigment of its own.

"Why do you want to live in Canada?" he asked, thumbing through my passport, and then he added, "You've been everywhere."

"I've done a great deal of writing since I came to Toronto, and the minefield here is not so thickly strewn with mines..." I said.

He looked up at me, then back down at my picture in the passport, chuckled, loudly stamped the passport page and waved me through.

Austin introduced me to the head of the CBC (Canadian Broadcasting Corps) and I submitted works to him which he accepted. I used to get a regular commission to do features and take part in literary discussions on radio and television. I lived in Canada for about five years, working on projects for the CBC, doing TV plays, and writing.

Toronto gave you the impression of being undecided as to whether it would grow upwards or spread out. It was a city suffering from what the Russians would describe as "Hamlet-ism," since it could not make up its mind as it did a balancing act between English, American and French cultures. Even its racial discrimination lacked the conviction that one was liable to find in Britain or the United States. Canadians preferred to practice their racialism slyly, behind closed doors. However, you began to realise how deep the racial antipathies were when you were looking for accommodation. People who had advertised rooms or flats would open their doors and you could see and smell the racial prejudice festering and oozing like pus out of secret sores. The lies and the dishonesty pierced your brain like daggers.

They would say, "Sorry that room was just taken. Someone came and paid down a deposit five minutes ago…" Or, if you were a man, "Sorry, but we really wanted a woman tenant." Or, if you were a woman. "Sorry, but we wanted a male…" The variations on this obvious self-deception were endless.

However, it was sometimes more merciful to be denied the accommodation, because many coloured tenants were "welcomed" and then charged a "colour" tax. In some instances, the landlord or landlady would subject a black tenant to a sort of cat-and-mouse racialism; what the wits in the Black barbershop would describe as "trying to find out if the colour rubs off on the sheets."

The petty affronts to my human dignity when I was looking for accommodation did not, however, blind me to the whole spectrum of discrimination. Racial prejudice is a disease which begins at the very roots of Western democracy. At one point, when I was living in the Wimbledon house in England and I had advertised one of the flats, people would contact me in some of the most curious fashions. After enquiring if it was available, they would assure me that their children made no noise. Obviously, this had been a problem in looking for other units.

To this, I would ask, "Well, what's wrong with them?"

Or, as Vidia Naipaul once commented on his unsuccessful attempts to find housing, when speaking to a potential landlady on the phone, he did confess that he was black.

To which she had enquired, "Are you very black?"

And, he had replied, "Regrettably."

At one stage, I found a residence in a district of Toronto where I was surrounded by Southern Italians who were, like me, recent arrivals to Canada. Most of them brought no racial discrimination with their scanty baggage and great expectations, but their children were already learning from the children of other Canadians to call black people names.

In Toronto, as true for elsewhere, the Black barbershops were meeting places, forums for ideas, and community social centres. While the barber, who invariably served as a master of ceremonies, cut hair with style and great expertise, one could learn much about life in Canada through the ebb and flow of conversation. The regular denizens of the barbershops were supreme realists, they never lied to themselves. I would visit the barber shops regularly and listen to these conversations; how this or that illegal immigrant was picked up by the Royal Canadian Mounted Police after a jealous girlfriend had tipped them off; how with the devaluation of the pound, people were catching hell down in the West Indies; how black people were drifting away from Nova Scotia, since the discrimination there was so intolerable it made America's Mississippi seem liberal by comparison.

I learned about the experiences of a certain man about-town who worked as a salesman for electrical goods:

"Man, I went after this room in Rosedale, saw it advertised in the papers, thought I'd put some distance between me and the folks for a while. So I get out of my car, walk up to the door and ring the bell. And old test came out and looking me up and down, he ask,

"Well, what you want, boy?"

"I wanted to see the room you advertised," I said, calm as hell, and the test look me full in the face and say, 'I don't rent my place to darkies, and it's not the neighbours that's prejudiced or the other tenants, but *me, I'm* prejudiced.' Man, I wanted to shake his hand. At least he was honest. The first honest one I met since I came to Toronto."

"Then there was this black girl from Jamaica, she had a white friend who was sticking to her like a tick, and this white friend, in order to show her what a big favour she was doing her by being her friend, take her on tour all over Rosedale looking for rooms so that the white people could turn them down and insult them. Boy, they have some peculiar whiteys in this man's town."

An uncle of mine, a minister of religion, who had lived in Canada for fifty-seven years, helped fill in the gaps about the social history of the black man in Canada – between the 1910 period and the 1960-era seminars I had heard at the barbershops. He claimed that the discrimination gap had narrowed. It had to, since the situation as recently as twenty years ago was abysmal – but that the generation gap had also widened. A younger generation of black people had been forced to shed the illusions of its forebears – and this applied equally to Indians and Blacks – they were now growing impatient with the palliatives and wanted cures instead.

Later, when I did settle in Canada, I was commissioned to write the opening play for the Toronto Workshop Productions, which was headed by George Luscombe. George and I didn't get along too well, but we managed to overcome our differences in the interest of the work. When the play opened in the company's own theatre it was called *Gentleman, Be Seated* and it dealt with the subject of Abraham Lincoln's assassination. It was later performed in Yugoslavia as Canada's contribution to the International Drama Festival that year.

In addition to my work with the Toronto Workshop, I was able to revive my television play production in Canada. I was under contract with the CBC to do a series of new plays. The first was a production in which the Black English actor, Earl Cameron, and the African American actress,

Cicely Tyson, acted. This was called *Behind God's Back*, and was an adaptation of one of Austin Clarke's short stories. This was the first TV play in Toronto where West Indians in Canada could see themselves in their own right and not as appendages. It was shown in 1969 in the 90-minute Canadian drama series *Festival*. I had heard that Cicely's family was from Nevis in the West Indies, but she had never shown it in her acting in the US. Yet, in playing the part of Belle in my play, all of her Caribbean background came out. Earl was a very talented actor, too, and very convincing in the part, and people would come up to me on the street to say that they knew "Brewster", the character in the play, that he was a denizen of such and such barber shop and loved drinking. Unfortunately, this latter part was true, as Earl did have a drinking problem.

But my play also explored some of the complexities of immigrant life in North America. In the West Indian immigrant community, women were more readily employed than men. There would be instances where West Indian men would have girlfriends who were working and whose salaries were going to pay the rent, and in some cases, were willing to support their men through medical or dental school. In these early days, many of these young women were delighted to have this new crop of West Indians in their midst. But there were those who exploited this. After benefiting from their largesse, these fellows would tire of their working-class girlfriends and end up leave them for the middle-class women they met in their new professional circles. I encountered similar stories at Howard in the US. While there were some who came from middle-class families and had funds, most did not have a lot of money and there was a constant search for jobs or other means to make it possible to stay in school and survive. If they didn't have women as their benefactors, some joined the US army, which would then pay for their schooling. Others found summer jobs where they learned a trade and could return to work in that trade over a number of years. One of the favourites was to work for a furrier.

I was rather busy, still freelancing for the BBC, and now working for the CBC, writing plays, poetry, and doing features on radio and television. Driving home one night, I had the car radio on. Much to my amazement, there was a broadcast from the BBC World Service and they were broadcasting my play *The Riverman*. One of the outstanding producers at the time, Charles Lefeaux, collaborated with me on this, and he had got a famous chanteuse to sing the Guyanese river songs. I could not help but wonder how many people were listening to that play around the world and what they thought of it. Because it was a story told by the Guyana river folk perhaps it might have struck a cord in the heart of other people who had rivers in their repertoire of songs and legends.

I was all set for a career in writing for television. One of the women from my production *Behind God's Back* in London, Mary Dalton, who had been my stage manager for my ATV productions, had moved to Hollywood. At one time she had been intent on finding some way to bring me to Hollywood, but she married a Californian and gave up the theatre.

I stayed with Austin Clarke initially, and then had apartments in other parts of Toronto. One of those locations was on Manning Avenue, off of College. My apartment there became a kind of meeting place for a wide variety of visitors, writers, other artists and activists, including occasional activist visitors from the US. C.L.R. James stayed there, and I lent him a copy of his own book, *World Revolution.* In fact, I loaned it to him on the condition that he would send me an autographed copy of the more recent edition. The rare copy I had given him I had picked up at a Toronto bookshop. Austin was a regular, as well as the poet Joe Rosenblatt, and Milton Acorn. When I became the editor of *Cotopaxi*, a new literary magazine, we used to finance it by holding concerts in a small theatre across from the Public Library. Winston and Mary Jane Young would sing, Joe would read some of his poetry and Milton would join in when his visits from Prince Edward Island coincided with our programmes. I was working on a new novel, "Cry Black Power" and would read passages there as well. This novel was an experiment. Rather than hand-write or type out the text, I was dictating it into a tape recorder and having it transcribed. But the task of editing my own words was almost impossible and so I ended up packing it away in boxes. I had either to write or talk, for never could the twain meet.

Despite the bureaucratic annoyances, the Canadian period was good for me as a writer. Even many decades later, Toronto remains enshrined in my psyche. It was a kind of creative and open city where imaginative ideas could take root, if one persisted. In the late 1980s, after I retired from the university, I was contemplating the prospect of living in Mexico in the winters and returning to live and work in Toronto in the late spring and summers.

Of course, in Canada, as in the US, there was an awakening of the Black and First Persons communities. This consciousness was being heightened by the anti-war and Black Power activism to the south. I began speaking out about the conditions under which people of colour were forced to live in the city and the *Toronto Star* accused me of bringing Black Power to Canada. This was alarming considering that black people had been in Canada for centuries.

I was developing another TV play, to be called "The Merchant of Manning Ave", but I didn't finish it. I wasn't fond of Shakespeare's *Merchant of Venice* and its merciless caricature of Shylock as some venal usurer. So, in my version, I portrayed Shylock as a Black Muslim with Antonio as a Toronto merchant and Portia as a Jewish Civil Rights Lawyer. I had written a draft of the first scene and been paid an advance for the play – this was the normal way of working and being compensated – but, once I moved to the US, the project fell through.

I had proposed to the CBC that I do a piece on the Black Power movement in the US, looking in particular at its effect on art in the inner cities. That proved to be an auspicious trip and one that would start a new chapter in my life. For the next several years, I would have two residences, one in the US where I was at Princeton and Rutgers universities, and other in Toronto which held my artistic and personal life.

"A Long Way To Go"

Globe Magazine, Feb. 15, 1969 (Toronto)

Can racial violence erupt in Canada? Of course, it can. There are many Canadians who cherish the fond colonial belief that the natives – in this case the Blacks and the Indians – are by nature docile and have an infinite capacity for enduring racial humiliations; that this state of affairs would continue indefinitely but for a handful of agitators "stirring up troubles". There is another attitude which is sometimes borrowed by members of the black middle class: "We all know that there is racial discrimination in Canada, but rocking the boat will only make things worse." It is an argument which 400 years of racial oppression on this continent has made hollow and hypocritical.

If there is racial violence in Canada, it will be home grown and it would be dishonest to blame it on our neighbours south of the border. For racial eruptions are never spontaneous. They are the result of coloured peoples having been goaded to the limits of their endurance by discriminatory actions, on the one hand, and by both public and official indifference, on the other.

White society has an extraordinary capacity for misjudging racial situations and for being taken by surprise when they explode in its face. The reason for this is simply that the majority of white society, in judging itself, is often the accused, the judge, the jury, the defence and the prosecution, and so a fair trial is impossible. In societies like Canada where the white majority discriminates against the coloured minority – the Black people and the Indians – the factories of press, radio and TV are geared to tell the white majority what it wants to hear and not necessarily to disturb it with the truth. And feeding the fantasies of the white majority, are black individuals and groups of middle-class Negroes. Malcolm X called them house niggers, and their Indian counterparts are called Uncle Tomahawks, trained like Pavlovian dogs to make the right kind of reassuring noises whenever they are prompted.

In dealing with the possibility of racial violence, one can apply this law of physics with equal validity to race relations: to every action there is an equal and opposite reaction. For violence in this context is always a reaction. If there are no acts of racial discrimination, there can be no possibility of violent reaction. Another fact which must be taken into account is that the victims of racism do not rush to confide in racists.

This does not mean that they do not trust any white people at all; after all, in Canada they work side by side with white people, live next door to them and most of the day, have some kind of contact with them. But it does mean that in countries like Canada and the United States, a certain caution about embracing every white man as your brother is eminently desirable. It was not so long ago that in both countries any white person in a "sensitive" position – whatever that is – who was known to have black friends, was suspected of being a communist.

Canada has a very small black minority. It does not have less prejudice than the United States, only fewer black people and a different history. Sugar, cotton, indigo, spices, tobacco did not flourish in this country and so slavery never took root. Before slavery was made illegal on the statute books, it had already phased itself out by being unprofitable. Of the thousands of black people who came here before, during and after the American Civil War of the 1860s, most returned to the United States. Those who remained, and the other black immigrants who came from the West Indies and Africa, gravitated mostly to both ends of the transcontinental railways or worked as seamen.

More important, Canada has its Native Canadians. In analysing race relations in this country, it is impossible to deal with the Black minority without references to this one. The two are indivisible since racism springs from the same tap root in this society – a history of exploitation and greed where profits were more important than human rights. The Blacks and the Native peoples were dispossessed for the same reasons: the European imperialists wanted their labour and their land, and they took both by unprecedented acts of violence.

Are white Canadians racists in their own right, or are they merely derivatives of the American and English systems of racism? Is the image of Canada as a peacemaker, a selfless bringer of aid and enlightenment to developing countries, a valid one? Is the holier-than-thou attitude which Canadians assume in talking about the race situation in the United States justified? How much freedom does the black man or the native Canadian really enjoy in Canada? In answering these questions, one has to say as the Guyanese Amerindian did watching the lengthening shadow of a thin ité palm: "There is much shadow and little substance."

My first encounter with Canadian racism was in Guyana, my home country. A Canadian mining outfit, the Demerara Bauxite Company, controlled and owned MacKenzie city on the Demerara River. The bauxite mined there is shipped to Canada. On my first visit in 1949, I was barred from entering the white section of this mining town by armed guards, for the racial divisions were as rigid as any in South Africa. And as I noted in a previous chapter, there was the case of Dr. Cheddi Jagan, having just returned from Northwestern University in Illinois, applying for the job of company dentist. He got the job, but when the company discovered that his American wife was white, they told him he would have to live in the coloured section of the town and his wife in the white section.

Things have changed a great deal since then. The nationalist movement in Guyana became so strong that it was impossible for any foreign company to discriminate against the local populations so blatantly. But that naked discrimination was like the tip of an iceberg, and removing it meant that the submerged nine-tenths of the problem of exploitation still remains to be solved. Racism inevitably has its roots in a system that breeds and sustains inequities between haves and havenots.

I also attended a Canadian Mission high school in Guyana. The head-master and one junior master were usually Canadians. It was a remarkably good school and, in many respects, a small but effective counterweight to the mining company. There is always this dichotomy in the Canadian racial scene – the good and the bad jousting with each other.

A psychiatrist in the United States has said that being a black man in that country is like living perpetually on the brink of a precipice. In Canada, the precipices also exist for black people and First Nations people, but the distance from the brink is greater, and hence the threat of falling over is less immediate. It is also said that the black man in the US who is looking for a job and a place to live is like a blind man crossing a mine-field. The minefields do exist in Canada for coloured people, but the mines are fewer and further apart and one stands a better chance of crossing them. So in comparing the racial situation here with the one in the US, one is a compelled to begin with a negative factor. White Canadians themselves are rather defensive about admitting how much racism there is in their midst. A CBC producer from Montreal, who turned out to be a remarkably insensitive and a not too bright individual, declared during a discussion with me on air, "At least no lynching took place in Canada." No black people were lynched in Canada, but certainly First Nations people were. There were not enough black people around at the time, and now the days of lynching are over.

I do not for a moment consider that fellow a spokesman for all white Canadians, but what was significant was that he began to argue from an extreme position on lynching, since after that everything else had to be judged as progress.

Lynchings were usually the result of pathological sexual fears and the jealousies of white Americans exploding into violence. Are white Canadi-ans free from these? I do not believe that they are, since they suffer from the same racist fantasies that afflict white Americans.

In Canada, these fantasies are reinforced by tourist propaganda and short visits to that exotic limbo world that tourists inhabit during short holidays in the Caribbean. Coloured women in Canada say that many white men tend to treat them not just as women and individuals, but as possessors of some secret sexual elixir; or as creatures who have, buried in their dark flesh, Ponce de Leon's Fountain of Youth. This can be very romantic in the abstract, but rather tedious when one is trying to establish genuine human contacts socially, professionally or otherwise.

But there is far more animosity directed at a black man with a white woman than against a black women with a white man. Frantz Fanon tells us that the white man regards the attractive coloured woman as part of the legitimate spoils of conquest. He, the white man, always dreams of a group of coloured women, a field of women, suggestive of the gynaeceum, the harem – exotic themes deeply rooted in the unconscious.

The Negro man, as distinct from the black man, however, is a creation of the white man, a figment of his imagination. And this creature's liaisons with white women are a kind of outlawry, poaching and theft. Just as the Russians built their izbas (wooden peasant houses) around a stove shaped like phallus, the Negro's body is built around his sexual organs. And having accorded the Negro an unlimited sexual prowess, the white man is then able to rob him of all human dignity, all claims to human intelligence and feelings. It is this kind of racist mythology that lays a basis for lynchings. I have heard of several instances in which black men walking down the streets of Toronto have been, particularly if they were small in stature, insulted and even attacked by whites.

It was this kind of racist cliché – the black man as a gladiator, a demon of sexuality – that the black athletes were protesting against at the Olympic Games, and the protest was long overdue.

There was a time when Negroes were constantly reassuring their white overlords that they had no intention of sleeping with white women. Many black men these days are no longer willing to offer these reassurances about white women, black women, brown women or yellow women. It is a private question which has to be dealt with by individual men and women and not by any public declarations.

Is Canada genuinely interested in finding solutions to its racial problems? One begins to wonder. For the majority of coloured peoples in this country, and no doubt for other groups, the just society promises to be always just around the corner.

Afro-Canadians – and one can use this label without any fear of being divisive, since until recently, black Canadians in the Maritimes were registered officially not as Canadians but as Africans – have made one significant gain in the last generation. They are better educated. But except for a minority that has migrated to other provinces, job opportunities and the housing situation have become worse. Under prodding by black militants, some rudimentary changes for the better have been introduced recently. But there is still a long way to go. Naturally, one cannot solve the black problem in that area, or any other, in isolation. First, there is the general problem of underdevelopment in the Maritimes, but there is also the particular one of the Blacks being among the poorest and the most deprived and having the additional blight of a harsh racial discrimination to contend with.

The government's cautious incursions into the field of race relations remind me of the student who arrived at classes late and, when asked by the teacher why he was late, said that every time he took a step forward he slid two steps backward.

"Then how did you get here?" the teacher asked

"I started going back home," the student said.

The incursions begin with the immigration policy and its mysterious points system. I have been assured that it is fairer system than the previous one. But the previous one was undisguisedly a "white Canadian policy" and the present one seems to have the advantage of mitigating and in some cases concealing the racist motives. There are also the hesitant steps being taken to make the First Nations people enjoy their full rights as citizens, their ancestors having been here for the past 25,000 years.

Although the racial situation in Canada is by no means hopeless at the moment, it can become so by default – the authorities and the public attempting to do too little when it is already too late. There is a subtle, underhanded violence being practised against all the coloured people in Canada daily. It exists in the schoolbooks which teach lies to children about black Sambos; about inferior native and superior white proconsuls; about treacherous "Indians" and noble cowboys; about white heroes who, be-cause of the large numbers of coloured peoples they have slaughtered, become super heroes.

Instead of patting themselves on the back and crowing about how liberal they are, Canadians can very profitably learn from and adopt some of the measures being taken in the United States in race relations. Spurred on by the Black revolution, and with the spectre of a racial apocalypse hanging over that nation, new textbooks are being written for black and white children; African history is being taught at all levels in the high school and university system, and at the same time, parallel steps are being taken to create a more honest image of the Native American, and to explain his culture and his proud past.

If genuine efforts are made to solve racial problems, not by restricting, but by extending the human and civil rights of coloured peoples, then there could be no possibility of racial violence.

"Culture and Rebellion"

Race & Class, volume 35, number 1, 1993 (London)

Millions are in silent revolt against their lot. Nobody knows how
many rebellions ferment in the masses of life which people earth.
— Virginia Woolf

God gave Noah the rainbow sign,
No more water, the fire next time!
— a slave song

I walked the streets of Detroit, Cleveland, Newark and Washington
DC immediately after the Black rebellions in the late 1960s. These
became euphemistically labelled "The Martin Luther King Riots", but
it was Malcolm X who had warned repeatedly that, given the all-pervasive
racism in America, rebellions would, inevitably, erupt in inner cities
across America – and they did.

The "fire next time" that James Baldwin had forecast in his apocalyptic
essay had burnt itself out by the time I walked up and down those mean
streets. The anatomy of America's inner cities was laid bare in the wake of
those cleansing fires. The culture of the streets then burst out of a humus
of decay like exquisite wild flowers flourishing in a dung heap. The poetry,
songs, drama, music – plus new creative infusions of words, images and
rhythms into the everyday language of the street – were an organic part of
the cultural regeneration that took place in the wake of those Black
rebellions and the nationwide protests against America's cruel, immoral
and deadly intervention in Vietnam. They proved once again that rebellion
against oppression, injustice and greed is as natural a part of the rhythms of
the oppressed as breathing.

The Black urban rebellions in the 1960s illuminated questions of race,
class, gender and the often ignored but visceral links fermented between
the Black Power movement, the martyrdom of Malcolm X and Martin
Luther King, the civil rights struggle, the struggle for women's rights and
the anti-Vietnam war campaign. In short, American imperialism was in the
throes of a crisis, and the primal impulse of this settler society was once
again to attempt to resolve its social, political, economic and racial crises,
at home and abroad, by force. But, since a changing kaleidoscope of racism
had always been at the heart of its concerns – from Plymouth Rock to Little
Rock – the patterns of resistance and oppression manifesting themselves in
the 1960s were at once as new as the "Days of Rage" in Chicago during the
bloody Democratic Party Convention, and as old as Sir Walter Raleigh's
predatory intrusion at Roanoke.

It was at this stage that I was inducted into the academic world. It was a time when irreverent and rebellious students were creating radical networks across the nation, demanding a say in the selection of professors, and compelling the universities to make their curricula more relevant. In short, it was a time when fundamental changes seemed imminent, when culture burst out of the confines of staid middle-class institutions and spilled out into the streets.

It seemed as if campuses would become catalysts for a revolution, but there were hidden factors that made this very unlikely at the time. The Cold War economy, in which billions of dollars were being fed into the maw of an insatiable military-industrial complex, had created a high level of employment and reinforced a class and racial hierarchy with white males at the top and minorities, women and poor whites at the bottom. This hierarchy, with its built-in racial and class antagonisms, gave the ruling class ample opportunity to play divide-and-conquer games; to contain and neutralise the motive energies of the anti-war, Black Power and civil rights struggles; to obfuscate the fundamental issue of women's rights and to pretend that the overall struggle of working people of all races did not really exist. In this divide-and-conquer game, privileged white male workers and a small, but vocal, coterie of Blacks was induced to jump onto a right-wing bandwagon. The rebellion, therefore, ran its course and petered out, and right-wing forces, far better organised than those of a fragmented Left, moved openly into the centres of power.

Jules Michelet, the great French historian whose writings both enthral and educate the reader, tells us in his *History of the French Revolution* that Robespierre, that archetype of a cunning revolutionary, never allowed "his mind [to] soar into the regions of speculation,"[2] and that, unlike other leaders such as Sieyes and Mirabeau "he [Robespierre] knew where power resided, and where he was sure to find it."[3] Michelet proceeds to describe the nexus of power that Robespierre had identified so unerringly:

> There were then two powers in France, two vast associations – one eminently revolutionary, the Jacobins; the other profiting by the Revolution, seemed able to be easily reconciled to it; I mean the lower clergy, a body of eighty thousand priests.[4]

Michelet goes on to tell us that, on 30 May 1790, when Robespierre proposed that priests should be allowed to marry, "his voice was drowned by the uproar of the whole Assembly". But that dry, academic voice was heard outside the Assembly and, in a month, Robespierre received "verses in every language, whole poems of 500, 700, and 1,500 verses, in Latin, Greek and Hebrew."[5]

The leaders of the Black Power and anti-war movements were never able to escape the euphoria that American capitalism, with its surfeit of baubles and trivia, induces. For, with four per cent of the world's population, America was squandering two-thirds of the world's resources. The distribution of loot from this capitalist plunder was unjust, unequal and unfair, but there was enough trickling down to confuse those single issue leaders so that they did not, or, indeed, could not, identify the real sources of power. They could not understand the basic tenets of class and race antagonisms and the importance of solidarity with advanced, unionised workers. When the anti-war leaders talked of "people's power", they really meant a more enlightened white male middle-class power, and the most articulate proponents of Black Power had equally narrow and myopic goals. Spokesmen for a plethora of movements that sprang up during that season of rebellion became, therefore, so many Don Quixotes tilting at windmills. I used this term "spokesmen" deliberately, because the women had different and more realistic agendas. It was no accident that Fannie Lou Hamer was a key figure in resetting priorities that were askew; with a symbolical journey to Africa and the founding of the National Woman's Political Caucus and the Freedom Farm Cooperative.

And yet, as I walked past long stretches of burnt-out blocks in Detroit, I remembered seeing an unforgettable picture on television – and I was certain that it had slipped past the editors in the cutting room by accident, because, having seen it once, I never saw it again. It was the picture of a black man perched on the shoulders of a white man, and reaching for merchandise in a store from which the plate glass window had been eliminated. The only other occasion on which I saw this unusual brand of black/white collaboration was during the Attica prison uprising. There was a clear underlying message in both of those very significant rebellions that Black, White, Hispanic and Asian leaders had chosen to ignore.

I made my way past burnt-out blocks and came to charnel rows of houses with weather-singed, peeling facades and broken windows that were like eyeless sentinels looking down at children playing on the sidewalk. But voices, warm and sparkling as sunshine, occasionally sang out from gloomy, cavernous depths, warning the children to be careful. I also noticed that, because of the burnings, sunlight was now invading spaces that had been innocent of its existence since the Whites had fled to the suburbs and the mansions they abandoned had been subdivided into warrens and dark cubicles where Bigger Thomases and their relatives, by the hundred thousand, had cotched and dreamed and survived. The poet, Frank Marshall Davis, in his portrait of a ghetto dweller, had said, "His life was a darkened cave where he had been shoved from birth", and "for countless carbon-copy days, he groped aimlessly, until, one day, quite by accident he stumbled into an exit of death."[6] But those children whose playground was the streets had learnt to dice with death from an early age, to dodge traffic and stray bullets, and circumvent the trafficking of pushers, prostitutes, hustlers and cops on the take. As they played their games on cracked pavements, they were oblivious of the requiem-in-advance that an ebony tower poet had written for them. Their poetry was in their bones, in their feet and in their laughter as they danced between multiple skipping ropes that whirred like hummingbirds' wings, and their laughter trilled like birdsong and occasionally hit the high-pitched notes of a flageolet. Why is it that outsiders invariably write such poignant poems and lyrics about the people of the inner cities, whereas the ghetto folk never write requiems for their own sufferers, but write and sing paeans of resistance and hope instead?

After a while, the facades of burnt-out buildings began to look like impermanent movie sets, and on street after street, blackened ruins looked like broken teeth stained with betel nut and grinning at the shining towers downtown.

Fires were still smouldering when I arrived in Washington DC to do a series of programmes for the Canadian Broadcasting Corporation on the culture of America's inner cities after the Black Power and anti-war rebellions. Transparent, silken scarves of smoke were rising from the ashes when the late Larry Neal, a brilliant and gifted black poet, took me on a guided tour. Years later, Larry would burn himself out like a comet to light up glooms that had settled on his spirit. He was one of those rare activist/ poets for whom rebellion against oppression was like the breath of life. But one could sense that despair was never far from his pristine elation. He pointed out those businesses that had been most ruthless in exploiting the poor. Special attention had been paid to them, and they had been reduced to rubble. He showed me a used-car lot that was empty and level as a tennis court. The owner, he said, had been notorious for selling cars, repossessing them and reselling them again and again. Every one of the cars had disappeared and the offices that housed records of loans were burnt to the ground. Larry had been an active participant in what he described as "our Black insurgency". He showed me a truck that had obviously been hastily abandoned. He had saved the white driver's life, he told me, by stopping him and advising him to run like hell in the opposite direction, since an unfriendly crowd was waiting two blocks ahead. The city was as familiar to Larry as his own face in a mirror, and he'd shown the terrified white man a safe escape route.

There was a festive atmosphere on the sunlit streets down which we strolled. Many of the folk recognized Larry as we walked along and greeted him with that careless, two-way banter so characteristic of black folks at ease. The rebellion had freed them for a moment in history from the thralldom of laughing to keep from dying, and an ineluctable surge of hope had possessed their spirits. They had struck out at the visible symbols and agents of their oppression – property that they could never hope to have owned, venal landlords, strong-armed rent collectors, bailiffs, the stealthy representative of loan sharks, the repo man who, backed by the police, could repossess cars in a matter of minutes – and they were feeling good. But they also knew that, in the coming tomorrows, the ruling class whom they had frightened during the days of rage would react like South America jaguars. One can frighten these creatures for a moment, but, after they've run away, they invariably return with fangs and claws at the ready to attack whomever or whatever frightened them.

Here and there, amidst buildings that were torched, an occasional forlorn sign pleading "Soul Brother" or " Black Owned" graced the front of a building. But, apparently, amongst them there were "Sold Brothers" as well as "Soul" Brothers, and venal owners as well as a few honest ones. Denizens of the ghetto, living close to the foundations of a towering edifice of exploitation, knew this only too well, because in some cases the signs were ignored and the building burnt down, while others were left alone.

Larry took me on tour of that other, often forgotten, Washington DC where black folks had clustered since before the Civil War. With wry humour, he recounted how the nation's capital had, momentarily, become integrated, and how whole communities of black rebels had imposed a racial democracy on this city for the first time since it had been founded. Motorists on their way home to their "whites only" sanctuaries, he declared, would offer rides to Blacks waiting at bus stops. The reason for this sudden surge of white benevolence, Larry explained, was that a black face was insurance against attacks by angry black crowds.

When we came to the end of the burnt-out sections of the city, it struck me that at the height of the burnings, the president of the United States could look out of his window and see the glow of night fires, just as Ho Chi Minh was doing night after night during US bombing raids. I cannot recall having read a single, inspired, Tolstoyan piece about what the president's thoughts were as he gazed at the city on fire from his seat of power. Presidential tapes, such as they are, have been banal, sprinkled with mundane ruminations, obscenities and mindless clichés. Profound thoughts or imaginative and original ideas have been conspicuously absent from them.

Joe Miles, a 19 year-old full-time official of the Socialist Workers Party, was my other escort during that historic visit to Washington. Joe had joined the SWP at 15 and was lively, intelligent, knowledgeable and utterly fearless, and, as a young black organiser, he worked with the youth of all races, colours and creeds. He took me to the most interesting community centre I had ever visited. Children, parents and people from all walks of life were there, and different groups of them were participating in classes in music, drama, dance, poetry, judo, karate, public health and childcare.

These folks, breaking free from the formal programmes that these centres usually sponsored, were designing cultural programmes that spoke directly to the needs of their community. The rebellion had opened up new intellectual spaces for them. There was even a class being run by architectural students, who, together with a group of slum-dwellers, were designing the kind of communal housing that people really wanted to live in. Looking at the designs and listening to passionate discussions, I could not help thinking of Carolina Maria de Jesus, that archetypal black Brazilian woman who had spoken for millions of the urban dispossessed in her book *Child of the Dark*. Carolina, with her three children by three different men, each of whom had, in turn, abandoned her, could be any of the women in the discussion groups I heard. For, like Carolina, there was a fierce, invincible, creative spirit locked up inside of their careworn and all too often abused bodies. After the success of her book, a reporter had asked Carolina how she felt about being a celebrity after years of foraging in garbage dumps to keep herself and her children alive. "Tell your readers," Carolina had said, "that I have merely re-entered the human race." These women who, a couple of days earlier, had taken to the streets to reaffirm their humanity, had also re-entered the human race. One of the Carolina incarnations, Mary Mason, slipped me a poem. Someone whispered to me that she had been a maid in white households all her life, and had, all of a sudden after the rebellion, begun writing poetry. Her poem was entitled "Silent Thunderstorm" and it told the story of her life and those of thousands of voiceless women in ten lines.

> Down there on my knees, scrubbing your floor
> You dangle me like a puppet
> I answer your questions honey-mouthed
> Questions 'bout my John and my church
> and my children
> and my hopes and dreams
> All my business…
> But make good use of me
> 'cause there ain't no more generations like me coming
> No more who'll bend down and scrub you floor
> while you kick them in the arse…[7]

When I left that group, I was drawn to other groups where older musicians were putting young ones through their paces. These groups were improvising riffs on a variety of instruments, beating out rhythms on drums, accompanying poems with music, reading rhythmic jazz poems, inventing scat lyrics and vocalising ballads and blues. It struck me, once again, that this language of music was the one that spoke the most eloquently from the souls of black folk. And having erupted from ancient rhythms of life and primordial memories, that music became the most universal of all cultural forms – melodic sounds that constantly echo and re-echo in the mind's ear of millions. The sounds are commercialised, saddled with inane and banal lyrics, but in their purest form, they still touch something visceral, haunting and unforgettable in the hearts of those who have an inner ear for the cries of anguish, of affirmation and rebellion. It was out of the seminal rhythms that this rebellious period fostered that we inherited rock and roll, the soul ballads of the 1960s, blue beat, reggae, soca, rap and hip hop and several other innovative musical expressions. When one listens with an inner ear, one can hear echoes of protest and affirmation in the best of all of these new musical creations, and one realises that, in fact, after the rebellions of the 1960s, *a luta continua!*

I brought back some other poems with me from that tour of the inner cities. They were written by men and women who could say, like the young poet in Watts, "From the ashes I came and with me many others." Theirs were pristine voices that had not been heard before. Their music can escape and echo across the globe, but they have to stage rebellions in order to make their written words leap across an infinite number of racist barriers.

Behind the façade of poverty and degradation in the ghettos, one can always find a turbulent and almost miraculous counter-culture. It is often hidden, buried, buffeted by despair. But on those all too infrequent occasions when the folk unite and rise up to stretch limbs stiff from too much kneeling, that counter-culture bursts out like flowers from cracks in a neglected pavement. Seeds of anger mutate and produce flowers of hope, and even the most despised and abandoned, like the prisoners the Black Muslims managed to rehabilitate, can be brought back to rejoin "the human race".

I close with the words of two other poets, Norman Jordan and Clyde Shy, both from the Hough district of Cleveland, Ohio. They emerged in the wake of the rebellion of the 1960s to write, recite and sing their poems to eager listeners.

Black Warrior

At night while whitey sleeps
the heat of a thousand African fires
burns across my chest.
I hear the beat of a war drum
and enchanted by this wild call
I hurl a brick through a store front window
and disappear.

Norman Jordan (1968)

The City

Blood and honey, wine and gunpowder,
innertubes and needles, marriage and murder
like the gutter for the drunk who sleeps
on his Bar-b-que box, and urinates in police cars.
This is unmistakably the city.

No one sees the lightning run and knock Mr. Jones down!
Cries from the children say he'll be O.K.
he's just new in town.
Friday nights and love affairs
fighting wenches and torn upstairs
This is unmistakably the city.

Clyde Shy (1968)

References

1. Virginia Woolf, *Selected Works of Virginia Woolf* (Hertfordshire: Wordsworth Editions Ltd, 2007), p. 606.
2. Jules Michelet, *Historical View of the French Revolution* (London: William Clowes and Sons, Ltd, 1883), p. 507.
3. Ibid.
4. Ibid.
5. Ibid, p. 508.
6. Frank Marshall Davis, "Three Average Americans" (in *De Kim* litterair pamflet, no. 3, Kraus Reprints, Nos. 1-6/7, 1950-1955, Nendeln/Liechtenstein, 1974), p. 8.
7. Mary Mason, "Silent Thunderstorms" (in *Cotopaxi*, Vol. 1, No. 1, 1968), p. 8.
8. Norman Jordan, "Black Warrior" (in *Cotopaxi*, op.cit), p. 8.
9. Clyde Shy, "The City" (ibid.).

CHAPTER EIGHTEEN

THE LURE OF EBONY TOWERS

I arrived in the US in 1968 to do a story on the Black Power movement for the Canadian Broadcasting Corp. Canada's small minority population was beginning to awaken. These were largely immigrants and their descendants from the former British Empire, along with a small Afro-Canadian population from Canada's early settlement and descendants of Blacks escaping the US. Though much smaller than the US, young people and not-so-young people were beginning to agitate for their rights, better jobs, education and health care, and more reasonable immigration policies. To some degree, the Canadians were worried that these activist groups were being influenced by the US. One of my best friends, who appeared frequently in the media, was dubbed "The Angriest Black Man" in Canada, but, as much as the authorities might deny it, there were many thousands more "angry" citizens.

When I arrived in the US, it was the first time I had put a foot in the country since the early 1950s. At that time, I was a member of the Laurence Olivier company, acting in plays in New York. Before that, in the 1940s, I had been a university student. In both instances, I had had to deal with the stultifying effects of US racism. Now, I was a journalist working for the CBC and curious to see how the cultural expression in the black community was being influenced by this Black Power activism.

I first went to Washington, DC where I connected up with my nephew, Nigel. Then, I did a tour of other major urban centres and interviewed leaders in the movement and had a lot of interchange of ideas from different groups. When I was in Cleveland, I also saw people at the Public Library. They remembered that I had worked there in the 1940s and Dr. Long was still there. I also met some other contacts there. I was crossing over between the white and black communities and they were glad to have someone who could cross this barrier in this tense period.

The anti-Vietnam war protests, the Black Power movement, and the waves of young people who were the children of the post-World War II generation were pushing for change. The GI Bill, following WWII and afterwards, had opened the door to higher education in ways not seen previously, and Blacks had been able to use the funds to attend the historically black colleges in greater numbers. Then, following Martin Luther King, Jr.'s assassination in April of 1968 and the riots in the inner cities of New York, Newark and elsewhere across the US, elitist and predominantly white universities, like Princeton and Rutgers, were compelled to open their doors to black students. The children of that earlier generation were now in the vanguard of the movement for change, compelling the universities to make the curriculum more relevant. They say "silence is consent", and that older generation, by not stopping their children from entering these universities, was demonstrating a silent acquiescence that would lead to a transformation of these institutions.

It was at this stage that I was inducted into the academic world.

Once these universities opened up, the next logical thing to do was to construct programmes, such as the Black Studies programmes, and make them integral parts of the universities' offerings. But you also needed to develop academic bridge programmes to help the students make the adjustment from their inner-city high schools to the demands of these institutions. From the late 1960s and into the early 1970s, universities like Harvard, Yale, City University of New York, among others, were very interested in what we were doing at Princeton and Rutgers, and I was involved in a number of programmes helping them develop summer and other programmes for their students.

In validating these programmes, we pointed to the question of Africa: how Africa is one eighth of the world's land surface and has over a billion people. That it has a vast reservoir of natural resources, and a plethora of languages and cultures, but that traditional histories had distorted, dismissed or trivialised these facts, lumping Africa's rich diversity into one big black amorphous mass. White historiography had even taken the Nile, which at 4,000 miles, is the longest river in the world, out of Africa, saying that the Nile Valley cultures had nothing to do with the rest of the African continent. They also tried to discount the fact that a hundred million African people were scattered in a global Diaspora of which the US was a part. These Africans and their descendants had faced the depredations of slavery as they were dispersed to the Americas and to Asia. It was also, as we pointed out, time to offer fresh perspectives on the impact that the peoples of this diaspora had on their new host cultures.

In formulating these studies, we had to decide whether to parochialise or internationalise them. An example of this was the discussions we had at Princeton of whether to have a "Black House" or a "Third World Center." Black students in many universities were pushing for a "Black House". I contended that a "Third World Center" would offer the opportunity to bring together a larger constituency and avoid the tendency of universities to provide a small space that could be shunted off to the peripheries of the campus. Happily, we were able to push this through and Princeton provided a building for it. I thought of the parallels with the struggle of Martin Luther to reform the church in the 15th century. Luther had nailed his thesis to the church door as he was formulating new ideas in a contest with Catholicism. The protestants needed to validate their new religion. To do this, they searched for a more all-embracing approach to avoid the tendency to parochialise their struggle. If they hadn't done this, Protestantism would have lost.

I thought that the focus of Black Power and Black studies, at the time, was very narrow and I felt that by bringing in a Third World perspective, local activism could draw on these outside contacts and have a more enduring effect. This is why I drew in some of my Third World contacts from England, such as Prof. Edward Scobie and Prof. Ivan Van Sertima. It was not only a question of a physical building or centre, but of developing a different kind of perspective. There were intense debates at both Princeton and Rutgers Livingston around these issues.

At one point, there was a crucial meeting at Livingston College, and the Black Muslims and cultural nationalists were out in force. I had brought Maurice Bazin and his wife, Nancy, to the meeting. Maurice was a French physicist whom I had last seen in British Guiana some years before, but we had stayed in touch. I spoke, then Van Sertima spoke, and Maurice was about to speak. When he began, the cultural nationalists complained, saying that they didn't want any white man to speak to them. Van Sertima was so angry at this, he broke the podium. He told them that they were going home to be brainwashed by white TV and yet, here was someone devoted to the struggle and they wouldn't let him speak. This was dangerous ground to be breaking at that time because the students had guns, but I was determined to talk the truth to them. I wanted to open the debate between concepts of the Third World and concepts of Black Power, while the cultural nationalists were intent on narrowing them. There were two factions which exist even to today. There were the Black Power faction that held that everything should be black – black leaders, black professors. Then, there was the Third World faction, which was attempting to broaden the struggle by dealing with the worldwide struggles, including the nonaligned movement – Nkrumah, Sukarno, Chou En-Lai.

The elms were dying on the Princeton campus in the late 1960s and early 1970s. Dutch elm disease was ravaging those opulent trees. Generations of students had for lazy moments lingered in their shade, and the roots of the oldest of those spreading elms had felt the vibration of footsteps hurrying to and from classes for over a century and a half. The roots had slept cold through many winters until the warm earth had awakened them, but you knew that the elms were dying from the way in which their leaves were changing colour prematurely when the breath of autumn was barely cooling the early morning air. By the time next spring came, they'd only be a memory; chain saws and crunching machines would turn their trunks, branches and roots into sawdust and mulch.

If you pressed your ear to the trunk of one of those dying elms, you might have heard them singing requiems long before the botanists discovered that a deadly virus was secreted in their sap. At the same time, if you were patient enough, you might also have heard echoes of affirmation that new and sturdy growths would replace the dying elms.

Matching these natural rhythms of life, death and rebirth on the Princeton campus were the profound changes taking place in the student body. All along, there had been, in fact, two Princetons: the idyllic one that F. Scott Fitzgerald had eulogised; and, the other, hidden behind its polite academic and social facade, that was infected with the virus of anti-semitism, racism and sexism. Now, for the first time since the university had been founded, this virus that had afflicted it from its royal colonial beginnings had been identified, acknowledged, and serious remedies were being attempted. With an unprecedented boldness, first women and then significant numbers of minority students were admitted. The heightened struggle for women's rights and the ferment of the anti-war and Black Power moments had, in fact, nudged this university (which black students had described as "the northernmost southern academic institution") into implementing dramatic changes. The result was that there never was and never will be again a minority student body like the one admitted between the late nineteen sixties and the early nineteen seventies. Over forty years later, I am still in touch with several of them and they've become remarkable people. I have a class photograph of the students and faculty who took part in that first summer orientation course and it provokes fond memories.

Princeton provided me with furnished living quarters in the Hibben apartments that overlooked Lake Carnegie, and it was a half an hour's drive on Route 1 to Douglass College at Rutgers. Badi Foster, who was a Ph.D. student at the time, and became the Acting Director of the Afro-American Studies Program, had set up a liaison between Princeton and Rutgers Livingston College and several faculty taught at both. However, after two years of the joint Princeton-Rutgers appointment, I became entirely committed to Princeton.

This entry into American academe not only offered the intriguing possibility of helping these new groups of students take advantage of the new programmes, but it also offered me the opportunity, for the first time in my life, of having a regular income. Now, I would have predictable funds and could send some money for Lisa and Christopher. Though my marriages to Joan and Sylvia had fallen apart, I still wanted to be involved with our children. After my sister's death, who had left four children, I had been at pains to do what I could to help from afar. I have a picture of the time when I had brought Christopher to stay with me. He was still in elementary school and my nephews Michael and Nigel were also in the area. Michael was doing engineering at Princeton – I had encouraged him to apply – and Nigel was working up the road as a research chemist at Exxon. I used to take all three of them jogging with me, and prepare a huge pot of cook-up rice for them on the weekend; before the weekend was up, the food would be gone. In my predominantly female family, it was a delight to have an opportunity for male bonding.

I was living in Canada at the time of the invitation to work at Princeton, and had hardly had time to pack my bags before returning to the US to teach. My invitation had been totally unexpected. I had visited a number of community centres as part of my research for the CBC programme I was doing, and it was when I went to New Jersey to visit LeRoi Jones' (Amiri Baraka) centre in Newark that I stopped off to see Maurice Bazin who was now teaching at Rutgers. He had been teaching at Princeton, but had got fed up with working at this elitist institution.

Just as I was about to return to Toronto, Maurice took me to a garden party at Princeton. It was at one has at these gatherings that I came across Sheldon Hackney, who was the Acting Director of Princeton's new Afro-American Studies Program. Sheldon was a white American from New Orleans and he and I hit it off. He told me that he'd like to invite me for a visiting professorship at Princeton, but I didn't take him all that seriously. I wasn't really interested in a permanent job at a US university, although I was open to a visiting post. I was on my way back to Toronto, and told him he could send me a letter. Much to my surprise, the letter arrived, and I got back in my car and returned to New Jersey.

In my romantic fashion, I had originally wanted to teach at Rutgers University, at Livingston College, which had just been set up and which was inducting students from the ghetto. In response to the riots in Newark, Rutgers was trying to provide a sanctuary for young people, following that old cliché about taking young people off the streets. But, after my interviews at Rutgers, a very interesting dean there told me that he was afraid he couldn't control me. I thought that this showed very good sense on his part. Princeton, for its part, didn't care about this at all. Princeton was more anxious to get a few black professors into its institution.

When I first arrived, H.H. Wilson, a professor of political science, sent me a newspaper clipping which showed that I was coming to Princeton at a time when the Afro-American Studies Program would be commemorating the memory of a black man who was lynched in Pittsburgh in 1911. Wilson was a revolutionary activist who was determined to tell me about the kind of country and environment, I was coming into by taking this job at Princeton. The man in Pittsburgh had been working at a factory and had

had a disagreement with a white worker which degenerated into a fight outside the factory. In the course of the fight, a factory superintendant was killed. The news spread around the factory and a mob chased this fellow. In the course of the chase, the black man was shot and taken to a hospital under police surveillance. They had actually arrested him. But, the white workers were determined to take matters in their hands and during the night, they broke in the hospital and captured him. They took him, chained him to a bed of straw, and burnt him alive. The next day, allegedly, children from the white neighbourhoods were playing games with the bones of this black man. This was the beginning of a major riot between black and white in Pittsburgh. Wilson, who also taught in the AFAM program, and had made it an act of honour to commemorate the occasion, invited me to discuss how they were going about it.

So, it was in this context that I came into Princeton and was given the widest possible terms of reference, practically *carte blanche*. Princeton had determined that 12% of the student body would be black. That, I thought, was an unfortunate sort of calculation. An assessment should have been made on the question of need, not simply on the question of population percentages. If you needed 50% black students in order to achieve a democratic balance, you should have had 50%. But that was also some of our own fault in accepting those percentages. We might not have gotten 50%, but perhaps we could have gotten more than 12%.

The campus was in uproar at the time. The students, black and white, in the anti-war movement and in other struggles, were challenging the whole university structure and the system at large. What I learned in this period was that academics get frightened very easily by outside forces impinging on their dreaming spires and the seclusion that the university offers behind wrought iron gates.

These gates, the wrought iron gates in front of Nassau Hall, look down the street towards the village of Princeton. That is Witherspoon Street, and Witherspoon leads directly to the black section of the town. This was the district where Paul Robeson grew up and he, as was true for most of the other children in his neighbourhood, had never been near that university campus, although it was almost within shouting distance from them. Here was the symbolism: those gates were always closed. In response to this, one of the first graduating classes of black students gave the university two metal spikes to be used to keep those gates open forever. So, the gates at Nassau Hall were opened, and they have remained open, symbolically, since then. But, there still remained a lot of invisible barriers across those open gates, even some twenty to thirty years later. They were not really all that wide open at all.

A good number of students have had the good fortune, or the misfortune, to have passed through my hands on these early programmes. I can trace them all around the country. One young woman, who came from Jersey City into Princeton, is now a lawyer and has also completed her Ph.D. She was having some trouble two years into her programme and I had to go and defend her. Then, later I got her a scholarship to study in Mexico because I felt the parochialism of Jersey City was overwhelming her, and she needed to be exposed to some wider perspectives. I thought she should go to another country with another language, to live and study for a while. Then, she could come back much better prepared to cope with the work needed to graduate from Princeton. In Mexico, she learned Spanish fluently, which served her well in her profession later on. But when this young woman came up for a scholarship, the Princeton officials said her grades were too poor, which they were – her starting grades. I pointed out that there had been a consistent improvement of these grades over time, and I assured them that her grades would improve even more with the time for study abroad. By the time she was due to graduate from Princeton, years later, she had begun studying law, and had done brilliantly.

At that time, the universities were not selective about whom they were inducting. They were throwing out a net and capturing for the university a wide range of students, some of whom were tremendously unprepared for the kind of educational rigour of a Princeton or a Rutgers. Students had attended high schools that had provided them with only rudimentary educational skills, and had left them ill-prepared for university-level work. While the students were keen to be at the university, we also had to keep them motivated and make them understand that they had to make tremendous efforts to overcome their educational handicaps. It was possible for many of them to get through the first year by riding on a combination of euphoria and an institutional "grace period". The crisis usually surfaced in the second year, when they had both emotional and intellectual problems.

Over and over again, I had to defend students who had been in my induction classes. For instance, on the question of plagiarism, I would meet the august committees of my colleagues who were judging these students for plagiarism. I prepared a mini-lecture on plagiarism and pointed out to my colleagues that plagiarism was a very new concept and that the famous 19th century French writer, Stendhal, was one of the greatest plagiarists to ever exist. Stendhal used to plagiarise entire stories, even down to the punctuation marks. Subsequently, he learnt to write better than the things he plagiarised and he stopped doing it. I argued that there were two ways of dealing with this problem: we could let the students plagiarise and then they might learn to do better than the things they plagiarised, or we could rap them on the knuckles. The concept of plagiarism was new to the students and so, in every case, the cases were dismissed and the students were sent back off with some threats and explanations on how to deal correctly with their research questions and writing.

The social, political and economic contexts of inducting minority students were also vital. You cannot just take statistics that begin some-where in the middle and *then* begin dealing with the problems of minority students. You have to see them in the context of the families they come from and of the overall social situation. I would not have been at Princeton as a professor without the anti-war and the Black Power movements and I never failed to remind my colleagues of this at meetings.

I said, "Look, ten years ago, I wouldn't have gotten an appointment as a doorman here."

The doors had been opened because the community had compelled the university to do what it should have been doing for a very long time. We were there to deal with the question of dropouts and improve educational opportunities for our students, and confront these immensely complex and difficult questions.

So at Princeton we began by setting up remedial programmes to help prepare minority students for university life. We had gotten funding from the university. I had the minority students for six weeks in the summer, when they would get orientation classes in writing, in mathematics, and in Basic English. I began to design a programme for helping them in using Standard English. One had to improvise, because there were not many models in American academia at that point. But, coming from the Third World, this was not a problem. I had been dealing with this in various ways back home. My mother adopted twenty-two children over the course of her long life in Guyana. These were all poor children and very poorly educated at the time they came into our household. In educating them, for eight of those twenty-two children, I had, at one time or another, taken them out of the school system and put them on a home reading course for two years. I made them expand their competence in the English language by simply reading novels and histories. After this period, they went back to school and had improved enormously in the whole business, not just in using standard English, but in mathematics and in all the other subjects. So, I brought some of this practice to my work with minority students in the US. It was a successful programme, and a high percentage of students who took part in it stayed the course and graduated.

I would ask them to list for me all the books they had read, in addition to the ones assigned in class, and the result was abysmal. Only a few of them had read more than half a dozen novels, biographies or nonfiction works. Ironically, one of the most widely read of the students I had during that period was an ex-convict who had come to Princeton after serving a number of years in prison for armed robbery.

"How on earth could this be? A convict? At Princeton?" people would ask.

"A bright young man," I would reply.

We didn't have many students who came to us from the penitentiary, but those who came, like this young man, were remarkable.

I did my best not to make the students feel self-conscious about handicaps for which they were not responsible, but I did begin to stress, when I could slip it in quietly, that reading and writing were part of a symbiotic exercise, and that the former fed the latter with ideas, examples, images, vocabularies and techniques. I provided them with a book list and told them that it was not just for the summer programme, but also for life. I added, that once they got hooked on reading, they would, hopefully, create their own reading lists.

I had them work on their writing skills by starting with essays written in their spoken language and then I had them translate these into a formal Standard English. I then showed them that their oral vocabulary was larger than their written one. This meant that in the new arena of the written word that they had entered, a new cognitive balance had to be established. I told them that some of the best examples of the juxtaposition of oral and written forms of English could be found in the contemporary Third World novels on the book list I gave them. I told them that some of the characters they would come across in their reading would be drawn from a vast and restless human tide of migrants, refugees, renegades, castaways, peasants moving from the countryside to the cities, individuals and peoples uprooted by wars, famine and pestilence. These were the faceless ones whom gifted writers, artists, musicians and creators of new art forms were bringing back into the human race by giving them faces and individual personalities. These were part of the unfortunate majority of the destitute who were erased from the pages of the books the white world regarded as universal, but who were now reappearing on the pages of Third World novels.

One element of the course looked at the dictionary, how it was made and how you added new words it. I had been living in England when they were preparing a new edition of the *Oxford English Dictionary*. Marghanita Laski, whose uncle was a famous Marxist at the London School of Economics, was an OED publisher and she had come to me to take words that I used in my novels. They tracked the etymology of words down, the meaning, the history. Researchers had to write an essay on the word and trace it in works by other writers. They then decided whether it should be entered or not. She was going to all the West Indian writers who had entered the literary arena. They chose a number of words that I had introduced through my novels. One word was "kinnah", a Guyanese creole word meaning that the person is a kind of poison to you. "The woman is mi kinnah." Their researchers tracked its origins to Africa. Another word was "cotching", which means that the house is full, but you're sleeping in a hammock or a sleeping bag in the passageway or on the porch. Guyanese linguist Richard Allsopp was working on similar words for his *Dictionary of Caribbean English* many years later. This came from an Old English word "escotch", which means a temporary stay.

The students believed that the dictionary was a magical thing, the last word on everything. We were trying to demystify it and make it less intimidating, so they could use the dictionary more creatively. We showed them there were racist descriptions in the dictionary, and how dictionaries could be subjective and distort the truth. The students got the message that this was one of the reasons we needed Black studies – so they could correct misinformation and other racist descriptions.

The summer programmes gave them strategies and tools so that they could manage with the regular courses once they started.

Outside the narrow parameters of this small educational experiment, the nationwide anti-war and Black Power ferment made it easier to motivate these students and, incidentally, to persuade Princeton to provide the resources to carry out the experiment successfully. We also had the collaboration of their parents. They made it clear that their sons and daughters had a rare opportunity to attend Princeton, and that they should work hard and listen to what we were teaching them. It was a time of exhilaration, passion, and great expectations.

The question of Black Studies coming into white universities was a vital one for inducting black faculty into academia, and for improving the quality of performance of the students in those universities. Where you still have good, strong Black Studies departments surviving, you have better quality students coming out. They are better motivated and their problems are more successfully dealt with. Now, some forty years later, a great deal of nonsense is being noised about when people ask, "Do we still need Black Studies?" But what they really mean is, "Do black people exist? Do black people have a history or a past of consequence? Do they still operate at a disadvantage?" Of course they do. It is not a question of whether you should study Swahili and go into some kind of mumbo jumbo, which is the racist thesis of Black Studies. Black Studies provide an important nexus, linking the past to the present and bridging the diasporan experiences of peoples of African descent.

Our fault in being quiet about fighting for Black Studies is reflected in the high attrition rate of Blacks in predominantly white institutions. True, many of these Black Studies departments were ill-conceived and badly financed. The planning was awful. Nevertheless, it was through such departments that we had Black faculty entering into these university systems. But, we now find ourselves faced with a situation Shakespeare described, when he wrote, "*When he doth attain the upmost round,/ he then unto the ladder turns his back,/ […] scorning the base degrees/ By which he did ascend.*" So, having got our black faculty into academe through the Black Studies programmes, they then become part of the mechanism for removing the possibilities of other Blacks getting into these universities. These are things that we should look at very seriously and very critically when we are dealing with the overall picture.

My work with my students in these summer programmes was, in a very real sense, a unique experiment. My day began with taking groups of students running along my favourite path between the lake and a canal; after breakfast, we had classes. The second break was for lunch, and then classes continued into the afternoon. The pivotal classes were in English and mathematics, and then there were others in race relations, the sociology of campus life, the development of good study habits, and the most effective use of the library. As a follow-up to this summer experiment, I was able to arrange study-abroad programmes to Guyana, the Eastern Caribbean island of Dominica, Jamaica, and to Tanzania in East Africa for a few of the more enterprising students.

This summer programme was a precursor to my courses, "An Introduction to Afro-American Studies" and "Contemporary Third World Literature", and these courses helped me to reach out more effectively to the more intellectually mature students in the class.

I remember that once, during a pause in our morning run, a student from the inner city, looking around with a bewildered expression on his face, had declared, "What am I going to do with all of this affluence!"

I did not say anything to him at the time, although I had to smile to myself over his use of the term. But, later in the day, I took him to the main campus and while we were standing under the neatly manicured elms I asked, "Do you see anything wrong with these trees?"

"The leaves are changing colour, but they look OK to me."

"Well, my young brother, they might look good on the outside, but a viral infection known as Dutch elm disease is eating away at their sap, and all of them will have to be replaced with new and healthy growths. You see, these elms are a metaphor –"

"Metaphor? You mean like a symbol?" he asked.

"Yes, a symbol of what you and other new presences are bringing to this campus. You are a part of the new healthy growths that Princeton needs to survive. Let's hope that by the time you graduate, and your sons and daughters follow in your footsteps, the virus will only be a bad memory."

"I don't get it all, Prof," he said, knitting his brow, "but I think I know where you're coming from."

I pressed my ear to the trunk of the nearest elm and there was a panicked look on his face.

"You okay, Prof?"

"I'm trying to hear the requiem music in the sap," I explained, and he laughed, excused himself politely, and hurried off.

Late at night, I could hear the sound of traffic on Route 1 and it reminded me of sound of surf. And the lake nearby was a constant source of magic and mystery, whether it was the sight of autumn leaves stirred by the wind and falling like a rain of butterflies, or trees rainbowed with colours and leaning over to stare at their reflections, or sculls with crews rowing in unison and splintering the still, sun-spangled surface while the coxes shouted orders. From the front verandah of my apartment, I could look across a narrow street and see a gently sloping hillside covered with untidy copses. As the autumn progressed, more and more of a tall ginko tree was exposed as the trees around it shed their leaves. Even when wind and weather had stripped the other trees naked, the ginko continued to cling to its brilliant yellow foliage. Then, when it seemed as if the ginko would remain immutable in its autumn garb, it shed its leaves in a single day and they lay in golden heaps on the ground beneath it. After being at Princeton for a while, it dawned on me that the ginko was telling me that, like Princeton, it was old, tough, stubborn, and reluctant to change, and was only willing to do so when relentless forces had borne down upon it.

Once the decision was taken to admit students of colour, for a heady period they comprised 12% of the student body, but thirty years later, when overt and covert attacks on affirmative action have come into vogue, the percentage is considerably lower.

In retrospect, after devising a student support programme, the establishing of Third World studies was probably the most important thing we achieved, when Badi Foster and I were able to push through the idea of the Third World Center which would offer courses such as my course in "Contemporary Third World Literature". I did, though, have to campaign for permission to use the term "Third World" for my course, since some administrators were not convinced that this was a legitimate term. A dean at Princeton called me in and asked if it wouldn't be better to choose a different title, because the term "third world" might be too controversial. I insisted that it remain with this title and they didn't require me to do otherwise. I took this same "Third World Literature" class with me to Rutgers and then later to Northwestern where I've taught hundreds of students. Some of them have written to tell me that this course changed their lives, or helped them get into their future professions.

A Third World Center, I told supporters, would induct black students into a worldwide arena. Black students were fighting among themselves in different factions, and I thought that establishing a Third World Center would help them avoid being locked into too parochial a focus by opening their awareness to a complex world of different peoples and new ideas. That is what, in fact, happened: it brought black students and international students together.

We had the support of a wide range of faculty, administrators and students, both black and white. Carl Fields, the first black dean appointed by Princeton, and Conrad Snowden, a vice provost, played significant roles in making the Third World Center a reality. Other advocates were Prof. Hackney, an historian and the person who first invited me to Princeton; engineering professor, Steve Slaby; Professor Wilson; law professor and international jurist Richard Falk; sociology professor Morroe Berger; Dean Joe Moore who was also an alderman; Dean Cecelia Drewry; history professor Henry Drewry; and visiting professor of art, Philip Moore of Guyana. There were graduate students who joined this campaign, such as Barbara Egypt, Aggrey Brown from Jamaica, and Colin Moore from Guyana; as well as some of foremost student activists at the time, like David Evans, Carl Barclay, Debra Jackson, Eric Lom, Richard Sobel, Juanita James, Michael Harris, Lionel Jean Baptiste from Haiti, and John Favors. There were, of course, many others.

Badi Foster's support for the idea of the Third World Center came from his exposure to the concept and the reality of the Third World in his early youth. A Chicago-born black American, Badi's family practised the Bahai faith and his father moved his family to Morocco when he was a youth. Returning to the US for college, Badi then did his undergraduate studies at the University of Colorado and his graduate studies at Princeton.

John Favors (Tsombe), one of our student activists, was also attuned to this global perspective. He was a most unusual inductee to the Princeton student body and one whom I came to know rather well. He hailed from the Midwest, had attended high school on the east coast, and was a former Black Panther. As was popular at this time, he had taken on the name of Tsombe to affirm an African identity. His widening consciousness of the Third World led to his doing a study-abroad project in Jamaica. Later, when he was about to graduate, I arranged for him to do his postgraduate studies at the University of Dar-es-Salaam in Tanzania. Years later, in the 1980s, when he visited me after I had moved to Northwestern University, I discovered that he had joined the Hari Krishna faith and become an important figure in the administration of this Hindu religion. John has passed away now, but he had risen to the position of the Swami Krishnapada and headed the global educational wing of the Krishna faith, devoting his life to travelling across oceans and continents preaching a message of peace, love, compassion, non-violence and spiritual harmony.

I had been instrumental in inviting the Guyanese artist, Philip Moore, to be Princeton's first black artist in-residence. One year, during spring break, when there was a lull in student activism, I persuaded a group of professors and administrators from Princeton and Rutgers to visit Guyana. Those accompanying me from Princeton included Gamel Lester, a lecturer in political science; Rob Fielding, a vice provost; and Professor John Marston, director of the Afro-Am program. Bill Roland, the vice president of Livingston college at Rutgers, also came. Our mission was to develop exchanges with the

University of Guyana, but this never got off the ground. Instead, I had taken them around to meet Philip and see his studio and they were so thrilled with his work that they helped me coordinate efforts to bring Phillip to Princeton with a joint arrangement at Rutgers.

The original vision we had as founders of the Third World Center at Princeton has been realised in the many positive paths chosen by students who passed through its portals. Of those who have stayed in touch with me, there have been a number of lawyers, some Ph Ds, and others who have travelled or settled in other countries where they have been able to make contributions. The Center served as a vital fixture and resource for generations of students after I left in 1973. I understand that, recently, the Center has been renamed after Professor Carl Fields, who was one of its early supporters, and I hope that it has been able to retain its global vision. In light of the catastrophe of September 11th, 2001, the mission of widening the student consciousness of a vast and complex the world outside of the US has become more urgent than ever.

The elms have gone and new growths sleep cold in the winter and awaken in the spring. The roots of those new growths once again feel the vibration of footsteps hurrying to and from classes. The idyll that F. Scott Fitzgerald created in his translucent prose resurrects itself with every new season. But the need for vigilance remains, for the viruses from the past are not dead, they're only sleeping.

CHAPTER NINETEEN

NORTHWESTERN BATTLES AND BEYOND

I was back in Guyana looking for some respite from the fray at Princeton and Rutgers. At the time Northwestern University's Dean Hanna Gray reached me, I was on a trip into the interior. I was visiting my mother who had gone into the interior as a missionary. At the age of 70, she had retired from a lifetime of teaching but instead of allowing herself to move into a comfortable old age, she became a Pilgrim Holiness missionary and started a school among the Amerindians at Paramakatoi. My mother had a co-worker, a medical nurse from Ohio in the US, who was also a Pilgrim Holiness missionary. The two of them, along with an occasional pastor and a teacher who volunteered to teach at the school, were the only non-Amerindians for many miles around.

I was travelling across a small section of the Guiana Shield, a vast area of savannah grasslands, rivers and plains. This is a magical area of Guyana. The name Guyana derives from the Amerindian word "waini", which means "land of many rivers". Lakes link themselves to springs and move from small beginnings as they gather strength and tumble down rocky staircases and are fed by tributaries, so by the time they reach the sea, they have become mighty rivers.

When the explorer Sir Walter Raleigh first saw Guyana, it was during the rainy season when the savannahs had transformed themselves into a huge lake. Looking at a golden sunset on the lake, he had declared that he had found "El Dorado". And so the myth of El Dorado was born and this myth has been kept alive by countless explorers since Raleigh's time. It is almost as though every new explorer has had to keep the myth alive by adding new embellishments to the tales that have proliferated through the centuries.

Paramakatoi had an unusual stretch of tableland with hills on all sides. This flat stretch had been levelled to form an airstrip for small planes to land. You had the choice of landing in an amphibious plane, which came down in the river, or on a small, dirt airstrip at the bottom of a hill. Then, you walked up a steep hill, which led to a community with a church, a school and a cluster of houses.

In order to visit my mother, I had to take a small plane and fly from Georgetown up to Paramakatoi. Often, I was the only passenger on the plane and would be surrounded by goods that my mother and her co-worker had ordered from the city. When we were about to land on the river, a parade of children would assemble along the river bank. Before the plane touched down, they would throw rocks into the water. The pilot explained to me that these children were performing a vital function. Near Paramakatoi, the river is like a mirror and pilots cannot gauge distances between the height of the plane and the surface when trying to landing on the water. When the children threw rocks on the river, they would break up the surface and the pilots could gauge it better. Then, the whole community would turn out to unload the goods. They had to do this very quickly in order for the plane to get back to Georgetown before the light faded.

The pilot was a small, wiry American who had been burnt to a crisp by the equatorial sun. He had been flying small aircraft over the rain forests of Guyana, Venezuela and Brazil for the past ten years and a high waterfall in Guyana, Angel Falls, had been named after him. He was the only white man that some of the Amerindian children had seen in their lifetime and they dealt with him with an easy familiarity. Since he had started flying over this vast region, he had memorised where the forest had been veined by the rivers and he knew, like no one else, where every airstrip was located.

Before we left Georgetown, the pilot had to make contact by radio telephone with an agent who would start up a generator and he would then talk with this agent at the time he specified. He had to make sure that everything was perfect, because one mistake could cost him his life. The rain forest had swallowed up many pilots and their crafts in the past decade.

As I've said, I was on a visit to my mother when the radio telephone operator announced that I had this call from America. It was a call from Northwestern University offering me a job. Here I was in this primordial setting, talking to someone in a distant world about a job in an American university. They were lucky to get through, because the generator was only going to be working for three hours on that particular day. Petrol had to be flown in to run it and supplies were limited, so the generator was only scheduled for certain periods. The call was from Hanna Gray's office. They were offering me a full professorship with tenure and I was to be the Chair of Northwestern's new Department of African American Studies. Dean Gray was a trustee at Princeton and she knew about my work there. They didn't know that I was in Guyana and had tried to get in touch with me in Princeton. When I talked to Dean Gray, I told her that I was in the middle of the rainforest and that this was not the best time for a discussion, but that I would get in touch with her when I returned to Georgetown.

When I told the administration at Princeton about the offer, they were interested in keeping me. There had been other offers at the same time. I'd been offered the head of the department of African American Studies at Rutgers University, too. The programme at Princeton was being reorganised, and Syl Whitaker had by now been made the head of a newly configured Program in Afro-American Studies. My good friend, Morroe Berger, was on the Advisory Committee for the Program. This was a time when Sir Arthur Lewis from St. Lucia was teaching in the Economics Department at Princeton. He went on to win the Nobel Prize for Economics in 1979. But, I felt that the politics of Princeton and Livingston College at Rutgers was very confused and I was ready to make a change to a more stable position at Northwestern.

Dean Gray was smart, able, and very much in charge. It was a great pleasure to work with her. She gave me free reign to build up and shape this new department of African American Studies. I arrived in the midst of a roiling controversy about what this department should be. I believed that since we were establishing a new discipline, we should have both long term and short term plans in order to make it an integral part of this renowned academic institution. Northwestern had only belatedly acknowledged that its student composition was predominantly white and that the black and other minority students were mere tokens.

The main campus of Northwestern University campus is in Evanston, north of Chicago. Its professional medical and law faculties are in downtown Chicago. Once this institution had decided to admit Blacks and other minorities in significant numbers, it was prepared to make a great effort to recruit the brightest and the best. "It was the best of times and the worst of times…" on the campus. The black students were restive and they were making it clear to the administration that "Yes we have been admitted to your august, lily-white institution, but we come here with special needs that are to be heeded if we are to succeed in this new environment."

I was brought in at the height of the unrest. A black student organisation, whose acronym, FMO, stood for "For Members Only", a rather curious name, seemed bent on setting up an exclusive secret society on the campus, not unlike the ones that Whites had used to keep Blacks, Jews and other minorities out for generations.

I accepted the Northwestern offer because it gave a considerably larger salary and to get a full professorship with tenure was unheard of – not only for Blacks, but for anyone. However, Northwestern was also fighting its own political battles, and the campus was even more divided than Princeton's. I didn't know this before I went, but once I got settled there I could see that they were in a state of turmoil, too. The Black student organisation wanted the Black Historian Lerone Bennett to be the chair. The university had appointed him, but he had only served for a couple of weeks before resigning because of illness. Later, when he got better, he tried to come back, but by then I was ensconced. I don't know why exactly, but the students were making unreasonable demands. Professor of History, Sterling Stuckey and Professor of Mathematics Joshua Leslie, and some of the black faculty, supported me as chair. But I was relatively unknown in the Chicago area and the students were calling on me to resign. It was very tense. They were talking about bringing guns – something I had heard and seen earlier at Rutgers when I was teaching there.

Nonetheless, I was appointed and the same week I called a meeting with the students. The hall was packed. I told them that I would be willing to resign if they gave me good reasons why I should. Instead, they decided to boycott my classes as means to pressure me. But, my classes filled up with other students. Eventually, the black students became jealous at the fact that white students were taking my classes. I used to have over a hundred students in my "Third World Literature" class. After a while, the black students figured out that there must be something interesting going on in that class and they made overtures to end the boycott. I welcomed them and told them that I would accept their decision to end the boycott on one condition: that they wrote a statement, explaining why they were ending it. I told them that it had to be well-written and I helped them craft the letter.

Also, since this was an academic institution, I told them that I would write an essay outlining what I saw Black Studies to be. I had written an earlier form of this statement and used it as an informal guidepost for the programmes we had set up at Princeton and Rutgers. But, now, as I was the Chair of African American Studies at Northwestern, and able to shape the department and our studies, I updated the statement and gave this to the students. The university published about 3,000 copies of this essay and had it distributed around the campus.

When I was appointed chair, the University had already hired Robert Hill and Cyrus Colter as associate professors. During my first few years, I added Leon Forrest, Barbara Fields and Joy Gleason to the roster. I had made these appointments in close collaboration with Dean Gray and Provost Ray Mack. I had a signed agreement with the University to have, over the next set of years, four full professors, four associate professors, three assistant professors, and one visiting distinguished professor who would be invited for a year at a time.

It was a matter of strategy and tactics. If the department, from its inception, was not firmly established as an integral part of the University when "the tumult and the shouting died", as it surely would, it would be very vulnerable to "the slings and arrows of outrageous fortune". For when the University ran into one of its cyclical fiscal crises and cuts had to be made, the African American Studies Department would be the first to go and the old adage of "the last hired and the first fired" would once more come into play.

I also proposed that a special African American studies collection should be established in the university library, in the same way that the Africana collection had been; and that the librarian in charge of this collection should be highly qualified. I was certain that this would be an enduring foundation upon which a new academic department could be built, because it would continue to be available to students no matter who was chair of the department. That collection, which was established in the early 1970s, has now become a notable section of the renowned Northwestern University Library collection.

In the late 1980s, I arranged for Professor Edward Scobie to place some of his voluminous collection of Ira Aldridge artifacts and books in the African American Studies Collection, so as to preserve them for future students and researchers. As I've mentioned in an earlier chapter, Aldridge lived in the 19th century, and was the first black Shakespearean actor to gain recognition on the international stage. He was so beloved in Europe that he was buried in Poland with full honours. These five boxes of items have been catalogued and are housed in the McCormack Library's Special Collections section.

Leon Forrest was an interesting addition to our faculty. Toni Morrison, whom I had known from the days when I was teaching at Princeton and Rutgers, had introduced us. Toni, who was working at Random House at the time, was editing Leon Forrest's first novel, *There is a Tree More Ancient than Eden,* when she told me about him. He had recently resigned as editor of *Muhammad Speaks*, the Black Muslim paper, and had applied for a job in the department.

Toni had warned me that in spite of his great promise as a writer, he made a very indifferent impression at interviews, and this turned out to be perfectly true. Leon was short, paunchy and he shambled rather than walked and when he spoke he did so in running monotones. But, mercifully, I had read his novel, which was a long poetic evocation of a black preacher's rhetoric, and I knew he'd be a good compliment to the department.

Toni was also working with Ivan Van Sertima on his manuscript of *They Came Before Columbus.* I encouraged Ivan to move to the US while I was at Princeton. Initially, he did graduate studies at Rutgers, then he was hired onto the faculty and also gave occasional classes at Princeton. I knew that he had a brilliant research mind and, though he was planning to do a book on Shaka Zulu, the great South Africa leader, I thought he could really develop the story of the early explorations of African seafarers in Ancient America. I had come across three volumes by the historian Leo Weiner, (*Africa and the Discovery of America* [1922]) which had these accounts, but which had been buried in the traditional Eurocentric myopia of not "seeing the forest for the trees". Here and elsewhere were periodic references to finding artifacts or comments made by indigenous people that indicated that other explorers had come into the region before the Europeans. As evident from the artifacts, such as those inimitable Olmec heads, there was no mistaking that these explorers were Africans. The choice of putting half of a contemporary West African face up against half of a stone Olmec head on the cover of Van's book was a strong selling point. Before Van passed away in 2009, the book had already gone into more than 20 reprintings because of its popularity. Van threw himself into the work, drawing from his linguistic and other training and this project, and his subsequent *Journal of African Civilizations*, became his life's work.

Toni Morrison, herself, was also working on her writing, but she hadn't yet become as well-known as she would become when she won the Nobel Prize for literature. She had taken over the editor's job from another black American, Charles Harris, who had gone on to become the director of Howard University Press. Toni's assessment of her predecessor was not exactly flattering. She said that he was a good salesman but when it came to being a literary critic, he was out of his depth.

Toni's opinion of her fellow writers could, at times, be forthright and trenchant, but it was never tinged with malice, because she had an intellectual honesty and a quiet consciousness of her own enormous creative ability. She said, for example, that Maya Angelou's autobiography, *I Know Why the Caged Bird Sings*, would titillate the senses of readers and play on white guilt for a season, but it would not endure as a work of literature. But Maya fooled us all. She had staying power and charisma and she continued to mesmerise audiences whenever she stepped onto a podium.

It is strange that after spending fourteen years at Northwestern, I remember so little about it over the long term of my period there. My classes remained popular among the students, but the soured bureaucratic climate was draining. Even after I stepped down from being chair, as the senior-most member of the department, I was constantly trying to force the university to live up to the agreements negotiated in the early days.

The memory of my early days during the turmoil and the shouting is more vivid than that of later years. This was also the Hanna Gray period which was both hectic and exciting. Hanna left Northwestern in 1974 to become provost at Yale for a few years, and then returned to our area to become the first woman president of the University of Chicago in 1978. Unfortunately, when Hanna left, the new dean, Rudolph Weingartner, did not possess the same vision or energy for change. Meetings to remind him of previous agreements were often less then cordial.

At one point, after some heated back and forth over various issues, in a peak of paternal effrontery, he insisted upon coming to one of our departmental faculty meetings. I told him that I would invite him to one that I thought was most appropriate, and eventually did. He came in and immediately took the seat at the head of the table and I placed myself directly across from him at the other end, with the junior faculty on either side. After a few introductions, I told him sternly that we'd already had four hundred years of apprenticeship in this country and didn't need anymore, and that the running of the department was my and my faculty's responsibility. His demeanour immediately changed to a more conciliatory posture and he quickly said that he was only there to get to know us better. I, too, had an agenda, and with backpedalling on his part, I knew I was in a stronger position to raise some issues on behalf of one of my beleaguered junior faculty.

Through the turmoil of the Princeton-Rutgers period, I had retained a presence in Canada. It was a respite from the ever-present vigilance one had to maintain at Princeton. In Canada, I could relax with my writing and my friends. But my personal life was unsettled, and I was travelling back and forth practically every weekend. My relationships were further complicated by the intractable divisions within Black Power activism in the US. But with my position at Northwestern, I had to acknowledge that I was now settling in the US and beginning a new stage in my life, and I knew I would have to make peace with this new reality.

One of the terms I had gotten Dean Gray to agree to was that after three years as head of the department of African American Studies, I would have a year off with full pay. I had gone from the tense years at Princeton and Rutgers into the protracted manoeuvring of Northwestern without a substantive break for retooling.

I wanted to study the descendants of those African communities who had won their struggle against slavery before slavery was abolished by whites. I wanted to visit the Black Caribs who had been expelled by the British from the islands of St. Vincent and Dominica in the Eastern Caribbean, and resettled on the islands off the coast of the Central American country of Belize. I wanted to visit the Maroon communities in Jamaica and in Suriname. I felt it was important to learn more about black people who had abolished their own slavery by fighting successful insurgencies against the slave owners and winning their liberty for themselves. I felt that the leaders of these insurgencies, both male and female, should be household names for black children. I was tired of reading about Blacks who fought and lost and Blacks who fought against each other.

In the fall of 1975, I married Joy Gleason and, as I have recalled in Chapter Thirteen we went off to spend a year with the Maroons in Suriname who had defeated the Dutch, British, Spanish, and French. These were descendants of escaped slaves who had maintained their communities for centuries by successfully resettling themselves in the more inaccessible regions of the Suriname rainforest.

The Maroons would also raid the plantations and slave ships to free other blacks, and laugh at the black mercenaries who were fighting on the side of the colonialists. The Maroon fighters would gather on one bank of the river and shout to the mercenaries, "We admire you, you are brave men.

You even fight for the white man while this white man is brutalising you and your people."

Another strategy was to make a lot of noise in the night so their enemies could not sleep and by the time morning came, the mercenaries would be exhausted. They also used to attack their enemies around 3:00 o'clock in the morning because they believed this is when human beings became the most vulnerable.

There was a Scottish captain by name of John Gabriel Stedman who was hired by the Dutch and the French to put these escaped slaves back into slavery in a territory that stretched over Suriname and French Guiana. In the end, after fighting great Maroon fighters like Boni, Stedman found himself admiring their bravery and strategies. He admired them so much that he wrote about them in his diaries, gave up the struggle, and went back to Europe. I came across a large folio reproduction of Stedman's diaries at the Surinaams museum in Parimaribo. I was shocked at the exorbitant price, but had to have it for my collection and, even years later, find Stedman's commentary and drawings fascinating.

When we were packing for our yearlong stay in Suriname, Joy and I ended up sending 40 boxes of books and supplies down. Unfortunately, these items took several months to reach us and we decided that they would be more useful to the educational programmes of Suriname than to ship them back to the US.

While I was concentrating on the Maroons, Joy, who is a linguist, was working with young teachers at the Teachers' Training School as they were wrestling with the issue of a national language. She later published some of her research in *Caribbean Quarterly*. Dutch Guiana obtained its independence while we were there – in the fall of 1975 – and the new Suriname was dealing with the choice of an appropriate national language. As a colony of the Netherlands, Dutch was the official language, although the local creole, Sranan Tongo, was more widely used. Importantly, this creole was the language preferred by the poets and writers and was used for all radio emergency or medical announcements beamed to the rural and interior populations. Now that the country had gained its independence, should it keep Dutch, which was only known by the elites in the capital and spoken by a very small minority in the world? Or should Sranan Tongo be given full recognition, like Papiamento had been in Curaçao? Or, should English be taken on as a primary language, as it would have greater currency in world affairs? Outside of the capital, English was not widely spoken, but luckily for us, learning Sranan Tongo was much easier than working with Dutch.

At that time too, as I have recalled earlier, I was interested in carrying out experiments with ancient agricultural technologies. I wanted to introduce local communities to organic farming. I wanted to wean them from plantation crops like palm oil and introduce them instead to crop rotations and to growing the winged bean from Papua, New Guinea.

When I returned to Northwestern in the fall of 1976, I was no longer the chair, but I continued to have a lively following from the students until my retirement as Emeritus Professor of African American Studies in 1987.

In the early 1980s, Northwestern, like many universities around the country, got embroiled in student-and-faculty-led campaigns to have universities divest themselves of investments that supported the South African apartheid regime. One of my Northwestern colleagues, English Professor Dennis Brutus, was in the midst of this. Dennis was a poet and South African in exile in the US. Because of his outspoken condemnation of apartheid and those who protected it, his activism provoked no small amount of consternation on the campus. At one point, Northwestern was planning to hold a conference to discuss South Africa and the divestment question with the purpose of thwarting the campaigns for divestment. Dennis was in the forefront of calling this exercise a sham and the officials never forgave him for it.

The students, too, were adamant in their activism, and in solidarity with them, I wrote a poem for the students who seized Rebecca Crown, the main administrative building, and staged a sit-in for two weeks. They renamed Rebecca Crown, NELSON MANDELA. The students were calling on the university to divest the $85 million dollars it had invested in companies dealing with South Africa. One hundred and twenty-four of the students were arrested and were then on trial for their brave and principled actions.

Rebecca Crown, after whom the building had been named, had huge investments in General Electric Corp., one of the main offenders in selling high-tech products to the South African regime. Ironically, the student protest was one of the first really high-tech ones, because they were in touch through computer link-ups with thousands of other students sitting-in at other universities – at UCLA, Columbia, Wisconsin, etc. – from coast to coast.

For Those Who Woke Up

The dreaming torpor is over
it is the season of awakening
the clenched fists of students
have opened
like bluebells in the morning
their tongues are pistils
pollinating exquisite blooms of truth
South Africa's abominations
can no longer be concealed

Bond certificates
neatly parchmented
have become slippery with blood
Rebecca Crown
fortressing obscene profits
has been set free
Nelson Mandela has risen
and shrugged off his chains.

Jan Carew, May 10, 1985

Not long afterwards, Dennis's visa was withdrawn and he was about to be deported. We formed the Dennis Brutus Defence Committee and drew people from Evanston and Chicago. Over the period of the campaign, we collected more than 30,000 signatures on a petition in his favour, including support from elected officials and other notable individuals. If the US courts had ruled that he should go back to South Africa, it would have been tantamount to a death sentence. There were malevolent men in the South African judicial system who wanted Dennis silenced and dead. Dennis, though, had the will to fight back against seemingly impossible odds, and he was fearless.

Initially, Dennis had a lawyer who definitely was not up to the challenges of facing down the US government, so we organised another lawyer. This young woman was not terribly commanding when you first met her, but once she was in the court room, she was on fire. One tactic she advised us to follow was to pack the hallways outside the courtroom so that the judge would have to pass through this gauntlet.

We took our protests to the streets as well, and the winter of Dennis's trial in downtown Chicago was a particularly brutal one. The wind was biting into any exposed human flesh like a flesh-eater with filed teeth. But the members of the Dennis Brutus Defence Committee were still demonstrating outside the courthouse, and we took turns trumpeting our message through a loud speaker: "Free Dennis Brutus!"

The only crime that Dennis had committed was that he wrote poems that called you to the barricades, and those poems had words that exploded inside your head like hand grenades. His poems were in such collections as *Letters to Martha* and *Sirens, Knuckles and Boots*. Dennis's use of language in both poetry and prose made you feel as if he had sculpted each word like a precious stone. We should be grateful to him for leaving a legacy that is more priceless than red diamonds.

In the 1960s, before coming to the US, he and others had formed the South African Non-Racial Olympic Committee (SANROC). By 1968, it had persuaded the International Olympic committee to treat South Africa as a pariah state and not allow it to compete. This ban stayed in effect until 1992 and South Africa was not allowed back in until the apartheid regime had collapsed. This had been a very telling blow against the regime, and they struck back against Dennis with rage and venom. A defector from the apartheid secret service told a friend of ours that Dennis was regarded as one of the twenty-five most dangerous enemies of their regime. For us, Dennis represented a person against whom we could measure our own sense of dedication.

I had already known Dennis for ten years or more when he told me anecdotes about his arrest and imprisonment in South Africa. He talked about those cruel events casually. One was about how Mozambiquan agents had arrested him when he escaped from South Africa. He was being held in a prison in Johannesburg after the Portuguese agents had handed him over to their South African counterparts. Dennis said that it was important for him to attempt an escape from that urban prison, because if his comrades did not know that he had been recaptured, the South African apartheid police could get rid of him quietly and blame his death on foreign agents. In his characteristically amusing way, he confessed that he had seen too many Hollywood movies, so he made a bold attempt to escape and to mingle with the crowds on the streets of Johannesburg. He figured that the police tracking him down would be more reluctant to shoot him when they would also be endangering the lives of white pedestrians. When he made the getaway, he knew that among those tracking him was the best sharpshooter in South Africa. So, with his Hollywood, Who-done-it scenes in his mind, Dennis ran in one direction and then tracked back in the opposite direction. Unfortunately, this manoeuvre merely brought him face-to-face with his pursuers. So, he turned to run again and suddenly felt as though someone that pushed him. He did not know that he had been shot until blood was pouring down his leg and into his shoes. He knew that if he continued running, he would bleed to death. The bullet missed his heart by an inch, and miraculously – with the minimum of medical attention – he survived. But, his comrades were alerted to the fact that he had been recaptured. Then he was incarcerated in the notorious Robben Island prison.

Something else he confided in me was that he was imprisoned before the wound was properly healed and that his comrades in the prison helped to nurse him back to health. It is a miracle that someone who had been shot in the back with a bullet that had barely missed his heart should have survived a lifetime of unbelievable hardships.

These stories were a manifestation of trust between us that would last for a lifetime. During the decades over which we swapped tales, they bound us together and give us an unassailable trust in each other. We were also drawn closer together during the time in the 1980s when I headed the committee that fought against his deportation from the United States. During his appearances in court, he was always calm, fearless, and eloquent. It was as if echoes of his poetry adorned his speech and gave it greater weight and clarity. The stakes were very high during that period and, yet, he always managed to be kind and gracious to those who defended him.

It took two years, but Dennis won his case and was not deported. He left Northwestern in 1985 and went to the University of Pittsburgh. We stayed in touch and would occasionally do joint readings at Robin's Bookstore in Philadelphia. He presided over my 80th birthday celebration there in 2000. The last time I saw him at Robin's was in 2007, twenty years after we both had left Northwestern. He was still an activist, being now engaged in the anti-globalisation protests against the World Bank and the International Monetary Fund. Little did we know, but that was the last time we met; he died in 2009.

In 1987, I retired from Northwestern. As much as I had enjoyed working with my many students, I was now 67 and looking forward to getting back to my writing full-time. For a number of years, I had been frustrated by not having the time and psychic space to write. In the late 1970s, there had been a dramatic rise in the interest in publishing my work – plays, poetry, stories, essays – particularly in the Caribbean, but Joy was finishing her Ph.D. and I thought that it was not yet time to make a dramatic move from Chicago. As the CSCS Grenada projects developed, I thought that we would relocate to Grenada, but, unfortunately, with the death of Bishop and the turmoil, Grenada was no longer an option.

It was still important to find a place outside the US, where the cost of living was manageable, the weather hospitable, and where our young daughter might be able to grow up without the black/white divide pressing down on her like the Du Boisian "double consciousness". The success of making this move was made patently clear to me when I watched her absolute self-assurance at the tender age of five as she would talk freely with any of the passengers on the many flights we took together.

We settled into a small village outside Guadalajara, Mexico and arranged for Shantoba to attend the German School of Guadalajara following the recommendation of a friend who lived in the area. This required a longish drive into the city from our village, Tlaquepaque, and after gamely doing this for a while, I hired my neighbour to take care of this run for me. I also hired a housekeeper to look after the basic household affairs since Joy had a project in Chicago and was commuting back and forth. I settled into my new novel. Our daughter rapidly picked up Spanish, and by the second year, she was helping us with the translations. Immersed in my work in English for the majority of the day, my Spanish was of the rudimentary type, although, over time, I found that I was able to go about my business with a fair amount of ease.

Living in Mexico, I can see why Eisenstein fell in love with the country. In Tlaquepaque, creative urges were flowing from every pore in the skin of this small community that was a sanctuary for the best of the *artesanas* from all parts of Mexico. I could not have found a better place in which to write, and my writing was gaining momentum. I had begun a new novel based on some of my early family history and in the first fall of my time in Mexico, I was invited to the Harbourfront Writers' Festival in Toronto. During my time there, I did a forty minute reading from this new work in a large concert hall. The effect on the audience was, for me, startling. The audience reacted to every nuance in the reading, and afterwards, I was surrounded by publishers and literary agents.

Over the next twenty-five years of my retired life, I have periodically agreed to come out of retirement. After two years in Mexico, I agreed to become a Robinson Professor of Third World Literature at George Mason University for two years, then went back to my writing. A few years later, in the early 1990s, Niara Sudarkasa, President of Lincoln University in Pennsylvania, prevailed upon me to take over the University's new Center for the Comparative Study of the Humanities, and get it off the ground. I agreed to a three-year term there, then went back to my writing. Joy also took over one of the other Centers, the Center for the Study of Critical Languages, which she headed for seven years. Then, when I turned 80, I thought I would do one more visiting stint, and so accepted the invitation to become Visiting Liberal Studies Professor of Pan-African Studies at the University of Louisville for a semester. In 2000, after years of moving to so many different cities and universities, Joy and I moved to Louisville, Kentucky, and never left.

Jan Carew in Evanston, 1980s, at Northwestern University, Illinois.
Photograph: Northwestern University Media Relations archives

"African American Studies at Northwestern University:
A Position Paper"
[1973] (Evanston)

All peoples have a right to share the waters of the River of Life
and to drink with their own cups but our cups have been broken.
— Lament of an anonymous Afro-Carib woman

The dispersal of millions of Africans throughout most of North, Central, South America and the Caribbean Archipelago was an important factor in the preservation of vital elements of African culture. The slave trade introduced the African presence into every territory in the Western hemisphere from Canada to Argentina. In some instances, as in Bolivia, Chile and Argentina, the African population was absorbed, leaving few physical traces in the complexions and features of the majority peoples or significant cultural ones in their music, cuisine, etc.

Large concentrations of African American peoples now exist in the United States, the Caribbean Archipelago, Brazil, Venezuela, Colombia, Guyana, Suriname, French Guyana, Peru and, in addition, the Central American Republics from Southern Mexico to Panama. Besides, there are significant Afro-Amerindian communities in several of the countries mentioned above and also in Bolivia, Uruguay, Paraguay and Ecuador. By far the largest groups of African American peoples, however, are to be found in the United States and Brazil.

African American Studies at Northwestern University, therefore, has a major focus – the particular experience of Afro-Americans. But from this important core, if these studies are to validate themselves, they must, of necessity deal with the other black peoples of the New World diaspora and with Africa, the continent from which the African American peoples derived. Our field of investigation in African American Studies must, therefore, embrace the Afro-American core as well as Africa and all areas in which the African presence exists.

It is held by many intellectuals, both black and white, that black peoples created nothing, that they had no part in humankind's technological revolution. This has led white liberals to talk of the greater spirituality and humanism of Blacks and some black intellectuals to emphasise that the black man made up in terms of his complex family and social organisations, his metaphysics, his legal systems, his music, his art, for what he lacked in technological invention. Hence, the creation of romantic stereotypes of a Negro who never knew anything about mathematics or machines or mines or metals. This is one of the most persistent and misleading myths of the Black past, and also one of the least questioned. Even great poets like Cesaire and his Negritude disciples repeat and embellish this myth.

The white European did not start the technological revolution. It was, in its initial stages, a revolution contributed to by men from all over the world. From Africa came mathematics and the first script; from outside Europe, too, came the wheel, gunpowder, the crucial basics without which the so-called "European" technological revolution would not have been possible. A process the anthropologists call "diffusion" sparked this revolution, one to which all major civilisations and cultures had contributed, from the American Indian to the Chinese. European technology, therefore, did not have its origins in Europe. Rather, it was from around the Mediterranean, Africa, Asia, aboriginal America, etc., that the seminal material for that revolution was taken.

In dealing with the mosaic of African culture after the era of slavery, European conquest and colonisation, one can make an analogy with Chinese culture after the Mongol conquest. By the thirteenth century, so many essential elements of Chinese culture were dispersed, scattered and in some instances obliterated, that one had to go to countries on the periphery of China, like Japan, in order to rediscover important elements of Chinese culture. Ivan Morris in his perceptive and scholarly work, *The World of the Shining Prince*, underlines this point when he writes: "Japan has remained a repository of many forms of Chinese culture, the stately court dances, for example, that disappeared in the country of their origin during the Mongol invasions and later disorders."

There is a living monument to Africa in the Afro-American, himself or herself. Civilisations can sometimes survive in the human person, in living beings, not merely in stone and wood, brass and steel. That living civilisation, that vital essence and nucleus of the international black experience, may be found, for example, in the rich oral tradition of black peoples – in language, in the myths, in the value-system and metaphysics of the folklore.

The richest repository of that oral tradition, the most enduring witness of buried black life, submerged black structures, are in speech, music and folklore. Rhythms and linguistic structures die hard; they are patterns ground into the being of men in a particular place, within a particular cultural complex, over a vast span of time. They can only be wiped out completely with the death of the species. Only in a superficial sense can we say that the African came naked to the Americas. He came with centuries of an immemorial culture embedded in his psyche. Even though his languages were many and various, there were certain common features linking large families of tongues. It was no wild Babel of mutually exclusive language structures.

There are remarkable similarities to be found in the various forms of Black English spoken by Afro-Americans in this hemisphere. There is a basic structure to which the variants may be reduced to establish a grammatical substratum with syntactical elements common to many West African and even Bantu languages. What was at first dismissed as a childish imitation of standard English or at best an archaic carry-over from an earlier English is now being seen as the accommodation of a body of African languages to the language of the conqueror, an accommodation that shows linguistic skills of a high order, reducing all foreign complexities (Portuguese, Dutch, French, English, etc.) to a minimum of regular rules and patterns for maximum flexibility, cross-fertilisation, i.e., "linguistic marriage," and rapid and effective communication.

African syntactical structures have stamped themselves upon the psyche of the Afro-American. Africanisms – that is, African words – may die out, become less and less with every generation, but the vocabulary of language even in its own home and setting changes dramatically. What is significant in language is its value as the means of communicating cultural values and beliefs and how it survives and transmits itself from generation to generation.

Any serious programme of African American Studies should, therefore, place special emphasis on cultural linguistics, social anthropology, literature, myths, folk music, oral traditions and folklore. Serious contemporary studies in these fields are at once confirming the international character of the black experience in the Americas, and also underlining the essential unity that African oral traditions imposed on the structure and form of rural and urban dialects spoken by black people throughout the Americas. Important pioneering work in this field was done by Lorenzo D. Turner, the Afro-American scholar, and is being continued by Richard Allsopp at the University of Guyana and Ivan Van Sertima at Douglass College at Rutgers University, and by others.

Black English, as spoken in the urban ghettoes, evolved from seminal African structures after being distilled by centuries of the American experience. To separate Black English from its roots, therefore, as some experts are inclined to do (in their educational experiments in urban Afro-American communities), is as meaningless as trying to deal with conventional English without its Latin infusions. And language is an important weapon in transforming the ghettoes from enclaves of deprivation into viable and healthy urban communities.

It has been proved that certain structures in syntax are common to Black English in the United States, Sierra Leone, Gambia, Ghana, the Nigerian coast and the Caribbean. If a teacher can be taught about the basic differences in the grammatical structures that exist in Black English (the synthesised oral English) and the conventional English, then the gap between the oral and the written language could be bridged more successfully, the learning process speeded up, and the scope of students' comprehension extended.

The international character of the Black experience and the cultural blood-knot that ties the Afro-American to his African past makes it imperative to view Afro-American and African studies as two parts of an organic whole.

The traditional belief was that slaves had their languages erased from their minds when they arrived in the New World and were forced to imitate the language of the white captors as best they could. This theory was first challenged by Lorenzo D. Turner, who drew attention to the dialects spoken by Afro-American communities on the South Carolina coast. The full extent to which Black English carries African structures and vocabularies is still to be fully ascertained; and this will, of course, throw new light on the question of African infusions into the American language as a whole.

There is a school of thought which sees African American Studies as a device for an escape by Afro-Americans into ebony towers. This school of thought does not see science and technology as an organic part of an African American Studies programme. There is in fact no incompatibility between African American Studies and science and technology. The two should exist as intellectual fruit from the same tree. For just as it is being acknowledged by scholars that there is Black English, one can in the same way envisage mathematics specially geared to the needs of black people. Once one deals with mathematics as a scientific language and understands that since it is the key to entering all branches of science and technology, familiar symbols and imaginative teaching aids could be devised to make it attractive to Afro-American students from elementary school upwards. Therefore, African American Studies can sponsor and encourage the writing of special texts in mathematics for Afro-American students, and also make available to these students teaching aids that relate to their environment and to their particular experience and cosmology.

African American Studies, based on a world view that links all creative impulses in the human mind and the human spirit to endless rhythms and harmonies of change, must take the precise and logical forms inherent in science and technology and use them for man's benefit and not for his destruction. The black scientist must, therefore, always assume full responsibility for the implementation and consequences of the science and technology that he masters.

In conclusion, African American Studies based on the international character of the Afro-American experience must of necessity deal with:

1). The African Diaspora and its many consequences in the Americas – the web of oral languages and traditions that the slaves brought from Africa.

2). Racism and the distortions and omissions that it caused to develop in Western scholarship: e.g., the vast dislocations that took place in African society as a result of the slave trade are seldom considered; nor is the

enormous resilience of the African cultures which survived the depredations of slavery taken into account. Even when it is admitted that the
strength to absorb cataclysmic shocks exists in the African and the people
of the Diaspora, these important factors are deliberately minimised. Knowledge of the history of African peoples on the continent of Africa and in the
Diaspora is essential to an understanding of continuities and discontinuities
in the African experience. The Afro-American has been especially sensitive
to the need to rediscover the lineaments and essence of the African past
precisely because in North America that past and the presence of things
African were mercilessly assaulted by the coloniser. The European scholars' postulate that African peoples lacked meaningful traditions was used as
a powerful rationale for enslaving Africans and subjecting them to un-
speakable horror, the most insidious of which was inducing many millions
to question their own humanity. Thus, the uses of history (and later
biology, anthropology, sociology, literature, art, and other disciplines) as a
weapon in the service of oppression must be given substantial treatment in
African American Studies. It is well to recall that the demand for "black
history" was at the centre of the concerns of those calling for "Black
Studies" after the assassination of Dr. Martin Luther King, Jr.

3). Oral languages, traditions and oral history, which are the keys to
understanding many undiscovered facets of the Afro-American experience.

4). African American song, dance and religious styles and the ancient
ritual and dramatic forms out of which they derive.

5). Building on the works of those Afro-American scholars and writers
who began examinations of the nature of colonisation and the psyche of the
coloniser.

6). The links that were forged between the African and the Amerindian
cultures in this hemisphere. The African, rapidly assimilating European
languages and facets of European culture and fusing them into his oral
traditions, acted in many instances as culture-bringer to the Amerindian.
He, thus, enabled the Amerindian to preserve vital elements of his culture
which would otherwise have been erased. In the Northern region of South
America, for example, there was a fusion in the folklore of the African and
the Amerindian, extensive intermarriage and a profound accommodation
of the two cultures. This is an area that African American Studies can
explore in North, South and Central America, since it could provide
valuable insights into a process of change that could teach lessons in
tolerance to all peoples of all races, colours and creeds.

African American Studies, then, must be both local and international in
character, must be based on a world view that is particular for Afro-
Americans and also universal; these studies must fearlessly cross new
frontiers of knowledge; and must allow no forces, no philosophy of
expediency, no plastic anger of superficial rage to divert them from those

goals of liberation which the anguish and the profound humanity of the Afro-American impels him to seek. And these goals are in no way secret or exclusive. They can be achieved by all men who would sincerely be the brothers and not the masters of men.

JAN CAREW: BIBLIOGRAPHY AND SPECIAL EXHIBITS

HISTORIES, ESSAY COLLECTIONS, MEMOIRS

Episodes in My Life: The Autobiography of Jan Carew. Memoir (Leeds: Peepal Tree Press, 2015).

Potaro Dreams: My Youth in Guyana. Memoir (Hertford: Hansib Publications, 2014).

Rape of Paradise: Columbus and the Birth of Racism in the Americas. History. (NY, Astoria: Seaburn Publishing Co, 2006).

A selection from JC's memoirs was published in *Trinidad and Tobago Review* in the fall of 2002.

Two chapters from his autobiography was published in *New Writing in the Caribbean*, A.J. Seymour, ed. (Georgetown: Guyana Lithographic Co., 1972).

Ghosts in Our Blood: With Malcolm X in Africa, England and the Caribbean. Memoir. (NY: Lawrence Hill Books, 1994).

Rape of Paradise. History. (NY: A&B Books, 1994)

Fulcrums of Change: The Origins of Racism in the Americas and other essays. Essay collection. (Trenton: Africa World Press, 1988).

Grenada: The Hour Will Strike Again. History. (Prague: International Organization of Journalists Press, 1985).

NOVELS, NOVELLAS, STORY COLLECTIONS, CHILDREN'S STORIES

The Riverman. Novella (NY, Astoria: Seaburn Publishing House, 2015).

Black Midas. Novel. (Leeds: Peepal Tree Press, Caribbean Modern Classics, 2009).

The Wild Coast. Novel (Leeds: Peepal Tree Press, Caribbean Modern Classics, 2009).

The Guyanese Wanderer. Collection of stories (Louisville, Kentucky: Sarabande Books, 2007)

The Sisters and Manco's Stories. Novella and a collection of stories for young adults (Oxford: MacMillan Caribbean, Schooner Series, 2002).

Children of the Sun. Children's story (Georgetown, Guyana: Guyana Book Foundation, 1999).

The Coming of Amalivaca. Children's story (Georgetown, Guyana: Guyana Book Foundation, 1998).

Black Midas, extracts used in *Guyanese Creole Continuum* by John R. Rickford (Stanford: Stanford University Press, 1984).

The Wild Coast. Novel (London: Longman Group, Horizons Edition, 1983).

Black Midas. Novel (London: Longman Group, Horizons Edition, second
  impression, 1981).
_____. Novel (London: Longman Group, Horizons Edition, 1980).
Children of the Sun. Children's book. (Boston: Little, Brown and Co.,
  1980).
The Third Gift. Children's book (Boston: Little, Brown and Co., 1975).
The Wild Coast. Novel (Nendeln: Kraus Reprint Division, Kraus-
  Thompson Ltd., 1971).
Black Midas. Novel (Nendeln: Kraus Reprint Division, Kraus-Thompson
  Ltd., 1971).
_____. Novel (London: Longman Group, School's Edition, 1970).
Green Winter. Novel. U.S. paperback edition of *Moscow Is Not My Mecca*
  (New York: Stein and Day, c1966, c1964).
_____. Novel. U.S. Edition of *Moscow Is Not My Mecca* (New York:
  Stein and Day, 1965, c1964)
Winter in Moscow. Novel. Special edition for readers for whom English
  is a second language. (New York: Avon Books, 1964).
Moscow Is Not My Mecca. Novel (London: Martin Secker and Warburg,
  1964).
The Last Barbarian. Novel (London: Martin Secker and Warburg, 1960).
A Touch of Midas. Novel. U.S. Edition of *Black Midas* (Coward-McCann
  New York: c1958).
Black Midas. Novel (London: Martin Secker and Warburg, 1958).
The Wild Coast. Novel (London: Martin Secker and Warburg, 1958).

FOREIGN LANGUAGE PUBLICATIONS – NOVELS, HISTORIES, MEMOIRS, ETC.

Geister in unserem Blut. German Edition of *Ghosts in Our Blood* (Bremen:
  Atlantik Verlags, 1997).
The Third Gift, second printing, Japanese Edition (Tokyo: Hopy Shoppan
  Publishers, 1985).
_____. Japanese Edition (Tokyo: Hopy Shoppan Publishers, 1983).
Black Midas: *Midas Negro* (Cuba: Casa de Las Americas, 1983).
Children of the Sun. Japanese Edition (Tokyo: Hopy Shoppan Publishers,
  1981).
Invierno Verde. Portuguese Edition of *Green Winter* (Rio de Janeiro:
  Distribuidora Record, 1971).
Black Midas. Georgian (USSR) Edition (publisher unknown, 1966).
Moskau ist Nicht Mein Mekka. German Edition of *Moscow Is Not My
  Mecca* (Munchen: List Verlag, 1965).
Prikosnoveniya Midasa. Russian Edition of *Black Midas* (Moskva:

Gosudarstvenoye Isdatelstvo Hudodjestvenoy Literaturi, 1963).

O Midas Negro. Portuguese Edition of *Black Midas* (Lisboa: Editora Ulisseia, 1961).

Wilde Kuste. German Edition of *The Wild Coast* (Munchen: List Verlag, 1961).

Schwartzer Midas. German Edition of *Black Midas* (Munchen: List Verlag, 1959).

SHORT STORIES

"But is Why Tonic Die?" in *Exile: The Literary Quarterly,* 24. 3 (Toronto, 2000).

"Ti-Zek", in *The Oxford Book of Caribbean Short Stories* (Oxford: Oxford University Press, 1998).

"Caesar in Paris", *Chelsea*, 1987.

"Tilson Ezekiel Alias Ti-zek", *New England Review and Bread Loaf Quarterly*, VII. 4 (Summer, 1985).

"Hunters and Hunted", *Anthology of Writing in English* (London: Thomas Nelson and Sons, 1977).

"Twins of Illora", *Bim*, 15. 59 (Barbados, 1975).

_____, *Guyana Graphic*, Georgetown, 1975.

"Tilson Ezekiel Alias Ti-zek", *Caliban* (inaugural issue), University of Massachusetts Press (Amherst, 1975).

"A Job with the Road Gang", *The Sun's Eye*, Anne Walmsley, ed. (London: Longman, 1973).

"Walking With Caesar", *CARIFESTA Anthology*, Georgetown, 1972.

"The Coming of Amalivaca", *West Indian Stories*, Andrew Salkey, ed. (London: Faber, 1971).

"Hunters and Hunted", *Island Voices*, Andrew Salkey, ed. (New York: Liveright Publishers, 1970).

"Walking With Caesar", *The African Review*, London, 1965.

"Klautkys, Allicocks, and Hamiltons", *The Listener* (London) Sept. 24, 1959.

"Forgotten Province", *The Listener* (London) Sept 17, 1959.

"Anancy & Tiger", British Broadcasting Co., Third Programme, London, 1956.

"River of His Night", *Kyk-over-al*, Georgetown, 1952.

ARTICLES AND ESSAYS

"A Timeless Truthteller", in *Savoring the Salt: The Legacy of Toni Cade Bambara,* Linda Janet Holmes and Cheryl A. Wall, eds. (Philadelphia: Temple University Press, 2007).

"Tribute to Martin Carter", in *All are Involved: the Art of Martin Carter* (Leeds: Peepal Tree Press, 1999).

"The End of Moorish Enlightenment and the Beginning of the Columbian Era", in *Race, Discourse and the Origin of the Americas* (Washington, DC: Smithsonian Institute Press, 1995)

"Moorish Culture-Bringers: Bearers of Enlightenment", in *Golden Age of the Moor*, Ivan Van Sertima, ed., *Journal of African Civilizations*, Trenton, 1993.

"Culture and Rebellion", *Race and Class*, 35.1 (1993).

"Columbus and the Origins of Racism in the Americas", *Race & Class*, published in two parts, vol. 29, Spring, 1988, and vol. 30. 1, 1988.

"The Third World, Its Facade and Its Landscapes Within", *Race & Class*, 1987.

"Of Writing and Risk", *Flare*, supplement to *The City Sun*, New York, November 18, 1987.

"Conversations with Diop and Tsegaye: The Nile Valley Revisited", *The City Sun*, New York, Mar. 26-Apr. 1, 1986.

"Tribute to Alex La Guma", *New Deliberations*, Chicago, Spring/Summer, 1986.

"A Tribute to Alex La Guma", *The City Sun*, New York, Dec.4-10, 1985.

"Harvesting History in the Hills of Bacolet", *Journal of the Association of Caribbean Studies*, Miami, 1985.

"The Indira Gandhi I Knew: A Tribute", *New Deliberations*, Chicago, 1985.

"The African and the Indian Presence: Some Aspects of Historical Distortion", *Race & Class*, XXVII. 1, 1985.

"Some Aspects of Historical Distortion: The African and The Indian", *Expressions of Power in Education: Studies of Class, Gender and Race.* Prof. Gumbert, ed. (Atlanta: Georgia State University Press, 1984).

"Fulcrums of Change", *Race & Class*, XXVI. 2, London, 1984.

"The German Elections From a Black Perspective", *Black Press Review*, Chicago, April, 1983.

"US Attack Against Grenada: America's Day of Shame", *Black Press Review*, Chicago, September/October 1983.

"Jonestown, Three Years Later", *Quaecumque*, Northwestern University Chaplin's office, Evanston, 1982.

"Estevanico, The African Explorer", *Journal of African Civilizations*, 3. 1, Rutgers University: April 15, 1981.

"Amaranth, the Miracle Grain", pamphlet for the Caribbean Society for Culture and Science, St. Georges, 1981.

"The Caribbean Writer and Exile", *The Pushcart Press* (1979-80 edition).

"Pre-Columbian African Colonies in the Americas", *Journal of African Civilizations*, 1. 1, Rutgers University, Spring, 1979.

"What the Cuban Revolution Means to Me", *The Mirror*, Georgetown, 1979.

"Introduction", *Synergein Project proposal*. Evanston, 1979.

"Caribbean Writer and Exile", *Journal of Ethnic Studies*, V.1, Hampton, April, 1978.

_____, *Journal of Black Studies*, 8. 4, London, June, 1978.

_____, *Caliban*, II. 2, Amherst, Fall, Winter, 1978.

_____, *Jamaica Journal*, CARIFESTA issue, Kingston, 1976.

"For Tolstoy's 150th Anniversary", commemorative essay. *The Mirror,* Georgetown, 1978.

"Suddenly Last Summer", *Caribbean Contact*, Trinidad, 1978.

"Caribbean Culture", Essay for schools commissioned by the Ontario Institute for Studies in Education, Toronto, 1978.

"The Evolution of an Educational System in the English-Speaking Caribbean", Essay commissioned by the Ontario Institute for Studies in Education, Toronto, 1978.

"The Fusion of African and Amerindian Folk Myths", *Bim*, 16. 64, Bridgetown, December: 1978.

_____, *Caribbean Quarterly,* 23. 1, Kingston, March: 1977.

_____, Publication of the Ontario Institute of Education, Vincent D'Oyley, ed. Toronto, 1976.

"Race and Class", essay commissioned by the National Council of Churches, Fifth Commission. New York, 1977.

"Identity, Cultural Alienation and Education in the Caribbean", *Commonwealth Caribbean Journal*, special issue, 1976.

"The Transition of Marginal Farming Communities", *UNITAR News: Internal Migration*, 8, New York, 1976.

"Season of Violent Change", *Pan African Magazine*, Northwestern University Press, Evanston, 1976.

_____, *Toronto Star*, Toronto, 1967.

_____, *New Day*, Georgetown, 1966.

"The Winged Bean, A High Protein Legume", *Bulletin of the Fifth Commission*, National Council of Churches, New York, 1976.

"Origins of Racism in the Americas", *Journal of Belizean Affairs*, Belize, 1976.

_____, *CARIFESTA Forum*, John Hearne,ed. Kingston, 1976.

_____, *Bim*, 15. 59, Bridgetown, 1976

_____, *African Themes* (Evanston: Northwestern University Press, 1975).

"You Can Grow and Miracle Bean in Your Backyard", *Bulletin of the Fifth Commission*, National Council of Churches, New York, 1975.

"African Literature: From the Breath of Gods", *New York Times Sunday Book Review*, New York, 1972.

"Guyana: Three Points of Eden", *Saturday Review*, New York, July 1, 1972.

"Being Black in Byelorussia is Like Being From Mars", *New York Times (Sunday) Travel Section*, New York, 1971.

"Look Bwana, in East Africa You Carry a Bicycle on the Bus, Eat Crocodile Tail and Get to Know the People Who Married the Wind", *New York Times (Sunday) Travel Section*, Part 1, New York, Oct. 24, 1971.

"The Growth of African Fiction", *Contrast*, Montreal, 1971.

"Journey to Dominica", *Saturday Review*, New York, 1971.

"Some Aspects of Life and Language in the Developing Countries", *Afro-Asian Writings*, Issue #5, Cairo, April, 1970.

"The Coup in Ghana: Season of Violent Change", *New World Fortnightly*, #40, Georgetown, 13 May 1966.

"The Story of British Guyana", *New Statesman*, London, 1953.

FOREIGN LANGUAGE PUBLICATIONS – STORIES, ESSAYS

"Chantal" in *Cuentos del Caribe*, Manuel Verdecia, ed. (Havana: Editorial Arte y Literatura, 2011).

"Fulcrums of Change", *Komparatische Hefte*, 9, (Bayreuth: University of Bayreuth Press, 1983).

"Tilson Ezekiel gennant Ti-zek," in *Die Entdeckung Westindiens: Ezrahlungen aus der Karibik*. Peter Schultze-Kraft, ed. Buchergilde Gutenberg, Frankfurt am Main, 1989.

"The Caribbean Writer in Exile", German translation. *Freibeuter*. Berlin. November, 1980.

"El Escritor Caribeno y el Exilio", *La Revista*. Casa de las Americas, no. 105, Havana, 1977.

"Vse Vozvrashchaetsya K Rodnim Holman", *Inostranaya Literatura*, vol. 2, Moscow, February, 1980.

"The Conversion of Tiho", German translation, *England Erzahlt*. De Mendelessohn, ed., Munchen, 1959.

PUBLICATIONS: POETRY AND POETRY COLLECTIONS

"Ten Years," in *Che in Verse*, Gavin O'Toole and Georgina Jimenez, eds. (Wiltshire: Aflame Books, 2007).

"The Dreamtime Lives Again" and "Tiho, the Carib" in *The Heineman Book of Caribbean Poetry* (London: Heineman, 1992).

Assorted poems in *The Caribbean Book of Verse* (London: Penguin, 1998).

Assorted poems in *The Penguin Book of Caribbean Verse* (London: Penguin, 1987)

Six poems, in *Black American Literature Forum*, 1983.

"Obote Must Return", special edition, Third World Center, Oberlin College, Oberlin, 1983.

"The History Maker", in *Pacific Quarterly*, 1982.

Sea Drums in My Blood. Poetry Collection (Trinidad: New Voices Publication, 1981).

"Nocturn for Roots", in *Journal of African Civilizations*, 2.1 (Spring, 1981).

"Nicaragua - Grenada: A Chrysalis of Rainbows", in *The Free West Indian*. St. Georges, 1980.

"Cuba-Angola" in *Viente Anos de Revolucion:* Palabras de Esta America. Vinyl 33rpm recording (Havana: Casa de las Americas, 1979).

"The High Road to Harare", *Bim*, 16. 63, Bridgetown, June, 1978.

"Letter to Neto", in *Caribbean Contact*, Trinidad, 1975.

_____, in *Caliban*, May, 1975.

"Ballad for Soweto", in *Caribbean Quarterly*, 25. 1:2, Kingston, March-June, 1979.

_____, in *Caribbean Contact*, Trinidad, November, 1979.

"Cuba - Angola", in *Bim*, 16. 61, Bridgetown, 1977.

"Requiem for My Sister", in *Nimrod*, 21. 2 and 22. 1, Tulsa, 1977.

"The Cliffs at Manzanilla", in *Caliban*, May, 1975.

"Africa - Guyana", in *Journal of Black Poetry*, 1973.

_____, in *Like It Is*. Penguin Books, New York, 1973.

"Ten Years", in *New Writing in the Caribbean*. A.J. Seymour, ed. Georgetown: 1972.

_____, in *Breaklight*, Andrew Salkey, ed. (London: Hamish Hamilton Ltd., 1972).

"Toussaint", in *Breaklight*, Andrew Salkey, ed. (London: Hamish, Hamilton Ltd., 1972).

"The Dyke", in *Bite In* (London: Thomas Nelson and Sons Ltd., 1971).

"The Cities", in *Bite In* (London: Thomas Nelson and Sons Ltd., 1971).

"Lovers", in *New World Quarterly*, III. 4, Kingston, 1967.

Streets of Eternity. Poetry Collection (Georgetown: 1950).

FOREIGN LANGUAGE PUBLICATIONS - POETRY

"De Kliffen bij Mazanilla" in *De Zee de Zee: Gedichten uit he hele wereld*. Kathinka van Dorp, ed. (Amsterdam: Van Gennep-Noviv-Ncos. 1998).

11 poems, in *Karibsky Majak,* Vladimir Klima, ed. (Prague: 1987).

"Cedars of Lebanon", translated into Spanish by Elisio Diego, publication
   unknown. Havana, 1983.

"Nicaragua - Granada. De une Crisalida de Arcoiris", in *La Revista*.
   Casa de las Americas, 117, Havana, 1979.

"La Carretera a Harrar", in *La Revista*, 1, Casa de las Americas, Havana,
   1978.

"Carta a Agostihno Neto", in *La Revista*, 99, Casa de las Americas, Havana,
   1976.

"Requiem for My Sister", translated into Estonian, in *Antillian Lunen*,
   Estonian Writers' Union anthology of West Indian Poetry, 1965.

"Ata", "Black Laughter", translated into German, in *Schwartzer Orpheus*,
   Janheinz Jahn, ed., Munchen, 1959.

"Manerabisi", translated into German, in *Schwartzer Orpheus*, Janheinz
   Jahn, ed., Munchen, 1950 - 1960, several editions.

PLAYS (STAGE, RADIO, TV, FILMS)

STAGE

"Black Horse, Pale Rider", in *Roots and Blossoms: African American Plays
   for Today* (Troy, Michigan: Bedford Publishers, 1991).

"Gentlemen Be Seated", sent on tour to the Venice Festival and to
   Yugoslavia by the Canada Arts Council, 1967.

"Gentlemen Be Seated", performed by Toronto Workshop Productions,
   Toronto, 1967.

"University of Hunger", performed by the Georgetown Theatre Guild
   to mark the occasion of Guyana's Independence. Georgetown, 1966.

"University of Hunger", option bought by Royal Court Theatre, London,
   1960.

RADIO

(These plays were all written for BBC radio between 1960 and 1969).
These plays plus lyrics based upon traditional Guyana folk melodies.
"Song of the Riverman":

"The Riverman"
"University of Hunger"
"The Legend of Nameless Mountain"
"Ata"
"Anancy and Tiger"

T.V. (London)

(Under contract to Associated Television, London, I wrote the following between 1963 and 1964):
"The Big Pride".
"The Day of the Fox".
"Exile from the Sun".
"The Baron of South Boulevard".
"No Gown for Peter".
"The Raiders".
"The Smugglers".
"A Roof of Stars".
"The Conversion of Tiho".

T.V. (Canada)
(written between 1966 and 1969):
"Gentlemen Be Seated".
"Behind God's Back".
"The Merchant of Manning Avenue".

FILM

"A Touch of Midas," the screenplay of my novel was included in the Screenplay Analysis Workshop. These screenplays are drawn from submissions from across the nation. 1985

REVIEWS OF OTHER'S WORK

Toronto Star: "*Proud Empires* by Austin Clarke", April, 1988.
Caribbean Contact: "*A Kind of Living* by Angus Richmond", 1979.
Canadian Journal of Education: "*Black Presence in Multi-ethnic Canada* by Vincent D'Oyley", 1978.
Journal of Caribbean Studies: "*A Double Exile* by Gareth Griffiths", 1978.

New York Times Sunday Book Reviews:

"*Anthology of Asian-American Writing*", 1974.
"*Long George Alley* by Richard Hall", 1973.
"*Natives of My Person* by George Lamming", 1973.
"*The Water-Method Man* by John Irving", 1972.
"*Die the Long Day* by Orlando Patterson", 1972.
"*No Resting Place* by Eugene Mirabelli", 1972.
"*The Polygamist* by Ndabaningi Sithole", 1972.

"*Panthermania* by Gail Sheehy", 1971.
"*Look for Me in the Whirlwind* by New York 21", 1971.
"*A Special Rage* by Gilbert Moore", 1971.
"*The Emergence of African Fiction* by Charles Larson", 1971.
"*Raise Race Rays Raze* by Imamu Amiri Baraka", 1971.
"*S.R.O.* by Robert Deane Pharr", 1971.

SPECIAL EXHIBITIONS

2005 Retrospective exhibition of art and writings, including paintings, manuscripts of novels, plays, clippings of productions. "Life Works of Jan Carew: Message from Manaharva – Save our Rainforest". Special Collections, Ekstrom Library, University of Louisville, Louisville, Kentucky.

1949 An exhibition of Jan Carew's paintings was held at the Cleveland Public Library, Cleveland, Ohio.

INDEX

Black Midas
ISBN: 9781845230951; pp. 267; pub. 1958, 2009; price: £9.99

Frustrated in his work as a doctor's assistant, Aron Smart decides to follow in his late father's footsteps as a gold and diamond prospector in the Guyanese interior. In the pork-knockers' untamed world of drinking, gambling and whoring, Aron has uncanny luck in making strikes and becomes the legendary 'Ocean Shark'. But when he attempts to set up house in Georgetown with his new wealth, he finds white colonial ghosts still in occupation – and sharks with far sharper teeth. In its energetic storytelling, outsize characters and sensuous poetry of place, Black Midas is a bawdy, picaresque epic of the male urge for dominance over land, wealth and women. It connects Shark and the ragged army of pork-knockers to the lusts for virgin land that Raleigh dreamed of in the 16th century.

The Wild Coast
ISBN: 9781845231101; pp. 236; pub. 1958, 2009; price: £8.99

Hector Bradshaw, a sickly child, is sent away from the city by his father to the remote village of Tarlogie. There on the wild coast between the Corentyne and the Canje rivers in Guyana, he is cared for by his kindly guardian, Sister Smart, and begins an education that will change him for ever. He receives dry book learning from Teacher La Rose that will win him a scholarship; struggles against the Christian precepts Sister bombards him with; and is challenged by the harsh African-centred vision of the old hunter Doorne and the sexual initiation he receives from Elsa. But above all, Hector is changed by his exposure to a nature disturbingly red in tooth and claw. As he matures, Hector wonders what kind of person he is becoming. Is he destined to become a man like his arrogant father, or can he find a new path for himself?

These and over three hundred other titles can be bought online from peepaltreepress.com